NkC

NkC

A Tribute To Yesterday

A
Tribute
TO
Yesterday

✦

The History of
Carmel, Carmel Valley, Big Sur, Point Lobos,
Carmelite Monastery, and Los Burros

by
Sharron Lee Hale

VALLEY PUBLISHERS
SANTA CRUZ

International Standard Book Number 0-913548-73-1

Library of Congress Catalog Card Number: 80-50118

This book is dedicated with love to my family...

Carmel—my mother, Rosa Lee Hale
Carmel Valley—my brother, Kevin Hale
Carmelite Monastery—Prioress Sister Francisca
Point Lobos—my daughter, Carmel Lee Hale
Big Sur—my father, Dale Hale
Los Burros—my grandmother, Vessie M. Deaver

Contents

Preface

This book springs from the heartfelt desire to see in print the story of an area and a village I have called home. In place of false facts, hearsay, misinformation, and in some cases a total lack of recorded history, I longed to see not only the reconstruction of childhood memories, but the fabric of recorded writings, incidents, and conversations with some now gone from our midst who were so much a part of our history. To me a town's most valuable resource is its people. Time and time again it has taken only one person to visualize a way to save a town's unique character. Then that spirit must spread and gather support, and in this respect Carmel has been fortunate.

Generally, reading allows us all a welcome escape from the fast pace and realities of our everyday lives. Reading about the past enables us to return for a time to yesterday and arouses pleasant recollections. For some, it brings a new awareness and understanding of almost forgotten days.

This book has been my labor of love and is the culmination of ten years of research, countless personal interviews, many trips to several counties, and the reading of vast supplies of materials.

Acknowledgements

The irrefragable love, support, patience, help, and loyalty of my wonderful family made this book possible.

There were many others, too, who helped in countless ways by offering a name here, a date there, and suggestions, and I would like to take this opportunity to express my heartfelt gratitude to all. Special thanks to the following individuals, many of whom not only gave generously of their time and knowledge, but opened their homes to me:

Joseph Hitchcock, Jr.
Sister Francisca and the Sisters
of the Carmelite Monastery
Carmel Fire Chief Robert Updike
Carmel Police Chief William Ellis
Fred Strong
Robert Norton
Joseph Mora, Jr.
Kip Silvey
Enid A. Larson
William Bishop
Pon Lung Chung
William Lehman
Daisy F. D. Bostick
Kenneth Goold
Giles G. Healey
Donald M. Howard
Robert Stanton
H. S. Mike Stalter
Mrs. M. Waters King
Richard Tevis
Clark Bruce
Robert Waldo Hicks

Ferdinand Burgdorff
Robert De Yoe
Mrs. Marjorie Marble
Hans and Esther Ewoldsen
Allen Griffin
Glenn Leidig
Earl and Myra Wermuth
Stuyvesant Fish
William Curtis Brooks
Ada Devendorf Reichard
Joseph Victorine, Jr.
Mayo Hayes O'Donnell
Mr. and Mrs. James B. Pruitt
Florence Josselyn
Mrs. Ruth Fisher
Josephine Childers
Mrs. William Askew
John Livingstone
Harry Downie
Gordon Campbell
Keith Evans
Mrs. James McGrury
Mrs. M. Ollasen Corpagno

And special thanks also to the following libraries and their research librarians:

Harrison Memorial Library
Monterey Public Library
Monterey County Library
Mayo Hayes O'Donnell Library
Watsonville City Library

Santa Cruz County Library
John Steinbeck Library
Hollister Library
King City Library
San Jose City Library

CARMEL

Friendly, familiar faces . . .

Quiet streets, some still unpaved, punctuated with children's laughter . . .

*Meandering paths to open forest places so perfect for a fort
    or a secret hideaway . . .*

Gentle days . . .

*The storekeeper who greeted you with a smile, and sometimes with a
    piece of candy . . .*

*The stables where you were always welcomed by a woman who endeared
    herself to all the children who knew her . . .*

*The Forge, where you could rest from play, chin in hands, and watch
    with wonder . . .*

*The Forest Theater, where no one minded if you pretended to be a
    princess with flowers in your hair . . .*

*Carmel cannot be captured adequately in words—its name and the
    thought of it call up deep private feelings from within me, the
    measure of my life spent in it and the awareness of the abundant
    blessing of having been surrounded since birth by some of nature's
    best works. It is as constant a joy to awaken to as to close your
    eyes in, thankful for yet another day in such a place.*

*Carmel is unique in the way it affects all those who know it—those who
    have made it their home and those who have known it for only a
    short time. It is an inspiration, both a haven and a passing fancy,
    and all who come here are touched by its magic.*

1

Carmel-by-the-Sea

From a rich pine-covered crest of a hill where the sun's silvered sheen strikes a billion pine needles rustling in the breeze, there is a view of the Carmel Valley, with a glimpse of what lies beyond Point Lobos. On a crescent of land where, shaped by the rolling surge of the sea and crowned by trees nestled in a fragile atmosphere, stands Carmel, encroachment (what has lightly been referred to as progress) surrounding it.

The battles for and against the shape of Carmel in the past, and the Carmel of the future, have been linked over the years. While the smoke of recent battles lingers, there is proof as well as hope that there are those who still treasure her unique flavor and charm among the commercial communities of our present times. Though much of what was the old Carmel has changed with commercial prosperity, we cannot turn back the clock or keep the present from becoming the future, but we can visit the past and thus treasure more keenly what we now hold dear.

Carmel's story began when Sebastián Vizcaíno, a man of humble birth, became a successful navigator. In the company of 200 handpicked men and a handful of Carmelite friars, Vizcaíno set sail in May 1602 in search of a suitable Pacific haven from Spain's rivals. On December 16, 1602, he landed in Monterey Bay, and later that day Father Antonio de la Ascensión said mass under a large oak. (The tree was later named the Vizcaíno Serra Oak. It died in 1905, after which the trunk was moved to the San Carlos Church in Monterey.) Spanish banners were unfurled and Vizcaíno began his survey of the land while the friars investigated the surrounding areas. After reaching the top of a hill where they found the topography almost a duplicate of Mount Carmel and the hills of Galilee, they persuaded Vizcaíno to call the river that traversed the land before them Río Carmelo and the rounded mountain above it Mount Carmel. These names have existed longer than any other in this country; Jamestown, Virginia was founded five years later.

The cross and Vizcaino Oak, now gone, below the Presidio of Monterey.

One hundred and sixty-eight years after Vizcaíno's landing, Father Junípero Serra arrived with a party that included Portolá, the governor of Mexico, a number of soldiers, and Father Juan Crespí. A few days later, on June 3, 1770, the Mission San Carlos Borromeo and the Royal Presidio were dedicated. The first mission building was on the site where San Carlos Church stands today.

Junípero Serra was born of humble parents in Petra on the Isle of Mallorca on the twenty-fourth of November in 1713. He received a religious education and entered the Order of St. Francis at a young age. At the age of thirty-six he was sent as a missionary to New Spain (Mexico) where he spent nineteen years before being sent to Nueva California to establish missions.

A year after the dedication of Mission San Carlos at Monterey, its location was changed to a more fertile area five miles to the south, near the Río Carmelo. At about this time, Don Pedro Fages, governor of Nueva California, began to question the lines of authority between himself and Fr. Serra. Serra desired only freedom in the construction and locations of the missions, while Fages desired total jurisdiction in all matters, spiritual or otherwise. To

Serra it soon became apparent that these matters could not be resolved and, despite his lame leg, which had been injured on an earlier trip and which never healed completely, he traveled on foot from Monterey to San Diego, then on to Mexico City where he arrived in February 1773, after a journey of almost six months. Before Spain's ablest viceroy, Bucareli, Serra laid the entire situation. Bucareli wisely understood the need for good relations with the native Costanoan and their rancherías of Ichxenta and Carmentaruka, as well as the visiting Rumsen from the south coast, and he knew that this peace would best come through Serra and the influence of the church with a minimum of governmental interference. The center of all religious control was to be at Mission San Carlos de Borromeo.

Serra's main purpose and the reason for his concern that the missions not be subjected to government interference, was the conversion of the natives to Christianity. In speaking of the purpose of missions, Serra's words to his close associate and good friend, Father Palóu, were, "Try to see to it that those who are to come are well provided with patience and charity and in that case they will have a joyous time and here become very rich . . . I say rich in hardships; but then, whither goes the ox that does not plow? And if he does not plow, how can there be harvest?"

By the time of his death on August 28, 1784, Fr. Serra, with the devoted help of Father Fermín Francisco de Lasuén and other Franciscans, had founded nine missions:

San Diego de Alcalá, July 16, 1769
San Carlós de Borromeo, June 3, 1770
San Antonio de Padua, July 14, 1771
San Gabriel Arcangel, September 8, 1771
San Luís Obispo de Tolosa, September 1, 1772
San Francisco de Asís, or Dolores, June 29, 1776
San Juan Capistrano, November 1, 1776
Santa Clara de Asís, January 12, 1777
San Buenaventura, March 31, 1782

The building at Mission San Carlos de Borromeo, which still exists in part, was begun in 1793 and was dedicated in September 1797 under the direction of Fr. Lasuén.

After the secularization of the missions, which occurred between 1834 and 1836, the Carmel mission fell into neglected ruins until 1882, when Father Angelo Casanova raised interest with the discovery of the graves of Frs. Serra, Crespí, Lasuén and López. Fr. Casanova was the priest at the San Carlos Church in Monterey at the time the Dutra-Machado family occupied the old "Pear Orchard" adobe in 1884, and he was responsible for the partial

John Martin's haystacks in front of the Carmel mission, before the start of the restoration.

The Carmel mission after restoration had been started. Lewis Josselyn photograph.

restoration and rededication of the Carmel mission. The rededication took place on August 26, 1884, the centennial of Fr. Serra's death, and two years later the graves were opened officially.

At the time of the restoration a peaked roof was built to replace the original tiled, arched roof. It safeguarded the walls until work was completed in 1888, and in fact remained on the mission until 1936. The first ceiling of the mission, according to Harry Downie, "was a vault of stone but was removed in 1814. Then a planked ceiling was put in, but it too fell in about 1851. Meantime a shingled roof had been put on. As late as 1936 nobody had the right information on the actual architectural details, but some documents came to light in my time and we made a proper study. We made patterns for the catenary arch and by letting a chain fall, we followed the natural line. One day, while working on the old choir loft, a piece of plaster was knocked out acci-

The mission from behind, after partial restoration.

dentally, revealing the original plate. It's from this that one gets a small clue."

Mr. Downie told of his talk with the well-known architect Bernard Maybeck who himself was not happy with the old restoration version of the mission roof. He and Downie agreed that the arches within "should be laminated" and when the job was completed they agreed that it had been "engineered properly." Some of the lumber for the final restoration was collected from old seating for an earlier Serra pageant and was considered well seasoned. When the present altar was put in, it required extra care because of the difference of several inches in the sweep of the building on the side where St. Anthony rests. There were three steps to the altar rail originally, which were altered to only one to make it easier for older parishioners, and radiant heating was placed under the new tile floor which replaced the original burnt tile.

Many of the statues and works of art which belonged originally to the San Carlos Mission have been returned, and one of its loveliest and most famous paintings is that of Pietá which was painted in 1777 by Miguel Roderíguez, who founded the Academy of Fine Arts in Mexico City.

Restoration and reconstruction of the mission school, still a school today, was undertaken in 1945. The pepper tree in the mission courtyard was planted in 1922, and the cypresses were planted by Harry Downie in 1938. All else has been reconstructed according to original documents, with Downie in charge of all restoration. He was commissioned in 1931 by Monsignor Philip G. Scher of San Carlos Church in Monterey—later bishop of Monterey—and was a devoted and faithful servant to the time of his death on March 10, 1980.

The present mission roof follows the general design of the original and within its walls in the sanc-

tuary lie the venerated bones of Fr. Serra. In the area which once held the original mortuary chapel on the opposite side of the church are the twenty sandstone steps which are deeply worn, not by modern day tourists as many think, but by the faithful padres and neophytes on their way to the choir loft, which is marked by its star window. The pulpit of our lovely mission today rises from its original base. To its left is an opening to a small chapel, and to the right is the sacristy with its beautiful old beams complete with wooden nails. The piscina is made of stone and is considered one of the finest mission carvings in California with its four separate pieces of native sandstone. Also remaining is the largest of the mission bells, which weighs nearly a ton. It was cast in Mexico in 1797 and brought up the coast by boat.

In 1921 Father Ramon Mestres conducted a "Cornerstone Ceremony," with descendants of original mission Indians placing the cornerstone. In 1924, a beautiful sarcophagus was dedicated in memory of Serra, having been lovingly designed and created by artist-sculptor Joseph Mora. Mora

Manuel and Alejandro Onesimo, descendants of an original mission Indian, bear the cornerstone at the October 2, 1921 cornerstone laying ceremony. Slevin photograph.

also created the statue of Serra which was unveiled and dedicated by Fr. Mestres on July 22, 1922, during the Serra Pageant. It is at the foot of Serra Road in the Carmel Woods, in the vicinity of what is said to have been a resting place along the Serra Trail between Carmel and Monterey.

In April 1925 there was cause for more celebration—two long-lost bells of the mission were found. The larger of the two was cast in 1799 and the other in 1808, and both came from Spain. They were taken away in 1830 during the Mexican regime, and the larger bell was sent to Soledad, the smaller to

3

Dedication of Serra statue in Carmel Woods, 1922. Lewis Josselyn photograph.

San Antonio. In 1862 they somehow arrived at St. Patrick's Church in Watsonville and were stored there for sixty-three years. Fr. Mestres, by then a monsignor, learned of their existence through mission records. It was also learned from the records that the larger bell was the one used to call the neophytes to prayer and could be heard clearly in Monterey.

There is great beauty and dignity in our Carmel Mission. Much work has been done by several individuals to preserve our heritage and make it possible for us to continue the sense of pride the mission inspires in us. A great deal of information has been uncovered through archaeological findings. In recent years the Monterey County Archaeological Society and its founder, Donald M. Howard, Esq., have added greatly to our knowledge of our heritage. The most notable contribution was that of Harry Downie, who for forty-nine years gave the ultimate in time, knowledge and devotion to the preservation of the missions.

After the secularization of the missions came the division of the lands into ranchos, rich in history of their own. Some of the ranchos lying near Carmel were San José Sur Chiquito to the south, El Potrero de San Carlos, San Francisquito, Cañada de la Segunda, Las Manzanitas, and the well-known El Pescadero. The latter was owned by John C. Gore from 1853 to 1860 and was the location of a colony of Chinese who set up a fishing village just south of what is now Del Monte Lodge. The old log cabin which had been Gore's home was later used for the sighting of whales by a Portuguese whaler who later worked for Captain Verisimo at Point Lobos. Old-timer Joseph Hitchcock, whose family moved to El Pescadero in early 1894, left us many

tales of the days he spent near the Chinese village before the Pacific Improvement Company forced its disbanding after the turn of the century.

In the early 1880s interest was shown in land for religious retreats and real estate subdivisions. In 1885, on behalf of various Catholic societies, Santiago J. Duckworth, a Monterey real estate man, opened a section of land which began at the top of Carmel Hill and ran past the Hatton Ranch down onto and along the present Ocean Avenue to Junipero, and called it "Carmel City." The land was purchased from Monterey businessman and settler Honoré Escolle. Escolle, a Frenchman, was the grandfather of Mrs. Kip Silvey of Carmel. He sold twenty-seven lots on the block where the old Carmel Theater of the 1930s stood (another lost example of Carmel Mediterranean style architecture), on Ocean Avenue between what is now Magnin's and the Bank of America, for the sum of ten dollars. Recently leased space in many shops in that area was $2.50 a square foot!

*Harry Downie
1904-1980
At work on plans for the mission restoration.*

The land was bonded by Duckworth in 1888, and was then promoted as a Catholic summer resort to rival the Methodists of Pacific Grove. Duckworth planned to build a theological seminary at the upper trail of La Loma Terrace, marked on the original map "college site." In April and May of 1888, W. C. Little of Monterey and his apprentice, Davenport Bromfield, were commissioned to do the survey work for Carmel City. Bromfield ended up doing most of the work while living in the small cottage he built for himself on the east side of Carpenter Street between Second and Third avenues. Directly across the road from Bromfield's was the second house built in the new town. It still stands today and belongs to Mrs. Elizabeth Diefendorf. It was built after the survey map was filed in May 1888 by Delos Goldsmith of San Francisco.

The sale of land began in July 1888. Corner lots were twenty-five dollars and inside lots twenty dollars and up, while lots within the business section were fifty dollars apiece. A brochure was put into circulation declaring that a "golden opportunity is here presented for men of enterprise to reap a golden harvest by directing their attention toward the advantages possessed by Carmel City for commercial purposes." Another brochure by Duckworth read: "As soon as the Pacific Grove branch of the Southern Pacific Railroad is completed to Pebble Beach, the transportation facilities will be first-class, as the distance from Carmel City to a railroad station will be about a 10 minutes' walk and probably less. The road is now in operation from Monterey to Lake Majella, a distance of five miles, and will be extended to Pebble Beach, and most likely to Carmel Mission within the next two years."

By the early 1890s it seemed that Duckworth's plans were failing, and his financial problems were on the increase. He turned to the support of a pretty green-eyed strawberry blonde, Mrs. Abbie Jane Hunter, who had formed the Women's Real Estate and Investment Company in January 1892. In April 1892, Abbie sent William T. Dummage to Carmel as her resident agent. Part of the land which Duckworth had purchased was Las Manzanitas Rancho, first owned and settled by Honoré Escolle. It extended from Junipero Street to Monte Verde on the west and ended at the Pacific Improvement Company line on the north. It included a 400-acre hillside. Other neighboring ranch lands were held by settlers Hatton, Sheriden, Martin, and Gore. A small parcel was owned by a Mathew M. Murphy and family, who were living in the area's oldest home, built in 1846. This parcel lay near the dunes at the end of Ocean Avenue and was "nestled in the eucalyptus trees."

Later the San Francisco Land Company bought part of the Martin Ranch between Twelfth Avenue and Santa Lucia, taking over Carmel Point (Point Loeb) and subdividing it, as well as acquiring the shoreline north. The land bounded by Santa Lucia, the mission, Carmelo, and the main highway was bought by San Franciscan Willis Walker. The road leading into Carmel City was at the top of the hill

The original house on the John Martin Ranch.

John Martin's Mission Ranch home as it looks today. Photograph by author.

where Carpenter and Serra meet, and was called Upper Trail. This was the original entrance to La Loma Terrace, later developed by one-time State Assemblyman Ray C. De Yoe. His son, Robert "Bob" Larue De Yoe, lives there today. The spot at the top of the hill was occupied by two tall posts with a gate for stock and a sign saying "Carmel City."

Meandering along through what was called, in the early days, Carmel's Tortilla Flat area, where Carmel Community Hospital stands today, the old road veered off to the south past the three cabins of Manuel Artellán, then past the home of his brother Frank, who married Phillaponda Soto. They had seventeen children, some of whom were often at odds with the law. Their house, known as the old Soto place, later became the home of Daisy D. F. Bostick. Just past the Soto place was the cabin of Manuel Boronda, son of the original owner of Rancho Los Laurelles, and next on the road was the Gómes house at Santa Rita and First, which stood until 1941.

Following more or less what was later known as

Onesimo (Panoche).

Forest Trail, now Carpenter, the road passed the adobe of Theodoro Escobar, son of Augustine, the hunter and trapper of early Monterey bull and bear fights, and a shack which belonged to Alfonso Ramirez of Carmel Mission Indian grandparents. It was Alfonso who recalled how another valley Indian, Alex Panoche, was once instructed by the teacher, in 1916, either to take a bath or no longer attend school. Further along the road, to what is now Second, was the home of Mr. and Mrs. Charles Berwick. Berwick was the brother of Edward Berwick of the Carmel Valley, and near their house on Fifth (the site located just inside the old wall of the De Sabla, Louie Lewis, Smith property) was a well which supplied water for that area when the wind blew. However, most of the water came in barrels from the Pacific Improvement Company's line off Ocean Avenue. Later "Mary's Well" was abandoned when a horse fell into it causing the water to be contaminated.

Past the Berwick house and barn on Carpenter and Lobos was the home of a bachelor named Barrows, and at Guadalupe and Second lived Canderlaria Escobar, Augustine's widow and Theodoro Escobar's grandmother. At Guadalupe and Third were two cottages which belonged to a Miss Robertson, niece of Delos Goldsmith who lived with her at the time. Nearby was the log house of Carmel's only woman mayor, Mrs. Eva K. De Sabla, elected April 19, 1920. She had come to Carmel from Marysville, where she had been known as Eva K. Couvileau, and was a survivor of the Donner Party. Mrs. De Sabla later sold her property to Louie Lewis, who

subdivided it and sold to Smith, who built the wall which still surrounds the property today. This property is also referred to as the "old nudist colony" because it was once proposed for this use by a local artistic group who knew Smith.

De Sabla's nearby neighbor, Delos Goldsmith, also had a colorful life. Goldsmith's mother, Abigail Jones, was born of English parents in Massachusetts in 1787. She lived to be 100, outliving her husband, a native of Milford, Connecticut. Delos Goldsmith was born in Painsville, Ohio, on September 3, 1828. He left Ohio at the age of nineteen for New Orleans. When New Orleans did not capture his youthful spirit, he moved to San Francisco in 1850 and was a witness to the great fire in 1851. A carpenter for two years in San Francisco, he worked on the first Presidio reservation, then left for Marysville, and later went to Yuma, Arizona. He worked in the oil business there until the outbreak of the Civil War at which time he was appointed citizen wagon-master of the Twenty-ninth Ohio Volunteers. His only surviving brother had joined the Ohio Sixth. Goldsmith was taken prisoner at Harper's Ferry and endured hardships until he managed to escape, which eventually took him south on a lumber expedition. In 1879, he became an agent for a Dr. Stockton who was involved in an oil concern.

Back in California again in 1888, Goldsmith came to Carmel in late 1888 where he erected a home for his wife's sister's daughter, Miss Robertson, in which he lived while constructing other homes for early residents—the Berwicks, Joseph Sley, and Miss M. E. Donnelly, among others. He built a shed for his carpenter shop on the southwest corner of Ocean and San Carlos, behind the Carmel Development Store. Between 1892 and 1894, acting on behalf of Abbie Jane Hunter, the wife of his nephew, Wesley Hunter, he constructed two lovely identical homes. One was on the northeast corner of Guadalupe and Fourth on lots 16, 18, and 20 of block 41, and later belonged to Mr. and Mrs. William Askew, Sr. Mrs. Askew still lives there. The other home, on the northwest corner, became the Goldsmiths' own home. It was the first house, and the Askews' the second, in the area next to what was known as Paradise Park. Paradise Park became a tract subdivision in February 1918, and was acquired in 1940 by James Doud and William L. Hudson. This area remained at that particular time the only undivided area within the city limits of Carmel. It lay in an elongated triangle between Carpenter and Hatton Fields with a narrow section extending south across the present end of Mountain View.

The Askew home on Guadalupe, when it was newly built.

Years later the Goldsmiths sold their home to Mr. and Mrs. Roy Nigh, who in turn sold it to a Mrs. Thatcher who sold it to her son-in-law, Carl Cherry, for the token sum of one dollar. The Cherrys' story began in 1920 when Dr. Alfred E. Burton and his wife came to Carmel with their three children, Ross, Virginia and Christine. Dr. Burton had been a dean at M.I.T. for twenty years, as well as having accompanied Commodore Peary on his North Pole expedition. Though Dr. Burton lived in Carmel for only six years, he endeared himself to many and was considered a "fair artist." He left after he was divorced by his wife, Virginia, who then married inventor Carl Cherry. Interested in art in its broadest sense, Mrs. Cherry sponsored many artists, playwrights and musicians, as well as art galleries, shops, laboratories, and non-profit organizations. She enjoyed composing poetry, but preferred painting, which she did profusely in a variety of styles, although she was considered an eccentric by many. Today, fifteen years after her death at the age of eighty-seven, her home, under the conditions of her estate, continues under the name of the Cherry Foundation.

The Cherrys did extensive remodeling to the Goldsmith house after they bought it, and there is little to hint at its past similarity to the Askew home. Mrs. Askew remembered how the workmen would come to work and drink most of the day until Mr. Cherry arrived to "inspect things," and how the roof sagged and the chimney cracked before the job was ever completed, yet "Mr. Cherry, being a very patient and kind person, never seemed to notice how little the men actually did for all they were paid." Also near the Askew home, at Fifth and Carpenter, was the home of Ivy Basham Sinclair, sister of M. J. Murphy. Ivy's husband, Walter, owned Carmel's early candy store known as Basham's, where Whitney's later stood.

Up to 1895, Delos Goldsmith and Abbie Jane Hunter's Carmel agent, William Dummage, had sold some three hundred lots in Carmel, most of them situated within what is now the business area.

Beyond the Goldsmiths' and Askews', there were no dwellings until you reached the area of San Carlos and Sixth, where the little cottage of Mr. and Mrs. John P. Cogle and Cogle's brother Harry stood. John Cogle worked with William Dummage clearing timber for Devendorf as a foreman. Next-door neighbors to the Cogles were Alfred Horn and his wife Lucretia. Their cottage was on the north half of the block facing San Carlos Street, while the Cogles owned the south half. Unlike the Cogles, the Horns did not live in their cottage all the time after they built it in 1894, but used it instead for vacations when Mr. Horn was not working at his job as a turntable operator at the western end of McAllister Street in San Francisco. After the 1906 earthquake, the Horns, as did many others, came to live permanently in Carmel. Mr. Horn helped drive the stage to and from Monterey, as well as delivering mail on occasion as a relief driver.

The Cogle home on San Carlos between Fifth and Sixth.

Mr. and Mrs. Alfred Horn at their home on San Carlos between Fifth and Sixth.

7

Another substitute mail carrier was Rudolph "Rudy" Ohm, a German man who was a house painter, and who built his home on the southeast side of Fifth and Monte Verde. Ohm also worked as a relief gatekeeper on the original Carmel Hill gate (which was removed and set back when the present freeway was put in), for the Pacific Improvement Company. He was also Carmel's poundmaster in 1915, and was an active volunteer fireman. One of Rudy Ohm's daughters is married to a popular present-day plumber, Paul Hazdovac. Paul's Plumbing Shop is one of the last of Carmel's businesses to be located in one of the old homes still standing in that block of Junipero. It was built by Giocente Re, a Swiss woodcutter who chose redwood board-and-batten for his home. Mr. Re died in 1937, two days after he was injured as an innocent party during a "fisticuff" which took place in front of the Carmel Smoke Shop. His cousin, Joe Martinoya, who was a Carmel gardener, inherited the property. Mr. Martinoya returned to Switzerland in the early 1950s, and J. O. Handley acquired the corner lot and the house was leased until the middle 1960s by a local professor. In 1966 Paul Hazdovac took over the little redwood as his plumbing shop, with Donald Berry joining him.

Along with Rudy Ohm and a Mr. L. H. Rask, Alfred Horn also worked as a relief gateman for the Pacific Improvement Company and drove on milk runs for the local dairies. In 1914, after a brief illness, Mr. Horn died at the age of seventy, and when his wife died at the age of seventy-seven, in 1927, their little cottage was sold and later moved south of Ocean Avenue to a location on Junipero. Over on Mission and Seventh was Carmel's first poultry man, T. H. Lewis, who later moved to Carmel Valley "when things got too crowded."

From 1895 to 1899 business was not doing well for Abbie Jane Hunter, and Delos Goldsmith was prompted to write to her husband, Wesley Hunter, telling of her financial difficulties. Efforts to get business to progress did not pay off, and Carmel remained truly a "paper town." Mrs. Hunter was finally forced to sell her holdings, a small portion of which she sold to her agent, William Dummage.

In late 1901, a man named Franklin Devendorf stood above a fern-studded canyon called Pescadero, surrounded by pine and oak, and viewed the land below him sloping down to a mile-long expanse of glimmering beach. Devendorf had come to inspect Mrs. Hunter's holdings. He was the owner of extensive property holdings in San Jose and the

Franklin Devendorf, left, founder of Carmel-by-the-Sea. Frank Powers, right, president of the Carmel Development Company. Powers and Devendorf were partners in the company.

Morgan Hill and Gilroy area, as well as Stockton, and had decided that trading some of his holdings for land in Carmel would be wise, as would plans to purchase further holdings from Honoré Escolle. Devendorf filed the first map of his land and plans for its subdivision in 1902.

Franklin Devendorf was a tall, large man who was "light on his feet with twinkling blue-grey eyes and seldom without a hat or a smile." He wasted no time in contacting his friend, Frank Powers, a San Francisco attorney, and in 1903 the men formed a partnership, the Carmel Development Company, which was to shape a jewel called Carmel-by-the-Sea.

The partnership was one of fairly matched personalities. Frank Powers had tall visions, as did Devendorf, and was a tall man physically, with a "deep voice and broad shoulders." An ardent lover of nature, he took delight in naming most of the streets we recognize today, and in planting palm trees on Mission at Fifth. Fifty years later, in 1953, they were removed for more parking. Powers returned from his travels with seedlings which he planted or made gifts of to various friends throughout California. He was a man who many said was "equally at home with a king or a panhandler," always ready with a smile, conversation and laughter. Like Devendorf, who felt more comfortable with a hat, Powers not only wore them but collected them in various styles and sizes. One small girl grown to adulthood remembered him for his "high laced boots and large hat."

Both Powers and Devendorf had a long and ardent love affair with Carmel and knew every path and every part of the forest. Powers had another love, a "preoccupation with the arts," and when in

Carmel, could often be found at the Forest Theater, either involved in a production or in the audience. A fascination with Father Junípero Serra and the restoration of the Carmel mission were also among his concerns.

Powers died in 1940. His son, the late Gallatin Powers, owned the Crocodile's Tail, a well-known restaurant. It existed on the right side of the present Highway 1 near Bixby Creek Bridge for many years until, after an unfortunate mass murder there by one of the waiters, it was pushed into the sea. Gallatin Powers is better remembered for his more recent well-known Gallatin's Restaurant in the old Stokes Adobe in Monterey. His sister, Mrs. Nelson M. Leoni, continues to live in the Carmel Valley.

Franklin Devendorf hired a man named Henry Fisher as the engineer responsible for laying out the village of Carmel. During this time Devendorf was having his own cottage built at Lincoln and Sixth while he boarded with Mr. and Mrs. Alfred F. Horn. The first property to be purchased by the newly formed Carmel Development Company was "bounded by 4th avenue on the north and on the east by the Hatton Ranch where it finally joined up with other Carmel Development Company holdings at Junípero." The prices of the property under the new partnership of Powers and Devendorf were $500 for a cottage, easily secured with a five or ten dollar deposit, or six dollars per month rental, and fifty dollars for a waterfront lot when these were added to the holdings. The first store to be erected in Carmel was known as the Carmel Development and Contracting Company and offered general merchandise and groceries. It later became Staniford's.

William T. Dummage, to whom Abbie Jane Hunter sold some property in Carmel, had at one time been employed by Main and Winchester Saddlery Company. He and his mother, Mrs. Inman, lived in their cottage on the lot he had purchased, which was bounded by San Carlos, Mission and Fourth streets. They had come to Carmel from San Jose in 1898. Before long Dummage had established himself as one of Carmel's first plumbers, having his early business where the old Carmel Delicatessen used to be. Also a past post office site, it is known today as Docklor's Canton Restaurant. It is interesting to note that the building next door to Docklor's which houses Swensen's Ice Cream Parlor once housed the old Corner Cupboard Grocery, Carmel's first and only cooperative grocery. This site, as well as that of the present Orange Julius, also became the Mission Laundry. In 1933 the basement of the building was the indoor range of the Carmel Pistol Club before it was moved to the Carmel Garage.

When Dummage first came to Carmel he worked for Devendorf along with John Cogle, A. F. Horn and George Foster, as a forest clearer for the Carmel Development Company. It was during this time that Carmel had its first labor strike. John Cogle became angered over the progress of his work crew while he was out of town on other business. The members of the crew felt they had met the quota of trees felled, and Cogle felt that they had not. The men, angry over the tongue-lashing by Cogle, refused to work. Devendorf saved the day, as he was to do many times, by creating four bosses instead of one.

In later years William Dummage married the widow Norton, the mother of Robert (Bob) Norton, who grew up to become one of Carmel's police chiefs. Mrs. Norton (Dummage) was a native of Illinois. She came to California in 1897 to take a position at Agnew State Hospital in San Jose, and she had come to Pacific Grove for a rest and holiday in 1899. Bicycling around country roads, Louise met and later married Melvin Norton, the proprietor of the Cash Package Grocery in Pacific Grove. One Saturday afternoon after their marriage, she was looking at the newspaper. "My eye happened to light on a full-page advertisement and I read 'Come to Carmel-by-the-Sea!' I had never been over the hill in the four years I had lived in Pacific Grove by that time and it suddenly sounded inviting. I made up my mind that we would go there on a picnic the very next day." Mrs. Norton was as good as her word. Accompanied by a neighbor, the Nortons made the trip to Carmel in their horse-drawn two-seater on Sunday, June 20, 1903, to see the town of Carmel, then thirteen years old. The route known as the "truck route" was being oiled, according to Mrs. Norton (Dummage) and it was necessary to detour through the eastern section of what is now La Loma Terrace and had been referred to as "Inspiration Point" because of the tremendous view.

W. T. DUMMAGE

Plumbing, Tinning and Gas Fitting

AGENT FOR

Acetylene Machines
Acetylene Burners
Acetylene Stoves
Acetylene Lamps
Acetylene Fixtures

Ocean Ave. Between San Carlos and Mission

The Nortons had their picnic at the foot of Ocean Avenue on the dunes and promptly fell in love with Carmel forever. "Others weren't so sure there would ever be a town here . . . but I knew it, and wanted to be a part of it!" On the return trip up Ocean Avenue, Mrs. Norton sought out Devendorf and inquired as to whether or not the lot on the southwest corner of Ocean and Dolores was unsold. The answer was yes, and for a five dollar gold piece as deposit, the Nortons made the purchase, returning the next day to finalize the transaction with the guarantee that Devendorf would erect a "stout floor 20 by 30 feet, side-walling it up to about three feet and topping it off with a canvas tent." The temporarily supplanted Nortons had a frame kitchen adjoining the tent and tent quarters for the family and whatever helpers would be needed, and thus were plans made for the opening of Carmel's first restaurant. The Nortons' Pacific Grove neighbors helped Mrs. Norton cut and hem napkins and tablecloths, and the opening was planned to coincide with the grand opening of the recently completed reconstruction of the Pine Inn on July 4, 1903.

The restaurant was a great success, but with the end of summer business slowed and the Nortons made preparations to return to Pacific Grove. When August came it was time to think of school for their daughter, Mabel. Devendorf, who was in favor of beginning a school in Carmel, begged the Nortons to stay so that Mabel would make the seventh pupil the law required and he could have his school. "It took a lot of clever managing, but we stayed." They lived in a little cottage on the southeast corner of Seventh and San Carlos, where they later built a more substantial house. By the time winter came, their tent had been taken down, and part of the flooring which had been used in it was used as the flooring for Carmel's second restaurant and first to serve Chinese food, opened by Pon Sing. It was next to Basham's candy store. Another part of the flooring from the Nortons' tent was moved to the end of the lot on Dolores Street where it was used as part of the flooring in the cottage which Mrs. Norton (as Mrs. Dummage) later made her home. She lived there until her death in 1952.

For a time after her death Mrs. Dummage's cottage was used as a studio by Carmel painter Ling Fu Yang. Then in 1957, after fifty-four years, when the building now housing the Shoe Box and Cachet was to be erected, Mrs. Dummage's cottage went for a ride to a new location at San Carlos and Ninth. The cottage had been purchased from Mrs. George H. Linsley, daughter of the late Mary Dummage, by Milton Eagleton, and he had it placed next door to

the original home of Mrs. Dummage's sister and brother-in-law, the Philip Wilsons. The Wilsons had built their home in 1906 and later sold it to a Mr. and Mrs. Gillette who raised a large family there. It remains almost as it was, with very little changed about it, across from the Carmel Women's Club on the corner. Eagleton retained the flavor of Mrs. Dummage's cottage, changing only a few items inside, just as he had done after his purchase of the old All Saints rectory when he had it moved to the same site. He lived in Mrs. Dummage's cottage after retiring from his Ocean Avenue business called "Joyce's" until his death in March 1978.

Mrs. Dummage also owned the land from the site of her cottage on Ocean Avenue back along Dolores to what was the popular Tom's Cafe, now Toots Lagoon, as well as the Ocean Avenue front section of her property where the tent-restaurant once stood and where the Corner Cupboard is today. This was where Mrs. Dummage had built a little plank building in late 1904, which she intended to lease as an ice cream parlor. Later it was used by Mr. Burnight for that purpose. However, at the time of the intended opening of the ice cream parlor, the prospective owners were unable to open their business, and hearing about the change of plans, Devendorf took over the lease, and the building was used for church services conducted by a Methodist minister from Pacific Grove, the Reverend Willis G. White. Mrs. Dummage recalled in later years that on Saturday nights a three-piece Spanish orchestra would come from Monterey to play for dances which were held in the building, and "often the dance would hardly be over in time to clean up the little hall for Sunday services, while poor Mr. Slevin two doors away used to grumble about the accordian music which kept him awake all night."

One of the first recorded weddings in Carmel took place in a cottage owned by a couple named Smith, which occupied the site of the later Asia Inn on Dolores, and the couple had a "wonderful dance party" in Mrs. Dummage's little place, complete with fresh pine boughs for decoration. Slevin's building nearby is also gone, but the old pine tree still grows on the corner, having been spared as the buildings have come and gone around it—proof that trees are still sacrosanct in Carmel.

The Women's Real Estate Company with Delos Goldsmith as builder was responsible for the erection of a bathhouse. It was started in 1888 and finished in 1889, complete with a boardwalk running from the main door to the beach, which was built with the help of Wesley Hunter. The bathhouse originally stood at the foot of Ocean Avenue

Carmel Bathhouse shortly after its grand opening, with Carmel Point (Point Leob) in the background. Slevin photograph.

near where the old restrooms later were, and until the late 1950s there was still an obvious depression which the sand and time had not yet obliterated. The bathhouse continued to serve the village of Carmel for many years after its opening, offering dressing rooms and towels, as well as peanuts, candy, special celery phosphates, popcorn, sandwiches and lemonade (courtesy of the Bashams). The cost of a rental suit, towel and dressing room was twenty-five cents. The scene of much gaiety and many happy times, including early day club meetings and church outings, the bathhouse was also the scene of the reception following the wedding of Delos and Catherine Curtis.

Thomas Burnight looked after the bathhouse until Mr. and Mrs. Waldo Hicks took over the job in 1914, living in a small building behind the bathhouse. There were other managers, one a "lovely lady" and hostess, Mrs. Agnes Signor, aunt of Harrison and Fred Godwin. She also became owner of the "Half-Way House" in the Carmel Highlands and the La Playa Hotel. It was said that next to Mrs. Signor, Walter and Ivy Basham were the most popular managers during the peak of the bathhouse's popularity. Walter was voted deputy marshal for the bathhouse and beach area on June 14, 1921. Eventually it was sold to the City of Carmel. After much debate between then-Mayor Ross Bonham and Perry Newberry about its upkeep (the city obtained only $100 annually from it) and the possibility of being sued should someone drown while using the life rope which extended from the bathhouse into the ocean, the City of Carmel voted to sell the building in April 1929. It was sold to Mrs. W. C. Mann, who soon afterwards had it torn down and used some of the lumber for her own home.

Shortly before the opening of the bathhouse in 1889, the Hunters, with the dependable help of Delos Goldsmith once again, opened the Hotel Carmelo, which had the distinction of being the first building to be erected in that part of town, on the northeast corner of Ocean Avenue and Broadway (now Junipero) where the Village Inn Motel and part of the Torres Inn site are today. It was an attractive two-story home-style wooden structure with six bedrooms upstairs and two down, as well as a front and back parlor with an open fireplace, a dining room, and a porch with stylish gingerbread. Mrs. Hunter hired a Mr. McLaren to run the hotel for her, and the hotel brochure boasted "two parlors on the first floor and a dining room to accommodate 50 people, with a total of some 18 rooms." Nearby, on the southwest corner of what is now Mission and Ocean, sitting back on the lot was an old barn which was used for rolling stock. This old barn, with improvements, became the well-known Manzanita Hall. Years later the hall was moved to San Carlos Street (where the present Wells Fargo Bank is), after it became the property of M. J. Murphy. Its old location site later became the Mission Laundry.

Eventually, like the bathhouse, the Hotel Carmelo was partly dismantled after its purchase by the Carmel Development Company in April 1903. It was moved down Ocean Avenue to Monte Verde where it became the nucleus of the present Pine Inn on the northeast corner of that intersection.

Hotel Carmelo at Ocean and Junipero, in 1903. It later became the Pine Inn Annex.

In 1898 the Hotel Carmel was erected by D. W. Johnson who, with his mother, built the rustic and lovely shingled two-story hotel on the corner of San Carlos and Ocean. They also owned the old Homes Best Cottage on Casanova and Seventh. The heavily shingled, rustic Hotel Carmel with its upper sun porch and potted palms, was later purchased by Dr.

Hotel Carmel at the corner of Ocean and San Carlos, in 1895. Sketch by author.

and Mrs. A. A. Canfield, who managed it as well. Before the hotel became the property of Mr. and Mrs. Charles O. Goold, other managers were the sister of M. J. Murphy, Ivy Basham, Mrs. Agnes Signor, and Mr. and Mrs. Lou Desmond (Mrs. Desmond was known later as Daisy Bostick).

In the early 1900s, the Coffey brothers, Oscar and Arthur, owned the livery stable on the site of the old Hotel Carmelo. They used the front of the Hotel Carmel for hiring their rigs for sightseeing tours and for a stage stop for their stages to and from Monterey. One of their first drivers was James Machado, who was remembered for his Carmel Bowling Alley, opened in 1906 on Ocean Avenue, where he also offered "Pool, Cigars and Tobacco," according to his advertisement. Later there were other drivers, of course, such as Alfred Horn, Charlie (Dad) Hamilton and Charles Olan Goold himself. Of all the drivers, Sam Powers was best remembered. He was

forced to retire to the position of gate keeper at the bottom of Ocean Avenue for the Pacific Improvement Company after one of the stages turned over and fell on him. Some old-timers remember that Sam was never without a pet parrot, nor his wit and wind to match, and his grandson Earl Wermuth recalled that his wit "matched his stubborness as well."

In 1912 Charles Goold took delivery of two sixteen-passenger buses from Shelly Pickles, the Buick dealer in Monterey. These were the first motor-powered stages brought to Carmel in competition with the horse-drawn stage driven by Sam Powers. The day the buses were delivered, certain citizens met Sam at the watering trough as he dismounted in "an unusually cheerful" manner. "Where's the Carmel-by-the-Sea bus?" they inquired. "Couldn't make the grade and rolled off the road," he gloated. "It's Carmel-by-the-Haystack now."

Mr. and Mrs. Sam Powers at their home in the grove of eucalyptus near the Carmel gate to Pebble Beach, 1921.

A few years later, in 1919, Fred Wermuth took delivery of a twelve-passenger bus, also from Shelly Pickles, as he began to enlarge his business prospects. By May of 1925, Wermuth's newly enlarged stage and transfer storage warehouse (next to what is now Sprouse Reitz) was completed and he was in charge of Carmel's first Western Union Telegraph branch, which he ran until his retirement in 1946.

The Coffey brothers later sold their stage and rig business to Charles Goold and his wife, the former Mary Machado, daughter of Christiano Machado. Coming to Carmel from the Priest Valley in 1905, Goold took a contract from Buck's Tannery to haul redwood and tanbark from the south coast through Carmel Valley along the old river route until he eventually reached what is know as Seventeen-Mile Drive and on to Pacific Grove. Goold had several teams, six horses to a team, and he worked hard building his stock to sixty horses. Known as an excellent driver, Goold soon earned himself the mail contract as well, and later formed a partnership with a Mr. Anthony for a time. They were given many freight and express contracts in the horse and buggy days of Carmel, and they operated out of an office in the Hotel Carmel.

In June 1915 Goold took over the stage and auto service previously conducted by Joseph Hitchcock for the Pine Inn, and in the following year he also purchased a chemical fire wagon which he generously loaned to the local fire department. On February 13, 1919, Goold was given a permit to run "auto" stages. In 1923, he was operating two large auto buses, White Company trucks with red bodies and black tops. One boasted "24 seats and 45 horsepower." Later, the Carmel bus stop and Greyhound stand was located at Dolores and Sixth streets until the new station at Junipero and Sixth was built. The new bus depot opened its doors on March 6, 1948. Designed by Jon Konigshofer, it was built of reinforced concrete and brick at a cost of $50,000 on what had been Goold property. The structure included a dispatching and information office where, following an old Carmel custom, dogs, children and baggage could be checked until bus time. The new building housed not only Bay Rapid Transit Company buses, but Greyhound's as well. Greyhound operated on a regular schedule from the new location. A popular added attraction was a lunchroom, open twenty-four hours. It was owned and operated by Joe's Taxi and was an exciting change for the taxi company after fourteen years at various locations. Joe Olivero started his taxi business in Carmel in early 1930, after leaving San Francisco. In 1957 it was acquired by Florence (Bobbie) Ammerman Reavis and Frank Gida.

Later, this new bus depot at Junipero and Sixth became the perenially popular Hearthstone restaurant. In the same block, some will remember Borden's dairy and also the old Purity Market with its wood and sawdusted floors which stood where the Goold family once had their home, now the site of the newest Crocker Bank. In 1914 Goold also owned the Carmel Garage at the southeast corner of Ocean and San Carlos, which later became the Standard Oil Station and is now leased from the Goold family as the site of Bruhn's clothing store.

Mary Goold worked hard beside her husband, and it was said that she could drive anything almost as well as Charlie. Men had to be hired to drive for Goold, and many of them (single ones) ended up being boarded by the young Mrs. Goold. Over the years the Goolds grew prosperous and invested in

Joe's Taxi stand at Dolores and Sixth in late thirties.

the land around them, as did other early day families. Charlie Goold never shirked his civic duties either, and was both an elected trustee and street commissioner for the city, as well as being a major organizer and the first president of the original Bank of Carmel.

In those early days, from the Hotel Carmel over to Mission Street, the block was somewhat built up under the ownership of the Goolds. After the dining room of the hotel was removed in 1916, Mrs. Goold rented this space to various businesses such as the Lucky Boy Market and Erickson's Dairy (where in 1925 milk was selling for twelve cents a quart) and to Kenneth Wood for his real estate office. Then in 1931 the Carmel Fire Department and the village of

Carmel turned out to view the end of the historic old building as it went up in flames. The Robert Ericksons (she was Irene Goold), who had spent the day in Salinas at the rodeo, returned to find that their upper-story apartment home, along with the rest of the building, had gone up in smoke. The fire was recorded in the old firehouse books and was indeed one of Carmel's spectacular happenings. Old-timers remembered fireman Manuel Pereira and his valiant efforts with a hose "atop a ladder which lay against the burning building."

The site remained vacant until 1935, when M. J. Murphy constructed a two-story white stucco building in Spanish style architecture for Mrs. Mary Goold. It was designed with the front to face Ocean Avenue and the back to face San Carlos and Sixth. However, only the front part was completed in 1935, and the back of the lot was taken up by the building which Goold had moved from Ocean Avenue which had formerly housed the bowling alley. This building was later rented to Steve Patterson who had the Chop House there until 1940, when he moved to a new site two blocks west at the corner of Sixth and Lincoln, which he had purchased from the Devendorf estate. Patterson had come to Carmel from San Francisco, where he had operated the Star Grill.

On the second floor of the front part of the new Goold building were apartments, reached through a small sidewalk garden on the San Carlos side. Their balconies displayed colorful potted geraniums for many years. After Patterson moved in 1940, the building was completed back to Sixth, and this section, facing San Carlos, housed offices for a dentist and doctor. The doctor was William Coughlin, who removed my tonsils when I was a small child. This newer section also contained an entrance to Decker's grocery through the corner of the building. Decker's also faced Ocean Avenue and later became the second Carmel location of Gladys McCloud's apparel shop. The occupancy of the building was completed with a real estate office on the ground floor, facing Ocean and San Carlos, owned by Kenneth Wood and Henry Pancher.

Next to Decker's was a small business, started in 1933, owned and run by Walter Tutnull. He sold beer and wine and had a card room frequented by locals in much the same way the popular El Fumidor owned by Harry Baxter on Dolores Street did in later years. Some Carmelites will remember Tutnull's place when it was owned by the Leidigs, who called it the Smoke Shop. Next to what had been the Smoke Shop was the dry goods business of Meagher and Company, which became the popular Putnam and Raggett in 1946, when Frank Putnam and Mark Raggett became partners. Later it was known as M. Raggett, which it remained until Mark Raggett retired in 1978.

On March 1, 1940, Mary Goold had construction started on a "reinforced concrete L shaped structure" for the enlargement of Victor Graham's Five and Ten, which fronted Mrs. Goold's land, next to what had been Wermuth's garage. (The garage had two gas pumps, for private use only, and upstairs the offices for Wermuth Transfer, established in 1919.) Guy O. Koepp of Carmel was the architect for Graham's new store. The 3,000 square foot addition included an iron-railed mezzanine with red chairs and a writing desk where customers could rest and wait for friends, while they looked upon shoppers below, and counters full of fascinating things that could be bought for a song. There was a sixty-foot hardware counter and a thirty-foot toy counter and counters devoted to glass and chinaware, as well as a complete line of gardening supplies. The new store also boasted a basement elevator, the second in Carmel.

William Bishop, who is a long-time Carmelite, told me about the days when his restaurant was on the southwest corner of Sixth and San Carlos, opposite his friend Patterson's Chop House. He said that they would often joke with each other over the fact that each time the fire bell rang, more than half of their respective customers departed. When Mr. Bishop retired, he sold his restaurant business to June Simpson.

There have been many changes to the Goold holdings. After Robert Norton resigned as Police Chief in 1940, he returned to real estate. It was Norton who was responsible for the removal of the stables once belonging to Lynn Hodges and the old barn that had been the site of dances as late as 1927. Also in 1940, another real estate transaction took

Blacksmith John Catlin at the door of Plaza Fuel, November 30, 1928. He served as mayor of Carmel for a time. Slevin photograph.

14

The earliest known photo of the Pine Inn, with campgrounds and the old Hotel Carmelo, which became the Pine Inn Annex, in the background.

place. The site of the proposed Gates-Phillips Carmel Hotel, to face Devendorf Plaza on the north side of Sixth, and the property extending to south of the Weaver Kitchen home and store, including the Keith Evans-Peter Carmalt Plaza Fuel Company property and John Catlin-Francis Whitaker Forge in the Forest property, went to the owners of the hotel corporation, Dr. Amelia Gates and J. C. Phillips. There have been many more recent changes to the Goold property, among others, and many of us have felt the loss of businesses which had long adhered to the way of life and pulse of the village. In 1956 the business census for Carmel was as follows: forty-seven apparel shops, thirty-three gift shops, twenty-eight art and craft establishments that did retailing, forty-six hotels, motels, inns and lodges, and thirty restaurants. There were fourteen businesses handling horticultural supplies and services, seven shops selling jewelry, silver, and clocks, six shops selling sporting goods, pets, and toys, one camera shop (my father's), three drugstores, six groceries, and three bakeries. Needless to say, a little over twenty years later the contrast is astounding!

In the early days and even in the 1940s and early 1950s it was not unusual to find merchants visiting with one another or sitting outside on a box, chair or even the curb in the sun with "half an eye" on the business. In very early days almost the entire village attended picnics at the beach and Point Lobos. Keys and instructions on how to find a place were left on the door of real estate offices. I well remember how for many years my father would leave a projector or screen or even a camera on his step at closing time for a customer who was a little late. The same items were returned in the same manner at times, and were found by my dad on the step in the morning. There was extreme faith in the basic honesty of man, and it held true all over the village when store deliveries were made or outgoing goods awaited pickup. Even houses were left unlocked until just a few short years ago, and businesses sometimes had notes to "serve yourself and leave the change—gone for a minute." Today Carmel is a potpourri of paradoxes with traffic so thick that neither squirrels nor people can get across the street at times, its locally-oriented businesses all but disappearing. It has become a tourist town, with a continuing art colony of aspiring and famous names.

The first property of the partnership of Devendorf and Powers to be sold was to a Mrs. E. A. Foster of Monroe, Michigan, a black woman who purchased two lots on Dolores and ten lots on the south side of Ocean Avenue between San Carlos and Mission. The total amount for the twelve lots was $1,000. Terms were not only easy, but simple, at five or ten dollars down and five dollars a month.

By the time July Fourth of the summer of 1903 rolled around, the Pine Inn was complete with tent grounds which began where the shops to the northwest of the present front steps are, and continued over to the present bank, which was once Beaux Arts, on Lincoln. The grounds were complete with first-class canvas tents for hire according to one's financial status. Tent rentals were one dollar to three dollars a week, and meals were available for forty-five cents.

15

The main building of the Pine Inn opened with Miss Mary DeNeale Morgan acting as temporary manager for her good family friend Devendorf. Her brother Thomas, an architect, had just finished helping Devendorf with the final plans for the Pine Inn. Later managers were George Shields in 1912 and Roy Newberry in 1916. The cook for the new Pine Inn was on loan from Mr. and Mrs. Frank Powers during the time that they awaited completion of their place (later named "The Dunes"). His name was Pon Sing, and he was a cousin of Carmel's beloved Pon Lung Chung. Pon Sing later did all the village laundry while living in a small shack behind the Grant Wallace home. His request to the then two-year-old City Council, on September 19, 1918, for permission to conduct his laundry at San Carlos and Seventh, was refused.

Lobos Lodge in 1920, during time it was owned by John Jordan, who also owned the Pine Inn. The lodge was razed in 1976. Sketch by author.

The Pine Inn on Ocean Avenue, 1908.

The history of the Pine Inn is an interesting one. At one period in its history, it displayed the name "Official Automobile Membership Blue Boar Hotel." John Jordan bought the Pine Inn in 1920 and was its owner for twenty years. He was a scholarly man, and an actor, and was remembered for "sounding out his lines" (in particular Shakespeare) while offering assistance to tourists awaiting rooms. Jordan served as a councilman and as mayor. He also operated the popular Lobos Lodge in connection with the Pine Inn until he sold it to Tirey Ford on April 14, 1923.

John Jordan also owned other Carmel properties and was responsible for the lease which enabled the Palace Drug Store to open on May 23, 1922, next door to the Pine Cone publication plant in the Storie Building. When Harrison Godwin took over the Pine Inn in 1940, it had become a rather dusty and rustic building which had begun to show its age. However, the main building still had a hint of its former charm, including the Carmelo Hotel

annex which had arrived via skids. One year after Godwin purchased the Pine Inn he had almost totally transformed it into a sparkling combination of old and new, with the old annex taking on a warmer, more comfortable charm while maintaining the same Victorian pattern throughout its interior. Harrison Godwin had been connected with Del Monte Properties between 1921 and 1929 and again from 1935 to 1940. He had been a cartoonist with the *Los Angeles Examiner* with two daily cartoon strips to his credit, and he was a popular Abalone League team member.

From November 1954 through May 1955 the halls and main lobby of the Pine Inn went through an extensive renovation. The old sun porch became the Red Parlor. In more recent years there have been additions and innovations, but the quiet, quaint charm which belongs to early Carmel has been retained.

The name Godwin was also connected with another popular Carmel landmark known as La Playa. Built originally as the home and studio of Chris Jorgensen, who had married one of the Ghirardelli girls, it was one of the first homes in that part of Carmel and boasted one of the town's first swimming pools and seaweed-insulated walls. In 1911 tragedy struck when Mrs. Jorgensen drowned while swimming in the Carmel Bay. Soon after his wife's death Jorgensen leased the house to Agnes Signor and left for a time to live with an artist colony in Yosemite. Mrs. Signor had already been part owner and manageress of three San Francisco hotels before the 1906 earthquake, and she set about making a success of La Playa. She built up quite a fashionable hotel with an equally fashionable line of clientele. Sending for her nephews Harrison and Fred Godwin, who were in Canada, Mrs. Signor enlisted their help in turning four bedrooms, a bath, a sitting room, and a twelve by thirteen foot kitchen into sought-after accommodations. More rooms were added on later. So popular was La Playa that at its first anniversary celebration, on May 25, 1922, 125 people were there, dancing to music furnished by Moffit's Orchestra.

In 1923 Mrs. Signor suffered a heart seizure which left her paralyzed, but until the time of her death she continued to keep up an extensive correspondence with many seasonal families who had been her faithful clients. Shortly before her death she transferred ownership of La Playa to her nephews, who remained joint owners. In December 1924 a spectacular fire almost totally consumed the hotel and showered burned shingles on the play yards of Sunset School. In 1925 the Godwins rebuilt the hotel and added thirty rooms, and during the depression they managed to hang on to it with a weekly room and board rate of five dollars and a reputation for delicious food. After the depression, the Godwins began to update the hotel gradually, and by 1936 another thirty rooms had been added, along with a four-room penthouse. Then just before

Looking east on Ocean Avenue in 1917. The Storie Building is on the left, then Cortland Arne's vine-covered barber shop, the Poeble-Leidig Building, and Hotel Carmel. Slevin photograph.

the war Fred Godwin bought out Harrison and continued improvements to the hotel with the addition of a new dining room in 1948 and by increasing the number of rooms to eighty. In 1952 Ashton Stanley became managing lessee, and today La Playa is run in keeping with earlier traditions by Howard E. (Bud) Allen.

Old ranch roads were the main cuts through the wilderness of early Carmel, with Ocean Avenue serving as a secondary street to Junipero. Most of

Oldest known photograph of Carmel/Monterey Hill.

the business took place at the crossroads of Ocean and San Carlos. Ocean was referred to as "the devil's staircase" because it was so full of ruts and holes, which can easily be seen in early photographs. It was quite a cause for celebration when in 1916 the Pacific Improvement Company representative, R. H. McKaig, threw open the Carmel Hill toll gates without charge while the construction of the highway between Carmel and Monterey took place. Anyone wishing transportation from San Francisco to Carmel during its early days had only to notify Mr. Powers when he was in the San Francisco area. He would notify Mr. Devendorf, or other prearrangements were made, so that the travelers' train would be met in Monterey by a surrey driven by one of Devendorf's colorful drivers, usually Joseph Hitchcock, who deposited them at the end of an almost two-hour journey up Carmel Hill at the doorstep of the Pine Inn. It was a great source of amusement to these same stage and surrey drivers when they later passed the "new fangled" autos whose drivers sometimes had to drive backwards up Carmel Hill in order to make it, while the horse and wagon passed them by.

Joseph Hitchcock was hired by Franklin Devendorf in March 1903 to take care of the necessary hauling and rolling stock belonging to the Carmel Development Company, and it was said that Joe "did it with style," endearing himself to many. Joseph Hitchcock was a rare link with our local heritage. Born in Carmel Valley January 9, 1881, he was the grandson of Lieutenant Isaac Hitchcock, who arrived with Commodore John Sloat. His grandmother was a Carmel mission Indian girl named Madelena Peralta, stepdaughter of James Meadows. Joe was linked still further to our local history by his maternal grandfather, Antonio Victorine, an early day whaler at Point Lobos.

In Joseph's long life he had many jobs, ranging from ranch and cattle worker, horse breaker and trainer, to working for W. L. Fletcher, a blacksmith and harness shop owner from whom he learned the harness and leather trade. His first work with Devendorf was as a surrey driver. From 1911 to 1916 he drove a four-horse stage from the train depot in Monterey to Carmel and back, until the stage and auto business was turned over to Charles Goold in June 1915. Joseph married the former Hazel Ayers in February 1909, and they reared three children. Later he spent seventeen years in Oakland as an auto trimmer. He returned to Carmel in 1933 where he had an auto upholstery shop on the west side of Mission Street between Seventh and Eighth. He remained there until the death of his parents and a brother in 1945. After 1945 he began writing for local weekly newspapers and lived in a little brown shingled cottage on Paso Hondo in the valley, with his mare, Laurel, and his two dogs, Phoebe and Pal. He died in 1968.

Joseph Hitchcock and Laurel, 1960.

Several things took place under the newly formed partnership of the Carmel Development Company. In the summer of 1902 Franklin Devendorf ordered four portable houses to be sent from San Francisco. Delos Goldsmith was given the job of placing them at the required locations. The first of Carmel's authentic board-and-battens was put up where the 1940 post office was located. This later became the stock exchange. The second was placed at the corner of Seventh and Monte Verde. The third portable, by prearrangement with the obliging Mr. Devendorf, was occupied by Mary DeNeale Morgan, her mother, Christine A. Morgan, her sister Jeanie, and her architect brother Thomas, during their stay the year before Miss Morgan took up permanent residence in Carmel. It was located on the west side of Lincoln between Fifth and Sixth, near another portable

owned by Mrs. Mabel Grey Young. Mrs. Young's old cottage has remained in the same location all these years. In the late 1940s Mr. and Mrs. Jose Fernandez lived there. The little cottage that had been Miss Morgan's also remains in its original location, next to the present library parking lot on the northwest corner of Lincoln and Sixth. A high fence has been added around it.

The cottage of "Uncle" John Staples, which had been nestled between the old Morgan and Young cottages, was moved for the third time in recent years. Originally it was situated across the street where the back entrance to Su Vecino Court is today. It was moved in the 1930s to make way for the new businesses which were to occupy that block, on the last two lots of the Devendorf parcel, sold in February 1940. John Staples, or Uncle John, as he was known, lived at the original location of his cottage until his death. He was remembered not only as a cousin of Frank Devendorf, but as the person who took care of all the mail at the Carmel Development Company Store.

In the spring of 1903, Devendorf purchased another twelve portable houses which were brought to his lumber yard located on Lincoln between Fifth and Sixth, almost on the site now occupied by the present Sans Souci restaurant. However, after the failure of another 100 to show up, a shipment of doors arriving instead, Devendorf sent for M. J. Murphy to do his building, and Murphy set up his own lumber yard. It was from Murphy's lumber yard that Joseph Hitchcock performed his hauling jobs for Devendorf. He worked with a William Cochran, hauling the heaviest loads with his four-horse team as the lumber supply increased, as more and more lots were cleared. Some of the early lumber came from the valley mill on land which is occupied by the Comings family today. During this time some of the first Japanese arrived. They had been hired to clear the land for the Pacific Improvement Company. They began at the old Hotel Carmelo site and went up the hill and along Ocean Avenue and Broadway (which we now call Junipero). It is interesting to look at some of the old saw blades which are now in my brother's possession and imagine those days when the land was being cleared.

By the time the second group of portable houses arrived, so did Mrs. E. Ury (born in Elk Grove, Wisconsin in 1838) and her daughter, Mrs. L. Brake. They came from San Jose with a black couple, Roland and Emma Henderson. Mrs. Brake settled in her cottage on Mission and lived there until her death in 1922. Mrs. Ury bought a lot on the corner of Ocean Avenue and Lincoln where she continued to live until her death on October 26, 1925. The Roland Hendersons opened a restaurant in the old carpenter shop on Dolores Street which had originally belonged to Delos Goldsmith. Goldsmith had sold the shop a short time before to Mrs. E. A. Foster, who lived there from January to September of 1903.

Perhaps it is a roundabout tribute to Delos Goldsmith, but his buildings were not only well used but long lasting. His original carpenter shop was put to use, following the Hendersons' occupation of it, as Carmel's first school, financed by Devendorf, with a Miss Westphal as teacher.

Through spring and summer of 1903, Carmel saw the addition of the Carmel Development Company Store and Contracting Office, which occupied the site of what later became "Doc Beck's" and then "Doc Staniford's" place. Until Louis Slevin's stationery store was built, the Development Company supplied everything from onions to hats, as well as dispensing the daily mail, with the exception of milk. According to all accounts, Carmel's first milk supply came from a couple of contented bovines belonging to the Charles O. Goold family. A later source was the Stewart-Martin property at the Mission Ranch with Andrew Stewart's cows doing the supplying and Stewart making the milk runs. About this time the Littlefield family made their runs from the Hatton Dairies at the mouth of the valley (where 100 gallons of milk from forty cows was the quota in 1924), and L. C. Horn also took turns as a milkman for the Hatton Dairies, with fourteen customers on his routes. In 1903 the Carmel Dairy was established. In 1916 Perry McDonald opened the first real commercial dairy in Carmel on the site which many years later housed the portrait studio of family friend Murle Ogden on Sixth. McDonald was responsible for the long-lived custom of milk shrines, which he stationed about every block and a half. Although McDonald had several drivers, Mr. I. B. Waterbury, who made two deliveries each day, stood out in the minds of many. Eventually McDonald sold out to a Mr. Ricketts who had his dairy where Luciano Antiques is now.

At about the same time the Ericksons had their dairy in the old Goold building. Later Earl Graft combined Ricketts' and Erickson's into Graft's Carmel Dairy, located where the Mediterranean Market is today. Graft operated his dairy business for twenty-seven years, and it was considered by all to be one of the most popular spots in town, not only for the quality of its dairy goods, but for its luncheons and the comfortable surroundings with the

Looking south on San Carlos toward Sunset School from Hotel Carmel at Ocean Avenue. Note watering trough at left center.

wonderful murals created by Jo Mora. The special Mora cow decorated the bottles and menus, much to my delight as a child. Later the locally-owned dairies and milk shrines gave way to the larger companies like Borden and Meadow Gold.

With the opening of the Carmel Development Company Store there were other arrivals. The F. S. Samuels family took over the management of the Pine Inn after Miss Morgan and her mother left Carmel. Mr. Samuels was then vice president of the Oceanic Steamship Company. He also took over the running of the Development Company Store, leaving a Mr. Pryor in charge of the Pine Inn. Mr. Samuels' son Fred worked with Pryor, who lived on Camino Real and Eleventh. Also coming to Carmel in late 1902 and early 1903 were Mr. and Mrs. Alf White; Dr. Peake, who was remembered for his donkey cart among other things; David Von Needa, who opened a bowling alley; Dr. Beck, who had his office and pharmacy in the Carmel Development Company Store building; Mr. and Mrs. Enoch Lewis and their son Louie. (Mr. Lewis later opened his paint shop on the site of the present Hansel and Gretel Candy Store owned by the Frank Robotti family); the Melvin Nortons from Pacific Grove; the John Turner family; F. B. Ackerman; Stephen C. Thomas; E. A. McClean; the Walter Kibbler family; the Arnds; and the Wyatts. In early 1904 new arrivals were the Wermuths, the Narvaez family, and the Michael J. Murphy family, whose son Frank had the distinction of being the first "white boy child" to be born in Carmel. The first white girl was born in the winter of 1903 to a French family by the name of Saville. They lived in a little cottage which became the second school, at San Carlos and Ocean. Another baby girl was born that winter, to the Utter family.

Michael J. Murphy was Carmel's leading builder after Delos Goldsmith and was well-known and well-liked for over fifty years, until his death in March 1954, which took place not long after his wife's. Originally from Minden, Utah, where he was born June 26, 1885, Murphy came to Carmel on a visit in 1902. In 1904, after his marriage to Edna Owens, he returned to live in Carmel where he became associated with Franklin Devendorf as builder for the Carmel Development Company. Murphy became a general contractor in 1914 and in 1924 he established M. J. Murphy, Inc., a business which sold building supplies, did rock crushing and concrete work, and operated a lumber mill and cabinet shop business situated between San Carlos and Mission streets (where the Wells Fargo Bank and parking lot are today). The Murphy lumber yard was located on what is known today as the Fenton Block. This location later housed the Mediterranean style Carmel Theater, built in 1935, and adjoining real estate offices and Pep Creamery, which were all razed in 1959. The site is now known as the Carmel Plaza and is considered by most old-timers to have been the beginning of the changes which have so drastically altered the face and tempo of Carmel. Mr. Murphy's yard stands out in my mind as a place where children were welcome to play nearby, as we often did, sending paper boats down the full culvert which ran alongside the Devendorf Park while a friend kept watch to see if the boats made their journey under Ocean Avenue and came out near Murphy's yard.

The Murphy's home was on Monte Verde at Ninth after they left the old house by the dunes, and there were few early Carmel homes that Murphy did not have a hand in either planning, designing or building. He had a part in the construction of the Pine Inn, Highlands Inn, Harrison Memorial Library, the De Yoe home at La Loma Terrace, Andrew Stewart's chalk rock valley home, the Pixley home in Pebble Beach, and many, many others. Many residents-to-be would simply send Murphy their specifications and he would go about his business of building according to their requirements, notifying them when the job was finished that they could take up residence. Almost without exception Murphy had a hand in all those homes along what has always been known as "Professors Row." His firm did the rock crushing and supplied wood materials for the construction of the Coast Highway in the 1930s.

Quietly active in village life, Murphy was also a city council member, at which time he helped lay plans for planting the trees along Ocean Avenue. He also was a charter member of the popular Manzanita Club. Though Murphy retired in 1941, and closed his firm down completely in 1954, he retained an interest in the M. J. Murphy Lumber Company in Carmel Valley, which his son Frank continued to operate for several years.

It was James O'Banion Handley who carried on the Murphy tradition. Handley came to Carmel in 1926 and worked for Murphy, and when Murphy retired, Handley opened his Carmel Builders Supply on Junipero. Like Murphy, "J. O." Handley and his crew have always welcomed children who came to hear the whine of saws and watch the work, or to gather scraps of wood for projects ranging from blocks to bird houses, and it was with much sadness that we noted J. O.'s passing in December 1978.

Louis and Joseph Slevin and their mother arrived in town and built their home on Carmelo in 1902. That fall they paid $325 for a twenty-five-foot lot where they built their store. Between Slevin's place and the property that was to become the Nortons' on the corner of Ocean and Dolores stood the little

Burnight's, to the left, and Slevin's, in 1910. Slevin photograph.

plank board building which housed the Carmel-by-the-Sea Bakery, a home bakery, which later became Thomas Burnight's Bakery and Candy Store. In later years Burnight moved across the street and the building was purchased by Delos Curtis. Burnight was remembered not only for the quality of his business and his "soope doope molasses," but also his many contributions of time and effort to Carmel's civic affairs for many years, even after his retirement. Joseph Hitchcock remembered that all the new buildings of this era were a cause for celebration, and Slevin's was no exception. While its floor was being put in and before the sidewall partitions went up, there was a dance there, with much foot stomping and the music of both fiddle and accordian, the air filled with festivity as both locals and visitors enjoyed themselves.

With the opening of the Pine Inn came the circulation of a now rare publication of the Development Company's brochure which read as follows:

"The prohibition clause in all deeds prevents the sale of liquor and insures the absence of the 'Sunday picnic' class.

"The sand dunes, with their 'toboggan slides,' and convenient lounging places, keep the babies and the invalids happy outdoors all day long.

"Sea Ozone and pine balsam combined have a wonderful recuperative effect on tired nerves.

"Most young women never wear hats the whole summer long.

"The town boasts of rugged, browned, and happy youngsters of the near-to-nature type physically and the aesthetically capable type mentally."

In 1911 the Pine Inn brochure read as follows:

"The regular railroad rates from San Francisco to Monterey are: Single trip $3, or return round trip as follows: Leaving Sunday, return Sunday $2.50. Leaving Saturday afternoon, return Sunday $3. Leaving Saturday, return Monday $4. Leaving Friday, return Tuesday $4.50.

"From May 1st to October 15th there is a round trip excursion rate, purchasable any day, good for 90 days, but not beyond October 31st, for $4.75.

"Thirty-ride commutation tickets, good for any member of the family, limit 6 months $60.00.

"During summer months a 90-day round-trip ticket is sold from interior valley points for about one and one-third of single fare.

"Accommodation rates: $2.00, $2.50 and $3.00 per day. $12.00 to $17.50 per week and $45.00 to $60.00 per month, with the $3.00, $17.50 and $60.00 rates including bath facilities. Children under 10 years one-half price and nurse maids three-quarter price."

A second brochure put out by the Carmel Development Company in 1911 read as follows:

"There are over 375 houses in Carmel. There are two hotels, several boarding-houses, two livery stables, a general store, a butcher and green grocery shop, a dairy, a hardware store, a notion store, Wells Fargo & Co. Express Office, Sunset Telephone Co., U. S. Post Office, a candy store, a bakery, a photo supply and several curio stores, a barber shop, a garage, a drugstore, several physicians, a lumber yard, and a dry goods store that supplies every clothing necessity for women and children with goods of a class not usually offered in country villages.

"Real estate demand has now been started for beach property, midst a pine forest, near historic surroundings, with neighbors of genial, sympathetic character, devoted to nature and her beauties.

"There is no other territory to supply this demand. The law of supply and demand governs real estate values, as everything else.

"The town has increased population over 80% each year for seven years. There are now over 400 permanent, regular inhabitants (by the milkman's census method), and several thousand people join them in the summer months.

"Over 60% of the residents of the town are devoting their lives to work connected with the aesthetic arts, as broadly defined. College professors, artists, poets, writers, and professional men find the surroundings conductive to their best work. The Arts & Crafts Club, The Free Library (over 2,000 volumes), the Town Hall, the Gentlemen's Social Club, the Ceramic Club, all show an unusual public interest in worthy purposes.

"All trees, shrubs and personal property on the streets, such as sand and stone, are reserved and preserved by the Development Company and listed on the Development Company maps which are filed on record. In this way the cutting of trees and hauling of heavy material over the streets is prevented, and so far as possible the natural appearance of the streets is safeguarded. Ocean Avenue has been parked with small enclosures in which shrubs and trees have been planted.

"Sports are offered at the Carmel River mouth through the ownership of the Development Company with a safe fresh water pool.

"Suggested excursions:

1. Walk to Carmel Mission, where the body of Father Serra and three of his associates and several Mexican Governors are buried.
2. Walk over a portion of the boulevard into the pine forest, to the north of the town, to the old Padre Rock Quarry in 'Timid Lovers' Glen.'
3. Walk to the mouth of the river and gather mussels from Abalone Point and have a 'mussel bake' picnic.
4. Drive around the Boulevard which skirts the town, past Abalone Point and the mouth of the river, and on the hill, whence in route from various points, you get the full sweep of the bay or of the mountain ranges which form the walls of the valley.
5. Walk or drive to Point Lobos (whose proper name is Pt. Carmel) and picnic near the articulated skeleton of a giant sperm whale.
6. Walk or drive to Yankee Point, with its Giant's Bathtub, Smuggler's Cave, Peninsula Tunnel, and Meteor Hole, and picnic on the 'Bay of a hundred islands.'
7. Drive up San Jose Creek to the redwood forest, and then walk to the Abrego Falls, in a granite gorge, forming a miniature Yosemite.
8. Walk to the Chinese Abalone Camp.
9. Drive or walk to the Cypress Forest and picnic on the open ocean shore.
10. Drive up the valley to the Laurelles Rancho, past some very interesting dairy and fruit farms.
11. Drive down the coast to Idlewild and the Sur river country, where there is some fine hunting. This road leads through occasional dense redwood forests, and past straggly, broken, wave lashed shores.
12. Walk or take horses over the Santa Lucia Hills, past the haunted house, to the Deserted Coal Mine, and thence down a granite gorge to the ocean road.
13. Take Seventeen-Mile Drive, and incidentally visit Del Monte, Pacific Grove, and the New Club House at Pebble Beach, about one mile, and enjoy the most modern, up-to-date accommodations.
14. Visit the Custom House, Colton Hall, Chinatown, Fishing Village, and other historical points about Monterey proper.
15. Take a launch and explore the arched rocks, coves, bays and irregular recesses carved by the ocean from the granite rock forming the coast.
16. Drive over to the dress parade given by the soldiers at the Military Presidio of Monterey every afternoon.
17. Fish for steelhead in Carmel River, or take a

boat for salmon and sea-fish for every kind in the bay.

> For further suggestions see
> J. F. Devendorf
> Manager Carmel Development Co.
> Carmel, Monterey County, California"

Not long after Slevin's store went up, the mail began to arrive daily from over the hill. It was brought in a leather bag by Sam Powers and left at Slevin's instead of the Development Company office. Among those receiving mail were Mr. and Mrs. P. Wall, Judge A. Carrington, and Mr. and Mrs. Walter T. Kibbler, who had come from San Francisco. Kibbler, a native of Boston, had been a resident of San Francisco for several years where he had established himself in two pharmacy businesses, one at Hyde and Truh streets and another at Truh and Larkin, where the Roos Brothers Store first opened. He had been active in San Francisco politics and had been a foreman for the San Francisco Grand Jury. After the 1906 earthquake the Kibblers came to Carmel. Kibbler traded his buckboard for two lots from Devendorf and built one of the first real unportable eight-room homes in Carmel. The Kibblers were popular early residents. Walter Kibbler served as mayor of Carmel twice and helped to see the town through its incorporation.

Other early mail came addressed to three of the seven Guichard sisters, Stella, Mai and Etna. There was also a building contractor, Chris Ambruster, the Weaver Kitchen family, a Mrs. Steave and her daughters Alma and Ella, the M. H. Bremners, and the Narvaezes, who were still camping on Junipero, near the Goolds, while their home was being built. Leon Narvaez worked as a painter, paper hanger and mason. Some of the chimneys he built are still standing. His grandson Ray is owner of the old Piccadilly Nursery on Dolores today. Ray Narvaez has roots in Carmel and has seen many of its changes, some of which may affect him in the near future when the Linharts (heirs to the Dummage holdings) carry out plans for a new complex of shops which will remove the office of Narvaez's business and the one-time home of Pon Lung Chung, the last of the two little cottages which have remained, and also Miller's Guild Shop.

In 1906 Mr. and Mrs. Henry Larouette and John C. Mikel arrived. Mikel, said to be a French Canadian, was an excellent furniture maker and also worked as a partner to Mr. Larouette in what was known as the "Fix-it Shop." The Larouettes' daughter Agnes later became Mrs. John Tennis and was responsible for the building of several charming Carmel cottages. The Larouette sons were Otto and

"Fix-it Shop" or "Noah's Ark," owned by Henry Larouette, built at Dolores and Seventh in 1904. Sketch by author.

Eugene. The family residence was built on Lincoln near Eleventh. They were known as "warmhearted while radiating a good old-fashioned understanding and hospitality." Mrs. Larouette was remembered not only for her good-natured kindness, but for her delicious home-baked bread and her sewing. She was responsible for many of the costumes worn at the masquerade balls given by the Manzanita Club in its early days.

Henry Larouette's shop was located on the west side of Dolores Street, where it remained for many years. It was demolished in January 1927 to make room for the $60,000 two-story reinforced concrete structure built by Dr. R. A. Kocher at Dolores and Seventh. Originally the Fix-it Shop was perched up on a rise, which Dr. Kocher had leveled, as he also did at the site of the Hotel La Ribera (now Cypress West) in 1929. Some referred to Henry's shop as "Noah's Ark," a nickname which was used by locals. Henry truly was a "Mr. Fix-it," as he fixed anything from fences to stoves and clocks to plumbing. He hung the shades in the 1918 City Hall, with J. C. Mikel's help. Henry's sole advertisement was a sign at the front of his store with another under it which read, "We mend everything but broken hearts." Quaint and highly individual, he was well respected for his old-fashioned integrity and good judgment both in serving on the town council and on a personal basis. Henry was also known for his "charming and prized" carvings which he made from the manzanita root. He and his partner, Mikel, and Mikel's faithful dog, Fritz, were an important fixture in early Carmel.

Not long after the Larouette's arrival, the Ralph Waldo Hicks family came, living for a while in the little place behind the old bathhouse. Mr. Hicks was the bathhouse manager for a time. The Alfred Hertz family, the Rev. Benjamin Fay Mills, H. W. Puden, Martel Stoney, Miss Alice Miller and her nephew, Allen Knight, were other newcomers. The boom was on for Carmel: animals both domestic and wild filled the dirt streets and paths; wagons and surreys began leaving wider ruts in the ground as new merchants set up their businesses, some in tents and others in both roughly made and well constructed buildings. It was a few short years away from the first automobiles in 1912, the first electricity in 1914, and the first gas in 1930.

An early day builder who had his hand in the construction of the Poeble Building was Arthur (Artie) Bowen, who worked for J. F. Devendorf for a six-year period during which he helped construct several other buildings. Bowen came from nearby Sotoville, a settlement on Jose M. Soto's Rancho Santa Rita in Salinas, where he was born in January 1887. Bowen was one of ten children born to parents who settled originally on land at the site of the Battle of Natividad. Later they moved to Cooper's Switch and his father became a foreman for Miller Lux. Eventually the family moved to San Jose where Bowen learned of Devendorf and the Carmel Development Company. After he went to work for Devendorf, "Bowen built a house for himself on the east side of Casanova between Ninth and Tenth, where he resided until his marriage in 1906." That cottage is still standing. Bowen is remembered today by several people, by some with high regard, and by some who not only called him a colorful character but a spinner of yarns. In later years Bowen went from carpentry to contracting and remodeling, with the Pine Inn on his list of remodeling jobs. He retired in 1955, after building his newer home on the northwest corner of Tenth and Torres, where he lived until his death at the age of eighty-two in September 1969.

Others who contributed to the building of Carmel in her early days were: Thomas Reardon, who had his business where the Mediterranean Market is today, and later in a building that housed Borden's Dairy at one time; Roy Babcock; S. J. Wyatt; Arthur E. Donnelly; Robert Franklin Gillette; C. S. Beck; Leonard Perry; Ernest Bixler; Percy Parkes; H. C. Stoney; J. E. Richards; Harry Turner; W. A. Van Horn; T. G. Feliz, paper hanger and decorator; J. E. Nichols; William A. Daggett; William Noggle; J. Kleugal; and William Plein, to name only a few. Electricians had their day, too, and some of them were S. J. Tice, E. E. Sirlee, and William H. McConnell.

Early day hauling and handy work was done by

Charles O. Goold (who also did repairs to the streets before William Askew, Sr. took on the job) and a Mr. Re Dante, who became Carmel's first paid garbage man. Others who were in the early hauling business were Tony Garcia, Roy Babcock, and C. S. Beck, who served as tree pruner for the city after incorporation, and Lester Thompson. Thompson also did street work, along with Albert Otey, Walter Basham, Thomas A. Oakes, and J. P. Lacey. There was even a local map maker and grader by the name of Henry F. Cozzens. However, there were no restrictions on building, no licenses or fees required before incorporation, and absolutely no zoning— Carmel was having her heyday. By 1904, a board-walk was built on both sides of Ocean Avenue, affording some escape from the dust in summer and mud in winter. During the spring of 1904, Devendorf had his Japanese work crew plant a row of young pine trees down the middle of Ocean Avenue. In 1906, when north Carmelo was still a sandy street bordered by a wooden sidewalk and the road now called Scenic, which went around Point Loeb, was completely treeless, he had his crew clear the hay field by the sea and plant again. This time the planting was of cypress trees along Scenic and San Antonio, and Devendorf encouraged all new residents to plant trees, too.

During those first years of the twentieth century, Louis Slevin had the distinction of being four "firsts" in the history of Carmel—first to open a general merchandise store, first postmaster, first express agent, and first city treasurer. He purchased eight lock boxes for mail customers and set them up under the north side of the roof overhang at the front of his store. He was worried that he had put up too many, but by 1906 there were not enough and he had to think about another order. Louis Slevin was a man of many facets, to say the least. He, his brother Joseph R., his mother, and his wife were all well liked and very civic-minded people. There were instances in which some considered Louis Slevin cool and businesslike—when his "principles" were threatened or his anger stirred he could be quite aloof—yet he was known for his keen wit and love of a good joke. He was a tall, dark haired man with a slight limp. His wife, Mabel, was said to be small, dainty and "sweet natured." Mrs. Slevin was also said to spend a great deal of time looking after their children at their home on Carmelo near the ocean. The Slevins had two children, a daughter who suffered from an undisclosed malady, and a son who became ill and died at the age of eight. The tragic loss of their son was keenly felt by the Slevins and their many friends, and it was said that Mr. Slevin leaned more heavily on his cane after the loss of this boy.

The Slevins' store, until it was sold in 1934, was a favorite place of many of the village children as it was "absolutely" full of curios, cameras, wonderful model ships in various shapes and sizes, coins and stamps from many lands, and numerous photographs which Mr. Slevin himself had taken, besides stationery, ink, picture postcards and the Carmel News Company.

When not at work, Slevin, in keeping with an old Carmel custom, was out about the countryside taking pictures of all the happenings, not only around Monterey County but other points north and south. Often there would be a sign posted on the door saying "Closed, gone to the countryside." Slevin's good and long time friend Cortland Arne, the barber, would accompany him, and his sign would read

Members of the Slevin family in front of Slevin's store in 1905. The post office was in Slevin's then. Slevin photograph.

"Gone for a picnic" or "Out with Slevin." Being modest, Slevin was not a man to talk about himself, but he had a unique and rare stamp collection as well as some of the finest rare books. In his collection of books was a first edition of *Cook's Voyage* published in 1784. He was the only person to have an extensive collection of photographs of Carmel from 1903 to 1940. He could produce a valuable or unknown subject from the depths of his marvelous collection, which often put him in the limelight, such as at the time the city of San Francisco was searching for a photo of the grizzly bear known as Monarch which had been kept in Golden Gate Park. After what seemed to be an impossible search by officials of the city of San Francisco, Louis Slevin came to the rescue with the photo he had taken of Monarch in 1899.

Mr. Slevin was a prolific writer of opinions and suggestions and many of his statements and letters appeared in local and Monterey publications, among them his historical outlines on sailing ships and the history of some of those same ships along our coastline. After the sale of his business to Mrs. Louisa Dummage, the Slevins took a trip to San Jose and in September of 1942, they purchased a home at 750 South Eighth Street, where they lived until Mabel became ill and died in January 1943.

Looking east on Ocean Avenue. On the right are Schweniger's, a bakery, Slevin's, and a grocery. On the left are the J. W. Hand office, Curtis Candies, and the Storie Building. Slevin photograph.

Her funeral was held in Monterey at El Camino.

It was said that Slevin was "truly" upset because his former business was remodeled so extensively by James Thoburn (it is now Spencers) and divided into two shops for Mrs. Dummage. It was the last of Carmel's false fronts to vanish, Schweniger's old place having become the remodeled Carmel Bakery the year before. Louis Slevin kept in touch with friends in Carmel, in particular a Miss Hadden. When his health and strength weakened so that he could no longer look after himself as he wished to do, he made the decision to move to the Casa Bella Sanitorium in Saratoga. It was during this final move that he offered much of his collection of books and photographs to the city of Carmel, while reserving his property in the Highlands and his stamp collection for his brother Joseph, a nephew and close friends. It is truly a loss for Carmelites that these marvelous collections were not accepted and that Mr. Slevin felt such resentment over the lack of enthusiasm for his offer, for today the only work of his that we have on our Peninsula are those original plates, speculated to number between 80 and 150, which Mr. Slevin personally gave to friends before his move to San Jose. There are also some on file at Bancroft.

Louis Slevin died in 1945, and not very long before his death he wrote to Miss Hadden: "I am resigned and have given up trying to do anything more but crossword puzzles and the like, and under the circumstances have no enthusiasm for this world

... to say nothing of being 'awful' lonely. I wish I could write more cheerfully but I'm hoping to be provided with a harp and wings before too long."

Carmel has had other excellent photographers, such as Emile Bruggiere, Arnold Genthe, Louis Josselyn (who became the official photographer for the Forest Theater), Johann Hagemeyer, George Seideneck, and Edward Weston, but Slevin's photographs were among the most highly prized.

Things began to happen fast for Carmel, and by 1908 there were 150 new residents despite the fact that the only conveniences in town were a stage and wooden sidewalks. However, James Franklin Devendorf's dream was becoming a reality. The three stores and two restaurants and public school which opened in the old Goldsmith shed no longer stood alone, for Devendorf and Powers had put Carmel into the hearts and conversations of many.

The first public school, opened by Devendorf in 1904 in the Goldsmith shed, was presided over by Miss Mary Westphal from San Jose, and her salary was paid by subscription while she taught the seven children who attended the school. When the little shed proved too small for the eighteen students who attended the following year, the classroom was moved to the M. J. Murphy lumber yard, across from where Devendorf Park is now, next to a big oak. This second location served until a new two-room school in the mission style, with curved arches and placements for nonexistent bells, was built on the present patio section of the old Sunset school at the corner of San Carlos and Ninth. One of the two rooms was used as a library at first. Franklin Murphy is credited with naming the new school Sunset. Classes began there in the late spring of 1906, with a Mr. Saxe as a new teacher. The term began with forty-eight students in eight grades, with two teachers. The first student to graduate, in 1907, was Mabel Stallings Norton, who later became Mrs. George Linsley. The first principal of the new school was Mrs. Willis White, whose husband, the Rev. Willis White, was responsible for founding the first, and now traditional, Carmel Kite Festival, on February 21, 1931. The Whites' home at the corner of Camino Real and Ninth was a popular place for children for many years. Their daughter, Mariam White Herrick, lives in that home as of this writing.

In 1916 there were ten graduates from Sunset. The former Guichard sisters, Etna and Mai, remember the occasion as the end of their first year of teaching at Sunset. In early 1926, Mrs. Joseph

Sunset School, built in 1906 on the southeast corner of Ninth and San Carlos.

Schoeninger was responsible for organizing a Parent-Teacher Association. She was its first president. The new association was responsible for the establishment of a kindergarten in June of 1927, as well as the first hot luncheon services, with lunches prepared in the homes of members and brought to the school. In late 1931 additional classrooms and an auditorium were built, which have served us well over the years. An article on the subject in the "Carmelite" on November 26, 1931, was written by Dora Hagemeyer. At first Mrs. Willis White was not only principal but taught the upper grades. Miss Genevieve Pratt taught the lower grades. During this time in the school's history, each graduate of

Sunset had the choice of attending either Monterey or Pacific Grove High School, as did students who attended the private school of Miss Emma L. Williams, namely Connie Heron, Phyllis Overstreet, David and Frank Lloyd, and Janie Hopper Vial.

The Sunset school, which I attended and later was graduated from, and then again returned to for my graduation from Carmel High School, was abandoned as a school on June 30, 1965, after being taken over by the City of Carmel and becoming the Sunset Cultural Center. Today, in outward appearance, with the exception of plants where there used to be climbing bars and sand piles, and a multitude of cars now parked on all the playing fields, it has changed very little. Inside, very definite changes have taken place, but faces and memories are there and emerge during concerts, ballet or art displays. Probably the most vivid of all memories came when I took my daughter Carmel to a Girl Scout meeting in what had been my old first grade classroom. I personally, and many, many others, were happy when the decision was made to put to use such a charming part of Carmel and of our lives, rather than tear it down as had been done to so many other buildings.

Carmel realized the dream of its own high school in 1938, when the Sunset School District voted 724 in favor of, and 252 against, the passing of a $165,000 bond issue for a new high school. Charles Van Riper was at the head of the committee for obtaining signatures which were needed on a petition for Sunset School District to secede from the Monterey Union School District. Vice president of the school board at the time was Shelburn Robison. E. A. H. Watson, owner of Watson's Nursery, was precinct chairman, and Robert Leidig, Mrs. G. Morehouse and Mrs. Arthur Strasburger were committee members. Peter Mawdsely and designer-builder Calvin Hogle were chief fact finders. Construction bids were opened in February 1940 with the lowest bid, $116,280, submitted by Harold C. Geyer of Monterey. On September 10, 1940, Carmel High School opened its doors on a twenty-two-acre campus.

Sunset School Song, 1916
(Words by A. Anthony)
Of all the schools in this district,
We love this best above the rest,
Because this school is just for
    ambitious boys and girls.
We're happy here with teachers dear;
There's some of us whose mothers
    went to Sunset years ago,
    yes long ago.

Our loyal hearts with love for dear
  old Sunset,
Will ever glow, will ever glow.

Chorus
Sunset, Sunset, that's the school we
  love,
Sunset, Sunset, that's the school with
  ranches above,
Tra-la-la-la-la-la-la-la
That's the school with ranches above,
Tra-la-la-la-la-la-la-la.
Some think it hard to come so far
  to school,
But we do not, but we do not,
We'd come a longer way with right
  good will;
To come to school, our Sunset school,
A monument is this our fine Sunset;
Oh, here's to you, oh, here's to you,
A monument is this our fine Sunset,
With such a view, with such a view.

Other schools were also available to the children of Carmelites in the '20s. In 1921 Forest Hill School, designed by Ralph Helm Johonnot, was opened by its founders, Mrs. Minna Steel Harper and Miss Mabel Spicker. Standing in a natural pine forest in the Carmel Woods at First near San Carlos, the school was organized for the purpose of applying new thoughts in the education of children, allowing them "independent thinking and expression while providing a natural atmosphere and wholesome surroundings for the instruction of music, dance, arts and crafts, languages, weaving, sewing and outdoor excursions." The school had facilities for both indoor and outdoor activities and was both a resident and day school with accommodations for twenty-five children from nursery to high school level. All staff members were accredited and the school also had a summer camp which lasted six to eight weeks beginning each first of July in the Carmel Valley.

In 1936 the five lots in block 12 of Forest Hill School were restricted to use as a park and playground which divided the ravine adjoining the land. Today the ravine and land strip, some of which has since been filled in, is used by the senior citizens of the community. In 1954 members of Carmel's retired community, my own grandfather Hale included, were searching for a place where they could set up horseshoes and shuffleboard, and at this time a small portion of the land was designated for their use. The surrounding property belongs to private individuals, and various other proposed uses for the park are a continuing topic of conversation.

Douglass School for Girls in Pebble Beach, in 1928. Today it is the Robert Louis Stevenson School.

Another school, the Douglass School, was established by Grace Parsons Douglass as a girls' camp in 1925 and became a school in 1928. William Raiquel was the architect for the Mediterranean style stucco, tiled building, which sat nestled in the trees. The school featured tennis and badminton courts, a theater, riding arena and barbecue area, and emphasized sports and the outdoor life. In 1948 Grace Douglass opened a 128-acre coeducational year-round summer camp twenty-two miles up the Carmel Valley which specialized in equestrianship and supplemented the normal school routine during the winter with the introduction of English riding classes. In 1950 a kindergarten was introduced into the program and the institution became known as Robert Louis Stevenson School for Boys. It remains under that name today.

By 1910 many changes had taken place in Carmel, with the gradual increase in population. In 1906, Mrs. Norton (later Dummage) opened a home bakery just up from Slevin's Stationery. A Mrs. Wise ran it for her. Thomas Reardon arrived in 1906, as did Carmel's first barber, Cortland J. Arne, who set up business first in a tent on the site of the first Carmel Bank Building, which later

C. J. Arne's shop being set back in place after having been moved earlier for the original Bank of Carmel in Carmel. The bank roof shows in the background. Franklin Devendorf, Frank Powers, and Sam Powers are watching M. J. Murphy do his job.

housed the second Wells Book Store run by Henry Meade Williams. Arne occupied this site until his tent was moved west ten feet to its second location, in 1923, to make way for the construction of the first Bank of Carmel. At that time he exchanged his tent for a vine-covered board and batten, which was then moved in 1928 to his home to be used as a woodshed. That same year Mr. Arne moved into his new shop building, which was ultimately to become Camera Craft when my father, Dale Hale and his partner, Thomas Tousey, opened it in conjunction with their business in Pebble Beach. When Mr. Tousey retired after nineteen years as my father's partner, my father and mother, Rosa Lee Hale, ran the business together with my brother Kevin, until after thirty-two years my parents decided to retire.

When my father and Mr. Tousey first opened their business, Mr. Arne's barber, Paul Mercurio, who had worked for him for twenty-two years, would come in while they were cleaning things up and reminisce. Paul had come to Carmel in 1918. He later went to work for the popular "Doc" Jones after Arne died. "Doc" Jones's, which opened in 1925 on Dolores, was the last of the old Carmel barber shops when it closed its doors in 1975 and became the Keane Gallery.

Very few changes were made to Mr. Arne's orig-

inal building when it housed my parents' business. From the first partition where the first fireplace stands was a lean-to addition which extended about nine feet back from the partition and included the second fireplace. Behind this lean-to was an open patio with the largest fuscia tree I have ever seen. This patio was later roofed and finished for additional merchandise display. The old bathroom and Mr. Arne's napping quarters were left intact. When my parents sold their business in February of 1978, some of the old tiles and patio windows still remained as well as the Dutch door (another old Carmel custom) and the brick wall of what was once the first Bank of Carmel next door. My parents, whose business depended upon the locals and not the tourist trade, also saw fit to retain staunchly another old Carmel custom by closing for lunch and a "siesta" if desired, while leaving a sign on the door stating simply, "Open when open, closed when closed." It was also a source of amusement to my parents and other old time Carmelites to hear comments by newcomers about "what an old-fashioned place of business" it was. My parents echoed the words of all old-timers when they said, "It's part of Carmel, the Carmel we've always known and loved, and we like it this way." The greatest compliment for my mother and father, in my opinion, came among the tears and bottles of wine and champagne from old and dear customers who, as they gazed around one last time, said, "I can't, I won't say goodbye, because it's like saying goodbye to the end of an era."

Cabbages and Kings, Walker Shoeshine, and C. J. Arne barber shop on Ocean Avenue in 1928. Slevin photograph.

At the end of 1905, the organization of many new village activities began, first with the founding of street fairs given by the Arts and Crafts Club with the festivities of the Dutch Markets. The

Arts and Crafts Club began with a conversation between Miss Elsie Allen, who had formerly taught at Wellesley College, and a Mr. Brewster, who was then a manager of the Columbia Park Boys Association of San Francisco. This group of 100 to 166 boys came to Carmel each July from the bay area for encampments in the vicinity of the Carmel Woods near the present Father Serra statue on Junipero, and also about a quarter of a mile east of Goold's

The Columbia Park Boys arrive at the Southern Pacific station in Monterey, in 1917.

Inspection time for the Columbia Park Boys during their 1917 visit to Carmel.

garage. The boys, always a popular group with the village, usually built a huge bonfire and delighted the entire village with a variety show. In appreciation for the response of the locals, the boys would help with local activities such as those of the Arts and Crafts Club.

The first meeting of the Arts and Crafts Club was held in Miss Allen's home in the summer of 1905. The club was established for the purpose of attracting artists to Carmel, and its policy was "dealing with arts and crafts in their most liberal sense." At the first meeting, Miss Allen was elected the president, with Mrs. Mary Braley as recording and corresponding secretary, Mrs. Frank Powers as vice president and Louis Slevin as treasurer. A resident of San Francisco for many years, Mrs. Josephine K. Foster, was elected president on September 4, 1906, and in turn appointed the following to be members of a committee to raise money for a site on which to erect a clubhouse: Mary E. Hand, Fannie Yard, Dr. J. E. Beck, Carrie R. Sterling, Sidney Yard, William E. Wood, and Arthur Vachell. At this time the club was incorporated under the official name of Arts and Crafts Club of Carmel. The club began raising money for its projects by holding "The International Dutch Market" in the park that once existed across from the Pine Inn. According to Ferdinand Burgdorff, "the group felt we were quite an internationally represented populace despite the fact that there wasn't one Dutchman among us, until Tilly Pollack and the Van Ripers came to town. In any event an open air market, Dutch style, seemed quite appropriate." It was always a festive occasion, drawing not only the locals, but outsiders. "There were always several booths, each well decorated, serving a variety of interesting goods." There were also booths with things to eat, and all participants wore colorful costumes according to the nation or character they were portraying.

One of these early day festivities was described by Clara Newton Nixon as follows verbatim: "Those in charge of booths were: Dutch, Mrs. George Sterling; French, Mrs. Joseph Hand; Spanish, Mrs. Sidney Yard; Irish, Mary Connelly; Arts and Crafts, Mrs. Henry Burlington; Japanese, Mrs. Michael Murphy; Colonial, Mrs. C. W. Hollis; Italian, Mrs. M. J. Foster; candy, Miss H. Gilmore; coffee, Mrs. M. R. Allen; cake, Mrs. Jessie Short; Scotch, Miss Isabelle (Bell) Martin; Dutch Chocolate Vendor, Miss A. Peterson, who was assisted by four little "flicks"; peanuts, popcorn and flower vendors in costume, while donkey rides were furnished by manager Mrs. Maxitone-Graham." Sinclair Lewis acted as master of ceremonies in his Dutch girl costume. A picture donated by Ferdinand Burgdorff (Ferdy, as we affectionately called him) was raffled off at a dollar a ticket, and a Mrs. Schumaker told fortunes. The affair was a huge success and at the end of the festivities at three o'clock, everything was "sold out, bringing the profits of the day to $145."

In the early part of 1907 two lots were being considered for the site of a clubhouse. One with an eighty-foot frontage was purchased for the sum of $600. By July of 1907 a clubhouse costing $2,500

one operator, and the Bloods reopened as the Dolores Grocery in 1927.) The museum held its first reception on Memorial Day, May 30, 1913.

The Arts and Crafts summer school continued to be a success, drawing specialists from Stanford University and the University of California at Berkeley, who contributed their time by giving lectures and demonstrations. Among them were Pedro Lemos, Ira (Rem) Remsen, whose Carmel studio was on Dolores, Thomas V. Cator, David Alberto, Jesse and Cornelius Arms Botke, and Blanding Sloan. Also at this time Mr. and Mrs. William C. Watts opened their gallery up on Dolores and were hosts to many who came to see the work of early Carmel artists. The Arts and Crafts Club was under the able leadership of Mrs. Mary Hand as its president for some sixteen years. She also helped to see to the building of the Arts and Crafts Theater in 1922. In 1927, the clubhouse was sold to the Abalone League, and later still its site became known as the "Green Room" of the second Golden Bough Theater, where the third Golden Bough now is on Monte Verde.

There were other happy occasions for fund raising for the Arts and Crafts Club. It was reported that one of the "most unforgettable" events was a May Fete given in 1922, when all the main thoroughfares were cleared of traffic and the Eleventh Cavalry Band of the Presidio of Monterey furnished the music for a "great parade" down Ocean Avenue, led by Carmel's one-man police force, Marshal Gus Englund atop "Billy." Also on horseback was Grace McConnell, who became Mrs. James Thoburn and owned the Carmel Riding School, also known as the San Carlos Riding Academy, until 1925 when she sold it to Lynn Hodges. Donald Hale led the group

Gus Englund, atop "Billy," and a motorist, on Ocean Avenue in 1930. Picture shows, from left to right, the Storie Building, the tiled roof of Cabbages and Kings, Arne's barber shop, First Bank of Carmel, Carmel Drugstore, and the hardware store.

had been completed at a location on Monte Verde. The Arts and Crafts Club thrived and in late 1910 established an arts and crafts summer school called Cedar Croft, with Mrs. Sidney Yard as its director. The following were its instructors: botany, Miss Helen Parkes; drawing and painting, Miss De Neale Morgan; pottery, china painting and art needlework, Miss Etta Tilton; dramatic reading, Mrs. Sidney Yard; and music, Miss Carrie Carrington. A Mrs. Pell taught art metal work. The club also sponsored what was called a "Museum of Yesteryear," with Miss Ida Johnson as its chairwoman and curator. She began her post asking for such items as "plants, birds, butterflies, moths, insects, animals, Indian pottery, sea creatures and organisms, geographical and topographical data, local geology and relics." Mr. E. G. Blood and his wife, Minnie, generously opened their grocery store for donations. (Their store at the corner of Ocean and Lincoln later became the first telephone exchange, with

The Wilson-McConnell riding party ready to set off on Turner Creek trip, June 11, 1921, in front of the Pine Inn.

of Helen Van Riper, Phyllis Overstreet, Kathryn Cooke, Betty Greene, Alice Greene, and Bonnie Gottfried, all on horseback. The rest of the procession starred the local fire department, school children led by Arthur Cyril (who impersonated Lady Godiva), and an organ grinder, Hilda Argo, complete with monkey. At the end of the parade a group gathered at the Soldiers Memorial to watch as Irene Goold was crowned Queen of May by "Doc" Kibbler, after which there was a Maypole dance and athletic events. There were also "gayly decorated booths" where various ladies of the community offered an array of "goodies" from their kitchens.

Entertainment was also provided by a dog show, with the winners "bitter, battle scarred enemies" Brownie Overstreet and Teddy Goold, Tiney Arne, Freckles Yates and King Tyrone Kuster. The good fun ended promptly after Brownie won the prize for the best behaved, and Teddy, reported as "jealous," broke into a fight with his arch rival, which "broke up the show and wrecked the booth." Pal, the only dog in the village allowed free roam of the streets, was rumored to have watched the entire proceedings with disdain, but then Pal was an unusual part of Carmel's history. Given to Bruce and Rupert Kendall by an Indian woman, he found in his old age a warm hearth and food in the valued friendship of King Mederos, who took care of him until he died in 1943 and was buried within the grounds of the Forest Theater. The daytime activities of the May Fete were brought to an end with the baby show held in the Leidig building which "had just been built for Stella's Dry Goods Store." (Also known at one time as La Accommodation, it was replaced in 1939 by the new Bank of Carmel.) The blue ribbons went to Jane Elizabeth Walker, Lawrence Leidig, Jr., June Lewis, and Forde Fraties, with the proud

parents looking on. Toward evening there was more entertainment and the Grand Ball.

Another entertaining event staged by the Arts and Crafts Club was the "Sir-cuss Day." One in particular was held in July of 1923, and the *Pine Cone* announced the following: "It's going to be a great day for the nuts. Jo Mora and Jack Jordan are issuing an open challenge for a potato race on the beach at 11 o'clock on Sir-cuss Day. Gifts of fog horns, buzz saws and other hideous noise-makers will be appreciated by Perry Newberry, the human calliope. The main show will be held under the big top on City Square (block 69). Nothing to equal it has ever been attempted." It seems that Fred Leidig was busy collecting sawdust for the ring, and Joe Hand was getting ready to play "Buffalo Bill." It was said he "was chosen wisely" since he had been a pony express rider once, carrying mail between Ragtown, California and Carson, Nevada.

Gus Englund had chosen his marshals for the Sir-cuss Day, and they were John B. Jordan, George Pollack, Frederick Godwin, Ernie Passailaigue, Mayor W. T. "Doc" Kibbler, Argyll Campbell, George Kegg, Harvey E. Russell, and Philip Wilson,

An old Carmel street sign in front of the San Carlos Riding Academy at Mountain View and Ocean. Slevin photograph.

32

Sr. Decorators of colorful circus wagons were Paul Mays, George Kegg and Daniel W. Willard, and all floats were done by local artists. Harrison Godwin and Albert Van Houtte acted as ringmasters. Alberta Langley was elected lion tamer, and Marie Gordon portrayed Joan of Arc. Elephants were portrayed by various citizens, with Tom Reardon and Richard Hoagland representing the lead elephant. Tilly Pollack guided an "educated bear," and Lynn Hodges was billed as Tom Mix's only rival. It was reported that various acts performed under the Big Top were both excellent and hilarious. The Ammerman brothers did a juggling act and a clown brigade was led by Harrison Godwin and Ernie Schweniger.

Not content with fund raising and other marvelous events which brought out the spirit and cooperation of the village, the Arts and Crafts Club also had a Civic Committee which took part in many major decisions affecting the growth of early Carmel. Some of its members were Thomas Reardon, Dr. Alfred E. Burton, Jessie Arms Botke, Susan Creighton Porter, and Charles Sumner Greene. Under the direction of the Civic Committee there were annual contests for garden beautification, as well as other endeavors such as the Christmas plays hosted by the Arts and Crafts Theater, which was also closely connected with the Forest Theater in the early days. The formal opening of the Arts and Crafts Theater was marked by the presentation of two plays by John Northern Hilliard, *Thrice Promised Bride* and *The Queen's Enemies*, under the direction of Dr. Alfred E. Burton. The two following nights' performances, presented by Perry Newberry, were the play by Charles Caldwell Dobies, *Doubling in Brass*.

Music for these special occasions was furnished by Arts and Crafts orchestra members Joseph Walter, F. A. Clark, Ralph W. Hicks, Felix Yangoo, Aubrey Sleeth, Austin Chinn, Mrs. A. B. Chinn, Fenton Foster and Josephine Culbertson. Josephine Culbertson came to Carmel in 1906 after the San Francisco earthquake with her friend and companion, Miss Ida Johnson. Both ladies were immediately accepted by the community and very well liked, and Miss Culbertson established herself in the local art community. The two soon opened a studio for the display of their art work. Their home, named "Gray Gables," was at Lincoln and Seventh. "Talented and warm hearted," they played hostess to many of the young boys of the village, and established a local boys' club named "The Dickens Club," its meetings held in the gardens of "Gray Gables." The many acts of kindness and help of these two

women were well remembered by men who were young at the time—Taggert Wermuth, Dick Botke, Douglass Scott, Robert Norton, Roy Fraties, the Machado boys, and Gordy Campbell. Miss Culbertson was also the organist for the Community Church for over twenty years. Her interest in Carmel never waned and was continued with regular visits from friends at the Murphy Rest Home in Pacific Grove up to the time of her death at the age of eighty-eight in April 1941.

Josephine Culbertson also had a hand in the formation of the local Art Association. There had for some time been a need for a local gallery where local artists might display their work, and a Mrs. J. Venestrom Cannaw, during a summer visit, had mentioned to her friend Josephine Culbertson that someone should organize such a place. In August of

Miss Josephine M. Culbertson
STUDIO NEAR LIBRARY

1927, Miss Culbertson sent invitations to various artists, seventy of whom were local or part-time residents. Meeting at Gray Gables, twenty artists made the decision to form a local art association. First president of the Carmel Art Association was Pedro J. Lemos, who was replaced by George Seideneck when Lemos had to go overseas. Josephine Culbertson was chosen vice president, with Kathryn Corrigan as her second. Homer Evans was secretary, William H. Norton was financial secretary, and William Seivert Smit, treasurer. Clay Otto was placed in charge of securing a gallery for the group in a central area of the village.

Among the association's early members were Myron Oliver, E. C. Fortune, C. Chapel Judson, Catherine Seideneck, Miss Celia Seymour, Mary De Neale Morgan, George Koch, E. Grace Ward, Isabelle Nicholson, Whitney Polache, and Zada B. Champlin. The motto was "Advance the knowledge and interest in art, create a spirit of cooperation and fellowship between artists and the people." This motto remains the same today, and many fine people, among them many great artists, have continued its purpose. On October 21, 1927, the Art Association opened its doors at the Art Gallery in the Seven Arts Court, with more than sixty paintings for public view, and the gallery, next door to the Seideneck's studio upstairs, was open every afternoon from two to five with Kathryn Corrigan as curator. By 1928 there were 149 members, forty-one of them active, and the association was renting extra space for exhibits.

In time the decision was made to purchase the Woodward studio which had been the home of Ira Remsen (later the Beardsley Gallery). The well-loved and remembered Forest Theater production, *Mr. Bunt*, was planned and written in this studio. By 1932 there was a total of $413.31 in the association fund. In 1938, under the leadership of attorney Ross, later Judge Ross, with negotiations by real estate man Barnet Segal, a new gallery was built. At about the same time, the Carmel Art Institute was started by Kit Whitman. Elsa Maxwell gave a fund raising event at Del Monte Lodge for the benefit of the new school.

In 1936 and for many years after, the clothesline exhibits held in the summer on the patio of the Pine Inn were a popular Art Association event. I remember the instructions from my parents before we arrived for these events—"Don't touch or make remarks if you do not like what you see." Over the years the work of our gifted artists has found its way from the Art Association to private collections all over the world, as well as into such places as the Metropolitan Museum in New York, the Petite Palais in Paris, Cleveland Museum of Art, Pennsylvania Academy of Fine Arts, and the Luxemborg Museum of Paris, to mention a few. Many members of the Art Association have belonged to the National Academy of Arts.

W hile purely civic associations were forming, a not so civic minded clubhouse (according to some) established itself where the Blue Bird, originally owned by Medora Schaffer, once stood, and it was called the Carmel Whirl. Though it furnished sightseeing tours and a news sheet, it was said to "flash the less delicate side of village life," becoming a "gamey road house" which was finally raided. A group of ladies belonging to the Arts and Crafts Club later came out with their version of an earlier copy of the ten cent newspaper known as "The Whirl," and in good humor mocked the earlier publication. The paper, printed July 24, 1909, with the title, "The Whirl Is On, Get Busy And Whirl Around! There is something doing all the time!" The following verse by Michael Williams began the front page article.

Oh, come and whirl around,
Whirl around, whirl around!
Come, bring your girl, and whirl
Happy and free!
Whoop it up, boy and girl!

Make joy's teetotum twirl
To the devil all troubles hurl
Here by the sea!
"We're off! Watch us whirl!"

"When Mrs. Josephine Foster organized the 'Whirl Around' which is tearing Carmel-by-the-Sea wide open today, it is safe to say that she had no notion of the size, noise, rambunctiousness, and general all-round whirl-i-giggle-ity of what she started . . . and which had so worthy an object, namely the betterment of the financial condition of the Arts and Crafts Club of Carmel. She will know today! And so will all of us!

"For the idea which Mrs. Foster launched has been developed and pushed on by Mrs. Foster and her helpers (in a word, it has been fostered) until it has grown into the dimensions which promise to make it the most noteworthy of all carnival stunts which have been so happily brought off in Carmel.

"Appropriately enough, the day's doings begin with the appearance of this paper, sold by Miss Helen Cooke and her band of whirling newsgirls."

The final paragraph of the story read, "Allen Beir is the bartender. Can you beat that name for the man on the job? No 'high signs' go with Mr. Beir. He can't give a straw for such! But he can sling coffee like a professional. We hear disquieting rumors as we prepare our account of the Roadhouse, that it has fallen under the suspicion of the law. Whether or not the Merry Widows are raided, it is safe to say that Attorney for All Ladies, William Greer Harrison, may be depended upon to bail them out in time for the Vaudeville Show. This will be given in the Roadhouse at eight o'clock in the evening."

Another new addition to the village in 1907 was Henry Warren's hardware store on Ocean Avenue in the middle section of the old Poeble Building. It has become known in recent years as the Village Hardware. Another earlier business in the same location was a furniture and hardware store under the ownership of Fred W. Ten Winkel, in charge of the furniture section, and Ernest Perkins, who ran the hardware division of the business. The same building was also later occupied by Holman's Carmel Store, complete with wringer-style washing machines of the latest model. R. G. Leidig was manager. The business was sold to Merrell Investment Company of Carmel in March 1928, and its name changed to the Household Store. Next door to the west was the space occupied by the Palace Drug Store which became the Carmel Drug Store, under the ownership of Thomas Bickle and the management of Peter Stuart Burke, with the same name and wonderful old marquee lighting. It was purchased by Burke and his wife, Virginia, in December 1937 Eventually Mrs. Burke owned and ran the business

Robert G. Leidig in front of Holman's Department Store.

with a partner, Ralph Castagna. On the opposite side of what became the Village Hardware was the building which housed Kip's Grocery for many years, until 1973. This same business had also been the Leidigs' grocery in days gone by, and it was behind this building that our early day firefighters stored their equipment. Kip's Grocery was a long time landmark, as was the old Market Del Mar which became Nielsen Brothers on March 13, 1932, when Harold and Walter Nielsen took it over. Neilsens still serves in the old Carmel tradition.

Also on Ocean Avenue, at the same time Henry Warren opened his hardware store, Thomas Burnight opened his ice cream and candy store in the building where Mrs. Wise ran the home bakery for Mrs. Dummage. Later Burnight moved across the street to the location which soon became known as Curtis's, when Charles Delos Curtis bought out Burnight in 1912. The old Carmel Development

Store went out of business in 1908 and Devendorf moved his office into the Otey building across the street on the site where Hobart P. Glassel built his stone building, also known as the Perry Building. Glassel displayed imported yarns from Scotland and his own hand woven wools and apparel. Eventually this building was sold to Mr. Constance S. Lowell and also housed Cabbages and Kings, Carmel Investment Company, and the Cinderella Shop. The Cinderella Shop was remembered as the "pioneer women's shop for Carmel." It was established in 1916 next door to what was known later as Basham's, and on Tuesdays and Saturdays the shop also carried baked goods, jams and jellies made by local ladies, until 1923. Then in late 1925, plans were made by Janet Prentiss to move the Cinderella Shop across the street to the Glassel Building where it remained for many years despite remodeling and changes in property ownership. In March 1976, then in the Swanston Building, built by Comstock Asso-

C. More Curtis, in white apron, leans against the popcorn wagon. Next to it is the Carmel bus. Slevin photograph.

ciates, the Cinderella Shop went out of business. The space became the front section of artist Danny Garcia's Gallery.

When the Carmel Development Company went out of business in 1908, the building was purchased by Dr. J. E. Beck of San Jose, who lived on San Carlos between Eighth and Ninth. He renamed it the Carmel-by-the-Sea Pharmacy. The business was threatened by fire in 1915 when a nearby meat market, owned by Mr. Dangerfield, burned. Dr. Beck ran his business at this location until January 1929, when he sold it to Donald "Doc" Staniford, also of San Jose. This transaction included two lots on Ocean, each 120 feet deep, as well as the buildings on them housing the Eureka Dairy Depot and the Carmel Shoe Shop. From 1929 until 1953 the business known as Staniford's was run by Staniford and his wife, although in December 1931 Fred Leidig became the owner of the property. Leidig

Carmel auto stages in front of the Carmel-by-the-Sea Drug Store on Ocean Avenue, 1912. Slevin photograph.

On March 11, 1937, Mr. and Mrs. Staniford posed in the doorway of their drugstore, which was in the oldest building on Ocean Avenue. The building directly behind is the Village Shoe Repair, which was run by E. Builder, and behind that is the McDonald Dairy Depot and then the Dodge truck and car showroom.

decided to tear down the building, and "Doc" Staniford moved to temporary quarters shared with the Mission Meat Market. However, instead of being torn down, the old building was purchased by J. O. Handley and was moved to his lumber yard on Junipero and Fourth where it is still being used as part of that business today. A new building then took the place of the old Staniford's. The name was kept for a while, before the building was leased to Frank Castagna for his pharmacy from 1955 to 1958, then to Womble's Drug Store. In the mid-1970s it became a tourist trade business, with the building still under the ownership of present day Leidigs.

The building next to what had been "Doc" Beck's had an interesting early history as a bowling alley, owned and run by Dave Von Needa. The building was divided in 1914, when the back part became the Pine Cone and the front part became the post office, with William Overstreet acting as assistant postmaster until 1922. After 1922 the building was enlarged to make space for ninety-six more post office boxes, and divided to house other businesses at various times, among them the Quality Market, which was later divided to house Bill Brady's Boys' Town (the Varsity Shop), which had been the second door to the west of what had become Womble's Drug Store, with the small space between occupied by Milton Eagleton's "Joyce's."

Next to what had been Hazelton's Electric in 1924, Quality Market and now the Varsity Shop, was a shoeshine parlor which was owned by a black man who shined just about everyone's shoes in Carmel over the years. He remained in that little business, his handmade sign, "Shoeshine Palor," (incorrectly spelled) over the entrance, until it and the building next to it (owned by James Doud, owner of the Blue Bird property, De Loe's Tap Room, Vinings Market, Carmel Grocery, and the old Montmorency service station) were remodeled to enlarge their neighbor Whitney's. The entrance to the popular Whitney's, which replaced Basham's in 1926, was originally shared with a real estate office.

Today the business known as Maxwell McFly's occupies the old real estate office and shoeshine "palor" site, and the present Peppercorn on the opposite side of the Doud Arcade occupies what was the cocktail lounge section of Whitney's. The restaurant was across the back of the three street side businesses. Near Whitney's was one of the last of the few old false fronts left on that block of Ocean Avenue. It had originally housed the Carmel Meat

Market with a Mr. G. Noller as its proprietor, and was on the site of Dangerfield's meat market which burned in 1915. Today on part of the old meat market site is James Rowe's Village Shoe Tree in the lovely Las Tiendas Building, owned by Robert De Yoe. This was also once the site of the office of the second Carmel Realty Company, which was later owned and run by Ray C. De Yoe. The first was opened in the old Storie Building by Mrs. Rose De Yoe in 1913.

The other portion of Las Tiendas was once occupied by Frank Charles's jewelry business (known as Frank's) and some will remember this site when it was the Economy Grocery, owned by J. G. Anderson in 1923 and T. L. Edler in 1924. After the death of Ray De Yoe, the site of the Carmel Realty first became the business of Conrad Imelman known as Imelman's Sports Wear Shop, then Mahar's, then Draper's. Today it is Gordon Robertson's business, known as Robertson's. Several years ago the business which is now Cork 'n' Bottle also housed Ewig's Grocery and later Carlton's Market. Next door to the Cork 'n' Bottle, on its west side and on the corner, is Fortier's Drugstore, owned by Florence Berrey. At one time this was the second location of the business run by one of the seven Guichard sisters, Stella.

The Carmel Meat Market on Ocean Avenue was established in 1914.

The following passage quotes Mai Guichard McGrury: "Originally Stella took over one side of the building when she first opened and leased from Mr. Arthur Storie, who had just put up the building across the street from the present Fortier's and that was in 1912. Then Sister took over the other half of the building and the upstairs, subleasing it to others, including Mrs. Rose De Yoe, keeping the upstairs for her living quarters which our youngest sister Etna and myself, who were teachers at Sunset,

The Carmel Realty Company and Charles Franks' were located where Robertson's clothing store is today.

shared with her. It cost sister twenty-five dollars a month to run her business there and she really did very well, making Mr. Storie and his wife happy with her management of the place until 1939, when she had to move her place because the new bank was going in on the site. Sister called her place Stella's Dry Goods. At the time sister had to move, I was married to Mr. McGrury and we lived on the fifty-foot lot where Ellie's Hay Loft is, and Sister bought the property next door where the post office later went in, and it was here that she took over the running of the little cottages which ran along that block to the end along Sixth. My husband, who had had previous experience with dry goods, was looking for a place for Stella to reopen her business, and it was at this time that Mr. Leidig put up his new place on the corner of Ocean and Dolores where Fortier's is today, and leased it to my husband who in turn bought Stella out, though she continued to work for us. We all agreed to call the new place L'Accommodation. In 1941 Mr. George Fortier outbid Mr. McGrury for the lease on the building and he had Mr. Comstock remodel it for him, while we relocated in our new store on our property next to our home on Dolores. This is where we stayed until my husband sold the business and Sister's old property when they were going to put in the new post office. The business became the Pioneer, Balzar's and Mason's, the last of which was located next door to the old post office and was referred to as 'Carmel's Department Store.'"

Also in 1925, the Leidigs (still owners of their family's property next to that of De Yoe's) erected a building which backed up to Las Tiendas and housed T. L. Edler's furniture store with studios on the upper floor. This attractive building remains standing today.

In 1900 the four sons of Elizabeth Leidig boarded a train at Vandalia, Illinois, bound for the west coast and San Francisco. The two older boys, Robert and Fred, were tempted to go into business together, while the two younger sons, Benjamin and Lawrence, wanted to go "somewhere where it resembled more like home," and Carmel was that place. The two younger boys were enrolled in Sunset School and in 1906 the two older boys went to work for Devendorf in his grocery located on the northwest corner of Ocean and San Carlos. It was later owned by the Leidig family and was the location of their future grocery. This same location also housed Espandola's, run by Byron G. Newell from 1927 to 1937, when it became Kip's Food Center, with its open air display of fruits and flowers, run by Kip Silvey. Kip's was later run by Tony Kastros, Louie Poulos, and then William "Bill" Arley Smith. Bill turned over the grocery business to the Brunos in 1973, and they moved the business to the original location of Pilot's Market, owned by Walter Pilot, on the northeast corner of Junipero and Sixth. However, as a grocery, Kip's was an Ocean Avenue landmark for seventy-one years, beginning in 1902 when it was built by Poeble. Today the old building with its painted wall murals and its oiled floor has given way to an outlet for Dansk where factory seconds are sold.

To return to the Leidig story—the older boys soon opened their own "Carmel-by-the-Sea Grocery" on Ocean Avenue between Lincoln and Dolores, where Derek Rayne is today, complete with blackboard (another Carmel tradition) where the daily specials, weather and tidbits of local interest were listed. Nearby was Ernest Schweniger, one-time Carmel sales manager for the Carmel Land Company, who had his bakery just east and across the open lot from the Leidig business. Earl Wermuth, one-time Carmel policeman, bears a scar made when he slipped and cut his finger while splitting up wooden crates from the Schweniger and Leidig businesses, in order to make some spending money as a young boy. Other old-timers recalled how much the Schwenigers were missed when in 1918 they were killed in their new car while returning to Carmel above Ocean Avenue before the cut was made. They swerved "after noticing a spark through the floorboard of their car, causing them to overturn."

Helen Hicks Schweniger had her own fond memories of this fine couple and their wonderful bakery, and of their parrot, which would yell at her brother Waldo, "Waldo, come home! Your mother wants you." Helen's parents took care of the beloved parrot after the death of the Schwenigers, and after Helen and George Schweniger were married she

Ocean Avenue looking east in 1916. Schweniger's Grocery, Carmel Bakery, and Slevin's are on the right side of the photo, with the top of Leidig's roof showing above Slevin's.

often joked that "George married me just to get old Polly back." After the Schwenigers were gone, their old building was given a face lifting and became known as the Carmel Bakery, under the ownership of Bernard Wetzel, who had come from San Francisco. In 1921 Wetzel formed a partnership with a fellow German, Carl Huseman, former owner of the popular Carmel-by-the-Sea Campgrounds. This building was destroyed by fire in 1923, rebuilt by L. E. Gottfried, and reopened the following April, remaining a Carmel landmark for over seventy-one years as the Carmel Bakery, before becoming a Purity Bakery in 1976. Some will recall a period beginning in 1956 when the bakery was under the ownership of the Otto Millers.

The Leidig brothers did well in business and became active in the community. Robert fell in love "at first sight" with Isabelle Martin, the daughter of John Martin, and married her in 1910. Their home sat just back of the present site of the Cork 'n' Bottle and Fortier's. Sitting back 100 feet from the present sidewalk, it looked upon pines and a small patch of meadow. Later the couple had a spacious apartment in the Las Tiendas Court area (on the same site as their original home), built by Edmund Sims, who also helped build the Pine Inn and White Cedars. The Leidig home was in its day something of a showplace. Sims was known for his love of auctions and through him the Leidigs obtained some large windows which had come from the Palace Hotel in San Francisco prior to the 1906 earthquake. In 1929 the Leidig home took a trip to a new location at the corner of Dolores and Fifth. It later became known as the Wermuth house, after Delbert Wermuth leased it. Its future became uncertain in 1965, and it soon succumbed to the bulldozer. A complex of shops were built in its place. The Leidigs' second home (before their Las Tiendas apartments) was a residence they built themselves at Casanova and Seventh.

Fred Leidig met a Salinas girl named Clara Black and brought her back to Carmel as his bride. Fred was one of the original members of the Manzanita Club and was its president in 1916, with Walter Basham as vice president and J. E. Beck and M. J. Murphy as directors. Both Fred and Robert were members of the Manzanita Club's Athletic Division, and Clara, Fred, and sometimes Robert, appeared in Forest Theater productions. Clara and Fred were especially remembered for their roles in *Twelfth Night* and their active participation in the Arts and Crafts Hall productions.

In 1909 all four brothers joined together in the grocery business. They later sold this business to Ernest Schweniger, who spruced up the place and reopened it in 1915 as a grocery, while retaining his bakery. In 1914 the Leidigs took over the store which later became known as Kip's. They took delivery of a Vim auto truck in June of 1916 for home deliveries. Ben Leidig opened Ben's Package Grocery, "on cash basis only," in early 1916 on the first floor of the old Storie Building, in competition with his brothers. Then in January 1917 he advertised, "Back to hardware, my favorite business," with the advertisement next to his brothers' "Leidig Brothers" ad, saying that he carried stoves, heaters, oil cookers and Hot Point appliances. In 1918 the old Kip's property was leased and Robert "turned his interests to fire equipment," becoming Carmel's volunteer fire marshal. In 1919, when Holman's was still in Carmel, he was its manager. Fred went into the lumber business, operating a coal and lumber yard for twenty-six years, called Leidig's Wood Yard, at Seventh and San Carlos. His son, Dale, later established his Texaco station there, next door to what had once been the home of a Mrs. Stewart.

Mrs. Stewart's home sat where Ron's Liquors is now, with Murphy's lumber yard to the north of her place, up to what is known to old-timers as "Goold's Alley." Next door to Goold's property and stretching back to Goold's Alley, where Adam Fox is today, was the bowling alley once belonging to J. Machado, where the young Wermuth boys would clean spittoons and sprinkle sawdust for pocket money. Recently Dale Leidig retired from his business and plans for the site of the Texaco station were revealed, showing an artist's conception of what it will look like when the last of Carmel's home gro-

cery stores, Neilsen's, will move from its long time location into a new and modern building approved by the owner of Nielsen's, Mervin Sutton.

Though Robert Leidig turned his attentions to the Carmel Fire Department, he later also opened a motor service station on the northeast corner of San Carlos and Sixth, with Thomas Reardon. In later years it became known as Grimshaw's Flying A, owned and run by Arnold Grimshaw and considered the first gas station offering a trade name gasoline, "Cycol." Later Grimshaw ran the station with his son Maurice, while the Leidigs retained the property and lived on a portion of it in the little house which has since become a savings and loan, soon to be replaced by a large building that will take up the site of the old station as well.

C. H. (Charlie) Grimshaw in front of his Flying A at the northeast corner of San Carlos and Sixth.

Benjamin Leidig settled in Salinas where he married Frances Mason. The youngest Leidig brother, Lawrence Beverly, occupied himself in the local grocery. Over the years the Leidig property grew, as did the family. Robert and Isabelle Leidig's children were Martin, Ted, and Jean, who became Mrs. Raymond Draper of Carmel and owner of Draper's, where Robertson's is today. Fred and Clara Leidig brought two sons into the world, Glenn and Dale. Elizabeth Leidig, who brought her sons to Carmel so long ago, lived to be ninety-six years old. She had eleven grandchildren, with eight grandsons to carry on the Leidig name.

The generous, warm-hearted "Devey," as he was referred to by many, endeared himself to countless numbers of people, and his name has come up often in my conversations with people about Carmel. Riding about in his surrey and later his "battered old Ford," chatting with possible customers and natives, or sitting on the walk outside his office, Devendorf was "always ready with a smile and conversation." Very little escaped his care and attention.

Born April 6, 1856, and growing up on the family farm just outside Lowell, Michigan, Devendorf first worked for his grandfather in his general store. When he was sixteen he left Michigan to join his mother, who lived in San Jose. He later established himself in the real estate business there, as well as in Stockton. His cousin, Ada Devendorf Reichard, said, "There was something about cousin Frank that made people feel very good just to be near him. I remember how warmly people greeted him when we walked down Ocean Avenue. The wide thoroughfare was bordered on both sides then by banks of fern, iris and other wildflowers. His daughters, Edwina (who was later known for her sculptures, including a bust of her father which had been placed in Devendorf Park), Marion, Myrtle, and Lillian (named after her mother), and I were all wading in Wildcat Creek the day Frank made his final decision on the site for the Highlands Inn. He had already moved the annex for the Pine Inn, with the help of his Japanese crew and a man in charge named Miyamoto, by moving it on rollers down to Monte Verde, by using a team of mules."

When Ada married De Forest Reichard of Pacific Grove in the spring of 1913, they honeymooned at the Highlands Inn. They later lived on Carmelo near Seventh, until they sold their place to the author of *Vagabond*, Don Blanding, and bought another not far away. "Frank had made the Inn the answer to a newlywed's dream," Ada recalled. "He was a dreamer, himself, but he worked and produced, too, and he loved Carmel so very much." Edwina, despite her handicap as a deaf mute, continued to live in the old Devendorf cottage at Lincoln and Sixth until the death of her father on October 9, 1934. Her mother returned to the Oakland area, where she died in 1940 at the age of eighty-one. Edwina retained the cottage until 1968, while living in Placer County, then sold it to W. A. Zingel. Cousin Ada, so full of memories, at the age of eighty-seven was still more than happy to relate marvelous bits of history and go over many treasured photographs. She died in September 1979.

While encouraging teachers, college professors, writers and artists to take up residence in Carmel, Devendorf did not see a real influx of new residents until after the April 18, 1906 earthquake. Up to that time, restaurants were seasonal, with only the Pine Inn serving meals all year long, but soon the sleepy village began to offer clubs, churches, the theater arts, and new businesses and associations, along with a variety of individuals who shaped and molded it into an oasis beside the sea. As several old-timers have told me, "there were lots of new faces after that quake."

The earliest writers to come to Carmel as residents or part-time residents, after David Starr Jordan, author of *Blood of the Nation, The Higher Sacrifice* and *The Strength of Being Clean*, and Robert Louis Stevenson, were Hal Lewis, who became known as Sinclair Lewis, poet George Sterling, and Mary Austin. After the earthquake, members of the so-called "Bohemian group" who lived in Carmel were Jimmy Hopper, Jesse Lynch Williams, Jack London, Raymond Stannard Baker, Lincoln Steffen (who came later, in 1927, and lived on San Antonio), Fred Bechdolt, William Rose Benet, Cornelius and Jessie Arms Botke, Redfern Mason, and occasionally poet Joaquin Miller.

Early artists were Charles Rollo Peters, Xavier Martinez, and Laura Maxwell, whose first studio was at Carmelo and Santa Lucia. Laura had been a student of Sidney Yard and, although she did not come to live permanently in Carmel until 1918, everyone thought she was crazy for building so far out of the village as well as for maintaining her custom of having her hair washed at Arne's and then sitting outside on the curbing until it dried.

Other artists were Josephine Culbertson, previously mentioned, George Bellows, Arthur Hill Gilbert, William Keith, Richard Partington, William Posey Silva (who built the Carmelita Gallery on San Antonio north of Ocean), and Ira Remsen. The Highlands colony of artists were John O'Shea, Theodore Criley, Thomas Shewsbury Parkhurst, William Clothier Watts, Armin Carl Hansen (painter and etcher who helped to organize the Carmel Art Association and became its president), and William Ritchel. Ritchel was a gifted marine landscape artist born in Nurnberg, Bavaria in 1864. He came to the United States in 1895 and settled in New York City. Having later visited the Peninsula and having fallen in love with the Carmel Highlands, Ritchel returned to have his "castle" built with the help of a Spanish stone mason. It was there that he and his second wife, Elanora (Nora) Havel, lived. And there was Chris Jorgensen, who built his well-known rockwork tower home and studio which later became known as La Playa Hotel, when after the death of his wife by drowning, he leased the home to Agnes Signor.

Another well-known early-day artist was Mary De Neale Morgan. Miss Morgan's association with

The Carmel Highlands home of artist William Ritchel, the "Castle."

Carmel was an early one through the visit with her family to the valley homestead of her grandparents, who had settled in Salinas. Born in San Francisco, De Neale Morgan attended the California School of Design from 1888 to 1890. She later exhibited throughout the United States. Opening her first studio in Oakland in 1896, she had her first showing in 1907 at the Hahn Gallery there. She had previously come to Carmel, in 1903, with her mother and brother Thomas and a group from the Pacific Coast Women's Press Association, and had helped run the Pine Inn for a little more than a month for Frank Devendorf.

Miss Morgan returned the following year and occupied a cottage on Monte Verde near the Pine Inn. Then six years later she established her permanent home and studio in the former Sidney Yard studio on Lincoln near Seventh. An avid painter in tempera and oils, active in the support of the Forest Theater and All Saints Church, and one of the founders of the Carmel Art Association, she was a generous hostess and dear friend to many. It was

The home of Mrs. Sidney Yard on the west side of Lincoln between Seventh and Eighth was built in 1928.

said that "nothing which touched Carmel failed to touch her." During World War II, Miss Morgan and her widowed sister, Jeanie C. Klenke, often opened their home and studio to servicemen who had missed their transportation out of Carmel, furnishing them with "bed and breakfast." After Mary De Neale Morgan died in October of 1948 at the age of eighty, Jeanie Klenke continued to display her sister's work until her own death at the age of ninety-three in 1970. Mrs. Klenke was also talented, in the arts of framing and bookbinding.

Another early artist and close friend of De Neale Morgan was Ferdinand Burgdorff. Born on November 7, 1881, in Cleveland, Ohio, Burgdorff had come to the Peninsula (Monterey) on a return trip from Santa Fe, New Mexico in 1908, to visit his friend and fellow Bohemian Club member, Charles Rollo Peters. "Ferdy," as he was known to us and other friends, claimed that the next day he left

Bechdolt, Maxwell, Burgdorff, Morgan, and Hopper.

Peters' home to hike to Carmel via the "Serra Woodland Trail" which led through Carmel Woods to George Sterling's, where he lunched, and what he saw made him return. "One look was all it took. Even though I have been around the world and seen many beautiful places, the protecting trees, the fields of flowers and the white lace of waves on the blue water still have the original charm of the first view." Soon after his first visit Ferdy did return and rented a small portion of the kitchen belonging to the Arts and Crafts Club, which he used as his first Carmel studio while often swapping notes with Sidney Yard.

Ferdy had a love affair with Carmel for over sixty years and with the desert and New Mexico, often returning there to live among the Navajo, to whom he had been introduced by his good friend Joseph Mora, while he painted.

The work of Ferdinand Burgdorff, with his broad

range of subjects, was well liked and received both in American and overseas circles. Burgdorff had a great affection for the outdoors, which was evident in his selection of a home on Boronda Road in Pebble Beach. One of his favorite pastimes was walking. Ferdy had his own style of dress; his earlier scarves gave way to Bo-lo ties with an interesting collection of stones, and a wide choice of hats. He was a generous man with his art, donating pieces to Sunset school, as did his friend De Neale Morgan, and to museums and libraries as well. We are fortunate to have many of his works in various places around the Peninsula. Out of a love for trees and plants, many of which he painted, he took to carrying around seeds which he tossed about him, and those who knew him well recall that he claimed to have been responsible for the abundance of Genista plant (not native, but prevalent) in and around the Peninsula. He thought it beautiful and took delight in spreading its seeds. When Ferdy died after a brief illness at the age of ninety-three, in 1975, he was greatly missed, as were his amusing stories and anecdotes about those wonderful early days of Carmel, many of which he shared weekly with my parents and me.

Musical expression found a niche early in the life of Carmel and has remained firmly entrenched. Some of those early musicians began by gathering at one another's homes to compare notes and mutual appreciation of their art. Teresa and Sally Ehrman, Allen Bier, Mrs. Lawrence Strauss, and Mabel Gray Young formed a nucleus which drew others, such as Thomas Vincent Cator, Antonio de Grassi, Nathan Firestone, Henry Cowell, Marian Ralston, Frederic McMurry, Evadna Lapham, Dorothy Woodward, Frederick Preston Search, David Alberto, and Katherine Vander Roest Clarke.

Later musical expression was nurtured through the efforts of two highly respected and well liked women, Dene Denny and Hazel Watrous, who came to Carmel to spend a few days in 1924. This first visit became a memorable one which stretched into a three-year stay, with a short absence at the end of the three years, after which they returned to Carmel. They founded the Bach Festival and, despite her ill health in later years, Dene Denny introduced the twenty-second Festival in 1957. She was also witness to the founding of the Carmel Music Society in 1926. Born in Callahan, California, she acquired her degree at the University of California at Berkeley where she met Alameda school system supervisor Hazel Watrous. Together they brought not only music and art, but drama and fine design to the village life. At first they concentrated on

Backstage at the Bach Festival, July 1949, left to right, are Russell Horton, Hazel Watrous, Mrs. Gastone Usigili, Mrs. Russell Horton, Nanette Levi, Gastone Usigili, Mrs. Montalban, William Henry, Charles Fulkerson, Jean Crouch Fulkerson, Ralph Linsley, and Dene Denny.

building their studio on North Dolores, designed by Miss Watrous. It boasted a free unsupported balcony which was thoroughly discussed by various architects—with some apprehension, it seems. The studio was the scene of a gallery where both informal recitals and exhibitions were frequently held, including the first exhibit in America of the famous "Blue Four" (later shown in every important gallery in the United States) and lectures by the well-known architect, Richard Neutra. There were lectures and courses by Henry Cowell, and previews of Aaron Copland's concertos.

During 1927 and 1928 these two women leased the Golden Bough Playhouse from Kuster and presented a total of eighteen plays. At this same time they were also encouraging the formation of the Carmel Music Society. By 1928 Denny and Watrous had a full-fledged partnership and formed the Denny-Watrous Gallery. It was in that gallery that what was known as "ultra music" was first introduced to the Peninsula, with compositions by Stravinsky. Also appearing in the gallery were Redfern Mason, Galt Bell's play, *The Drunkard* (before it went to Hollywood), Countess Tolstoi, Richard Buhlig, and Irving Fichel. Tent dressing rooms were at the rear of Vining's Meat Market and Minges Grocery. Among the most interesting of the gallery activities were the rehearsals of the Neah-Kah-Nie Quartet and later those of the Monterey Peninsula Orchestra, under the direction of cellist Michael Penha. The Neah-Kah-Nie Quartet was attributed as directly responsible for the formation of the Bach Festival organized by Denny-Watrous in 1935, and given annually the third week in July. In 1935 the

Denny-Watrous Gallery moved into the Murphy building on San Carlos, and the first official Bach Festival was presented, with Michael Penha as conductor of a chamber orchestra.

In 1937, as project supervisor for the local group of Federal Musicians, Dene Denny was witness to Carmel's second labor dispute. Members of the Tipica Orchestra, which was a small unit of the larger Federal Music Project, decided to strike because of what they considered incorrect payment for their work. However, the strike (the only one of its kind to occur with the Federal Project) was soon smoothed out and things returned to normal. Gastone Usigli was Festival Director from 1939 until his death in 1956, when direction was taken over by Sandor Salgo. In 1958 the Bach Festival was incorporated, with Miss Denny as its president. Not

In addition to her involvement with the commercial arts, music, and the theater arts, Hazel Watrous also had the design of thirty-six Carmel houses to her credit, and among them she presented the village with its first "red roof," as well as the house known as "the house with the chartreuse outside walls." Another credit to Miss Denny's twenty-two years of effort was the dedication of the First Theater in Monterey as a state historical monument on June 3, 1937. There is no question that these two ladies were remarkably well-blended early day personalities who brought fine art and rare quality into the lives of the people of the Peninsula which will not be forgotten.

The theater found its day with Herbert Heron and Edward Kuster, and numerous others came later and contributed much in their varied fields. Among them were Robinson Jeffers, Charles and Kathleen Norris, and Harry Leon Wilson, who was known for his best sellers, *The Spenders* and *The Lions of the Lord*, as well as for his years of service to *Puck* in New York, as a contributor and then its editor. Wilson's daughter Helen married Edward Weston in 1939. Among others were the Josselyns, Samuel Blythe, Gouvener Morris, sisters Alice MacGowan and Grace MacGowan Cooke, Helena Opal Peet Heron, Harry Lafler, Perry Newberry, and Catherine and George Seideneck.

George and Catherine Comstock Seideneck were both highly skilled and talented individuals who made themselves an important part of the village life. George was for a long time a staff artist with the coastal laboratories of the Carnegie Institute, and was known for his fine landscapes and portraiture works as well as his photography. Catherine was a teacher of leather work at the School of Fine Arts at the University of California at Berkeley, where she also filled orders for the 1915 Exposition. She was known internationally for her work in tooled leather. It was said that "pastel is a glove to her hand," and she was much sought after and admired for her pastels of children's heads.

George Seideneck belonged to the group which organized the Carmel Art Association, and he was not only a charter member but its first president. Active in the Forest Theater, Catherine handled arrangements and designs for the local garden club and made costumes for the "Nativity" which was given in the old Golden Bough on Ocean Avenue. At the same time, George was actively helping to form the Carmel Music Society. It was also George who trimmed and shaped the cypress trees on Scenic Drive and designed the walls and corners of Devendorf Park. Although the Seidenecks opened their studios in the Studio Building on Ocean Avenue on August 17, 1922, which was considered a "new phase of activity in the creative arts of Carmel and the Monterey Peninsula," they drew criticism when they built their home on their thirty-acre "retreat" up the Carmel Valley with a bright red outdoor light.

While various organizations had brought the theater to Carmel in a small way in the very early days, it was not until Herbert Heron arrived in 1908 that the theater arts began to be fully realized locally. Heron, who was born in 1883 in New Jersey, had been a professional actor with Belasco and Morasco

First Theater of California was erected by Jack Swan as a saloon and boarding house for sailors, in 1844. It became a theater in 1847. Sketch by author.

Stock Company in Los Angeles, and had first visited Carmel in July 1908, on his way to San Francisco. One year after his first visit to Carmel, he returned, building his home across on Guadalupe and Mountain View, where he settled in and wasted no time in formulating plans for an open air theater which was to be the first of its kind in California. He chose a site in the eighty acres for his new venture and presented his choice to "Devey," who turned over the property to him on a long lease basis without rental and advanced money to build a suitable stage and auditorium. In fact, Devendorf was so delighted with the idea that he even "tossed in the remainder of the block and two workmen as well to help Heron clear the grounds." The Forest Theater Society organization began in 1910, its ideal "to produce plays by local writers, and to give local writers the opportunity and experience of writing, producing, acting and directing, as well as stage and costume design." The original members of the Forest Theater Society were a remarkable group, small by today's standards since the village itself boasted only 600 in population, but they were gifted, efficient, eager and talented people. Among them were Joseph and Mary Hand (who had their home

Mr. and Mrs. Joseph Hand on their fiftieth wedding anniversary in 1924. Slevin photograph.

nearby where the Hofsas House stands today), Helen Parkes, George and Carrie Sterling, Lucia Lane, Maud Lyons, Stella Vincent, Jessie Francis Short, George Boke, Virginia Smiley, Mary De Neale Morgan, Fred and Clara Leidig, Saidee Van Bower, J. E. Beck, Thomas Reardon, Nellie Murphy (who became Mrs. John Montague), Ferdinand Burgdorff, Frederick Bechdolt, Helen Cooke and her aunt, Alice MacGowan, and Perry and Bertha Newberry. (Bertha was the originator of the Carmel "tin can" lantern.)

J. W. Hand home.

The first production to grace the newly founded theater was the play *David* by Constance L. Skinner, directed by Garnet Holmes. It was said that nobody in the village was quite prepared for what they were about to witness that historic night, July 9, 1910, as they headed toward that spot in the forest and passed through the rustic gate, carrying lanterns and blankets. The long awaited evening began as a star-studded, clear one, but it ended up foggy, with the specially acquired calcium floodlights transforming the stage sets, designed by Ferdinand Burgdorff, into something magical. The actors and actresses were well costumed in outfits from Goldstein's Theatrical Company from San Francisco. It was a great start for a theater said to be the first open air theater of its kind. Plays were constantly in production, and 156 were produced in its first eleven years.

Listed among its offerings were thirteen plays written for and played by children, eighteen short plays, thirty-two of three or more acts, twenty-eight that had been produced elsewhere, seventeen by Carmel authors, and thirteen by foreign language authors, as well as a total of thirty-five plays staged by local producers. Presented during the history of the theater were twenty-two Shakespearean plays, six by George Bernard Shaw, and eight dramatizations of stories written by Robert Louis Stevenson. Others whose works were presented were Percy MacKaye, William Butler Yeats, Harry Leon Wilson, Frank Pixley, Maurice Maeterlinck, Edward Knoblock, A. A. Milne, John Millington Synge, Anatole France, Alfred Noyes, Edmond Rostand, Euripides, and Aristophanes.

Some of the 150 productions written and presented by Carmel people were: *The Toad* by Bertha Newberry, produced by Garnet Holmes; *Runnymeade* by William Greer Harrison, produced by Frank Matthiew; *A Wife of Nippon*, written and produced by Redfern Mason; *Aladdin* by Elizabeth

44

Field Christy and Perry Newberry, produced by Frank Matthiew; *Fire*, written and produced by Mary Austin; *The People's Attorney*, written and produced by Perry Newberry; *The Arrow Maker*, written and produced by Mary Austin; *The Spy* by Herbert Heron, from J. A. Altsheler, produced by Alice MacDougal; *Tusitala* by John Northern Hilliard and Herbert Heron, produced by Herbert Heron; *Montezuma* by Herbert Heron, produced by Porter Garnett; *Junipero Serra*, written and produced by Perry Newberry; *The Columbine*, written and produced by Helen Parkes; *Serra* by Garnet Holmes, Booth Tarkington, and Harry Leon Wilson, produced by Glenna Hughes; *Confounding of the Witch* by Grace Wickham and James Hopper, produced by Grace Wickham; *Inchling* by Ira Remsen, produced by Blanche Tolmie and Rem Remsen; and *Mr. Bunt* by Ira Remsen, produced by Rem Remsen and directed by Blanche Tolmie.

Between 1910 and 1920, the census on plays read as follows: eleven directed by Garnet Holmes, seven by Perry Newberry, six by Herbert Heron, who started Carmel's Shakespeare Festival in 1926, and some fifteen more by others such as Mary Austin, Helen Parkes, and John Northern Hilliard.

In the early days of the Forest Theater, the music was furnished by Frederick Preston Search, who had come to Carmel to spend time perfecting his art while living at his "Casa De Roses," and "in earnest good nature" provided his musical abilities for the theater. He and his wife established their home on the corner of Thirteenth and Monte Verde in 1914. Frederick Search was the child of musically talented parents and was acclaimed one of America's and Europe's finest cellists for over twenty-five years. He was also noted for his musical compositions, one of which was played at the 1915 Exposition. During his Navy service, Search earned the title of First Musician. From 1920 to 1933 he directed the orchestra at the old Del Monte Hotel. He later made his home on the Jamesburg Road in upper Carmel Valley. In 1952 he donated his library of chamber music scores to the Harrison Memorial Library, and when he died in November 1959, it was the passing of a brilliantly gifted individual.

Others who contributed their time and brilliance to the music of the Forest Theater through the early '40s were Raine Bennet, Thomas Vincent Cator, and Allen Bier. Costumes were provided by such names as Rozeltha Greeley (Douglas Greeley's wife), Lottita Corella, Jeanie Morgan Klenke (De Neale Morgan's sister), Lita Bathen, Margaret Williams, Jeanne Barlow, William T. Wise, Rhoda Johnson, Helena Heron, and various unnamed women of the village who gave generously of their time and talents. Scenery and sets were the works of such as Ferdinand Burgdorff, Arthur Vachell, Daniel Willard, William S. Cooper, De Neale Morgan, William P. Silva, and Cornelius Botke, along with Paul Mays, Grace Yenni, Richard W. Johnson, Winsor Josselyn, Perry Newberry, Jimmy Hopper, Henry F. Dickson, Jr., Carleton Lehman, C. G. Lawrence, George Seideneck, and Clay Otto. Dance direction was provided by City Attorney Argyll Campbell, Jeanette Hoagland Parkes, Daisy Fox Desmond Bostick, Alice Miller, Dorothy Woodward, Willette Allen, Ruth Austin, and Ruth Allerhand.

The actors and actresses were many, ranging from the local plumber, shopkeeper, doctor, carpenter, writer, artist, seamstress, and half the children in the village, who always played to capacity crowds, capturing a certain magic which prevails even today. The 1912 children's play, a dramatization of *Alice In Wonderland* by Perry Newberry and Arthur Vachell, under the direction of Garnet Holmes, brought overnight fame to the theater. Then upon the newly expanded stage in 1912, Bertha Newberry brought further fame and popularity with her production of *The Toad*. The most widely acclaimed spectacular of all productions was said to be Perry Newberry's *Junipero Serra*, a pageant which was produced in 1915 with a cast of 400, including visiting vacationers, locals, and a machine gun group from the Presidio in Monterey to help fill out the numbers, since the village population was only 600 in total. Among the cast of players of this memorable event were Fred Bechdolt, who played Serra; Winsor Josselyn and Talbert Josselyn as Spanish dancers, with Jeanette Hoagland Parkes as a solo dancer; Phillip Wilson as a friar; and Phyllis Overstreet, Catherine Cooke, Fred Leidig, and Thomas Reardon, to name only a few. The pagaent, an overwhelming success, was selected for repetition and performed again successfully on July 30 and 31, 1915, at the Panama-Pacific Exposition.

There was, for the most part, general harmony among the writers, producers, and cast members of the early days of the Forest Theater. However, there were flareups of artistic temperaments with one difference in particular between the MacGowan and Austin factions. The MacGowan faction desired conventional behavior, including the prohibition of alcohol. The Austin-Sterling group purchased their liquor from the "local" druggist and desired the more "liberally interpreted productions," such as Sterling's *Triumph Of Bohemia*. Sterling lost the battle of wills and by 1912 he claimed to have "crayfished" again where his views on the Forest

45

Theater were concerned. The next flareup came in a particular difference between Herbert Heron and Perry Newberry, with Newberry's group splitting away from the main group for a period of time and forming an organized group of its own, the Western Drama Society. At this same time Newberry suggested to Edward Kuster that he too should leave the Forest Theater. Kuster did sever relations with the theater within weeks of Newberry's leaving, but for totally different reasons. Eventually both sides saw the need to reunify, and they decided to merge with the Carmel Arts and Crafts Club of 1924, with the Forest Theater Society operating as acting branch of the older, earlier organization.

In thinking back on the active days of the theater, old-timers recalled many humorous occasions, such as the time when Thomas Reardon, dressed in a new suit, was solicited from the audience by Perry Newberry to occupy the front legs of an elephant in the play *Aladdin*. Newberry gave Reardon some quick instructions, thanked him, and retired to the sidelines to administer other last minute directions. Well, Reardon occupied the legs just fine, but not without uttering a list of unprintables as the fresh paint, still wet, began to ruin his new pants. But, deciding to make the best of it, he took his place on stage. What happened next brought the house down with laughter and brought forth another volume of expletives from Reardon. It seems Kenneth Goold, who was the elephant keeper, was not aware that he should be steering the stand-in across the stage, and Reardon went the wrong way, separating himself from the other half of the elephant and getting himself tangled up in the trunk of a tree.

Another funny incident which has often been mentioned was the time that Xavier Martinez, a painter of note and fun-loving personality of early days, came down with his wife, Elsie, from San Francisco for rest and relaxation and to visit with their friends Perry and Bertha Newberry. Bertha had written her play, *The Toad*, and friend Marty, as they called him, was given the role of chief assassin with a one-liner: "I stabbed him to the heart," which he practiced faithfully, preparing for his big moment on stage. The night of the performance, all was running smoothly until it came time for the villain to speak, at which point Marty began to stutter and stammer, and finally emitted the line as "Oh Gawd! I keeled heem weeth my steeck!" The curtain was rung down on the laughter.

Other such moments of uncontrolled laughter, and times of near separations of the cast in the thickness of foggy evenings, have become a part of countless memories.

Artist Xavier Martinez in 1910.

During the depression the theater was deeded to the village of Carmel in order that the Public Works Administration might rebuild the stage and continue its upkeep. During this time quarried rock was used to face the concrete in the dressing rooms and original stage, the plain wood benches were replaced by two-inch redwood plank seating, and a new fence was built around the property. After the depression, plays were given again until 1942, then stopped during the war (with the exception of afternoon performances which were given by a locally founded drama school) until 1945, when *Distant Drums* was staged by Dan Totheroh, native Californian, playwright and author. By 1949 some thirty plays, staged at the theater by local writers with local talent, had taken place, and by 1959, Herbert Heron had a fifty-year record as producer and director in connection with the Forest Theater. When he died after a brief illness at the age of eighty-four, in 1968, his contributions had been phenomenal. The tradi-

The seating at the Forest Theater is shown in this photograph taken during a rehearsal of "H.M.S. Pinafore."

46

tions of the Forest Theater have continued to today, through the fine efforts of many locally born and raised individuals, along with the devotion of newcomers who have dedicated themselves to its cause. In support of the theater, the tradition of the Guild has continued, and there are those of us who continue to take blanket, flashlight and ceremoniously filled thermos and sit beneath the stars on a summer eve, or in the foggy mist, listening to the crackle of the fires while we wait for the play to begin.

While Herbert Heron devoted his abilities to the Forest Theater, he also supported other forms of art, and having a great love of books, he opened Carmel's first genuine book shop in 1918. In later years Heron was also on the City Council and served as mayor from 1930 to 1934. He was responsible for the creation in 1925 of the lovely building built by Percy Parkes and engineer Clay Otto which we know as the Seven Arts Building on the corner of Ocean and Lincoln. At the first location of Seven

A 1979 rehearsal of "H.M.S. Pinafore" by Carmel Middle School on the Forest Theater stage.

Arts, in the eighty acres, Heron specialized in rare editions as well as new books. Later he moved it and took for a partner Miss Helen Conger, who was later replaced by John Pairtz. The Seven Arts Building as we know it today housed several early businesses when it first opened and was a popular choice of many merchants over the years, even after Heron and Pairtz broke up their partnership and sold the Seven Arts in October 1940. Before and during the 1940s, the Seven Arts housed, among others, Edward Weston's shop, Merle's Treasure Chest, before it moved onto the Dummage property across the street, Jack and Jill Children's Shop, the Wells' Music and Rental Library, and Parsons' Antiques and Vanity Fair, which remains today.

The other important theater in Carmel was the Golden Bough, the dream of Edward G. Kuster. He came to Carmel for the first time in 1919, from Los Angeles, with twenty years of successful legal practice behind him. Kuster, who was known to his friends as Ted, gave up his lucrative practice to take

Edward Kuster's home at Carmel Point.

up the study of dancing and acting with a former client, Ruth St. Denis, who later became his second wife. (Una Call, his first wife, married Robinson Jeffers.) Kuster soon became a stage manager and lighting expert for the St. Denis-Ted Shaw Troupe out of San Francisco. He also studied acting under Mme. Henrietta Hobey and the theater arts with Maurice Browne, spending two seasons in Berlin and Munich, where he learned a great deal about the foreign theater. Returning to Carmel in 1920, Kuster began to cultivate the artistic resources of the Carmel Village, while he appeared in short plays by Herbert Heron and tried his hand at co-directing as well as composing music. His break with the Forest Theater, mentioned earlier, was over a "run-in with pathological tree worshipers," as he called them, who would not allow him to remove certain trees which interfered with his elaborate set for *Caesar and Cleopatra* and also with the production of *The Countess Kathleen.*

Kuster went to New York to study classical and medieval architecture, and later enrolled in the San Francisco School of Theater. He returned once again to Carmel to become involved on weekends with the Arts and Crafts Theater, which Newberry had organized during his absence. In the meantime, Herbert Heron had also organized the Carmel Repertory Players.

During this period Kuster was busy drawing his plans for the Golden Bough, which was later to become known as "the crown jewel of small American theater." It opened at Ocean Avenue and Monte

Verde on June 3, 1924. Try to picture, if you can, what it looked like originally, without buildings in front of it—a rose-colored stucco building looking almost like the backdrop for a play itself, without the actors present. Inside, the Golden Bough featured large, comfortable wicker chairs with muted toned cushions for comfortable viewing, and a grill backstage which permitted music to drift up from the dressing rooms below. Later Kuster's wife had her little weaving shop (which is now the Cottage of Sweets) moved in front of the theater, and she would use the little window on the left rear as a ticket office.

The Golden Bough became famous almost overnight with the celebrated Maurice Browne and his wife, Ellen Van Volkenburg, as directors of its acting school. The first class to enroll consisted of the following people: Irene Alexander (who later became the *Monterey Peninsula Herald*'s art-drama critic), Rhoda Johnson (who became costumer for Monterey's First Theater), Mrs. Marie Gordon, Ruth McElroy and Jadwiga Noskobiak (Mrs. C. Stanton Babcock). The instructor of dance was Ruth Ford, wife of Byington Ford. The first productions were *The Princess Who Wouldn't Say Die*, Philip Barry's *You and I, Beyond the Horizon, The Nursemaid of Heaven*, Ibsen's *The Master Builder*, and the world premiere of St. John Irvine's *The Ship*. The Golden Bough was successful, but in order to survive, Kuster leased it first to Dene Denny and Hazel Watrous, while he went to Berlin to

study in the early winter of 1927, and then to the Abalone League Players, although he was at odds with them at the time. The Abalone League, which called itself the Filmarte Group, leased from Kuster until it acquired the Arts and Crafts, though Kuster bought it out in 1929. In 1930 and 1931 Kuster used the Arts and Crafts as an auxiliary to the Golden Bough while he used the Golden Bough for experimental theater.

Kuster felt he was never truly understood locally, despite all his efforts in the community. He brought *Karl and Anna* from Germany and obtained the first U.S. rights to *The Threepenny Opera*, which was not seen on Broadway for another seven years. The local clergy scorned Kuster when he presented Saroyan's *They Knew What They Wanted!* and *Beggar on Horseback*. Restless and unsatisfied once more, Kuster took off in 1931 for San Francisco. While he was away, the group calling itself the Carmel Community Players was formed. One member of the group, Laurence d'Etie Grenier, joined Galt Bell in the opening of his legendary play, *The Drunkard*, in Los Angeles, which ran for a then unprecedented twenty years. Kuster returned to Carmel briefly to lease to this group before returning to San Francisco.

From 1933 to late 1934 Kuster was director of the Fresno Players and produced a huge success, *By Candlelight*. He returned to Carmel to find his lessee in debt, went back to Fresno, and in May 1935 brought back with him the cast of *By Candlelight*, including Barbara Collins, who later married Gunnar Norberg. Within a few days of the first run of the play, the theater burned to the ground. Arson was definitely indicated, and there was a story linking a mentally disturbed young man to whom Kuster had recently refused to lease the theater. However, the

After the May 1936 fire at the original Golden Bough Theater on the south side of Ocean Avenue. Josselyn photograph.

young man was not prosecuted because of certain conflicting conditions. Kuster used the insurance money for the installation of the very best motion picture projection equipment in the Arts and Crafts building and then promptly left for San Francisco to establish a new Golden Bough on Sutter Street. In later years Kuster would refer to the arsonist with the comment, "The person is now one of the biggest personalities in the American theater," yet he would never mention a name. The San Francisco Golden Bough enjoyed success until union difficulties arose, at which time Kuster joined Ma Reinhardt in Los Angeles for a two-year period, directing British and American plays.

In the summer of 1941 Kuster was again drawn back to Carmel, where he opened still another new school. In the middle 1940s he had a new Carmel Golden Bough constructed on the site of the present theater of the same name, on Monte Verde between Eighth and Ninth. The new Golden Bough offered foreign films, with alternate plays, until May 21, 1949, when during the run of—again—*By Candlelight*, the new theater burned. I remember the excitement and discussion at the time among my parents and their adult friends, many of whom were friends with Ted Kuster. There was much speculation about the fire and arson was of course strongly suspected, though the fire was blamed on overhead lighting.

A new theater came into being with the subscription of 400 families in stock for the building of an intimate Circle Theater with 150 seats. Its entrance was on Casanova, and the movie screen was between the dressing rooms and the reconstructed

Golden Bough. The Circle at the Golden Bough was very popular for a time, and I remember how thrilled I was to have dancing lessons there, as was our teacher, Joanne Nix, after her previous location on Mission. The entire class was delighted to give our performance on the stage of the Golden Bough with its seating for 299 people. Beginning in 1955, the theater was used as a motion picture house exclusively and not long after, the group of Circle Theater stockholders dissolved and a new group took over with Kuster as managing director. Kuster had dreamt of a fine community theater but his dream was not realized. In later years he was known to remark, "There's a lack of interest and a lack of understanding in Carmel."

The history of dance in Carmel began in 1907 when Saidee Van Brower came to Carmel with her niece, Jeanette Hoagland, who was later Mrs. Parkes. Saidee became Carmel's first dance instructor and arranged the ballet and dance numbers for the Forest Theater in its earliest days. She performed a solo dance for one of the theater's first plays, *David*. Saidee was also active in the Manzanita Club and Arts and Crafts productions. She continued as a dance instructor until she was elected city clerk in 1920, a position she retained for almost twenty-two years. Her niece, Miss Hoagland, was also a dance instructor for the Forest Theater for several years.

Another early instructor of dance was Portia Mansfield Swett, who called her school by the same name. She held classes in the woods and on the beach in what we call today a "modern dance" style. Then in 1924 Betty Merle Horst came to Carmel, having been hired by Kuster for his school for the theater. She was closely followed by Dorothy Woodward, Willette Allen, and Ruth Austin. June Delight Canoles arrived in Carmel in 1933 and held her classes in the Arts and Crafts Gallery until she built her own studio in 1937. Well liked and community conscious, June Canoles also provided many performances for the U.S.O. and Red Cross on the Peninsula. Others to follow on the Carmel dance scene were Russian dance instructor Una Hollet and the well-known Joanne Nix, who continues to inspire and create dance on the Peninsula.

During the period when musical expression and the theater were finding their places in Carmel history, many talented people came here, contributing and leaving so much behind them. The awesome and compelling beauty of rich forests, pristine sands, billowing, pounding surf, fields of wildflowers, and unequalled simple pleasures were a continuing magnet and source of inspiration.

49

George Sterling home in "Eighty Acres."

Poet George Sterling was given credit for luring others to Carmel as he gathered kindred souls about him. Sterling, who came to California in 1890 from Sag Harbor, Long Island, was considered the black sheep of his family. He had studied for the priesthood for three years, then left that and went to work for his uncle, Frank Havens, as an insurance agent. He married pretty, blond Carrie Rand, and they settled in Piedmont. Not content with his line of work and feeling at odds with a "vague sense of a different calling," he found himself taking twice daily trips on the ferry and writing verse for the sheer pleasure of it. Encouraged by Carrie, Sterling casually mentioned his pleasurable pastime to friend and critic Ambrose Bierce, who helped him print his first collection, in 1903. With encouragement from Bierce and from established writers such as James Hopper, Joaquin Miller, Harry Lafler, and Jack London, Sterling began to devote every spare moment to his writing. It was London who had the most profound effect on Sterling, and it was London who introduced him to Mary Austin. Mary in turn introduced Sterling to Carmel, in the early summer of 1905. Acting as her chauffeur, Sterling drove Austin to Carmel, and together they spent long hours climbing at Point Lobos and hiking and strolling in the surrounding countryside. Though they went their separate ways at the trip's end, Sterling was drawn to return to Carmel.

Though Carrie was not immediately intrigued with the idea of moving to Carmel, Sterling did return to build his house, with the aid of Jimmy Hopper and Michael Williams, on a wooded hilly slope in what was known as the "Eighty Acres." Using some of the red brick from the kilns owned by the Plaza Fuel on Torres, he built "Sterling's Castle" with its wonderful view, on Torres Street between Tenth and Eleventh. Needless to say, the footbridge across the ravine at Torres and Vizcaino saw much foot traffic by the Sterlings. Work on the house began in July 1905, and by October a wonderful thirty-foot living room, with Carmel chalk rock hearth and fireplace, was completed. This was to be the setting for many lengthy conversations with friends such as Lincoln and Ella Steffens and Jack and Charmaine London (though Charmaine, because of her dominating manner with London, was not popular with the local group). The favorite place for the many gatherings at the Sterlings' was the stone-pit in the forest behind the house, which became the focal point of most festivities there. Roasted mussel and abalone was washed down with muscatel, a favorite of Jack London, or with ale. George grew a vegetable garden which he called "my potato patch," and he and Carrie were lauded for "finding such a place." They offered hospitality and suggestions to new arrivals, including Sinclair "Hal" Lewis, who was undergoing rough times and used their porch to sleep on during 1907, until he moved in with William Rose Benet near the present Golden Bough. In later years, good friend Jimmy Hopper took over the Sterlings' place, living there until it burned down in 1924.

After the fire Jimmy rebuilt on the same site. His house was nicknamed Cottage 9009, after one of his books, at the suggestion of a friend, Fred Bechdolt, whom Hopper had talked into coming down to Carmel in 1907. Mr. and Mrs. John Porter Gilbert purchased the house in 1939 from Hopper, who moved down near the point with his wife, Elayne, an accomplished musician who was remembered for her fight to save and beautify what is now Devendorf Park.

James "Jimmy" Hopper, born in Paris July 23, 1876, was in and out of Carmel from 1898 to 1901. He finally came to stay after the San Francisco earthquake (his vivid account of which was published in *Harper's Weekly*) and rented a cottage at Dolores and Ninth. Hopper had already created a reputation for himself by being one of the trio who stole the Stanford Ax in 1898, when he was a quarterback for the University of California, and for his first book, *Caybigan*, a collection of short stories which was published in 1906. For a while Hopper taught school in the Philippines. He returned to the United States and took up writing full time, successfully completing more than four hundred stories and several novels for popular magazines such as *Collier's* and *The Saturday Evening Post*. He was also a newspaper and foreign correspondent. Hopper met and married Elayne Lawson of Monterey in 1938.

Jimmy Hopper was loved by many and was extremely close to George Sterling, who dedicated his poem "Beyond the Breakers" to Jimmy, known for his daring swims beyond the breakers of Carmel Beach. To quote Hopper, "I was the swimming contingent here; I used to swim out every day in the bay, and must have gone out a thousand times at least. It was a mania of mine to go every day. I got so I could take the heaviest waves and swim way out.... Why, in our group, we would walk our guests to the Monterey train station after an all night party on Carmel Beach, then walk back, doing as much as twenty miles a day and think nothing of it." Hopper and Sterling were steadily in each other's company, with Michael Williams often joining them, as they would ride horseback to Point

Left to right, Fred Bechdolt, James Hopper and Michael Williams, on March 8, 1913. Slevin photograph.

Lobos or swim off the rocks at Point Loeb, diving for mussels or abalone. When George Sterling committed suicide in 1926, Jimmy was deeply crushed, as was Fred Bechdolt who, with Sterling's encouragement, had collaborated with Hopper on one of Jimmy's first books, *9009*. Though he traveled a great deal, Hopper once remarked, "I am sighing for the golden aridity of Carmel land," and he chose to spend the closing years of his life in Carmel. His death came in 1956.

Frederick Ritchie Bechdolt, affectionately called "Bech," was loved for his unflagging optimism and "peppery ways." Born on July 27, 1874 in Mercerburg, Pennsylvania, where he received his formal education, he later went from placer mining in the Klondike, through cowpunching, to rubbing shoulders with criminals at San Quentin and Folsom. Fred Bechdolt was a western writer whose experiences lent reality to his work, which included my favorite, *When the West Was Won* and, in collaboration with Hopper, *9009*, based on his study of

prison life. Other books for which he is remembered are *The Hard Rock Man* and *Tales of Oldtimers*. He also wrote for various newspapers, including the *Seattle Star* and the *Los Angeles Times*.

Bechdolt, who was Kathryn Overstreet's brother, was an ardent supporter of Carmel causes, and did service as postmaster, city councilman, and police commissioner. He also had an active interest in the Forest Theater. When he first arrived in Carmel in 1907, he rented what he called his "studio-shack" in the eighty acres, for eleven dollars a month, until he met and married a "lovely local lady," Adele Hale, and became stepfather to Bonnie Gottfried (wife of Lee Gottfried) and Donald Hale. The marriage of Fred and Adele was said to have given them the happiest thirty-five years either of them spent. When Adele became ill in 1948, "Bech" cared for her lovingly until death, and when he died two years later, he was hailed as "one of the oldest, most dear and distinguished of early Carmel citizens."

During the period in which the Sterlings were enjoying their spot in the eighty acres, the famous photographer Arnold Genthe arrived to build his redwood studio hide-away. Not long afterward, Mary Austin returned to Carmel, where, in her typical unconventional way, she had a quaint log cabin built on North Lincoln with a studio platform around the limbs of the oak in which she had it constructed. Designed by Louis Mulgardt, and known as her "wick-i-up," it became a conversation piece among residents and fellow writers, while the prolific Austin, who "dressed in long Grecian robes" and other unusual costumes, would work in her wick-i-up on her latest novel. Some called Mary Austin "plain Jane"—Raine Edward Bennett referred to her as a "rugged faced woman with glasses, who looked like Teddy Roosevelt in skirts"—but all were in agreement about her individuality.

Mary Austin on Sterlings' property, 1912. Slevin photograph.

When on April 18, 1906, the earthquake created its terrible devastation on San Francisco, it also had its effect on Carmel, which was still very much in the horse and buggy days. All communication lines as well as rail transportation were lost, leaving Carmelites to worry and wonder how everyone else had come through. Carmel received a good jolt which damaged stone work, fireplaces and chimneys, and left a large crack in the building which would one day house Kip's Grocery. The worst local effect of the quake was at the Hotel Del Monte, where one of the huge chimneys fell into the room of a couple, injuring a man and killing his bride.

Hotel Del Monte, 1885.

Before long there were other arrivals "without help from the National Catastrophe." One was Harry Lafler, who lived down the coast most of the time while writing for local papers and working on the publication of poems by Nora May French after her death. Another was Geraldine Bonner, a writer for the *San Francisco Argonaut* whom we remember today for her books, *The Pioneer* and *The Emigrant Trail.* Michael Williams, "journalist extraordinary," one time city editor of the *San Francisco Examiner*, and special correspondent during the fire and earthquake, also came to live in Carmel. He was noted for his collaboration with Upton Sinclair on two books in 1908 as well as his own books, *The Little Flower of Carmel* and *The Little Brother Francis of Assisi.*

Nora May French, a protegé of George Sterling, came to Carmel as a guest of the Sterlings in 1907. Sterling built a small cabin in the woods of the eighty acres not far from his and Carrie's place so that Nora May could write there. Lover of horses and fond of riding, French could often be seen riding along the beach in one of her few "unmelancholy" moods. Her fits of melancholy later led her to take her own life. Sterling wrote "Ashes on the Sea" as a commemoration of her memorial service.

THE SINGING HEART

Oh heart of mine, the tears are on my face,
Grief on my eyelids for all eyes to know,
And bitter tremblings that all smiles displace,
Then heart of mine, why art thou singing so?

Oh faithless heart, that all its care forgets,
If but a sea wind stir the grasses rare,
As though we still were gathering violets
That in the wood of Carmel grow so fair.

Oh foolish heart that would its joy renew
If but this hour the silvered rain would fall,
Or through the desert dawnings hot and blue
We heard dim-breasted doves begin to call.

O heart of mine, though tears are on my face,
And if the Lords of Life be kind or no,
The white stars shining in the twilight space
Beyond all griefs would keep thee singing so.

—MARY AUSTIN

TO ONE A-MARRYING

Aye, pluck a jonquil when the May's a-wing,
  Or please you with a rose upon the breast,
  Or find a violet chosen from the rest
To match your mood with blue caprice of Spring;
Give windy vines a tendril less to swing—
  Why, what's a flower? a day's delight at best,
  A perfume loved, a faded petal pressed,
A whimsey for an hour's remembering.
But wondrous careful must he draw the rose
From jealous earth, who seeks to set anew
  Deep root, young leafage, with a gardener's art—
To plant it queen of all his garden-close,
  And make his varying fancy wind and dew,
    Cloud, rain and sunshine for one woman's heart.

—NORA MAY FRENCH

Harry Leon Wilson was an early figure and collaborator with Booth Tarkington on *The Man From Home.* He lived in a picturesque residence high atop the rocks down the coast, near William Ritchel. Wilson's wife's mother, Grace MacGowan Cooke, and Grace's sister, Alice MacGowan, came with the second influx in about 1910, along with William Rose Benet. Grace and Alice MacGowan wrote separately and together, and though their work was referred to by many as "pulpy," they were well known for *The Last Word, The Power and the Glory*, and *The Joy Bridges.* John Kenneth Turner had his studio-bungalow beneath the pines situated near the residences of Bechdolt, Hopper, and Socialist Mrs. Dell H. Munger, author of *The Wind Before the Dawn.*

The unconventional Mary Austin, George Sterling, and Jack London were more than ever in each other's company. It was during this short and carefree, yet prolific, period that the famous abalone song came to be, as the group pounded at the abalone, had their "ambrosial, unquotable talk," and braved the cold sea, accompanied by "vacuum bottles filled with cocktails and red wine in huge demijohns," to use London's description. The noise from the pounding of the abalone was said to have a definite rhythm.

The Abalone Song

Oh some think that the Lord is fat,
And some that he is bony
But for me, I think that he
Is like an abalone.

Oh some drink rain and some champagne,
And whiskey by the pony
But I will try a dash of rye
And a hunk of abalone.

Oh some like ham and some like jam,
And some like macaroni,
But our tom-cat he lives on fat
And juicy abalone.

George Sterling

Some stick to biz, some flirt with Liz,
Down on the sands of Coney
But we, by hell, stay in Carmel,
And nail the abalone.

Sinclair Lewis

The more we talk, the more they make,
In deep-sea matrimony.
Race suicide will ne'er betide
The fertile abalone.

Michael Williams

I telegraph my better-half
By Morse or by Marconi
But when in need of greater speed
I send an abalone.

Oh Mission Point's a friendly joint
Where every crab's a crony
And true and kind, you'll never find
The faithful abalone.

He wanders free beside the sea,
Wher'er the coast is stony.
He flaps his wings and madly sings,
The plaintive abalone.

George Sterling

Some live on hope and some on dope
And some on alimony
But bring me in a pail of gin
And a tub of abalone.

Anonymous

We sit around and pound and pound,
But not with acrimony,
Because our ob-ject is a gob
Of sizzling abalone.

Oh some folks boast of quail on toast
Because they think it's toney,
But I'm content to pay my rent
And live on abalone.

Opal Heron Search

Changes occurred which left the golden group both shaken and divided. Charles Rolo Peters, who was responsible for beginning Monterey's art colony, and who later owned the Peters' Gate subdivision just south of the junction of Cass Street and Munras in Monterey, became seriously ill. Charles Warren Stoddard, who was a brilliant correspondent, educator, and author of the famous *South Sea Idylls*, also became seriously ill within a short period of time. Mary Austin, certain she had cancer, left for Italy. In 1914, after a rather "outrageous affair," one of many infidelities which broke up his marriage to Carrie, George Sterling left Carmel permanently for Greenwich Village. Jack London, battling with "John Barleycorn" and in ill health, died quite unexpectedly on November 22, 1916. While the "inner group" suffered its misfortunes, the ebb and flow of village life continued on around them. In reflection, Jeffers recalled Sterling with the following four lines:

"I did not meet him in the gleaming years
That made the great friendships and the early fame
The Carnival time when wine was as common as tears
The fabulous dawn was darkened before I came."

In the second wave, during the 1920s, there were other names: Herbert Bolton, educator and historian who, as a University of California faculty member, wrote the five volume *Anza's Expedition Into California*; Leonard Bacon, writer of satirical verse, "Guinea-Fowl," "Lost Buffalo" and others for *Harper's Weekly*; Ralph Pearson, noted etcher from New Mexico; landscape artist Amos Engle; Dorothea Castelhum from Massachusetts, who published the series for girls, *The Penelope Books* and collaborated with Daisy Bostick on *Carmel at Work and Play*. Dorothea was the wife of Willard K. Bassett of the former *Carmel Cymbal*.

There were also Grace Wallace, who lived in her "Wee Gables" on Camino Real near Thirteenth and was known for her plays, *Sun Gazers* and *Poorest of the Poor*, as well as lyrics set to music by Thomas

Vincent Cator; M. M. Murphy, author-paleontologist and Navajo Indian Reservation official, who lived at Twelfth and Casanova; actors Frank Sheridan and Frederick Burt; actress Helen Ware and playwrights Martin Flavin and Perez Hirschbein; novelist and author of *The World of H. G. Wells* and *America's Coming Of Age*, Van Wyck Brooks; musician-philosopher Dane Rudhyar; Eunice Gray of *Cross Trails and Chaparral* (who lived in one of Carmel's first beach cottages, "The Barnacle"); and others such as Donald MacLeod Lewis, who made his home at Peter Pan Lodge, and Philip Nesbitt and Anne Porter.

Studio home of Isabel Chandler, 1910.

New real estate businesses opened—that of Joseph Hand (originally an associate of the Carmel Development Company) in 1912, the Carmel Realty Company, established in early 1913 by Mrs. Rose De Yoe, and Philip Wilson's. The Carmel Development Company had in the interim extended its holdings even further with the addition of a portion of the old Martin Ranch which encompassed the area called Point Loeb, or as we know it today, Carmel Point. In these early days even the merchants and the real estate people were in agreement that the new Carmel "should grow slowly." Electricity and gas were "forbidden" and paving was considered "disdainful."

In 1908, when the Carmel Point was a rolling grass meadow, Florence Wells, one-time president of the San Francisco Women's Press Club, came to Carmel. She was the builder and owner of "Driftwood," which belonged later to actress Jean Arthur and her mother, Mrs. Greene. Originally the house was small and square with a slightly peaked roof, and weathered looking, as it sat out on the Point alone. Today it is very much changed after its third remodeling, with the exception of its fireplace which had always been a focal point of the house. At the

time Mrs. Wells built her home she also purchased six acres of the beach below, which she later sold to the State of California. It is interesting to note that she had the beach in front of her house marked on the deed maps as Reamer's Point and that the beach below was called Reamer's Beach by old-timers at that time. The Reamers, who were from San Francisco and were dear friends of the Wells, owned property there next to Mrs. Wells but had not yet built upon it. Later when the Reamers did build their home, the second on the Point, the two good friends won a battle against the Sanitary Board, which wanted to use the beach below their respective properties for a pipe to dump effluent into the lagoon beach. Later a relative, Mrs. Sara (Sis) Reamer Elber, lived in the home she affectionately called "Nannu's house."

Other early homes built on and around the Point were the Charles Van Ripers' lovely Norman-French home, the R. B. Long home, Perry Newberry's home on two lots at Allen Place at the end of Monte Verde, the Philip Wilsons', the Jeffers', the home of Elizabeth K. Elliot, and the seven-room Praegar home on Bay View between Martin Way and Santa Lucia, as well as the wonderful Dutton home down from the Jeffers', nicknamed "The Warehouse."

The old Dutton place, "The Warehouse," on Scenic Drive, 1953.

Of the personalities on the Point, perhaps those of Charles Van Riper and Perry Newberry and his wife, Bertha, were among the first to influence profoundly the thinking of the village. Charles Van Riper was steadily involved in village matters and referred to as "solid as a rock."

Perry and Bertha Newberry were married in 1892 and came to Carmel in 1910, she a well-known poetess whose work had appeared in magazines all over the country, and Perry an art staff member of

54

the *San Francisco Examiner.* He claimed to have first heard of Carmel over a glass of wine at Coppa's in San Francisco, from George Sterling, Mary Austin, and Jimmy Hopper, all singing its praises. Newberry was assistant editor of the *Pine Cone* and later its owner until he sold it in 1935. In his editorials, he always fought for the preservation of the "different quality" of Carmel, and for a long time Carmel continued to maintain its freedom from the bustle of civilization which surrounded it. Perry loved all the arts, children, trees, and "mother nature," and he wholeheartedly embraced all facets of life in Carmel Village and remained always a champion of Carmel causes. He fought for regulation and zoning, and against "regimented architecture," house numbers, mass sanitation, planned building, and progressive schools, while all the time fighting conventional progress.

Perry was even involved in the fight to make the famous "Block 69," now Devendorf Park, a reality. The story as it was related to me, goes as follows: In 1922, Devendorf tossed in Block 69 with the purchase of the dunes and beach property by the City of Carmel. For a considerable time the lot stood up under a multitude of uses—as a polo field, for horseshoes, a local circus, and even a campground. However, two things about it stood out in several people's minds as they recalled the story—it was a dust bowl in summer and a quagmire in winter, and there was always a great deal of discussion about what to do with it. It seems that there was one woman in particular who championed the cause to make something of that lot, and that was Mattie Hopper, wife of Jimmy Hopper. Mrs. Hopper stopped at nothing to publicize her fight, and even sponsored a Spanish Fandango to foster funds for a park improvement program. It was a beginning, and soon M. J. Murphy pledged 100 yards of top soil, Dr. R. A. Kocher offered chalk rock and benches, and some citizens met to decide on a name. Some villagers felt the block should be the site for the construction of a fire house, city hall or police station, and the idea of a park at one time seemed very distant. However, by 1928 it became apparent that beautification could be realized through the support of the local Women's Club, the Abalone League, and the P-T.A. The city fathers soon approved the plans set before them, and finally in January of 1932 the project was underway and planting had begun. Supervised by councilwoman Clara Kellogg, the park soon looked like one, but in April of that year there was once again a movement underway to make the park a civic center. Yet amazingly, before the measure could be voted upon,

the Monterey Water Works, which had long before been granted easement in "perpetuity," disputed the right of the City of Carmel to use the land for anything other than a park so that no construction of any kind would interfere with the company's right of free access. Needless to say, the measure for a civic center was rejected by all voters and for all time a park it is and a park it must remain.

Of course the "Dunes" story went hand in hand with that of "Block 69." Both stories began in the spring of 1921, when Talbert Josselyn, De Neale Morgan, Perry Newberry, the James Hoppers, the Taylors, the Silvas, the MacGowans, Miss Prentiss, Arthur Vachell, the Seidenecks, and forty other staunch citizens met at De Neale Morgan's studio and decided that the purchase of fifteen acres of dunes lying to the north of the 100 by 600 foot section of land already deeded to the City of Carmel was simply a must, in order to preserve it for all time. Fred Bechdolt, De Neale Morgan, and Tal Josselyn "went down the road to Devey's that night." The deal was set at the price of $15,000 and the people of Carmel cast their vote four to one in favor of the purchase of the dunes, beach and Block 69, now Devendorf Park.

Perry Newberry's loving wife, Bertha, stood beside and behind him in every cause and even went so far as to throw a pot of geraniums at councilman

Perry Newberry in 1921 in the house he built. Slevin photograph.

55

George Dorwart when he roused her ire during a town meeting. Newberry loved Carmel dearly, and so afraid was he that progress would ruin the village that he ran for the Board of Trustees in 1929, and won with the slogan, "Keep Carmel Off The Map." He had urged village residents *not* to vote for him if they desired commercial success and street lamps for their city. Bert Heron ran on a similar platform in 1938, and also won. In fact, once upon a time, Perry L. McDonald petitioned the council for the "privilege" of blowing a steam whistle at twelve o'clock noon, "the same to made musical as a fairy chime." Perry Newberry rose to the occasion and pleaded for the peace and content "of that portion of Carmel who had fled from whistles and maddening crowds and trolley cars." "Why keep account of time in Carmel?" said Perry. "People come to her to get away from it." The petition was denied.

When not devoting himself to causes (which was rare indeed), Perry was busy building stone and brick houses and cottages around town. When ill health came to him, he and Bertha were living in Hatton Fields, and when he died in December of 1939, Bertha scattered his ashes at Stillwater Cove, and a "bright and shining champion of village fighters was gone." Today Perry Newberry's words still echo the personal feelings of many of us as we have watched the changes in our own time—"Nearly everyone that comes to Carmel wants the town to remain 'different,' and hasn't the slightest conception of what its 'difference' is. Some people think it has to do with holding back the town's population, being old-fashioned, keeping things primitive, getting along without the comforts and luxuries that modern life demands. NOT A BIT. The idea of holding back progress has nothing to do with the notion of keeping Carmel different, for difference, as far as its definition applies to our town, means originality. Community originality is what has made Carmel a different town from its neighbors, and is what you found here that decided you to make it your home."

Another couple who lived on the Point in the early part of this century were Philip and Laura Wilson. He had been a rancher and she a schoolteacher. They were married in 1890 and came to California and Carmel via Texas, with three young children: Grace Hood Wilson III (later Mrs. James H. Thorburn, wife of one of Carmel's earliest mayors), Philip Wilson, Jr., and James Wilson. Laura Pearce Wilson, born in 1865, was the sister of Mary Louise Norton, who later became Mrs. Dummage, wife of early plumber William Dummage. Laura and Philip Wilson opened a real estate office and

built their home in 1905 on San Carlos opposite Sunset School. In 1912 they purchased their Point Loeb home and property at Fourteenth and San Antonio, where they lived for forty-three years. This included the little cottage which had been built earlier by writer John Fleming Wilson (not a relative) which they later used as a guest house.

Philip Wilson was responsible for the building of Carmel's first and only golf course, which was located south of the village and followed the ocean

Carmel's first golf course, on Point Loeb, was laid out and run by Philip Wilson, Sr.

front from the end of the beach to the mouth of the Carmel River, where he also had twenty rowboats for rent during the spring and summer months. The golf course consisted of nine, then ten, holes of "natural hazards," and a clubhouse was constructed at what is now Fourteenth and San Antonio, maintained under Mr. Wilson's management. He took delight in explaining how it was modeled after the well-known Berwick Golf Course in Scotland. The course was abandoned during the First World War. It was later sold and the land subdivided, and the open beauty which surrounded those early homes was lost. I remember how soon after the death of Mrs. Laura Wilson at the age of ninety, in 1956, the beauty around the Jeffers, Arthur, and Reamer homes seemed to change almost overnight. Property owned by the Philip Wilsons also played a later part in the story of Carmel, for at the northwest corner of Ocean and Dolores there is a building still

First official City Hall, in Philip Wilson Building. The flag pole was erected on June 6, 1917. Sketch by author.

standing which became the first "official" Carmel City Hall after incorporation. Its flagpole, now long gone, was erected on June 6, 1917. The same building, where Mr. Kinji's Oriental Shop is, was used by the early Red Cross organization of Carmel, and it was in this building that August Englund was nominated by George Beardsley for City Marshal, and was appointed at ninety dollars a month. It was also in this building that the official seal of the City of Carmel with the old mission design was adopted. In June of 1915 another piece of the Wilson property opened up with a new garage on Dolores at Sixth which later became the site of the Browse Around Music Store, Mary Mays, and more recently a third additional expansion of the old Glennon's, and is now known as Oxbridge.

Another influential personality of the Point Loeb was Robinson Jeffers. All manner of things have been written about Jeffers, some fitting and some not. I remember the Jefferses as I knew them, and in particular I remember them together—Una, with her hair in silver braids and a secret smile on her face, and he with bleached blue eyes, tall, thin and bent but agile—as they made their way along the path and across to the rocks below the house early

one morning. I have kept these memories of them and of Tor House when it still stood in their loving care.

Robinson Jeffers was born on January 10, 1887, to Annie Robinson Jeffers and William Hamilton Jeffers, a professor of ancient literature. For Robinson, schooling began under his father's guidance at home, where he learned Greek at the age of five. A well-seasoned traveler with his parents, he came to California in 1903, and received his B.A. at Occidental College at the age of eighteen, as a most distinguished scholar of Biblical literature. Later he attended the University of Southern California, taking medicine and forestry. He did post graduate work at the University of Zurich in Switzerland, and in 1939 he was given an honorary Ph.D. from the University of Southern California. Jeffers had begun writing poetry in his earliest years. His first publication was "Flagons and Apples" in 1912, followed by a second in 1916. None of his first works won him any public recognition. However, when "Tamar" and other poems such as "Roan Stallion" came to public light, along with "Descent to the Dead," "Give Your Heart to the Hawks," and "The Loving Shepherdess," he became the center of public criticism and controversy.

In 1913, Jeffers took Una Call Kuster as his wife, and they purchased a five-acre site for $500. In their intense love of the place they built the stone walls and tower which was their beloved Tor House. Tor House was and still is an anachronism, infinitely more beautiful when it was not surrounded by present day structures which crowd it. I remember the beauty of it when is seemed to grow out of the land it occupies to become a part of the craggy granite, sun, fog, and sea below. Jeffers was to say later of their decision to stay, "When the stagecoach topped the hill from Monterey and we looked down through the pines and seafog on Carmel Bay, it was evident that we had come without knowing it to our inevitable place." The house was constructed of granite boulders from the Carmel shoreline, much of it coming from below their property, and Jeffers worked alongside the stonemason and M. J. Murphy, learning as the house was being built. The first section of Tor House was finished in 1919, but over a period of time they continued to add to the place. A year after they had moved in, Una suggested the building of the tower. Of his own design and labor, Jeffers built the three-story forty-foot tower. He used it as a place in which to do his work by lamp light, refusing to accept electricity until 1949. Una chose its second floor as a place to keep and play her organ. This granite home, this "place apart," was the center of their lives, and Jeffers described it well in this verse from "A Westward Beach":

"There is no house for
    miles around:
There is no human chatter;
The waves give tongue, the
    cliffs resound,
The pines along the water
Murmur together, and on
    high
Seagulls call and curlews
    cry,
Wheeling low in vacant sky."

Tor House, 1932. Julian P. Graham photograph.

The favorite walk of the Jeffers was along the grass-covered "track" which wound around the Point. The only houses then were Reamers' Driftwood and Philip Wilson's; otherwise the view was one of unbroken acres of green, with poppies, lupines and other wildflowers, and of distant horses grazing across the lagoon, or "moor," as Robinson called it, and the mission on behind. Robinson described the feeling of the place: "All about us here was pulsing life and motion . . . flighting birds and pounding waves and cloud shadow fleeing across grasses bent and woven by the winds. There was a special night wind from the valley that wuthered unhindered around our exposed little house . . . now it seldom wins through to us." It is a lovely description and one you can picture if you know the land and love it. It was the perfect place, the perfect complement for a couple whose vitality and love of nature belonged in such a place. This couple were also a complement to each other, she a force and comfort in his need to create. Together they traveled widely and explored both literature and culture, raised two sons, and contributed to the community around them. Some called Robinson Jeffers a recluse and unfriendly, and he made this comment in

rebuttal: "It's not that I don't like to see people, but total strangers are constantly coming to the house merely out of curiosity. Being known as a recluse prevents many a boring afternoon."

Una died in September 1950 and Robinson in January 1962, and the loss of each was keenly felt. A private and humble man, Jeffers once had this to say in reply to a publisher who asked for biographical material: "The only things of consequence that a man can do are to plant a tree, get a child, build a house, write a book. I have just finished a book, have built a house, gotten two children and planted two thousand trees but none of these things are biographical material." Today the fate and state of Tor House are controversial. Of his beloved home, Jeffers wrote:

"If you should look for this place after a handful of lifetimes:
Perhaps of my planted forest a few
May stand yet, dark-leaved Australians or the coast cypress . . .
Look for foundations of sea-worn granite, my fingers had the art
To make stone love stone, you will find some remnant . . .
My ghost you needn't look for; for it is probably
Here, but a dark one, deep in the granite . . ."

The Carmel Point had another claim to fame when an activity formed which probably organized and included more of the local gentry for longer than any other Carmel has ever seen or will ever see, and it was a league of softball teams, called the Abalone League. Its name was derived from its place among the abalone at Point Loeb (Carmel Point). The games began soon after the First World War on a rough diamond at the Point, near Charles Van Riper's house, but a man named Thorn Taylor was actually responsible for getting the ball rolling, along with Talbert Josselyn. The games began as a purely social affair of good spirit and fun where amateurs could "swat away balls (many ending up in the abalone cove) to their hearts' content." Thorn Taylor had been an athlete in pre-Carmel days, and his idea soon captured the entire town. Good friends Van Riper, Tal Josselyn, and Lee Gottfried helped commandeer the local populace, and soon the stage was set, as Van Riper and Taylor placed the players—men, women and children—around the field. It was truly Carmel's social and athletic event, and it was the first organized softball league ever in the Western United States. Talbert Josselyn was quoted in later years as saying he had been "dragged" into one of those "impromptu" plays at the Forest The-ater in 1919 where he saw ex-fighter pilot Thorn Taylor outfitted with a broomstick-sized bat and a casaba-ball, asking the cast to join him. "The cast enjoyed themselves so much they were all home late for dinner."

By 1921 the games were held twice a week and a regular league was formed. Whole families played and there were two games in session on Sundays. Lee Gottfried was one of the first players, and jour-nalist Robert Wells Ritchie was the league's first umpire, who it was said was chosen "because he had just returned from Arizona with some broken ribs and everyone thought he would be safe from getting into a fight." The lineup of early players sported the following names: Dr. R. A. Kocher, Tad Stinson, Donald Hale, William "Rosie" Henry, Norman Marshall, Harry Leon Wilson, Jimmy Hopper, Bob Pinkerton, Philip Wilson, Jr., Fred and Harrison Godwin, Hilda Argo, Jimmy Doud, Kit Cooke, Helen Wilson Charyis, Elliot and Marion Boke, Samuel F. B. Morse, Colonel Fletcher Dutton, L. Wycoff, Charles Van Riper, Ashton Stanley, Eugene Marble, Clay Otto, Winsor Josselyn, Ralph Todd, Happy Byford Hoehn, Gordon Campbell, Joseph Hooper, Frank Sheriden (writer of the lyrics for the song "Marquita"), Hal Geyer, Paul Hunter, Byington Ford, Trevor Shand, Frenchie Murphy, Fred Ammerman, Sis Reamer, and "Doc" Stani-ford. Pon Chung served refreshments from the side-lines and helped Hilda Argo stuff newspapers in the gopher holes.

Eventually a home run, and a ball through a window, caused the league to move from the Point to the Carmel Woods, which in Gordon Campbell's words "was a triangular shaped area bordered on the north by Camino del Monte, on the south by Serra and on the west by Portola which runs into Guadalupe on what would be the eastern tip." The site known as the Mission Tract and Hatton Fields was also used for games. There were a dozen or more teams, such as the Shamrocks, Reds, Giants, Tigers, Blues, Pilots, Robins, Sox, Rangers, Cres-cents, Eskimos, and Sharks, and distress among the players as families found themselves divided. As one ex-player stated, "families were broken up in the resulting controversies as to where each was to play on a certain Sunday. Children were lost and the dogs and cats went insane." In order to purchase land for a permanent field, the league bought the Arts and Crafts Theater (where the Golden Bough is now) and staged plays to raise money. Eventually the league was able to purchase ten lots in the Carmel Woods. In 1930 that diamond was aban-

doned, and in 1938 the last games were played in the Mission Tract, approximately where the River School is today, though there was a short revival of the games in 1947.

Before the games gave way to another time, they blazed in glory, complete with press box (packing crate) on the third base line, courtesy of William Overstreet. One of the teams included a squad of football players who had the motto, "You name the game and we'll win it!" Among them were future Stanford "great" Gordon Campbell, Jack Eaton, Goldie Goldstein, Bob Stanton, Jimmy Doud, Tad Stinson, Happy Hoehn, and Winsor Josselyn. An-nual dinners were held, and trophies given, such as the "Silver Hooper Cup," named after the league's most active senior player, Joseph J. Hooper who, in his sixties then, played behind home plate and "blocked 'em hard." The Herald Cup was an ornate stove top which Tal Josselyn and Hilda Argo "pre-sented with great enthusiasm."

Games were played seriously, and there were injuries. "Doc" Staniford supplied his special brand of crutches for those with broken legs, including "Doc" himself, Louis Beiset, and Harrison Godwin. Sam Morse sustained serious facial injuries as a result of his playing. Hilda Argo was noted for her valiant efforts at stuffing newspapers in all the many gopher holes to help avoid as many broken legs as possible.

The Abalone League was the first softball league in history ever to get a ruling from Judge H. Kene-saw Mountain Landis, the commissioner of base-ball. The decision was handed down after a dispute arose when a player scored from second base on an overthrow. Players on the opposite teams claimed the man should be sent back to third base, and Talbert Josselyn said he would write Landis. The judge ruled that the player should indeed return to third. This decision earned Tal Josselyn the nick-name of "Landis." At the peak of the league a hundred cars were known to circle the diamond on a Sunday, and at its closing, when the life styles and encroaching housing gave too much competition, Winsor Josselyn was heard to remark, "It's getting so you can't stand in the middle of Ocean Avenue and read your mail any more."

In December of 1905, the first meeting of the Manzanita Club, formed by Thomas Burnight, was held in his candy store up the street from Slevin's. There were several more meetings in the candy store, then the club was moved to the Carmel Hall, the old barn which had been a part of the

Escolle property. In 1916, the proud officers of the Manzanita Theater, under the ownership of Mr. and Mrs. Douglas Greeley and their son Robert, began the showing of movies. Paul Funchess and another man by the name of Cunningham were projectionists for the silent movies played upstairs, where ex-prizefighter Charles Delos Curtis, acting manager, would sell tickets for ten cents and furnish the "eats." Whenever a film was available, Curtis would hook up his pony, Peanuts, to his cart and drive around with a sign stating "Movie Tonight." After selling tickets until he felt the barn was full enough, Curtis would begin the show. Known for his love of children, he always reserved the front row for "little ones," as he called them, while city clerk Saidee Van Brower tickled the ivories in accompaniment to the silent films.

Delos Curtis advertising "movie tonight" in front of the park which he made for local children between his and Hand's offices, 1927. Slevin photograph.

Curtis was also remembered for his almost single-handed conversion of the vacant lot between his and Joseph Hand's office into a playground for local children, and for both his and Catherine's contributions of small gifts for the village children after the annual Christmas tree lighting ceremony on Ocean Avenue.

Several Carmel youths were treated to the job of assistant projectionist; one who remembered those days fondly was Waldo Hicks. The theater became a regular source of enjoyment to the villagers when, in cooperation with the Carmel Hall Association, the decision was made in 1915 to bring moving pictures to Carmel as a business. Selected to handle the matter were Murphy and several friends and associates, W. L. Overstreet, T. B. Reardon, B. W. Adams, R. W. Hicks, and Fred Leidig. It was their plan to give "first class" movie shows every Saturday. Up to that time everyone had to go over the hill to Monterey for first class shows. The committee approached Douglas Greeley, who had just advertised that he had acquired "one of the new improved projectors allowing all films to be shown clearly without interruptions, and the installation of a new screen." The next advertisement in the *Pine Cone* after the meeting stated "there will be three shows a week Tuesday, Thursday, and Saturday with special High Class features shown on Saturday. Admission 20¢, children 10¢, with other shows at 5 & 10." Moving pictures had come to Carmel to stay.

Eventually a clubhouse was built for the Manzanita Club on Dolores Street between Eighth and Ninth. It was built in 1926 by Murphy, the plans having been drawn up by G. O. Koepp. In later years the Manzanita Hall was moved to San Carlos just south of where the original Carmel Garage owned by Goold, then the Standard Oil station, later stood. Many young men pumped gas after school and during summer vacations at the service station while their girl friends would sip sodas and Coca-Cola in the adjacent creamery first known as Blewett's, then Konrad's and then Hilbert's, until it and the old station were leased by the Goolds. It is known today as Dick Bruhn's Carmel store. In 1934 the new Manzanita Club became a "little theater." Later it was under the direction of Dene Denny and Hazel Watrous, and in the end it became M. J. Murphy's Cabinet Shop. Members enrolled in the original Manzanita Club were Thomas Reardon, O. H. Lewis, Dr. J. E. Beck, Edward Payne, L. S. Slevin, J. F. Devendorf, Philip Wilson, Sr., M. J. Murphy, Thomas Lisk, Ben Turner, and Dave Von Needa. The club was incorporated in 1925, exactly one year after the formation of Carmel's Athletic Club. The Athletic Club was under the direction of T. Nichols as president, Wesley Dickenson as secretary, and Waldo Hicks as treasurer. Sherman Sorow and Manning Tarr were executive committee members. The club was responsible for many plays and outdoor athletic events as well as a summer camp.

By 1916 there were four religious denominations meeting in Carmel: Catholics at the mission, with Father Mestres celebrating masses; Methodists in their Community Church, which later became the Church of the Wayfarer; Episcopalians, who met in what is now City Hall; and Christian Scientists, who were the first to hold services within the city limits. Those first religious services were conducted by Henry Fisher, the engineer responsible for laying out Carmel for Devendorf, and they were held in the original Hotel Carmelo.

The next religious services in Carmel were offered by Edmund Sims, a builder, painter, and collector of antiques. Devendorf had hired Sims to help with the preparation for the opening of the Pine Inn. At the time, Sims occupied a tent across the street from the Pine Inn in which he had a small organ which he would play, without prompting, as he sang "fervently," welcoming all who would join him.

Then in 1904 came the Reverend Willis White and his wife Sarah, along with his aged mother, who encouraged him to do something about the lack of religious order in the village—"at the very least a Sabbath School should be established." The cause was taken up by Sarah, who acted not only as teacher, but superintendent, organist, and janitor, while her mother-in-law took care of baby Mariam. John Staples was teaching the Bible classes which were first held in a tent-covered building at the southwest corner of Ocean and Dolores, just slightly behind where the present Corner Cupboard is today.

The local Methodists first met for worship in 1904, under the trees on the corner of Dolores and Sixth where Mausita Jennings would one day have her Browse Around Music Store. Then before long the sound of their singing voices accompanied by an organ was heard coming from the barn belonging to Mr. Horn at San Carlos and Sixth, where the brother of Cortland Arne, Edmund, acted as a singing evangelist. The Reverend George Clifford was hired by Devendorf as the pastor of the Methodist Church. He occupied John Staples' cottage and was paid the yearly salary of $300. The First Methodist Episcopal Church of Carmel was incorporated with the following members: J. F. Devendorf, William Gilchrist, Lucretia C. Horn, Lillian Hanson, Mrs. M. A. Potter, C. E. Rogers, John P. Staples, and Mr. and Mrs. Edmund Arne. Devendorf, in his customary generosity, donated two lots on Lincoln

Methodist Episcopal Church, later known as Carmel Community Church, 1905. Sketch by author.

near Ocean Avenue. During its first year the group grew, and with Mrs. Edmund Arne as director, was able to collect sufficient funds to build a church free of debt. The dedication of the church took place in 1905, with the Reverend John Kirby officiating at the dedication service. A church bell was donated by the village of Carmel, and a Reed organ was presented as the gift of William Gilchrist. Miss Josephine Culbertson held the job of organist for a period of twenty years. At the time of the dedication the Rev. Clifford was reappointed at the same salary of $300. The Reverend Wesley Dennet and the Reverend Robert Ladd served the church in 1906 and 1907. The Reverend Wilfred Kent served from 1907 to 1910, and in 1910 a house was purchased at Lincoln and Seventh for $700, for a parsonage.

The Reverend J. J. Pardee was minister from 1910 to 1915, and during his service the debt on the parsonage was cleared and electric lights were installed. When the Rev. Pardee was forced to retire in late 1915, due to poor health, he was replaced by the Reverend S. C. Thomas from San Leandro, who served until September 28, 1919. Thomas was credited with the organization of the local Camp Fire Girls in connection with the church. Beginning on October 10, 1920, the Reverend Fred W. Sheldon served a one-year term, and at its end was asked by the board to remain as permanent minister, which he did. During Sheldon's term several things occurred, the first of which was the building of a new room for Sunday services, a kitchen and recreation hall. The rooms were built by M. J. Murphy in 1926 and dedicated by Bishop Leonard after a presentation speech by Dr. E. A. Sturge. A new furnace was installed, the gift of Mrs. George Beardsley who, as did her husband, contributed much in both time and materials to various causes. The church also purchased a new piano and several chairs for the choir, at the cost of $4,000. Also in 1926, the Rev. Sheldon retired and the Reverend I. M. Terwillinger took his place, staying until September 1929.

In September 1924 the Rev. Sheldon helped to organize a group of Masons, including William Titmus, Ross E. Bonham, W. T. Kibbler, Walter T. Basham, A. F. Meckenstock, and M. N. Wild. The Rev. Sheldon was acting chairman, D. L. Staniford was elected vice president, F. O. Robbins secretary, and Charles L. Berky treasurer.

Between 1929 and 1940, the Methodist Church was served by the Reverends T. Harold Grimshaw, September 1929 to October 1933; Melvin Dorsett, October 1, 1933 to December 31, 1935; Homer S. Bodley, Jr., February 1, 1936 to June 1938; and W. W. McKee, June 1938 to May 5, 1940.

The new Carmel Community Church was dedicated on March 3, 1940. Robert (Bob) Stanton was the architect for the new building. Several years earlier, Stanton and his mother had attended an auction of the collection of Mrs. Millard from her estate, La Miniature, designed by Frank Lloyd Wright. Stanton's mother, also a collector, purchased the set of lovely wooden panels that you see in the present church for $1,000. When Stanton was selected as architect for the new church, he suggested that the church could make arrangements to purchase these panels at the original cost, and that he could incorporate them into the design. The purchase was made, and the church and the old-world panels have continued to complement each other. The marvelous concrete vault was designed by Stanton for the choir and music chamber, and the cross was done by Tom Mulvin. The tile which Stanton skillfully used in the flooring came from the Hearst estate. The new building also housed four classrooms and a recreation hall with a kitchen, and at its dedication by the Reverend T. H. Palmquist, Robert Stanton read "The Work is Planned," and soloists were Edith Anderson, Robert Stanton, and Andrew Sesink, with A. M. Michaels from San Francisco accompanying them on the new Hammond organ, the gift of Mrs. Anne Winslow. Other ministers who assisted the Rev. Palmquist on this occasion were Dr. W. W. McKee, the pastor, and the Reverends J. F. Follette, Elwood Hunter, S. C. Potter, and C. J. Hulsewe, and Father O'Connell.

After the formal dedication of the church at Lincoln and Seventh, the Rev. McKee retired, after forty years of service in the ministry, in June 1940, and Dr. J. E. Crowther took his place. He served for seven years, and during those years the Carmel Community Church was given its new name, the Church of the Wayfarer. In 1919, Dr. Crowther had written a musical pageant which he titled "The Wayfarer," and the congregation of the church at the time was made up of members from around the world. In 1941, through the inspiration of Mrs. George Beardsley, a Biblical garden was planted. Dr. Crowther, a talented carpenter, built a new altar with panels which were left from the building of the church. Dr. Crowther celebrated his golden jubilee as a minister of the church on September 7, 1945, at which time he was given a gift of fifty silver dollars in recognition of his service. On the ninth of March, 1947, the Rev. Crowther announced his retirement, and on March 13, 1947, he passed away. His wife had died in 1940.

In June 1947, Dr. K. Filmore Gray came from St. Stephen's Church in Oakland, with his wife and

Church of the Wayfarer on Lincoln Street, 1940.

sons, to give his first sermon at the Church of the Wayfarer.

The first Sunday school at the church, begun by Mrs. W. G. White, also prompted her to begin Bible classes. Mr. H. W. Askew was the Sunday school superintendent after the church was first built, and then Dr. E. A. Sturge, a retired missionary, took over the job. The primary department was presided over by Miss Frances Farrington until Mrs. D. E. Nixon took her place for a period of twelve years beginning in 1919. When Mrs. Thomas Douglass became teacher with Miss Farrington, they also started the Girl Scouts in Carmel. The church also had an extensive Ladies Aid Society and a Women's Auxiliary, with both groups listing the names of the majority of the village's female citizens from 1901 to 1930.

This is a good point at which to tell how Carmel's Girl Scouts came to be. In 1922 Carmel's Girls Club was organized by Mrs. Eva Douglass. Miss Frances Farrington offered to have the meetings in her home instead of in the Sunday school rooms of the Community Church. The girls were instructed in homemaking, and Mrs. Douglass also often opened her kitchen to cooking classes. After a year of successful meetings, an accredited representative of the Girl Scout organization came from Palo Alto to visit with the Girls Club and help to organize a local Girl Scout group. By the spring of 1923, Mrs. Arthur Hannon had been appointed leader of the first Girl Scouts of Carmel, and for six months she contributed her time and efforts to the group. The first scouts, many of whom continued their affiliation with scouting over the years, were: Mary E. Douglass (Mrs. Richard Elliot, Carmel); Florence Edler (Mrs. Jack Volkers, Carmel); Violet Payne (Mrs. Paul Brookshire, Carmel Valley); Helen Ward (Mrs. Arthur Norbey, Santa Barbara); Jane Foster (Mrs. Louis H. Carne, San Francisco), deceased;

Mildred Pearson (Mrs. M. J. M. Doyle); Mary Wetzel (Mrs. Walter Mueller, San Francisco); Evelyn Arne (Mrs. Lynn Frisbee, San Francisco and Fresno); Jane Lowler (Mrs. Richard Allen, East Coast); Wilma Bassett (Mrs. Theodore McKay, Southern California); Helen Turner (Mrs. Gene Ricketts, Carmel); Virginia Rockwell (Mrs. Robert Elliott, Marin County).

The story of All Saints Church began on September 25, 1907, at the Pine Inn. The Carmel Missionary Society was its guiding force. Regular meetings began at the Bathhouse, and then, it may surprise some to know, church services were held in the basement of the Pine Inn, with hymns sung in the lobby. In late 1906 Bishop and Mrs. Moreland came to stay at the Pine Inn, and funds raised during their stay amounted to $2,000, which was held in a building fund by a Dr. Himmelsbach. In 1910 the

All Saints Church in 1949. George Cain photograph.

rector of St. Mary's-by-the-Sea in Pacific Grove, the Rev. Maloney, held regular services in the basement of the Pine Inn. First members were Mrs. Rose De Yoe, Miss Mary De Neale Morgan, Miss Etta Tilton, Mrs. Fowler, Dr. and Mrs. Himmelsbach, Mrs. Cummings, Mrs. Emma Rendtorff and her hus-

band, Professor Carl Rendtorff, Mr. Rosenbloom, Mr. Wolks, Mr. and Mrs. William G. Harrison and daughter, Miss Lichtenthaer, Mrs. Charles Clark, Mrs. Dorwart, Mrs. Ashburner, and Mr. and Mrs. William Overstreet. During these first meetings a guild was formed with the following as officers: president, Miss Mabel Thompson, secretary, Miss Etta Tilton, treasurer, Mrs. William Overstreet, and committee members, Mrs. Charles Clark, Mrs. William Watts, Mrs. Hughes, Mrs. Abby McDow, Mrs. Rose De Yoe, and Mary Cummings, all of whom were in charge of fund raising events. Once again the goodwill of "Devey" was felt when he agreed to give deeds to two lots at Mission and Eighth whenever building was to take place.

On Easter Day of 1911, the Rev. Maloney and the Rev. Gardner came to Carmel, bringing with them a choir and organ, and services were held on the stage of the Forest Theater. By July of 1912 the Ladies Guild was holding regular meetings at the studio of Miss Tilton on the northeast of San Carlos and Sixth for the purpose of discussing the organization of regular church meetings and fund raising events. Mabel Thompson and her sister, Mrs. Wingate, were strong leaders in the fund raising efforts. When $1,200 had been raised, it was used as a deposit on a building which was designed by Albert Cauldwell, a San Francisco architect, and built by M. J. Murphy. The two lots at Mission and Eighth originally offered by Devendorf had been exchanged for a site on Monte Verde, and the first All Saints Church building is City Hall today. The name of "All Saints" was suggested by Mrs. Charles Clark at one of the meetings of the Ladies Guild. After the building was completed in July 1913, it was dedicated by Bishop Nichols and named All Saints.

Mr. Rosenbloom was elected as senior warden, E. A. Walker as clerk, and William Overstreet as treasurer. Until a full time minister could be obtained, the Rev. Maloney continued to come from St. Mary's to officiate at services each Sunday. The first full time minister was the Rev. Darwall, whose service started in the fall of 1914. He was followed by the Rev. Moffitt, who served a very short time, and then the Reverend Francis Williams, who was the minister for four years, until his death. In 1924 the Reverend Austin B. Chinn became minister of All Saints, and it was during his term that the church truly developed. A new parish house was built in 1928, and a church bell was cast at the Meneely Foundries of Troy, New York, the gift of Mrs. Charles W. Thatcher in memory of her daughter, Edith Cherry, for whom the Cherry Foundation is named.

In 1931, Mrs. Paul Prince, who was for many years an active participant in Carmel's community affairs, suggested the founding of a boys' choir, which was organized with Edward C. Hopkins as choirmaster and organist and Mr. Gillingham as choir counselor. Three ladies made possible the acquisition of choir robes—Mrs. Kilpatrick, Mrs. Louis B. Hill, and Miss Ada Howe Kent.

After the retirement of the Rev. Chinn in 1937, the Rev. Hulsewe was appointed. He served for the next nine years and was followed by the Reverend Alfred B. Seccombe. The Rev. Seccombe and his family made "White Cedars" their home until it was purchased as the site for a new church. The old church was purchased for use as the City Hall, which it remains today. At the September 6, 1946 meeting of the city council, Mayor Fred Godwin stated that the vestry of All Saints Church had offered an option to the city for the church, parish hall and rectory, and two adjoining lots, for the purpose of a City Hall. Godwin also stated that council members felt that the general public should exercise their expression, and thirty citizens, as representatives of the village, expressed their enthusiasm for the acceptance of the building for a new City Hall. The motion for authorization was made by Allen Knight and seconded by Charles Childen, with Mrs. Talbert Josselyn, Hugh Comstock, and Herbert Heron expressing the opinion that the option should be "exercised immediately."

"White Cedars" was built in 1904 on the corner of Ninth and Dolores by Edmund Sims, with a Mr. Samuels and William Polk, both from San Francisco, as the architects. It was originally the home of Mrs. M. E. White, and was the setting for the founding of the Carmel Missionary Society on September 25, 1907, when the Reverend W. J. Clifford met with some ladies to form an auxiliary of the San Jose Presbyterian Society. At this time the president was Miss Margaret White, the vice president was Mrs. Philip Wilson, Jr., and the secretary was Mrs. Philip Wilson, Sr. The constitution of the group was adopted in October 1907, and some of the projects of the group were a box for the Lake County Indians, quilt blocks for Miss McKay's work with the Kentucky mountaineers, the sale of articles made by the Navajo Indians, and the gathering of clothing for an orphanage at San Anselmo, California. According to the secretary's minutes of March 25, 1908, all meetings were then being held in the Bathhouse, where luncheons were provided. That day the group hosted the Monterey Presbyterian Society. In February 1911 work had begun on the Carmel Missionary Society's chapel at Ninth

and Dolores, with the Rev. Hicks doing the supervising. The San Jose chapter donated $400 towards the building of the chapel, which was completed in April 1911. The formal dedication took place on July 30, 1911, with the opening sermon given by Dr. Noble. The years from 1912 until the Carmel Missionary Society was disbanded in 1951 were eventful, with the Society accomplishing a great deal by the organized efforts of its members.

In 1912 a tradition was established when the Ladies Aid Guild of the Carmel Methodist Episcopal Church was invited to a meeting of the Society held at the Pine Inn, at that time under the management of Mrs. Wingate. At this meeting the idea of a federated society was discussed. A Mrs. Butcher suggested a plan of organization, which was presented as a motion by Miss Sybel Young. On February 22, 1922, officers of a federated group were elected: president, Mrs. Butcher; vice president, Miss Mariam E. White, and recorder and secretary, Mrs. Thomas Douglass. The four groups that made up the federation were represented as follows: Mrs. Fred Sheldon, Methodist; Miss Josephine Culbertson, Congregational; Mrs. E. L. Taylor, Presbyterian; and Mrs. D. E. Nixon, Christian. Mrs. Nixon later became the first chairman for the Church of the Wayfarer, with Mrs. Florida Holm, Mrs. Walter Kreisler, and Miss Olive Swezy succeeding her. The All Saints chairman was Mrs. Walter Lehman. After the disbanding of the society, the idea behind its existence was carried on through the auxiliary groups of the Carmel churches, and the little chapel was removed and transported to Salinas, where it became a section of the Presbyterian Church of Filipino people.

The first Church of Christian Science meeting, Carmel's first meeting of a religious group, was held in the old Hotel Carmelo. Later meetings were held in the newly built Pine Inn, in 1903. A non-resident group of members met in the home of Agnes Miller, where the Sun Dial Court now stands, from 1904 until they disbanded in 1909 for the organization of the church proper. After the disbanding of the earlier group, eight members of the Christian Science church held meetings on San Carlos between Ninth and Tenth avenues in the home of Mrs. Edna Bloom, which was later owned by Mr. and Mrs. Fred Wermuth. Mrs. Bloom was the first reader, with Miss Helen Parks acting as the second reader. Miss Bell Kant took Mrs. Bloom's place when she moved to Los Angeles. Other members were William Silva, Miss Stella Vincent, Miss Mary Mower, Miss Jesse Swift, and Mrs. Albert Otey. By July 1913, organized meetings were being held in the Arts

This photograph of the First Church of Christ Scientist was taken in 1918 by Clara N. Nixon.

and Crafts Hall. A regular Sunday school was being held in the Arts and Crafts Hall by 1914, with the children of M. J. Murphy—Franklin, Fay, and the twins Kathleen and Rosalie—and Walter Basham in attendance. Mrs. Caroline B. Silva was the teacher. She and her husband William opened their home for Wednesday evening meetings the following year.

Incorporation, with the name First Christian Science Society of Carmel, took place in 1917. Mr. and Mrs. Albert Otey (who owned the property where Cabbages and Kings used to be, and the original Hill's Corner property at San Carlos and Eighth) took an active role in the excavation for the building, as well as the laying of the cornerstone in December 1917. A debt-free dedication ceremony took place in August 1918. The building was on the site of today's Christian Science Church, and a small studio on the property next door was purchased for use by the Sunday school. In 1927 a dream was realized

The Christian Science Reading Room in the court of the Golden Bough in 1922. The building is now Robert Talbott Ties.

for Carmel Christian Scientists when their society became "First Church of Christ Scientist, Carmel, California." Many will remember the reading rooms in the quaint little building in the court of the Golden Bough, which were established in 1936, with Miss Helen Parks as reader. This same little building became the first business site of Mr. Talbott for his ties. The present reading rooms were erected in 1950 at Monte Verde and Fifth. Incidentally, the quaint little building next door to Talbott's, now occupied by the Cottage of Sweets, had its original home on Dolores Street on the Dummage corner. It was built for Ruth Kuster by L. E. Gottfried in September 1922 for her weaving shop, where fellow weavers Vivienne Higginbotham and Iris Alberto joined her. It was later moved out front of the court of the Golden Bough where Ruth continued to use it as her shop while using the window at the back left for a ticket office for her husband's theater. Years later, after the theater was gone, the billboard out front, a touch typically Kuster, still read "Now Playing."

First Presbyterian Chapel, built in 1911 under the supervision of the Rev. Hicks. Located on the southeast corner of Dolores and Eighth, it was used by local Chinese. Sketch by author.

The newest of Carmel's churches is the Carmel Presbyterian Church, which held the ground breaking ceremonies for its present church building at the site of the old stables at Mountain View and Junipero in June 1954. I was present at the first wedding held there.

Along with the establishment of the first school and churches, Carmel's early residents organized to provide themselves with a library, hospital, and fire fighting service. The founding of Carmel's library took place in early 1904, when Mrs. Helen Jaquith began a library at her cottage by soliciting books as gifts while giving those who contributed the privilege of exchange. Mrs. Willis White, the Reverend Willis White's wife, took charge for Mrs. Jaquith until a large enough collection of books was acquired to engage a librarian for a part of each day, and meanwhile various fund raising events were sponsored to meet expenses. On October 5, 1905, ten residents gathered with Frank Powers as leader to form a group to work towards the beginning of a library. Each of the ten contributed annual dues of one dollar. The name chosen by the group was the Carmel Free Library Association. Among its charter members were Edmund Arne, Mrs. Helen Jaquith, Mrs. Frank Powers, Miss Parmele, and Miss Annie Miller, whose family cottage was converted in later years to a retail shoe shop for I. Miller and Company on Dolores Street. (The franchise for this shoe outlet was owned by Mary and Jack Miller.

Carmel's first library, at Lincoln and Sixth.

These Millers were all unrelated, except Mary and Jack by marriage.) Other members of the library association were George Beardsley, Miss Anne Gray, and her mother, Mrs. F. H. Gray. By the end of 1906 the membership had grown to seventy. By August 1907, the library contained 450 volumes and by 1909, 1,526. In August 1911, Josephine Culbertson, Emma Williams, Ida Johnson, Mrs. Hollis, Mr. and Mrs. Joseph Hand, a Mr. Pudan, and Mrs. Greer Harrison retired as trustees, the constitution was rewritten, and a new name, "Carmel Library Association," was given to the group. By-laws and amendments were adopted in 1912 and again in 1915 and 1924. After Mr. Powers' term as first president ended, Miss Ida Johnson served in 1911 and 1912, and Miss Caroline Hancock in 1912 and 1913. Mrs. Frederick Dutton was president from 1913 to 1928, and in 1928 Miss Etta M. Tilton served for a short time, then she became secretary while Miss Hancock became president. From then on

records appear to have been written by someone else, but there is no name. The Carmel Development Company of Powers and Devendorf, forever generous, agreed to give a building and the use of the lot on which it was built.

That first library, with a personality all its own, stood on a sandy expanse with wild flowers scattered around it. The building itself was quaintly shingled, with narrow windows on each side and a long board walk stretching from its seven short steps across the sand to the street. A special corner in that little shingled building was devoted to children, and there was a weekly story hour which has remained a tradition through my own childhood and later my daughter's. As a child I always felt welcome among the books, doll cases, and paintings of Chief Red Eagle and of Carmel dog "Pal." As I grew, the narrow rows between bookshelves became my place to study alone or with a friend. Today, with the recent remodeling of the library, my memories have been banished to the basement.

The charming little shingled library had many donors who gave not only books but furniture. In October 1915 the *Pine Cone* stated that "the library asks for financial support of the permanent residents of this town and their personal interest as well. Library dues are 25¢ per month or $3 per year." The largest single donation of 800 volumes came from Miss Caroline Hancock (who became Mrs. Eichrodt). George F. Beardsley donated a "loan library" which eventually became the property of the library, and he was also responsible for the collection of *Pine Cone*s of which the library became owner. Beardsley worked with great devotion, giving time, personal labor, and money, before, during and after his term as vice president of the library association.

The lady to whom all Carmelites owe thanks was the very generous Mrs. Ella Reid Harrison. Mrs. Harrison was a new resident in the days when the library was forming, yet she soon became widely respected and was considered an "extremely cultured woman." At the time of her tragic and untimely death in a fire in her home, it was found that she had left her entire valuable collection to the City of Carmel. Though much of it was lost in the fire, some of the collection which was saved still sits on the library shelves today for our enjoyment. Mrs.

Mrs. Harrison's generosity did not end with her collection of books, for her will contained the following statement: "I give, and bequeath to the board of trustees, City of Carmel-by-the-Sea, Monterey County, State of California, in trust for the purpose of building in said city, the Ralph Chandler Harrison Memorial Library, $21,000 in bonds of the

Harrison Memorial Library, 1930. Slevin photograph.

City of San Francisco; lots 7, 8, 9, 10 all of block 72, Carmel; all of my books and much furniture in storage in San Francisco as it is to be placed and kept in the Ralph Chandler Harrison Memorial Library with my husband's photograph." Four years after Mrs. Harrison's death the board of trustees of the library decided that Bernard R. Maybeck would be the architect for the new building and M. J. Murphy the contractor.

By the time the shingled library had neared its capacity, funds had been donated for the purchase of the lot next to the little building, as well as for the building's removal. In 1921 it was moved diagonally across Sixth Street, to the site now occupied by the library parking lot. With remodeling, plastering, and other improvements, it became the Girl Scout House. Painting and furniture were donated by Mr. and Mrs. Richard Johnson.

At the last official Library Association meeting, which was in 1927, the association gave the books to the Harrison Memorial Library, the land and building to the Girl Scouts, and the remaining money in the treasury to the Boy Scouts. One year later, on March 31, 1928, Carmel had a new library complete with concrete walkway. Members of the board of trustees for the new library were Winsor Josselyn, Miss Clara Kellog, Paul Prince, Frank Woolsey, Mrs. Herman Spoehr, and Mrs. John Dennis. Mrs. Karl Rendtorff replaced Miss Kellog in 1930. Many have served on this board over the years and upheld the traditions and quality of our library while preserving its character, through its $40,000 modernization in 1949 and its second remodeling in late 1976 and 1977. Though it has changed, it continues to reflect the quality of our community.

Some of the faithful early librarians were: Miss Hayt, 1908 to 1911; Miss Stella Vincent, 1911 to 1915; Mrs. Sidney Yard, 1915 to 1918; Miss Margaret Clark, 1918 to 1919. From 1919 to 1924 there were several short terms held by Miss Janet Prentiss, Miss Grace Wickham, Miss Gregg, and again Miss Wickham. Miss Margaret Clark served from 1924 to 1925, and Miss Kissam Johnson and Miss Grace Roberta Wasson from 1925 to 1928. After Miss Wasson there were more short terms until Miss Hortense Berry took over for a five-year period. In 1935 Miss Elizabeth Niles became the librarian, and she remained through the 1940s.

Although no provisions were made in the early days for the general maintenance of the library, the city council took on this responsibility.

Another library which early Carmelites enjoyed belonged to writer Dora Hagemeyer, who became Mrs. Herbert Comstock. It was called Woodside Library, and was a charming little place in a small

Woodside Library

THE little green cabin on San Carlos avenue north of Fourth, where one can find books which are being discussed by book-lovers everywhere.

All suggestions for new books given careful consideration.

Library Hours
2:30 to 5:00 and 7:30 to 9:00

Dora Chapple Hagemeyer
Librarian

cottage owned by the poetess on San Carlos Street north of Fourth near her home. It was open daily from 2:30 to 5:30 and 7:30 to 9:00. Then in January 1927, due to Mrs. Comstock's desire to enlarge her popular place, the little library was moved to Monte Verde. It remained there until, with the growth of the Harrison Memorial Library, there was no longer a need to continue it.

The story of Carmel's hospitals began in the home of an early day Carmel doctor by the name of Himmelsbach on the northeast corner of Dolores and Ninth. Dr. Himmelsbach's home had been built by his parents in 1902, with Willis Polk as the architect, and the name the doctor gave his hospital was the Pine Sanitorium. In later years the home belonged to a very pleasant little lady whom I remember from my childhood, Mrs. Clara Newton Nixon. Dr. Himmelsbach's hospital was a success, as there were still those who came for the benefits of our climate, and those who came to serve them as physicians. One such visitor to our area in the early

Pine Sanitorium at Ninth and Dolores streets.

1900s was Grace Deere Velie Harris, the granddaughter of inventor John Deere of tractor fame. Coming first to Pacific Grove and then Carmel on visits, Mrs. Harris, heiress of a vast fortune and the victim of an incurable blood disorder, chose to establish a clinic in Carmel for the purpose of research on diseases like the one from which she suffered. During her frequent visits to Carmel she came to know and respect young Dr. Rudolph A. Kocher. With his encouragement and help, her dream became a reality when the Metabolic Clinic was incorporated in 1928. The president of the new clinic was, of course, Mrs. Harris, and her attorney was the vice president, while Dr. Kocher was both medical director and secretary-treasurer. At incorporation various articles were drawn up to make the institution a gift to be held in perpetuity and operated as a non-profit research facility under the management of Theodore Martin and Dr. Kocher, and the sum of almost a million dollars was set aside as an endowment fund. The land for the clinic was purchased at Valley Way and Highway 1, where the building still stands, with some external alterations, as a convalescent home.

It was unfortunate that Mrs. Harris died before she saw the completion of her clinic, which opened its doors in September 1930 with twenty-five beds. In the processing of Mrs. Harris's will an endowment of only one hundred thousand dollars remained, and at one point the director of the clinic,

who was appointed by a Los Angeles company, advised the closing of the clinic, but by the decision of Mrs. Harris's heirs, it continued as a research clinic with expanded facilities until the depression years almost closed it once more. Fortunately several citizens had come to the conclusion that the Carmel Hospital in the woods, owned by Mrs. Edith Shuffelton, was overly crowded and that there was a need for a larger, fully staffed hospital. Dr. Rudolph Kocher organized a meeting with physicians of the peninsula and asked them to pledge their support of such an undertaking, agreeing that he would resign as medical director and take up private practice. This he did, taking offices first in the Las Tiendas building and later in his own building on Dolores, which now houses the Dolores Pharmacy. It was decided that funds could be raised through public subscription and in October 1934, with remodeled articles of incorporation, the Grace Deere Metabolic Clinic became Monterey Peninsula Community Hospital (Carmel Hospital), a strictly non-profit organization governed by a board of directors composed of "community-minded citizens."

Upon reorganization of the hospital in 1935, Miss Katherine Smitts from Baltimore, Maryland became the new superintendent. During Miss Smitts' tenure as superintendent, a nurses' home was completed and furnished through the donations of Miss Ida House Kent and Mrs. Kilpatrick of Carmel Highlands. The old nurses' quarters then became the new maternity wing of the hospital along with a second new wing with two additional rooms and a large nursery with "individual table care service" for newborns. It was at this site that I was to leave my tonsils as a small child, under the care of Dr. Coughlin, and that later my brother Kevin was to come into the world.

In 1937 Katherine Smitts was responsible for

Carmel's ambulance and part of the crew in 1937. Left to right, B. France, Bill Askew, Sr., A. Lockwood, B. Bracisco, Fred Mylar, and B. Black.

68

making up stretchers and procuring equipment for Carmel's first ambulance. In 1936 Clarence W. Lee and other concerned citizens had founded a fund raising committee. In 1937 Mr. Lee and Colonel T. E. Taylor accompanied the new $2,000 ambulance home to Carmel. A reception was held at the Carmel Fire House, with Miss Clara Hinds as chairman, assisted by Mrs. Herbert, John Morse, Mrs. Alfred Mathews, Miss Patricia Lee, and Mr. John Albee. Members of the first volunteer crew for ambulance duty were Fred Mylar, Al Lockwood, Jim Williams, Robert (Bob) Leidig, Jack Black, Birney W. Adams, Stanley Clay, William (Bill) France, Earl Walls, and Barney Bracisco.

The original Carmel Hospital is another story. Today it resembles for the most part what it originally looked like as the fulfilled dream of Mrs. Edith Ballou Shuffelton, who came to Carmel as a private nurse in 1924. Mrs. Shuffelton came from Palo Alto, and shortly after her arrival appealed to the citizens of Carmel for financing through personal notes her dream to build a small hospital on her Carmel Woods property. With the selection of plans by architect Robert Stanton, and construction by M. J. Murphy, Mrs. Shuffelton's dream was realized. The hospital opened September 2, 1927, and was staffed with nurses who were friends from Mrs. Shuffelton's nursing days at Stanford. The hospital was supplied with equipment and X-ray units as well as a large surgery, given through the legacy of Grace Deere Velie Harris, who had befriended Mrs. Shuffelton and felt her cause should be supported.

Years later, after its equipment had been sold to Monterey Peninsula Community Hospital, Carmel Hospital was converted into a small hotel called "Forest Lodge" and became a popular place with the guests of local residents. Later, during the war, Mrs. Shuffelton offered her property to the armed services as a convalescent home, and though her offer was declined, she still had hopes that it would eventually become a convalescent home. However, before her death in July 1948, she gave the property to Stanford University which in turn leased it to the Community Hospital. It became known as the Convalescent Annex, which it remained until the late 1950s, when it was sold to a private individual.

Today the Grace Deere Velie Clinic, which became the original Community Hospital, is used as the Carmel Convalescent Hospital, while the lovely newer modern Community Hospital of the Monterey Peninsula occupies a wooded site off the Carmel Hill on the Pacific Grove "cut-off" (as it has always been known to old-timers, though it was rededicated in 1976 as Holman Highway). The in-

The Grace Deere Velie Clinic became Community Hospital in 1948. Dale Hale photograph.

firmities of age were not ignored in Carmel's early days, as the aged of the area were given excellent care and allowed to convalesce for a small fee in the Carmel Convalescent and Rest Home just off Ocean Avenue on Camino Real, under the ownership of a graduate nurse by the name of Catherine Morgan.

The scientific society also had its place in Carmel's early history. The often referred to and once well-known "Professors Row" had its beginning in 1905 on Camino Real. It was said that Dr. David Starr Jordan, who came to Carmel for the first time while taking the U.S. Census in 1880, was responsible for the settling in of other professors after he built his home on two lots at Camino Real and Seventh. At that time he was a professor and naturalist at Stanford University. Dr. Jordan's home was "comfortable and stately." It was remembered that Jordan's beloved son Eric, who died tragically in an accident, wrote an entire college textbook on shells at the age of nineteen. Some of Eric's shell specimens were found in neat boxes under the house many years later when the house had given way to time and termites. George Whitcomb had been contracted to tear it down and build an English-style home in its place for Charles Eytings of Greenwich, Connecticut.

Between 1905 and 1910 almost all of the first block and a part of the second on Camino Real were overflowing with "mostly Stanford professors." There were no trees between Camino Real and the beach in those days, and all the homes were afforded excellent views of the beach below. In 1910 Dr. Karl G. Rendtorff and his wife, Emma, built their home on north Camino Real, and they became very active in village life. Their home "was always filled with various people of varying intellect," and their daughter Gertrude was later dean of girls at Monterey High School and was also chosen woman of the year in 1965 by the Quota Club of the Peninsula.

With the exception of Professor O. V. Lange of the University of California, the "row" consisted mainly of Stanford men. Some of those early names were: Professor J. L. Fish, whose home became author Don Blanding's and then the home of Mr. and Mrs. Robert Spencer; Dr. and Mrs. George J. Pierce; Dr. William S. Cooper, plant ecologist; Dr. Beverley Clark, an authority on photosynthesis; Dr. Edward Free, soil physicist; Professor Benjamin M. Duggan, physiological pathologist; Professor Guido Marx, whose home became the "Holiday House"; Professor Raymond Allen; and Professor James Worthington, a fellow of the Royal Astronomical Society of Great Britain and conductor of eclipse expeditions. There were also Professor and Mrs. Gilbert, whose home later became the Old Cabin Inn with its special dinners, lunches, and teas; Dr. William L. Tower; Professor Vernon Kellogg, noted zoologist, and his popular wife, Charlotte; Professor and Mrs. George H. Boke; Professor Francis E. Lloyd, botanist and professor emeritus, and his wife and sons, Francis and David; Dr. Forest Shreve, who was known for his map of North American vegetation; Dr. Alfred E. Burton, former dean of Massachusetts Institute of Technology; Dr. H. W. Fenner; and Dr. Stillman, early experimenter with vitamins.

The Coastal Institute was also responsible for the local accumulation of many of these names. The Institute base was in Washington, where it was founded by Andrew Carnegie on January 28, 1902 as an endowment institute with twenty-two million dollars. The purpose of the corporation was the "organized prosecution of scientific work in all fields." The corporation was presided over by Professor Robert S. Woodward with a governing board of twenty-four trustees, and contained ten departments: Botanical Research, Economic and Sociological, Experimental Evolution, Geophysics, History, Marine Biology, Meridian Astronomy, the Mount Wilson Solar Observatory, Nutrition Laboratory, and Terrestrial Magnetism. The institute also had many research associates and collaborators connected with universities and colleges. Those on the staff who lived in Carmel were Dr. Daniel Trembly MacDougal, director of botanical research, Dr. W. A. Cannon, Dr. Spoehr, and Mr. G. Sykes. The work in Carmel was "prosecuted" depending on the nature of the varied work done

Left to right, Dr. MacDougal, an unknown lady, Mrs. Seideneck, Perry Newberry, and George Seideneck, in front of Walker Shoe Shine and C. J. Arne's.

locally. The Carnegie Laboratory at the eastern end of Twelfth Street closed its doors for the last time on July 1, 1940, to move to Stanford. Dr. Daniel T. MacDougal had been its director for thirty years. Dr. Francis Lloyd was closely associated with Dr. MacDougal at the institute's Desert Laboratory in Tucson, Arizona in 1906, and the two men worked closely together in Carmel. In later years both had laboratories in their respective homes—Lloyd on San Carlos where he studied carnivorous plants, and MacDougal at the Carmel Highlands in further study of the Monterey Pine, with local Harry Aucourt acting as his "daily minister and custodian."

The beginning of Carmel's Fire Department was a humble one. Until 1908, Carmel had no established fire protection, but that year twenty volunteers with twelve one-gallon buckets, sacks and twelve long-handled shovels were organized under the leadership of Robert Leidig at a meeting with the twenty men and "twenty-seven dogs" present. "The meeting had to be halted several times on account of the dogs." The equipment was kept in a leaky half-tent, half-shed affair on the southwest corner of San Carlos and Sixth behind what became Kip's Market and the Village Hardware. The fact that the makeshift tent building was not entirely the best was well remembered by Pon Lung Chung, whose association with the fire department spanned some forty-six years, and who still today wears his honorary badge with pride as he walks the streets of Carmel, Monterey, and Pacific Grove.

In the early days the village lived in fear of grass fires, a great threat for everyone outside of the main business area, since everything beyond the main street was tall, dry grass soon after the end of each rainy season. The only available source of water during these times was either the Carmel Water Works holding tank or the water trough at Ocean and San Carlos, which is now occupied by the recently rebuilt War Memorial designed by Charles Sumner Greene. Despite many grass fires, the first serious fire the village experienced was the burning of Dangerfield's Meat Market in late 1914. The fire destroyed his market while Mr. Dangerfield was across the street visiting with Devendorf, and although it was caused by the explosion of his oil stove, it made even more obvious the need for a more effective way of protecting the village from any further losses.

A campaign was begun in April of 1915 for more adequate fire equipment to protect the village, with William Overstreet at his recently established *Pine Cone* office appealing to the village through his editorials, the first of which stated, "The plan is to purchase what is needed in the way of apparatus, house it where it will do the most good, and then organize a crew of experienced firemen." Also at this time the men of the community, who had thus far assigned themselves to the task of fighting village fires, decided to organize and name themselves as a company (once legal requirements were met) so that they might have this authority and no longer be known as a volunteer fire department. Though the city of Carmel had already formed a fire commission, this commission did not have the legal ability to obtain funds for the purpose of buying needed equipment until March of the following year. Under the circumstances it was agreed that the only way to accomplish what was needed was to solicit the aid of all interested citizens. Overstreet's editorial did its job, and within days a citizens' committee was formed by property owners. Birney Adams (father

of the late Floyd Adams, Carmel Building Inspector), who was a state fire warden and United States forest ranger, came to the meeting to outline the most economical way the villagers could achieve their goals. A committee was appointed to secure the subscription of funds for the needed apparatus, and it was learned that the Carmel Development Company had decided to contribute support in the form of a building to house the purchased equipment at the southwest corner of Ocean and Lincoln.

Between April and August of 1915, the newly formed Citizens Fire Protection Committee obtained $293 in subscriptions from the following village citizens, as their names appear in the record book:

J. F. Devendorf	$25.00	G. W. Creaser	$10.00
T. B. Reardon	5.00	Mikel & Larouette	3.35
A. P. Frazer	5.00	W. Beardsley	5.00
R. G. Leidig	5.00	L. S. Slevin	2.50
Dr. J. E. Beck	5.00	Fred Leidig	5.00
L. Dangerfield	2.50	H. L. Warren	5.00
C. Moore Curtis	5.00	Mrs. Hamlin	5.00
F. S. Schweniger	1.00	Mrs. J. H. Gray	5.00
J. L. Williams	2.50	Misses Hutchinson &	
L. Desmond	1.00	Keeler	3.00
M. De N. Morgan	1.00	Miss Tilton	2.50
Mrs. H. L. Tevis	1.00	Mrs. C. E. Yard	2.50
Mrs. J. E. Beck	1.00	R. B. Cherrington	5.00
R. W. Ball	5.00	R. M. Alden	5.00
Ellen S. White	5.00	A. F. Lange	5.00
William Silva	5.00	Dr. D. T. MacDougal	
Mary E. Mower	2.50	(personal)	5.00
J. H. Hand	5.00	(for laboratory)	10.00
Walter Hansen	5.00	Prof. Purse	5.00
Mrs. A. D. Signor	2.00	Mrs. Cobbe	5.00
Mand Lyons	1.00	Dr. Gardner	2.00
J. R. Rogers	1.00	Mrs. S. A. Young	1.00
Lena Brake	2.00	Mrs. L. A. Pudan	5.00
Miss E. Williams	10.00	Mrs. Dutton	2.00
W. W. Johnson	5.00	Mrs. Trethway	3.00
M. J. Murphy	5.00	Miss Stant	2.00
Prof. Parks	——	Mrs. Bremmer	2.00
Prof. Fish	1.00	William Kibbler	2.50
Mrs. Ury	5.00	Miss De Sabla	5.00
Ethel Burk	5.00	Miss Dawson	15.00
Miss Jackson	3.00	Mrs. Darling	5.00
Miss Brown	2.00	Miss Agnes Miller	5.00
Mrs. Short	5.00	L. A. Holbrook	1.00
Misses Lynch &		Miss Edmonds	5.00
Williams	5.00	Miss Duffy	2.50
Mrs. Rice	5.00		——
		Total	$293.00

With subscription money in hand the decision was made to purchase a forty-gallon Stempel at the cost of $200, and on July 7, 1915 Overstreet proclaimed in the *Pine Cone*, "It's here! It's here! Carmel's Chemical fire engine! Protection at last. It was hauled out from Monterey last Wednesday

Left to right, E. Walls, D. Machado, B. Adams, and R. Leidig, in back of the firehouse at Sixth and San Carlos, 1936.

morning by Fred Leidig and in the afternoon, under escort of the Columbia Park Boys Club, was paraded up and down Ocean Avenue." In the meantime, because of the early arrival of the Stempel, the committee accepted the donation of property by Robert Leidig near his home on Ocean Avenue at the site of the present Cork 'n' Bottle. The Stempel was soon housed, with the donation of lumber by various citizens and the construction of its new home by Birney Adams and J. E. Nichols. On Friday, July 16, 1915, in the Manzanita Club rooms, a meeting was held to organize a permanent fire company which was to call itself Carmel Chemical No. 1. The minutes of that historic occasion and those which followed soon afterwards give us a clear picture of what took place. Following are the official minutes, which were written in the hand of Douglas H. Greeley. They are copied verbatim without spelling corrections, beginning at page one of the official fire book.

Douglas H. Greeley:
Members of the Carmel Chemical Co. No. 1
(organized July 16, 1915 in the Manzanita
Club Rooms at Carmel, Calif.)
Constitution and By-laws on Page 2
Charter members marked with X

1. Eugene Gillett X	10. H. P. Larourette X
2. W. L. Overstreet X	11. B. W. Adams X
3. Delos Curtis X	12. W. H. Butter
4. George W. Creaser Jr. X	13. T. B. Reardon
5. Douglas H. Greeley X	14. R. W. Hicks
6. J. E. Nichols X	15. Ernest Schweniger
7. R. Bowen X	16. Benjamin H. Leidig
8. S. J. Wyatt X	17. Leo Narvaez
9. Robert G. Leidig X	

The following officers elected for the first term.
B. W. Adams - Foreman
J. E. Nichols - Asst. Foreman
Douglas H. Greeley - Secretary & Treasurer
R. G. Leidig
S. J. Wyatt   )Trustees

Constitution and By-laws

Article I

This organization shall be known as Chemical Company No. 1 of Carmel.

It object shall be the protection of property from and during such fires as may occur in Carmel and vicinity.

Article II

The officers of this company shall be a Foreman, Assistant Foreman, Secretary-Treasurer and two Trustees; all of whom shall be elected at the annual meeting and shall serve for the ensuing year.

Article III

Duties of officers. It shall be the duty of the foreman to be at all fires if possible, and to direct the activities of the company and especially the play of the Chemical engine.

The Assistant Foreman shall direct the use of the auxiliary equipment and help carry out the orders of the Foreman.

The Secretary-Treasurer shall act as quartermaster and take charge of the supply of chemicals for recharging the engine.

Section II

Duties of officers at meetings: At the annual or called meetings of the company, the Foreman shall act as President, the Assistant Foreman as Vice-President. The Secretary shall keep a record of all proceedings of the company and handle the necessary correspondence—and he shall also act as Tresurer [sic] and have charge of the funds and collection of fines.

The two Trustees shall make an examination of records and audit the accounts at the annual meeting; they shall make a careful inspection of equipment at least one week before the annual meeting and prepare a report to be presented at the meeting.

Article IV
Membership

Any resident of Carmel, of good character and standing shall be eligable [sic] to membership. Any member may present the name or names of candidates at any meeting and upon the acceptance of a three quarter (¾) vote he shall be selected.

Section II—Duties of Members

It is the duty of all members to respond promptly to all alarms and assemble at once at the engine house.

When on duty at a fire all members shall give prompt and willing obedience to the command of their officers.

Members who are not assigned to special duty in connection with the engine shall take the auxiliary equipment to the fire and place themselves under the direction of the Asst. Foreman.

The first member to arrive at the engine house shall assume command of the company until the arrival of the Foreman or the Asst. Foreman and shall have all the authority of such officer.

The Foreman shall personally supervise the use of the engine at a fire and may detail the necessary number of men to assist them.

Article V
Care of equipment

All members shall be required to return equipment at engine house after a fire and see that it is in its proper place before leaving.

No office member shall take any article of equipment from the engine house for his own use or for any purpose except to use at a fire or shall any article of equipment be loaned to non-members.

The Foreman shall see that the engine is properly cleaned and recharged after use, and that it is all times kept in servicible [sic] condition.

Members to whm [sic] keys to the engine house are issued must keep them available for use at all times.

Article VI
Fines

A member violating any of the sections of Article V shall be liable to a fine of not less than fifty cents ($.50) nor not more than two dollars ($2.00). The fine for losing a key to the engine house shall not exceed fifty cents ($.50).

Membership

Philip Wilson	W. H. Basham
W. L. Overstreet	R. W. Hicks
Leo Narvaez	Eugene Gillett
Earl E. Alds	C. Haskell Warren
Robert G. Leidig	S. J. Wyatt
Fred Leidig	T. B. Reardon
H. P. Laurouette	Leonard Sinclair
George Schweniger	T. F. Lisk
J. E. Nichols	

Minutes of First Meeting
Carmel, California
Friday, July 16, 1915

The meeting was called to order by Mr. W. L. Overstreet, who took the Chair until Mr. B. W. Adams was elected Foreman, after which the business of the meeting was attended to.

The Constitution and By-laws were read by Mr. Overstreet and duly adopted by all of those present.

The following officers were then elected: Foreman, B. W. Adams; Asst. Foreman, J. E. Nichols; Secretary-Treasurer, Douglas H. Greeley; Trustees, R. G. Leidig and S. J. Wyatt.

Signed:
Douglas H. Greeley
(Secretary-Treasurer)

Minutes of Second Meeting
Carmel, California

The meeting was called to order by President B. W. Adams.

The following bills were passed and paid (by check) by the Secretary-Treasurer.

J. E. Nichols (Ribbons etc.)	$1.40
D. H. Greeley (Hall rent)	$5.00
W. L. Overstreet (Printing)	$3.00
Delos Curtis (Refreshments)	$5.10

After the preceedings [sic] were over there followed a general discussion of the possibilities of a fire alarm but nothing was decided upon definitely.

The meeting adjourned at 9:40 o'clock.

Signed:
Douglas H. Greeley
(Secretary-Treasurer)

Third Meeting (called)
October 22, 1915
Rooms of Manzanita Club—Carmel-Calif.

Meeting called to order by Pres. Adams at 8 pm. Minutes of previous meeting and financial report to date read and approved.

Motion by W. L. Overstreet to give a dance on Thanksgiving eve failed to carry.

R. Hicks was assigned to see about pulling an electric light in Engine House also to investigate the possibilities of an electric Klaxon for an alarm.

It was decided that the Company should keep Mr. Goold's Chemical engine supplied with chemicals in return for its use if needed.

The need of raising a maintenance fund was discussed fully; it was suggested that every owner of improved property be asked to pay 25¢ per year on each house owned, this would bring in approximately $75.00 per year. No action taken.

A motion was made and seconded that Mr. Laurouette see Mr. Frazer regarding our rights and authority.

Suggested by B. W. Adams that several members be recommended for appointment as State Fire Wardens.

Meeting adjourned at 10 pm.

Signed:
Eugene Gillett

Fourth Meeting (called)
January 11, 1916
Rooms of Manzanita Club, Carmel, Calif.

Meeting called to order by Pres. Adams at 8 pm. Minutes of previous meeting were read and approved.

B. W. Adams presented his resignation as chairman which on motion was accepted,

Moved and carried. Eugene Gillett be Secretary by unanimous vote.

Nominations for election of assistant foreman ensued. The majority of ballots were cast in favor of Delos Curtis.

Needs of securing a legal footnote were discussed fully. Moved by B. W. Adams and carried that a committee of three be elected to confer with Carmel Development Co. as to securing a legal standing for Chemical No. I of Carmel.

Mr. Fraser, Mr. Nichols and Mr. Wyatt were elected for the said committee.

Mr. Hicks & Mr. Basham were appointed to confer with C. O. Goold as to the arrangements of a fire alarm at his garage.

Sec. was instructed to record all fires.

Meeting adjourned at 9:30.

Signed:
Eugene Gillett
(Sec. & Treasurer)

During the interim between the last minutes of the company on January 11, 1916, until April 12, 1916, there were no further meetings until the legality of the organization of the company could be settled. At the first official meeting of the organization as Carmel Chemical No. 1, April 12, 1916, the minutes were written as follows by W. L. Overstreet, who was acting as secretary:

Meeting of Carmel Chemical No. 1. called to order at rooms of Manzanita Club, J. E. Nichols in the chair.

Twenty-three persons present, including the newly appointed Carmel Fire Commission.

Owing to the fact that in order to comply fully with the law relating to the organization of fire companies, this organization, after transfering [sic] all of its property to the fire commission, went out of existence.

W. L. Overstreet
Acting Secretary
Carmel, Calif. April 12, 1916

An organization, the purpose of which is to protect and save property from Fire was organized at the rooms of the Manzanita Club.

Twenty-three residents signed the roll and took the fireman's pledge as administered by Fire Commissioner W. L. Kibbler.

The property of the former fire organization was turned over to this new organization by the Carmel Fire Commission.

Election of officers resulted as follows:
Treasurer, W. M. Basham
Foreman, J. E. Nichols
1st Asst. Foreman, R. W. Hicks
2nd Asst. Foreman, H. Aucourt
Secretary, W. L. Overstreet
Trustees, R. Ohm, H. P. Larouette, R. G. Leidig
Committees were appointed as follows:
Constitution and By-laws: J. E. Nichols, R. Ohm, W. M. Turner
Certificates and Badges: H. P. Larouette, R. Ohm, J. E. Nichols
Meeting Place—W. L. Overstreet
R. G. Leidig gave written consent that present location and firehouse may be retained.

Motion offered and adopted that meetings be held every two weeks.

Adjournment

W. L. Overstreet
Secretary

In 1915, there was some question and argument as to how best to warn the citizens of Carmel that a fire had started, and during this time William Overstreet once again used the *Pine Cone* to ask the village to purchase an alarm, since the signal used at the time, which was the bell at the Methodist Church, was not adequate and was much too confusing to the populace. However, by the end of November of 1915 the funds raised by subscriptions totalled only $19.00, and had been given by: A. Stewart, $1.00; Mr. Roseboom, $2.50; L. H. Rask, $1.00; I. B. Waterbury, $1.00; Pon Lung Chung, $1.50; Mrs. M. J. Thomas, $2.50; Miss Stella Guichard, $1.00; George W. Collins, $5.00; J. K. Lynch, $1.00; and Mrs. Sarah White, $2.50. This left the volunteers of Chemical No. 1 to "pony" up the remaining amount needed for the alarm, which was eventually installed in Goold's garage.

In 1916 the company changed over from the usual certificate form of membership to card membership and a new committee was formed to find the "modus operandi" for a better water service. In October 1916 a motion was made by R. Leidig that the firehouse should be lighted, and I. B. Waterbury volunteered to do all the work with the department supplying the materials. At the time elections were as follows: R. G. Leidig, Captain; R. W. Hicks, Vice Captain, with I. B. Waterbury as "Assist and A. A.

Decker as Assist. to Captain of Engine Co. and entertainment committee." Charles O. Goold still continued to furnish transportation to and from all fires as well as renting his chemical engine and remaining in charge of the alarm, until further debate took place about obtaining an "air whistle" with the installation being seen to by Mikel and Larouette in August of 1917.

During its first years the fire company met in a variety of places, the most popular being R. J. Wyatt's store, where the rental was two dollars a month. Shaw's restaurant and Larouette's store were also favorites. The Manzanita Club rooms were used, as were the rooms of the City Hall, after incorporation, which were in the Philip Wilson building on the corner of Ocean and San Carlos streets. After being moved from pillar to post and back again, the second temporary Carmel firehouse was on the site later occupied by Earl Glennon's clothing store, which became another clothing store in the early 1970s by the name of Oxbridge. Carmel soon obtained her first ten fire hydrants, five of which were installed on Monte Verde and five on Ocean Avenue, along with 500 feet of new fire hose. On January 10, 1917, a meeting was held to discuss the advisability of turning over the equipment and effects of the department to the municipality, which would terminate the department's connection with state and county authorities and place it totally under the control of the City of Carmel. The action was taken and since then the Carmel Volunteer Fire Department has remained a department of the city's government and is supported by our property taxes.

In 1915, the newly formed Chemical No. 1 had the opportunity to put itself to the test when a fire occurred in a two-story house at the corner of Casanova and Eleventh. Although the men had to pull the new Stempel wagon to the scene, they succeeded in doing so in time to extinguish the fire in the attic and save the house.

In 1920 the fire department acquired a 750-gallon Mack pumper, and when the question arose as to where to house it, Pine Inn owner John Jordan donated the shed which had housed the McDonald Dairy on Sixth between San Carlos and Dolores (where later Murle Ogden had his portrait studio until 1973). Although these firehouse facilities were not exactly ideal, they far outshined the half-tent half-shed affair of 1908. Within a few short years the village had outgrown not only its Stempel but its Mack pumper as well.

The department was growing also, and on May 26, 1920, Chief J. E. Nichols, who had come from Oak Grove by horse and buggy so long before,

In front of the equipment sheds on Leidig property in 1934 are, left to right, the Mack engine, Ford engine, Luverne engine, and the police motorcycle. Josselyn photograph.

called a meeting to order for the enrollment of the department members, who appeared in the record book as follows:

1. Arne, C. J.	15. Leidig, Robert G.
2. Ammerman, E. F.	16. Leidig, Lawrence
3. Adams, B. W.	17. Larouette, H. P.
4. Curtis, Delos	18. Nichols, J. E.
5. Coffey, A. R.	19. Pickham, R. Allen
6. Dummage, W. T.	20. Sinclair, Leonard
7. Donnelly, A. E.	21. Stoney, Burdette
8. Englund, August	22. Stoney, A. C.
9. Fraties, Roy	23. Reardon, T. B.
10. Gtolzbuck, Loya F.	24. Thompson, L. S.
11. Graska, F. W.	25. Waite, Cameron
12. Hicks, R. W.	26. Wermuth, Marshall
13. Hand, H. C.	27. Zinc, E.
14. Hodges, Leonard	

At the same meeting there was election of the following men as officers:

Chief	J. E. Nichols
Asst. Chief	B. W. Adams
Chairman	H. P. Larouette
Secretary	Lile Stoney
Treasurer	W. T. Dummage
Trustees	C. J. Arne, Ralph Hicks and Herbert Hand

Committee on Finance
A. E. Donnelly   E. Zinc
Lawrence Leidig

Members of Chemical Company
Robert G. Leidig, Captain
Leonard Sinclair, Lieutenant
Lawrence Leidig, C. J. Arne and Marshall Wermuth, Auxiliary

Members of Hose Company
Herbert Hand, Captain
Lloyd Glotzback, Lieutenant

Auxiliary

L. D. Thompson	Cameron Waite
A. R. Coffey	Allen R. Pickham
William Graska	E. F. Ammerman
Burdette Stoney	Edmund Arne
Roy Fraties	Lile Stoney

Members of Hook and Ladder Company

Ralph Hicks, Captain	W. T. Dummage
A. E. Donnelly	Delos Curtis
Leonard Hodges	T. B. Reardon

New Members

Joseph McEldowney	W. T. Overstreet
Joseph F. Cline	Leo Narvaez
Bert Comstock	E. H. Lewis
Fred Machado	

Also at this time a motion was made and carried that the department hold a meeting the first and third Thursdays of each month.

The department formed its first official drill teams on May 18, 1921, with Mayor Walter Kibbler and Trustee Coleman acting as judges. The losing team paid for ice cream for the winners.

No. 1 Team	No. 2 Team
John J. Gillis	R. F. Ohm
Lester Branch	Robert G. Leidig
James Chappell	B. W. Adams
Winsor Josselyn	Harry Johnson
Clyde Johns	Leo Chappell
Marshall Wermuth	Earl Ammerman
Leo Narvaez	Roy Fraties
Armstrong	Cameron Waite
Holhn	Frank Lee

The fire drills, as well as being useful, were popular among the members. They also enjoyed many social events, which ranged from picnics at Point Lobos and the Carmel Highlands to parades and

75

dances, and they had refreshments, reported as delicious, at the end of regular meetings. Also very popular were pinochle games and a baseball team. Ten baseball uniforms, used but in excellent condition, were purchased from the Salinas Fire Department for the sum of $150, towards which Robert G. Leidig, secretary and captain, personally advanced $74. The baseball team was quite impressive, it was said, and to make certain that there were enough team members a ruling was put into effect that members could be secured from outside the department.

On October 5, 1921 a new electric siren arrived, which the city trustees promised to install, along with twenty-five official fire badges from the La France Company at the cost of $1.25 per badge. By November 2, 1921, the new siren had been installed and the time of 7:30 p.m. on meeting nights was decided upon as the time to blow it. This was published in the *Pine Cone* as an official notice to the village. At this time there was growing discussion of a need for more fire apparatus as well as an official meeting hall, and the possibility of the Bathhouse was suggested. It was pointed out that there had been several chimney fires and also that there was a lack of properly filled extinguishers at the school. Though the needs of the village were obvious, the city did not wish to go into debt over the purchase of further equipment. The bank could not lend the necessary money outright for new fire apparatus, and a bond issue to meet the payment failed to pass. It did not look as if it would be possible to buy the needed equipment unless back-

ers would be willing to take loan notes through the bank. Three local men took it upon themselves to enlist the support of backers. One of them was one time city attorney Argyll Campbell, a champion of many Carmel causes, and father of now retired Superior Court Judge Gordon Campbell. The others were Fenton Foster and Robert G. Leidig. Within a short time the following community conscious citizens had offered their support for the purchase of new fire apparatus: Mrs. Isabelle Leidig, E. G. Kuster, F. P. Foster, C. H. Yates, Mrs. P. K. Gordon, Ray C. De Yoe, and the Rev. J. H. McKee, who by their support saved the city "upwards of a thousand dollars."

On October 18, 1922, a Mr. Brown, representing the American La France Company, and a salesman for the White Truck Company attended the department meeting, each attempting to sell his respective equipment. Robert Leidig presented the case for the Luverne Company. A vote was cast of eleven for the No. 15 White and five for the Model 6 Luverne, and a committee of three, Rudy Ohm, Robert Leidig, and Miller, was elected to take this decision before the board of trustees. The board favored a Luverne, and decided to take over the equipment of the department and to pay off the loan for the new engine over a stipulated period of time. In 1923, a Luverne engine was driven over the hill from Monterey and ceremoniously driven up and down Ocean Avenue while the village turned out to admire and inspect its marvelous new machine. At the time of the arrival of the new engine, the temporary fire house was still at Wilson's Garage, where Glennon's

Shown with the Luverne engine are Fred Machado, Fred Ammerman, and Bill Askew, Sr., in front of the cab; John Weigold and Delos Curtis in back; and left to right, in front, Albert Coffey, Sid Smith, Harry Turner, Robert Leidig, J. Machado, Lynn Hodges, Ben Wetzel, Machado, Vince Torras, Manuel Pereira, Rudy Ohm, and policeman Charles Guth on motorcycle. Josselyn photograph.

76

In 1930 the firehouse was located on the lot between the present location of Pernille Restaurant and the Zautman gallery at Sixth and San Carlos. Slevin photograph.

was later to be, and the advertisement in the *Pine Cone* still read: "IN CASE OF FIRE, From 6am to 8pm telephone Curtis 602 W 3; from 8pm to 6am telephone City Marshal Englund 374 W." Generally the job of turning in alarms fell to Curtis, who would run around the corner and sound the siren. Mrs. James McGrury, the former Mai Guichard, said, "Sister and I would simply howl with laughter at Mr. Curtis who looked like he was going to fly around the corner with his apron flapping about his knees." Later another shed was built for fire equipment, again on Leidig property, this time at Sixth and San Carlos back of Kip's.

Shortly after the arrival of the new Luverne engine there was a fire at the Carmel Bakery next door to the Wells Fargo Express Company office, which put the men and the new engine to the test. Next was a fire in Henry Hitchcock's Stanley Steamer, and in December 1924 one at the La Playa Hotel. Two fires which were well remembered were the one at Jimmy Hopper's home and the one in which Mrs. Harrison died. Hopper's home was on the southwest corner of Camino Real and Ninth. There was great criticism of the department and in particular Chief Nichols because the fire hose, though stretched across two lots, was not long enough to fight the fire at Mrs. Harrison's adequately. In the end Nichols turned in his resignation, and Robert Leidig took his place, becoming chief of the department officially in January 1925.

On October 31, 1925, a secondhand water wagon was added to the equipment for $250. Over the next few years there were many accounts of interest in the department's record books, far too many to list, but some stand out, such as the special banquet for Pon Chung, champion pinochle player of the department, before he left for a trip to his native China. At

this time Pon was elected an honorary member for all his hours of service. It was often said that Pon never missed a fire, and on one occasion when all else had been removed from a burning building, Pon took wrench in hand and began to remove a bathtub, protesting that it too was salvagable. It was also Pon who made a memorable "leap for life" from the second story of the La Playa at the time of its fire, and Pon's own special retelling of that episode is marvelous. I feel that Pon Chung's story is not only a part of the Fire Department story, but of Carmel's. It is a story filled with a mixture of humor and poignancy.

Pon Lung Chung in 1931, at the age of thirty-seven. At that time he was said to be the only fireman of Chinese ancestry in the United States.

Pon Lung Chung came to Carmel aboard the S. S. *Siberia* in 1908 at the age of thirteen, under the impression that he was a United States citizen. Pon began his adventures in the United States as a cook and then a cannery worker, from San Francisco to the San Joaquin Valley. Eventually his travels brought him to Carmel where his cousin Pon Lung Sing was already in residence. Pon took on all kinds of odd jobs, among them service to the Fire Department. As the years passed, Pon worked quietly and diligently, and he was soon ready for his first return trip to China, which he took in 1916. There he married for the first time. He remained in China until early 1920. Returning to this country, Pon opened a restaurant in San Francisco, but after only seven months he came back to Carmel, where he remained until 1926, when he went back to China to visit his wife, only to learn that she had died. However, before the visit was over, he married again. His new wife was Goke Chan.

On his return to Carmel, Pon lived for many years in the little cottage now used for the office of Picadilly Nursery. In 1947 he moved from there to the Carmel Legion Hall on Dolores, where he was caretaker. Then, finally leaving Carmel, he moved to his place on Lighthouse in New Monterey. Not long after Pon's return to Carmel after his marriage to Goke Chan, he learned that he had become the father of a son. Desiring his family to be with him, he set himself upon the path of a task that was to take forty-five years. Pon, who had worked, voted, and been a model citizen, was suddenly confronted with the fact that the Department of Immigration and Naturalization Service could find no record or proof of his citizenship, nor proof that his father had been born in San Francisco. Eventually, with the help of Paul Mercurio and Robert Leidig, with whom he had been closely associated in 1920, Pon was able to prove that he had resided in Carmel since at least 1920. He continued to work among the residents of Carmel, a model citizen and American at heart, all the time working to bring his family to be with him.

In 1968 it seemed that Pon's dream would not come true, for unable to prove his citizenship, despite the testimony of friends and thirty years of voting, Pon had to start all over as an alien. With his usual good humor, humility and patience, he began again, and finally, at the age of seventy-four, after sixty-one years in the United States, he was declared a United States citizen by Superior Court Judge Ralph Drummond. This was in December 1969, and on Saturday, January 30, 1971, Pon was reunited with Goke Chan and the son he had never seen, Pon Sheung Kwen. For Pon the joy and good fortune were almost more than he could endure. The three were seen together constantly for almost a year, until quite suddenly Pon Sheung Kwen died of a heart attack.

Today Pon and Goke live together in their little place in New Monterey, and talk of returning to China for the last time someday. You will often see them together, or you may see Pon alone as in the past, always ready with an embrace or smile and handshake for those who know him. He has etched himself vividly on the hearts and in the memories of many and has the distinction of having been for

Pon Lung Chung in 1963.

many years the only Chinese in an American volunteer fire department. Pon was immortalized in *Carmel Nights*, which was staged as a musical comedy at the Forest Theater in early times. Also a special edition of the *Carmel Cymbal*, under the direction of then owner Willard K. Bassett, was devoted to him.

Pon has somehow always been at the heart of village activities, from the Abalone League softball games, where he would serve coffee and hot dogs, to the "Halloween Capers" at Sunset playfield, and even as the favorite write-in at elections. He has had a special place in our family memories over the years because of almost daily visits to my parents' store, where he would light up his pipe and the faces of many local customers while he imparted the latest happenings in his life and around the Peninsula. Today Pon's prized mustache is turning white, but the twinkle in his eyes and his smile are always present, and he proudly continues to wear his honorary fire badge and small American flag. Of all that has been written about Pon, the following, as it appeared in the *Carmel Cymbal*, is by far the best: "All these years Pon Chung has been living, working, dawdling, manifesting simple generosity of spirit among us, with a malice toward none of us, an unassuming charity toward all of us, and a consistent unaltering integrity that should shame so many of us."

To return to the story of the fire department, an entry in the books of 1927 tells us that the Carmel Woods Tennis Court was opened and "offered for the use of the department," and public

Kneeling, left to right, Birney Adams, John Catlin, unknown, R. Leidig, Dave Machado, J. Weigold, Paul Mercurio, Machado, W. Askew, and P. Funchess. Standing, left to right, Charles Guth (policeman), Torras, unknown, B. France, F. Mylar, Pop Warner, B. Bracisco, Lockwood, unknown, Fred Machado, B. Black, two unknown, and Chief of Police Robert Norton. Josselyn photograph.

works contributed some one hundred feet of new hose to the fire department. In 1929, the department devised a system in which it gave out "honorary dollars" for merit points. Also in 1929 there were fires at the Blue Bird Tea Rooms, the Daggett home at First and Carpenter, and the Romylane Candy Store on Dolores Street. Appreciation of the fire department continued, and in 1929 and 1930, the following donations were made: Tilly Pollack, $10; Dr. Davidson, $15; Mrs. Smartt, $10; and Miss Fanny Reeves, $5. Slevin's donated stationery, and there were letters of thanks, such as one from John Scott who in 1931 was manager of the Mission Ranch (John was the owner of Scott's Silver and Leather for many years, until his death in 1978), after the department had helped during an after-flood salvage job. The Espandola Grocery donated food supplies for the department's socials in appreciation of its efforts.

The members of the fire department were a closely knit group in those early days, with an attitude of one for all and all for one, and their good spirits and good natured antics were often welcomed at affairs. They received an open invitation from J. Bells when he held the grand opening of his milk depot on December 6, 1929 and were often invited to such

events. In January 1930 the department purchased its first "official" stationery, which for many years remained the same. In 1934 the local Boy Scouts were invited to drill with the department under the supervision of Birney Adams, and on April 18, 1934, the department celebrated its twentieth year at a social with five surviving original members: Delos Curtis, Cort Arne, Harry Turner, Henry Larouette, and Rudy Ohm. In May 1934, Robert Norton was elected new fire commissioner, and on June 20, 1935, the department lost a long time friend when James Machado died. Most of the members attended the funeral and offered financial help to the family, as was typical of the men in the department.

On July 8, 1935, a special meeting was called and a committee of Willard Whitney, John Catlin, Bernard Rowntree, William Palache, and John Jordan selected to confer with the mayor, James Thorburn, on "pertinent facts" concerning the building of a proposed new fire house. The February 7, 1936 *Pine Cone* carried a bold message which read, "Vote 'YES' For Firehouse Bonds Monday," with accompanying paragraphs devoted to the opinions of various locals, all of whom were in favor: Perry Newberry, Jack Abernathy, James H. Thorburn, Byington Ford, R. E. Brownell, Elizabeth McClung

White, E. H. Ewig, Bernard Rowntree, "Doc" Staniford, Kenneth C. Goold, Mr. and Mrs. James McGrury, Willard Whitney, Ross C. Miller, Herbert McGuckin, Mr. and Mrs. Weaver Kitchen, Frank Townsend, Iris D. Taylor, Harold Neilsen, John Jordan, Earl Graft, Kent Clark, C. L. Berkey, John Catlin, George Walters, Donald Hale, Barnet J. Segal, Walter L. Gaddum, and Joseph A. Burge.

The bond passed, 664 to 75. The $12,000 bond and a W.P.A. pledge of $9,046 brought the total to $21,046, enough to begin construction in September on the fire house for which the village had waited twenty-one years. Gone were the days when Charlie Goold furnished the team and wagon and skids to move another shed to another location. It was quite a time for celebration. Although each attempt by the city council to combine a fire department with a city hall or jail had failed, by itself the fire house was a winner. Work on the fire house, which was designed by architect Milt Latham, progressed well for about two months until on November 14 a portion of the floor of the second story section collapsed, taking with it part of the west wall and four feet of the upper story wall as well. There was an extensive investigation into the matter, and wet concrete was thought to have been the probable culprit, although there were other possible causes.

The Carmel Fire Station soon after its opening in 1937. Robert Leidig is on the left front seat of the Luverne engine; William Askew is on the left front seat of the Ford engine; and Vince Torras is on the left front seat of the Mack engine. Josselyn photograph.

Rebuilding of about twenty per cent of the building was necessary. The whole project was finally completed in June 1937. The department held its first meeting in the club room of the new fire house on June 3, 1937, and the following people were thanked for their generous contributions: the *Christian Science Monitor*, the *Monterey Herald*, Jack

They'll Do It Every Time   By Jimmy Hatlo

Eaton, Billy France, Miss Fanny Reeves, Fred Mylar, Robert Leidig, the Josselyns (for their donation of a rocker), Joseph Briggs for a large mirror, Elizabeth White, Mr. Trask, Paul Flanders, Stella's Dry Goods, Fred Wermuth for magazines, Mrs. Pettiford for an American flag, and Mrs. Anna L. Winslow for two chairs and a lamp. Special thanks were given to Jack Black, who made several tables, and to Winsor Josselyn for the donation of an ax from the historic Hotel Del Monte fire. The new fire house boasted a Carmel chalk rock exterior, and it had a large upstairs hall and three bedrooms, as well as the Chief's office. There was a stairway with wrought iron railing at its west end and two fire poles. The lighting fixtures were all hammered copper. Also made of copper was a plaque designed by Spohn which depicted action scenes in the life of a fireman. This was completed in 1938 and hung over the mantelpiece in the new assembly hall.

The fire department of Carmel has, through the years, made every effort to instill an awareness of fire prevention in its young citizens by making the fire department a place to visit during the annual Fire Prevention Week in October. Children as well as adults are invited on an inspection tour of the fire house, rides are given on the engine, and there are safety demonstrations. A radio system was installed in 1958, allowing direct communication between the firemen and the Carmel Police Department, and also including "buzzer boxes" for communication within the department. There have been other additions in recent years—a new ambulance and, in 1963, the long waited-for, 300 horsepower, $27,000 La France engine, which was made to order. The newest engine arrived in 1975, a Crown Coach with snorkel which cost $88,000.

In 1965 the Carmel Fire Department celebrated

At the Carmel-by-the-Sea Fire Station in 1980. Leaning out of the engine door to the left is Captain Bill Hill. Kneeling, left to right, are Captain Vince Rogers, Captain Tim Connell, Assistant Chief Vern Allred, Chief Bob Updike, Batallion Chief James Kelsey, and Captain Paul Artellan. Carrying on the Leidig tradition is Ron Leidig, who is standing behind Capt. Kelsey.
Jim Cox photograph.

its fiftieth anniversary and the culmination of many fine years of service to the community under the leadership of the following Carmel Fire Chiefs:

Birney Adams, July 1915 to January 1916; Jess Nichols, January 1916 to December 1925; Robert Leidig, December 1925 to December 1941; Vincent Torras, December 1941 to December 1956; Robert E. Smith, December 1956 to December 1965; James R. Baker, December 1965 to December 1966; Rollie Belvail (acting chief), January 1966 to December 1970; and Robert Updike, December 1970 to the present.

In early October of 1916 it was reported that "everyone jammed all together like cattle" at Cort Arne's barber shop to sign an incorporation petition. Fifty-four residents signed, including the following: Laura Maxwell (one of Cort Arne's best customers), Cortland J. Arne himself, Mary Machado Goold (Carmel's oldest resident at the time), Fred Leidig, Robert Leidig, Albert Comstock, H. P. Larouette, J. C. Mikel, Isabelle Leidig, Delos Curtis, Harris D. Comings, David Von Needa, Charles Hamilton, J. F. Devendorf, Mary Beck, Dr. J. E. Beck, Mrs. Frances Leidig, Rose De Yoe, Mary De Neale Morgan, Roy Newberry, Jennie Coleman, Mrs. Charles Clark, Mrs. W. L. Overstreet, Helen Schweniger, L. S. Slevin, E. A. McLean, A. A. Decker, Janet Prentiss, Margaret N. Clark, John A. Machado, Martha A. Kibbler, Lorena Underwood,

Josephine Foster, Mary R. Allen, John P. Staples, Stephen C. Thomas, Ernest Schweniger, and E. M. Tilton.

There had been much controversy previous to the move for incorporaton, with two schools of thought on the subject—some wanted to preserve the paradise of Carmel, and some wanted to be annexed into the commercial area. However, the first step toward incorporation had been taken, and the County Board of Supervisors approved the move for incorporation in early October 1916. On October 26, 1916, the residents of Carmel cast their votes at S. J. Wyatt's store, and it was said the register was missing in the crowd several times. Four days later, when the votes were all tallied, the results were 113 in favor of incorporation and 86 against, and on October 31, when Carmel-by-the-Sea was entered in the California State Archives, it officially became an incorporated city.

At the time of this election the village also voted for its trustees, city clerk and treasurer. The tallies were as follows: for treasurer, L. S. Slevin, 117, J. E. Beck, 62; for city clerk, J. E. Nichols, 74, J. W. Hand, 57, H. P. Larouette, 54. Out of eleven running for the trustees' posts, the following five were elected: A. P. Fraser, Peter Taylor, G. F. Beardsley, Mrs. E. K. De Sabla, and D. W. Johnson. Johnson beat M. J. Murphy by two votes. Perry Newberry also ran, but was not elected until another election several years later. There was no treasury for the newly elected treasurer to take care of, so each trustee chipped in a dollar, establishing Carmel's first municipal funds. The *Pine Cone* continued to be the voice of the village for many years, while it published all official business of the city as well as a list of suggestions and improvements.

With incorporation came the need for ordinances and regulations, and with them the need for law enforcement. The first ordinance prohibited "any horse, mare, colt, ass, jack, mule, ox, bull, steer, cow, calf, goat or hog from running loose in the town or being pastured in any street, alley, park or other public place." The next ordinance prohibited "the cutting down, removal, mutilation and injury of trees, shrubs and bushes on any city-owned land." Closely following was another ordinance and law forbidding the discharge of firearms, fire crackers, Roman candles, skyrockets and the like, as well as prohibiting bonfires or campfires within the city limits, unless, in the case of bonfires or campfires, written consent had previously been obtained from the marshal. Ordinance number four set the monthly salaries of city officials as follows: city clerk, $25; city treasurer, $5; city marshal, $90; city recorder, $5; and city attorney, $20. Trustees served without pay, and the newly elected trustees were named to posts by the president, Alfred P. Fraser, as follows: Peter Taylor, Judge; George F. Beardsley, public health and safety; Mrs. Eva K. De Sabla, streets, sidewalks and parks; D. W. Johnson, lights and water.

On December 11, 1916, County Assessor George S. Goold gave the assessed value of Carmel-by-the-Sea as $350,000, and on January 9, 1917, Philip Wilson's building on the northwest corner of Ocean and Dolores became the official City Hall. Also at this time the official seal for Carmel was chosen with the old mission design. On January 16, 1917, Gus Englund was given the oath of city marshal, Charles O. Goold (who had leased the northwest ground floor) took bids for all hauling and repairs for the newly incorporated city, and Henry Warren was appointed as city recorder. On January 23, 1917, Trustee De Sabla asked the board for permission to contract an approach to the county road known as Berwicks Corner, and her request was granted. The only road to Monterey at this time was San Carlos to Fourth and up to the present truck route. On April 13, 1917, a two-party telephone line was ordered, one for the residence of the city marshal and one for the office of the clerk in City Hall, with a montly rental of ten dollars. (The Carmel Telephone Exchange was established in 1913 in a section of Bloods Grocery on the corner of Ocean and Lincoln, the four hundred and seventy-sixth in the

Waldo Hicks' birthday party, 1913. In back are Helen and Waldo Hicks. In the middle row, left to right, are Marion Plein, Julia McEldowney, Violet Payne, Vera Basham, Eugene Roehling, George Leidig, Fay Murphy, and Franklin Murphy. Bottom row, left to right, Dale, Ted, Glen, and Martin Leidig, and the Murphy twins, Kathy and Roselyn.

state. There were thirty-five customers. By 1928 there were 880 subscribers.)

Also in 1917, H. P. Larouette was appointed head of the Carmel Sanitary Board, and a Mr. Alexander was placed as head of an encampment known as the School of Forestry located off Junipero. On May 1, 1917, Trustee Johnson announced that the flag had arrived for the city hall and that M. J. Murphy had been hired to erect the flag pole and install the flag. Also at this same time dog tags were ordered, six new chairs arrived from Louis Rudolph's furniture store at the cost of eighteen dollars, and Louis Slevin's mother took on the task of supervising the installation of "rubbish barrels" on Ocean Avenue. On November 6, 1917 the following bills were submitted and paid: W. L. Overstreet, publication and printing, $23.65; August Englund, police, $93.00; W. P. Evans, extra police officer, $5.00; Carmel News Company, stationery, $1.45; L. S. Slevin, salary for stamps, $5.50; Ed Rommandia, hauling garbage, $.50, H. G. Jorgensen, salary, $20.00; J. E. Nichols, salary for writing receipts, $73.38; Mrs. Philip Wilson, rent on City Hall, $20.00; W. A. Daggett, pipe nozzle, $17.50.

Mr. Re Dante was also paid on occasion for hauling garbage. Roy Babcock, who was a contractor, also hired himself out for auto service driving, and C. O. Goold was paid for his livery, freight and hauling, while A. E. Donnelly and Tony Garcia worked with teams. T. B. Reardon was responsible to the city for installing a faucet in November of

1917 at the watering trough at Ocean and San Carlos. During this time, C. B. Beck was the city tree pruner, J. W. Hand served as notary, and Fred Leidig furnished the soda for the chemical engine belonging to the fire department.

The first year after incorporation was a busy time with all concerned taking their positions seriously and working in earnest toward a successful government. The things which unified everyone were also those which caused division as to what was best for Carmel, and that situation has not changed since.

The history of zoning in Carmel is something of a legend in itself. It began with early grumblings in 1915, before incorporation, and continued with force in 1916 as a means for the protection of the village from what was termed "success and banality." There were battles between two opposing village factions, the art group and the business-minded, with a bitter gap between. The business faction had finally gained a hold by 1922. Many suggestions have been made during the battles that have continued over the years, beginning with the idea (which has been falsely attributed to Perry Newberry but was actually made by Argyll Campbell, city attorney) that walls should be erected around the village. Newberry then said that "toll gates should then be erected" to coincide with the walls. A recent suggestion is that Ocean Avenue should be closed and shuttle buses used to convey both tourists and locals around the village.

There has often been resentment towards the city council for the loss of a tree or meandering path. At

one point, in 1928, so bitter was the reaction to a proposed traffic pattern for Carmelites, which had been outlined by Charles Chaney, that the offending city council was voted out and a new "business oriented" council with Mayor Bonham at its head was voted in. Soon the old zoning ordinances were revoked and in June 1929 a new zoning act called number 96 cut four zones to two, one for residential and one for business. Another act concerning the "one kitchen" per single family dwelling was effected, with the city having the right to limit the number of "paying guests" in a guest house or rental home as well as building height and land coverage. (It all has a familiar ring, doesn't it?) By 1939 there had been a breakdown of zoning, people having rented rooms to augment their incomes during the depression. This created a concern for the city council which had established ordinance number 96 in the beginning, and forced amendments of the ordinances with clauses for the city. The procedure took place in the Superior Court in Salinas.

It was said that the merchants had been agreeable to removing the center parking so long as they could have safe diagonal parking at the curbs as agreed upon by Mayor Herbert Heron and Commissioner Fred Bechdolt. It was Bechdolt at that time who pointed out that all diagonal parking would be eliminated in time. The cost of carrying out the change was estimated (in the request for a restraining order) at $1,500. There was a compromise one week later when the width of the strip was set at twelve feet (less than the city council had authorized), losing the court battle for the local businessmen. After another debate in 1940, Junipero, after long being a wide dusty lane which was only partly cut through and partly oiled, was finally opened all the way through to Camino del Monte. I remember how we children used to collect bottle caps from the dairy and stamp them into the newly oiled surface until our fun was spoiled at the end of the 1940s when Junipero was finally curbed and paved.

In Carmel's zoning and parking history, the city attorney responsible for drafting many of the zoning laws and ordinances which affect us today was a very popular man, Argyll Campbell. This brilliant and gifted man was born on December 2, 1892 in San Jose, California, the son of James Havelock and Mary Faulkner Campbell. Argyll Campbell's father was a leading jurist of San Jose at the time of Argyll's birth, and dean of the Institute of Law of Santa Clara University as well. Arriving in 1914 via motor stage with his wife, the former Mabel Phelps, and later made this comment about his arrival: "As

83

California is the garden of America, so to me is Carmel its Eden." An avid reader and seeker of knowledge, Campbell was also distinguished as attorney for three cities during the course of our local history, and when he died in 1943, the man left behind not only his personal touch on the shape of the peninsula, but two sons, Gordon and John Douglass, who grew to be respected in their own chosen professions—John as a member of the Monterey High School faculty, and Gordon as Marshal for the U. S. Court in China, nominated by Roosevelt in 1938, and as a Monterey County Superior Court Judge after many years as a highly respected attorney. In a statement in regard to Carmel's zoning and ordinances, Argyll Campbell was remembered for the following: "The City of Carmel-by-the-Sea is hereby determined to be primarily, essentially and predominantly a residential city wherein business and commerce have in the past, are now, and are proposed in the future to be subordinated to its residential character."

Now, many years later, change is again in the air with the "second kitchen clause." A post war council was responsible for the creation of a planning commission whose need was keenly felt with the 1946 boom in building activity and the need for some type of effective "stop-gap measure." The committee members for Carmel's new planning commission were P. A. McCreery and Herbert Heron, both former mayors, Mrs. Florence Josselyn, Ernest Bixler, Hugh Comstock, Miss Clara Kellogg, and Donald Craig, along with popular building inspector Floyd Adams, City Clerk Peter Mawdsley and City Attorney William K. Hudson. Perhaps this group did more than any other to set the "first line of defense" against the forces wishing to undermine what had made Carmel unique. The commission and the city council were a compatible working team for approximately six years. In 1952 certain new council members created heated discussions over what was the best way to "govern" Carmel. However, high principles and good judgment won in the end, with the important decision to devise an alternate route for the proposed "high-speed highway" at the Ocean and Carpenter junction, with Chaney's previously vetoed plan of 1928 being the one chosen. To study further some way to combat the impact of parking and travel overflow, due to the tourist element and the residential-commercial elements, another committee of fifty citizens was appointed in 1956 by Mayor Horace Lyons. Once again heated discussion took place, with the council bending to public pressure. New zoning and some rather "expedient" changes were effected in 1959

Ocean Avenue with center parking.

with the "General Plan for the Conservation and Enhancement of Carmel," drafted by people like the late Floyd Adams, who not only grew with the town but knew its aches and pains in depth.

There have been other topics of debate, too many to list. However, as the topic of parking and the lack of it continues, it is interesting to note that the village did once have center street parking in what is known today as the garden strip that begins in front of Devendorf Park and continues, with spots to rest or pass through, down Ocean toward the sea. This pleasant "garden strip" caused debate at its beginning and on several occasions since.

The story of Carmel's Police Department began with the incorporation of the village of Carmel, as Carmel-by-the-Sea, in the autumn of 1916. The enforcement of laws and ordinances after incorporation fell on the shoulders of Carmel's one-man police department, and it was agreed that August Englund performed his task admirably. He was both efficient and alert, which gained him the esteem and confidence of the village. Born in Sweden on November 16, 1868, Gus grew up to become a member of the Swedish army as a sergeant in the King's Dragoons. In 1892 he came to the United States and soon enlisted in the Eighth U.S. Cavalry. Serving from 1896 to 1899 in the Spanish-American War, Englund campaigned in the Philippine Islands under General Lawton until his discharge. Upon his return to the United States he became a policeman for Yosemite National park and then for the Quartermaster Department in Vancouver, B.C. In 1900, he served again as quartermaster, this time in China. After a short period in Sequoia National Park, Englund left in 1902 to prospect for gold in Dawson, Alaska. A year later he arrived in Monterey, where he was instrumental in helping to establish the Post at the Presidio of Monterey. He was a member of the police force of Monterey in 1905 and 1906. After the San Francisco earthquake and fire, he joined the well-known Pinkerton Detective Agency to help maintain law and order in that city. From 1911 until 1913 Englund served as Chief of Police in Monterey, then returned to San Francisco where he worked for a year and a half as a special police officer during the Panama-Pacific Exposition. Termed a "soldier of fortune," "handsome and proud" as he sat upon his black steed, Billy (one of his three horses), Englund was said to "sport a wonderful humor." His wife, the once-widowed Ella Albright, was very well liked.

Despite the size of the village of Carmel in 1916, Gus Englund was a busy man according to entries in his personal arrest book, written in his own hand. Two of the first arrests he made were for the sale of chickens without license and for an assault and battery charge. His days were never dull, and they began early. His routine consisted of administering directions and giving advice on gardening techniques and hunting methods, as well as tax collection, licensing and revoking of licenses, returning lost pets, children and husbands, assisting the milk delivery, and lighting oil stoves. Once he was invited to test a husband's sanity.

Carmel's early citizens were not all an orderly group, and there were arrests made of upstanding members of the village such as George Graft, Clark Bruce, George Aucourt, and C. R. Gilkey for disorderly "disturbance of the peace," when after a good get-together, their not so quiet voices were heard to boom through the pines, breaking the peacefulness of the village night with loud song. Then, too, there were the almost monthly arrests of the Philliponda-Soto boys. Later there were arrests for reckless driving which stemmed from "my machine can beat yours any day," and for the violation of the newly formed ordinance to regulate traffic in 1928. Pacific Grove was the model for this ordinance, which called for traffic signs at all boulevards, and pedestrian markers. Double parking was made a misdemeanor, and Jacinto Re, H. P. Larouette, Fred Machado, Ernest E. Arnold, and Walter Pilot were all in violation. H. E. Bixler was cited for driving without a license.

On March 4, 1932, there was a burglary at Imelman's sport shop of $500 worth of goods between 1:00 and 2:00 A.M. Another time there was a blown safe at the meat market. There was also an entry in Englund's book of Carmel's first case of petty larceny when five Monterey fellows came over the hill and removed several chickens from Duvall's Carmel Poultry Market in May of 1932. There were two unfortunate murders to be investigated, and a couple of drownings, including controversy over the disappearance of evangelist Amy Semple McPherson. During rescue attempts following a drowning in 1928, Englund suffered a severe cut on his leg on

Marshal August Englund and Charles Van Riper in conference at Carmel Point.

the rocks at Cooks' Cove. A diabetic, he never recovered fully from that injury.

On August 28, 1932, Paul Flanders was arrested for burning grass on his property and turning in a false alarm. It seems Paul was trying to put the new fire equipment to the test by seeing if it could reach his property in time in an emergency, and it cost him a twenty-five dollar fine to find out that it could. There were also fines for driving over the fire hose during the terrible fire at La Playa Hotel.

Englund recorded two marriages in his book, one in 1922 between Russell Sigard and Vivian Parrett from Los Angeles, and that of Dr. Rudolph Kocher and Alice E. Knight of Carmel in September 1928.

With the paving of Ocean Avenue in 1922, one of the most humorous arrests took place on April 21, 1923, when Englund, atop Billy, had to chase Stanley Sweeny and arrest him for reckless driving and possession of a slingshot. The fine was fifty dollars for the slingshot and $150 for the reckless driving, plus fifty days in jail. It seems Sweeny put out many lights and did other damage with great accuracy.

An instance which Daisy Bostick recalled involved a real fisticuff between two locals in the area of the old Soto place, which had become her home. So wild was the fight that it took several other men to assist Gus in hauling them down to City Hall, and witnesses said the more the parties argued the higher Englund set the fine. Finally when both parties realized what it was going to cost if they continued, they became very quiet. On collecting the $120 fine Gus was heard to remark, "This will make a good deposit toward a fund for a proper city hall one of these days." Some thought Gus very clever over the settlement of the problem, and is was said the two warring parties gave each other plenty of berth after the incident.

George Seideneck was arrested for violating the city ordinance by cutting down two trees on Eighth Avenue between Torres and Junipero, with the top of the trees being offered in evidence. The jury consisted of R. H. Hoagland, Ellis Rigney, M. McDonnell, R. H. Durier, Irene W. Rapier, Mrs. A. Grimshaw, Mrs. B. Nixon, Leo Narvaez, W. S. Eroili, William T. Kibbler, Mrs. M. Dawson, and P. C. Piinic. Seideneck was found guilty and fined fifty dollars.

City Marshal Englund found himself right in the middle of a village dispute over the proposed paving of Ocean Avenue in 1919, after he had gone about town on Billy posting election notices. The favorable vote was successfully contested by the artist element of the village, led by Perry Newberry, in court in Salinas. After a long hearing, Judge Bardin found the election to have been unfairly conducted and stated that Englund had posted all the election notices "too far up on the sides of pine trees for the populace to read."

Englund never missed on handing out a speeding fine, much to the dismay of the driver who, thinking himself safe because Englund was on a horse, headed up Ocean Avenue toward Monterey, only to find that the marshal had taken the shorter horse trail through the Carmel Woods, coming out by the old Carmel Hill gate where he would be waiting for the driver, ticket in hand. In August of 1926 the Board of Trustees met and decided that the local traffic officer, Charles Guth, should give out "courtesy notices." The new notices read, "You have failed to obey traffic regulations as follows: [the date, name, license, and nature of offense]. This is not a notice to appear before a Police Judge, but your car number has been taken, and in the future we respectfully request that you be more careful in observance of the police regulations of our city. The purpose of this notice is to warn minor traffic law violators in a friendly way and thus enlist the co-operation of automobiles."

One young boy, long since turned man, remembered how he thought the marshal had some kind of superior powers after Englund chased him and his friend through the bushes out on the Point one evening when it was dark. The boys did not believe the marshal could see them, and after being caught were convinced that he could see in the dark. It wasn't until several years later that they found out the secret—one of them had had a turned-on light in his hip pocket.

Another humorous happening was the time Marshal Englund was awakened at 1:25 A.M. one morning by the sound of a car stopping in front of his door. Hurriedly throwing on his clothes to go out and investigate, Englund soon found that the car had been stolen and placed the driver under arrest. It was later remarked that "the thief couldn't have picked a better place to park."

In early June of 1932, Gus Englund, with his customary composure, took the decision of the town council to cut salaries ten to fifteen per cent calmly by "lighting a cigar and polishing his badge," while he led Billy out to pasture near Point Lobos. His only comment was that he couldn't dig into his pocket for the extra that was needed to keep Billy on the job. Despite a troubled leg, he continued his regular duties, with the assistance of Charles Guth. Billy's retirement didn't last long. The July 29, 1932 *Pine Cone* read, "Horsefeathers! It Just Ain't Right . . . . Gus To Ride Nag Again." It was unanimously agreed in the village that even if house to house solicitation were necessary, Englund was to ride Billy again, because all the visitors to the village were grumbling and complaining over his absence, and all the old-timers were threatening an uprising if something weren't done about the matter. It was almost immediately agreed that Mayor John C. Catlin would bring up the issue at the next council meeting, which he did. The whole matter was resolved for a while, but eventually Englund retired Billy permanently, saying that times and traffic had changed too much for him to continue.

Gradually Englund's health deteriorated due to the injury to his leg which had not healed, and he was forced to retire in 1935. His illness took him to the Veterans Hospital in San Francisco, where efforts to improve his health failed and he died. He was buried at El Carmelo Cemetery where a host of friends paid their respects.

When Englund retired, Robert Norton, who was at the time on the town council, was elected to the position of Chief of Police by the recommendation of Rudy Ohm, T. Moore, and others. Norton continued in that position until 1940, when he resigned over the controversy which had arisen over the words and actions of Police Commissioner Everett Smith. It was the first time there had ever been any discord in the department. Briefly what happened was that two officers, Leslie Overhulse and Earl Wermuth, were quite suddenly informed that they would be retired from the force, and an editorial headline in the October 5, 1939 *Monterey Herald*,

Carmel Police Department in 1952. Left to right, Bill Weeks, Noel Clarabutt, William Ellis, James Kelsey, Sgt. Earl Wermuth, Dan Throp, desk officer, Chief Clyde P. Klaumann, Andrew Del Monte, Verdie Herdine, Clint Colburn, reserve, and Carl Patnude, reserve.

written by Winsor Josselyn, read, "Officer Says Two Men Fired; Council Says It Is 'Rumor.'" The officers in question, well liked by the populace, were incredulous over the matter. The chief insisted that he was only passing down orders, and Commissioner Smith declared he had never passed down such orders. The popular Argyll Campbell represented the two officers in court proceedings which lasted three hours, and won the case. One hundred and twenty-five citizens jammed City Hall to observe. Norton soon resigned as chief and was replaced by Robert Walton from Monterey, who acted as chief for a six-month period until the war interrupted his duties. From 1940 to 1950 Roy C. Fraties was Carmel's police chief. He was replaced by H. S. "Mike" Stalter, who served on an interim basis until thirty-eight-year-old Clyde Klaumann, a fourteen-year member of the Monterey Police Department, could come over the hill to fill the position. When Klaumann's retirement was announced in September 1975, Captain William H. Ellis was named as his replacement and is our present chief.

Carmel's Police Department has had a colorful and proud history since its beginning. The first police station was at City Hall in Philip Wilson's building. Englund took arrested parties there long enough to legalize his papers, then accompanied them to Monterey. Carmel's second station was between Mission and San Carlos in the building which later housed Carmel's Hobby Shop (now Adam Fox). It was to this location that Earl Wermuth remembers helping Gus Englund carry the body of a man who had been killed in a car crash and "placing him as neatly as possible on the chief's table, the only place we had to put him until other arrangements could be made."

The third station, occupied in 1927, was in the Thomas Morgan building above the Dolores Street post office, in the council chambers. According to ex-officers Nupper, Stalter, and Fraties, it was small and cramped. Stalter remembered that when he returned from military service in late 1945, a new station was half completed at Mission and Seventh. The move to that station, where the Security Pacific Bank is located today, was made on April 9, 1947, according to official records. Years later, while plans for another new station were being drawn up by Robert Jones, the department used the temporary location of the City Hall, which had been All Saints Church. In 1966 Carmel's newest station, in combination with the public works department, was constructed at the southeast of Junipero and Fourth Avenue. Upon its completion in late April of 1967, dedication ceremonies took place. The pledge of allegiance was led by Herbert Heron, a former Carmel mayor.

William H. Ellis, who is the present Chief of Police in Carmel, was a captain when this picture was taken. Clyde Klaumann, left, was the chief at that time.

Some other early day police officers in Carmel were Frank Hay, Dave Nixon, Van Orcan, Paul Funchess, and Willard Dufur. Many others have joined the ranks over the years, beginning their duties as "door shakers" who walked their patrols. Charles Guth, who served under both Gus Englund and Robert Norton, left the police department to become one of the village's first paid firemen, in March of 1937.

The police department became motorized under Robert Norton, and Earl Wermuth, who had begun his service with the department in July 1928, remembered the occasion well. Officers were paid five dollars a month for gas and used their own cars, paying for all repairs themselves. It wasn't until 1938 that Chief Norton was able to get the council to agree to a token payment of ten dollars a month toward car maintenance. Wermuth rode around on a motorcycle for a long time, but got his first car, a Model A Ford, during World War II. "I managed to put 158,000 miles on my car in a very short time and I had to put synthetic rubber tire recaps on about every six weeks. I remember in 1947 the first person to get an overtime parking ticket was the owner of a black Buick coupe with the license number 18 H 170, and soon after came the addition of a new traffic officer and patrolman, Verdie J. Herdine." (Some will remember Herdine doing beach patrol atop his horse in Englund style.) Wermuth served his years as a policeman with both pride and determination, under the jurisdiction of five chiefs. The last was Clyde Klaumann, who was his favorite of all. "I've never worked for a better man than Clyde Klaumann," Wermuth said, and the feeling was mutual. Wermuth has seen a great many changes in Carmel, with his earliest memories stretching back to 1913. He came to Carmel in 1906 when his family moved here from Oakland. They lived in a little home where the entrance to the Sunset School cafeteria was, until they later moved across the street just below Ninth on the west side of San Carlos. Wermuth remembered with pride the 1940 motorcycle the department acquired for him to ride, and all the courtesy cards he bestowed over the years for parking infractions. He was so well known for not letting a law breaker pass his scrutiny that Robert S. Vance published the following poem about him in October 1938:

> Wermuth Will Give You A Ticket
> Bob Norton froze—things were tense,
> (A barking dog is a grave offense)
> The Force rushed to the Chief's defense
> and
> Wermuth gave him a ticket.
>
> The town drunk guzzled whiskey and gin;
> Knowing the enormity of his sin,
> Then the Chief of police came rushing in
> and
> Wermuth gave him a ticket.
>
> If you park too long in front of a shop
> Or stay in a red zone you'll soon meet a cop,
> They'll drive alongside with a skidding stop
> and
> Wermuth will give you a ticket.
>
> O criminal beware and stay far away,
> You'll regret Carmel to your dying day.
> Our cops will show you that crime doesn't pay
> for
> Wermuth will give you a ticket.

In October of 1939 the Carmel Fire Department, in cooperation with Carmel's three-man police department, made use of a twenty-four-hour radio (call letters KQFI) with the installation of receivers in the cars of the officers on duty, which made the job of the police much easier.

Our police department has come a long way and

seen many changes since those early days. It has maintained an excellent record and has had many fine men whom we have considered special and who have devoted themselves to their duty and contributed to a strong sense of community pride and well-being. Beginning with one man in 1917, today the department has a full complement of twenty-five employees, making it Carmel's largest municipal agency.

The history of Carmel's post office began in 1889 in Monterey, where the mail came from Salinas three times a week, then found its way over the hill by stage, in leather pouches. It was left with postmaster Antonio Nunes of Carmel Valley in the small building which became known as White Oak Inn. This arrangement was discontinued after a year, but was re-established in 1893 in what is believed to be approximately the same location, with Burritt Cahoon as postmaster. Then in 1899 John Hibbrom relieved Cahoon, and in 1902 Montgomery Whittock took charge and the post office was moved to what is now Rancho Carmelo. Although the post office officially bore the name of the new settlement of Carmel, it was still up the valley when Whittock suddenly resigned and moved away, leaving no replacement. Hearing of what was happening in the valley, Frank Powers journeyed to Washington without further delay to make Carmel the official post office. (Collectors will note that all the early cancellations bear the name Carmel, not Carmel-by-the-Sea.)

Frank Powers' visit to Washington was a success, and on December 5, 1903, John Staples, or "Uncle John," as he was known, took charge of doling out the mail that came in on the stage and was left with the Carmel Development Company. On September 27, 1904, Louis Slevin became the first official postmaster at his store. Stage drivers at that time were Alfred Horn, Charlie (Dad) Hamilton, Samuel Powers, and Joseph Hitchcock. Both Slevin and Hitchcock recounted how those on horseback in the early days would simply "ride up, insert their key into a locked box, remove their mail and ride off."

L. E. Payne became the second Carmel postmaster on September 16, 1914. It was during his term that the post office was moved to the part of the Beck building which adjoined the pharmacy run by "Doc" Beck, later Staniford's. During Payne's tenure there was great excitement when assistant postmistress Stella Vincent arrived the morning of April 14, 1915, to find the safe, which had contained large amounts of money as well as stamps, blown open. It was said to have been the talk of the town for years. In October of the same year Charles Howland relinquished the mail appointment down the coast to Corbett Grimes of Big Sur.

In 1918 Stella Vincent was appointed to take Payne's place when he resigned. She filled the position until 1929. In 1922 the post office was moved to the Tom Morgan building on the west side of Dolores north of Seventh, next to what became Monterey County Trust and Savings Bank. In April of 1924, Earl Percy Parkes and Jeanette Hoagland were given clear title to the building as block 15. Helen Parkes, who was Stella Vincent's dearest lifelong friend, became clerk in Stella's place, and also served several terms as assistant postmistress, in addition to her duties on the city council and the first planning commission. Stella and Helen both later recalled how Bob Leidig's chickens often "came running in and out of the post office," and the dog fights which "occurred regularly" at the front door or in the lobby.

Others who served during Stella's reign were a Miss Nash, Mrs. Grace Wickham, and Theresa Ratliff, all of whom worked half days. After Stella Vincent's long term, William Overstreet served as postmaster until 1933, when Irene Campbell Cator became postmistress. In 1934 the post office was moved again, this time to the southwest corner of Ocean and Mission. Irene Cator served as postmistress until 1939, when Ernest Bixler took up the position.

In 1941, during Bixler's tenure, the post office was moved to Robert Leidig's building on the south side of the old F. A. Darling family home on North Dolores between Fifth and Sixth, with Rollo H. Payne's Village Candies as its neighbor. From 1942 to 1946, Frederick Bechdolt did the honors as acting postmaster while Bixler was away at war, serving with the Seabees. When Bixler returned in 1946, Bechdolt stepped down and Bixler continued in his former post until 1951, when he returned to his one-time building trade, and Alfred Mollner became the acting postmaster. In 1951 the post office took up its present location, and in 1953 Fred J. Mylar (grandson of Isaac Mylar, pioneer author of San Juan Bautista), who had served for twenty-four years as a popular postal clerk, became acting postmaster.

In October 1957 Fred G. Strong became acting postmaster, and then the following March he became postmaster. Strong saw the present building through its remodeling which doubled it in size. He remained in service as our popular postmaster until he retired in 1969. William P. Woolsey then became the assistant postmaster and was in charge until 1970. Since then, those in charge have been Melvin E. Taylor, 1970 to 1971, Sam R. Haley, in 1971, and Frank Ledesma, our present postmaster. Ledesma is now seeing to an end the construction of a new $1.4 million post office building, which is almost completed on an 85,619 square foot site at the northwest corner of Rio Road and Carmel Rancho Boulevard. On old Hatton family valley land, it will serve all of Carmel Valley and the coast south of Malpaso Creek excluding the zip code area served by the Carmel Valley Village post office. The present village of Carmel post office will remain open and be called the Carmel-by-the-Sea Station—all a dramatic and overwhelming change from not-too-far-past days when we all met each other at the post office or on the way to it.

I t was apparently often said, "If you don't hear about it on a trip to the bulletin board or the post office, you'll read it in the *Pine Cone.*" In 1915 when Irving and Lundborg established Carmel's first stock exchange, another significant first was the establishment of William Overstreet's *Pine Cone.* Prior to the founding of the *Pine Cone,* the local and national news had to come from elsewhere, although local news could be read from the "Bulletin Board," which had originated on a board fence between Slevin's store and the Carmel Bakery. The next stop for the historic news center was a board fence between the Seven Arts building and Mrs. Harry Leon Wilson's Bloomin' Basement, where it remained until 1925, complete with canine "hitchen post" to which the following early day Carmel dogs found themselves attached: Bruno Curtis, Reddy Gottfried, Brownie Overstreet, Domino Yates, Buddy De Yoe, Rags Bechdolt, Cubby Wallace, Delilah Wells, King Kuster, and the Goolds' white bulldog—but never Pal, who had free roam of the village.

When the Bulletin Board was removed, the following comment on its passing was printed in the *San Francisco Chronicle* on November 15, 1925: "For a long time the demise of the board which had sported notices of the mysterious disappearance of lipsticks, gloves, hats, maids and butlers as well as lost loaves of bread, was a bone of contention."

Retired stage driver Sam Powers in front of Carmel Bulletin Board on Ocean Avenue.

According to Mr. Slevin, the board found its way to a temporary short term home "across the street from my place near the library." In 1932 the town was once again without its news spot until 1939, when it found a home on the north side of Dolores next to what would become Rollo H. Payne's Village Restaurant. When in 1947 Rollo Payne purchased Joe Olivero's little residence which had sat at the rear of Curtis' Candy Store, and had it moved next to his restaurant to become his Village Candy Store, the Bulletin Board remained between the candy store and its next door neighbor, the post office. Finally when the last and newest post office was built up from James McGrury's, Stella Guichard's, and J. F. Darling's old property, the board found its final spot of faded glory. Today what is left of our Bulletin Board rests between the United Nations Shop and the Helen Baker Gallery, and many pass by without ever knowing its place in early village life.

In 1910 the William Overstreets, who had been previous visitors to Carmel, came to live permanently. Overstreet, ex-San Francisco news reporter, clerk and correspondent, had a love affair with print and a dream of owning his own newspaper. He opened a job printing business in the spring of 1914. Not long afterwards, Overstreet said that his good friend Lou Desmond (then husband of Daisy Bostick) came into his office with the rumor that a Los Angeles man was shortly to publish a weekly newspaper in Carmel. Overstreet was to say of that day, "Auspicious time or not, I was not minded to allow anyone to beat me to it after my five years of preparation." He grabbed the bull by the horns, and touring the village, he collected ads, acquired news, and arranged type. To use his own words: "I sacrificed to purchase the secondhand plant, borrowed money and spent two hectic weeks of hand-type setting." His press was operated by foot power. On February 3, 1915, Volume One of the first *Pine Cone* was printed. The newspaper got its name because of Overstreet's affection for the pine trees (collecting pine cones was one of his favorite pastimes). The small four-page newspaper, on ten by eleven inch paper, had sixteen advertisements and had to be "kicked" off the press four times, a total of thirty-three copies at 1,200 times through the press. Kathryn (Kitty) Bechdolt Overstreet wrote the "Pine Needles" column and did the folding. With the opening line, "We have come to stay," the *Pine Cone* quickly sold out its first edition. The first paid subscriber to the newly founded paper was the Overstreets' neighbor, Birney W. Adams. James Franklin Devendorf became the first "paid-in-advance" subscriber, and the first five-year subscription, for five dollars, came from Harry Leon Wilson. Overstreet once recalled a remark made by one of his early subscribers, "If you don't run a year, I'll take it out on your hide." He was noted for his fair and impartial coverage of all issues and his support of local merchants in the advice, "Spend your money where it will do the most good, for you owe it to yourself, no less to your village, to patronize the home merchant." One year after he began publication, Overstreet printed his publication rules as follows:

"Editor's Publication Rules"
"To Be Explicit"

FIRST—It was resolved never to publish anything having in it the element of malice.

SECOND—The paper must be clean. There should be no questionable advertisements or matter.

THIRD—The Pine Cone is not to be used by the publisher as a personal political organ.

FOURTH—We feel it is not only our duty, but our privilege as well to place before the world the superior advantages of Carmel.

"If you see it in the *Pine Cone*, you may safely repeat it," was the pledge. Overstreet, known as a tremendously energetic and enthusiastic man, loved Carmel fiercely. His editorials most often reflected the latest needs or desires of the village, with his suggestions often being made fact, as happened in November of 1915. In one of his editorials Overstreet suggested that the mails should be carried by auto, and the town immediately adopted the idea, with "Dad" Hamilton making the arrangements whereby F. M. Wermuth's autos were used.

Advertisers in the first issue included the follow-

The Leidig family's first grocery store, on Ocean Avenue between Dolores and Lincoln. Robert is in dark-trimmed sweater, Fred is standing with the hand truck, and Benjamin and Lawrence are at right back.

Charles Goold and driver with Goold's taxi, in 1927.

ing: F. S. Schweniger, whose bakery and grocery advertisement announced that he carried "Sunkist goods"; Fred Leidig, who advertised his coal, hay, wood and grain business; the Carmel Drug Store, which advertised "Big Baby Ben Clocks"; Thomas B. Reardon, who offered his electric work and plumbing; and C. O. Goold, who advertised auto tours for hire along with his livery stable, hauling, storage, hay and grain business. There was even an advertisement from Monterey Bank telling of its four per cent interest on savings and deposit accounts, and one from Pacific Grove Building Company announcing their new name and address. Articles featured in the first edition covered rehearsals for *Junipero Serra* at the Forest Theater, the latest report on the Carmel Boys Club, and fire protection.

The *Pine Cone* continued faithful encouragement of support for the Carmel Boys Club. Douglas H. Greeley, Sr., previously a supporter of the Columbia Park Boys Club, was directly responsible for the start of the Boy Scouts in Carmel, which began with a visit to the Monterey Peninsula of the founder of the organization, Sir Baden-Powell, in 1910. At the time of his visit Baden-Powell stayed at the Presidio of Monterey and "bivouacked" with a group from the presidio which at the time included some visitors from the Boys Club of Carmel: Douglas Greeley, Jr., Louis Lewis, John Machado, Rowan Rapier, Tom Warren, Dave Machado, Walter Warren, Robert Raigge, and Scott Douglas. All of the boys and their leader, John Neikirk, became official scouts, with the help of Douglas H. Greeley, Sr. and Fred Leidig. Eventually, through the fund raising efforts of Louis Levinson and F. L. Veatch, and the support of the *Pine Cone*, property was purchased at Eighth and Mission where M. J. Murphy built a clubhouse. Also sponsored by the American Legion, in 1925 the local troop received the official number of 86. Later the troop met under the direction of Otto Bardarson and continued to meet for many years at the Mission and Eighth scout house.

What had begun for Overstreet with a second-hand press in a room behind the post office became the voice of the village, while between issues Willaim Overstreet acted as postmaster. Well loved and respected by the community, as was their daughter, Phyllis Overstreet Appleton, the Overstreets took an active part in village life. William Overstreet was remembered for his work as chairman of the school board and as an active member of the Carmel Volunteer Fire Department, along with being its secretary and constant supporter of its causes in many editorials. The Overstreets retired in 1926 and moved into their home on Junipero across from what is now Carmel Plaza Shopping Center. For many years after William Overstreet no longer ran the *Pine Cone,* it continued in his tradition, with owners like J. A. Easton, who ran it until he encountered financial difficulties. Then Allen Griffin agreed to purchase the paper from Easton "if it was agreed that a friend . . . Perry Newberry, would be editor. Easton agreed and I told Perry he could have half interest in the paper if he made a success of it for me . . . he did, and eight months later he came to me and asked to buy my half and I sold it to him!" said Griffin. All of this took place in 1926, and by December of 1926, Perry Newberry was owner and editor of the *Pine Cone* and the cry went out around the village, "The Pine Cone's out!"

In 1925, Willard K. Bassett, a colorful, outspoken individual, began his career in Carmel with the establishment of the *Carmel Cymbal.* He left in September of 1927 for "private reasons" and publication was suspended. Ross C. Miller and Herald Cockburn took over the *Pine Cone* in 1935. Then in 1940, Archibald MacPhail became editor and publisher, with Francis L. Lloyd as assistant editor, and ran the newspaper until 1941, when Clifford and Wilma Cook took over. They continued with it until 1961. In 1955 the *Pine Cone* moved from the De Yoe building site on Dolores to another site on Dolores, next to Oliver White and Associates, Interior Decorators, and the Carmel Drive-In Market. As of this writing, the *Pine Cone* has been sold to relative newcomers from New York, the A. Eisners, who have been residents of Carmel for seven years. For the present the newspaper offices occupy the upstairs of the Goold building on the corner of Ocean and San Carlos.

There have been competitors to the *Pine Cone* and other attempts at local news publication. Some were quite popular and lasted for some time, yet the *Pine Cone* has outlasted them all. A list of some of the competitors is interesting. There was the *Carmel News* (1914-1917) next door to Slevin's, the *Carmelite* by Stephen Alan Reynolds (1925-1931), begun as a liberal weekly, and the *Daily Carmelite,* begun in 1931 by O'Brien at about the same time the Carmel S.A.R. came out. The *Bohemian* was housed next door to architect Robert Stanton's office on the site now occupied by Merle's Treasure Chest. Others were the *Village Press,* published from 1926 to 1935, with William D. Cooke as editor and Peter O'Crotty as managing editor, and the *Front Page,* published by the Abalone League in 1928. The *Front Page* had four single front pages, "depending on how you folded it," and a first issue "loaded" with theater news. The *Village Daily* was published from 1930 to 1935. The *Carmel Sun* began February 2, 1933, at five cents a copy each Saturday, and was run by Mr. and Mrs. F. E. Bunch. In close competition with the *Carmel Sun* was the *Villager,* selling at fifteen cents a copy each Wednesday, beginning publication in March of 1937 with editor Rosslyn Cowan, Julia Park as assistant editor, and Larry Grenier in charge of advertisements and circulation. The editorial board consisted of Lincoln Steffens, Herbert Heron, Charles Aldrich, John Catlin, Marjorie Mac-Evan, and Dr. D. T. MacDougal. Still other publications were: the *Acorn,* the *Pine Nut,* the *Town Crier, Controversy,* the *Pacific Weekly,* the *Fairways,* the *Chukker, All Arts Gossip,* the *Spectator, Game and Gossip* (originally issued as a monthly publication by Del Monte Properties), which later merged with *Sports and Vanities,* the *Californian, Panorama,* the *Scintilator,* and in more recent times, *Gazette* and *Old Carmel.*

An interesting lady whose connection with Carmel

spanned many years and endeared her to many was Daisy Fox Desmond Bostick. She became a member of the *Pine Cone* staff in 1921 with William Overstreet and continued with J. A. Easton, Allen Griffin and Newberry, who with his wife Bertha had become Daisy's good friend.

In 1966 Daisy was ninety-four years old, and she had seen fifty-six years of changes in the village of Carmel-by-the-Sea since her arrival in July 1910. When she first came to Carmel from San Jose she was a guest of the newly settled Newberrys, and it wasn't until a return trip to Carmel from a three-month tour of Europe in 1918 with a friend and fellow antique collector, Tilly Pollack, that Daisy made Carmel her permanent home. She became assistant to real estate man Arthur Shand in his office, after which she worked for Ray C. De Yoe along with others, including Robert Norton after he retired as police chief. At this time Daisy worked on her book with Willard K. Bassett's wife, Dorothea Castelhun, and lived in a garage she remodeled into a quaint cottage for herself on Lincoln. Later she remodeled another cottage at Ocean and Santa Fe, and still later bought the old Phillaponda-Soto place on Monterey Street below the old Grace Deere Velie Clinic, which she fixed up most charmingly. There was nothing wrong with Daisy's memory in her last years in Carmel, and her bubbly personality, along with her many recollections aided by scrapbooks, memorabilia and the charming setting of her home, will be remembered by many. Carmelites owe her much, for she was either at the scene of or a part of much of what was going on, and took the time to make notes about it all.

When Daisy first came to stay with the Newberrys, it was the year of the founding of the Forest Theater. During her first years in Carmel there were arguments against the paving of Ocean Avenue, some opposition to Carmel's changing its name to Carmel-by-the-Sea (because of the popular saying around the Peninsula at the time, "Pacific Grove-by-God, Carmel-by-the-Sea, and Monterey-by-the-Smell"), "singing, dancing and parties that went on all over the town, spilling into the streets and ending up on the beach"—even fist fights in front of her residence. Daisy managed the old Hotel Carmel for a time with her husband, Lou Desmond. She recalled a "gay young bachelor," Allen Knight, who lived in a prefabricated cottage at Seventh and Monte Verde, and the difficulty he got into after attending an all night studio party. It seems Knight, who returned home late, did not realize that the cottage he lived in had already been placed on wheels to be ready for moving in the morning. At

precisely the right moment, as the sun was beginning to come up, Daisy happened to look out her window to see the cottage passing by, with Allen Knight standing at the window "in shock," and then, clad in pajama bottoms, jumping from the window to the curb below. The whole happening became a joke they shared privately over the years.

Daisy had another friend of long standing in Franklin Devendorf. "One thing was certain, if you were a stranger in Carmel, James Franklin Devendorf inevitably got hold of you. In his old rickety Ford Devey took you to a lot you couldn't help buying for ten dollars down and five dollars a month. I succumbed, like everyone else. If Devey had a flock of customers in his car, he would take them all to Pop Ernst's on Alvarado Street in Monterey for an abalone steak dinner. There was a great closeness between Carmel and Monterey in those days."

Of her association with the *Pine Cone*, Daisy was to say, "I broke into newspaper advertising by visiting the Christmas decorated shops and writing about them for the *Pine Cone*. The columns I wrote seemed to please both buyer and seller, and I was most grateful for the results. I soon became known as the Pine Nut, and that was back in 1921 when Bill Overstreet was editor, with his wife Kitty as bookkeeper, along with Brownie, their dog, as mascot, and Bill Nye as typesetter. Ivy Basham furnished our coffee and our courage."

Prior to 1922 there had been a desire on the part of various local citizens to see the formation of a village oriented building and loan society, and in August of 1922 such a society was organized with its headquarters in the Carmel Realty Company offices. The board of directors included such names as Dr. H. W. Fenner, Calvin C. Hogle, J. F. Devendorf, and Ernest Schweniger. The committee of appraisers consisted of John B. Jordan, Charles Olan Goold and Harrison W. Askew. The following subscribers were responsible for its assets, having themselves subscribed for twenty to forty shares each, with the par value of each share $100, and a monthly payment of fifty cents per share:

J. F. Devendorf	H. P. Glassell
R. C. De Yoe	R. A. Johnson
Percy Parkes	L. S. Slevin
T. B. Reardon	J. B. Jordan
T. L. Elder	Carl Huseman
C. C. Hogle	Bernard Wetzel
L. E. Gottfried	P. K. Gordon
M. J. Murphy	Stella J. Guichard

H. W. Fenner   Helen W. Parkes
C. O. Goold   Stella Vincent
H. A. Spoehr   E. Schweniger

With its continued growth Carmel had the greatest proportionate increase in population between 1920 and 1930 of any town or city in northern California, and this created the need for loans and banking expansion. In May of 1923 work on the original Carmel Bank structure was begun after the sale of shares created capital of $25,000. The building was to sit next to the Wright Building, and arrangements were made with Bernard Wetzel, who owned the lot west of the bank, for a "partnership concrete wall," and the relocation of C. J. Arne's barber shop to "ten feet west of its then present site." The officers of the new bank were Charles Olan Goold, Barnet J. Segal, Thomas A. Work, Silas W. Mack, and J. A. Sparolini. Carmel stockholders were J. F. Devendorf, A. H. Roseboom, Helen W. Parkes, L. S. Slevin, Helen Van Riper, E. B. Bragg, Henry Leon Wilson, Ray C. De Yoe, Carl Huseman, C. O. Goold, Barnett Flanders, Stella Vincent, and Dave Wolters. Stockholders from Monterey were P. J. Dougherty, J. K. Oliver, C. A. Mertz, T. A. Work, Silas W. Mack, and J. A. Sparolini. On July 23, 1923, the Bank of Carmel opened its doors. It served the community with pride from this location until it moved on June 3, 1939 to a new building at the northeast corner of Ocean and Dolores.

Historical plaques by Paul Whitman decorated the front face of the first bank building. The bank was staffed by Thomas A. Work, C. L. Berkey, Arne Halle, Harry C. Hilbert, Donald A. Lyon, James J. Williams, Thomas N. Hooper, Mrs. Mary A. White, Miss Mary Wheldon, and Mrs. Florence Elder. It boasted three vaults, one of which was a twenty-six by fourteen foot vault, along with telephone booths at the right of the entrance for the convenience of clients, and the first night depository on the Peninsula. I well remember my pride as a child in having an account in our local bank, and how impressed I was with the wonderful Burgdorff painting which covered the back wall (long since painted over), and how your footsteps always had a hollow sound as you walked across its floor. The village experienced a feeling of sadness in 1959, when our local bank joined with the First National Bank of Monterey and First National Bank of Pacific Grove and became Crocker-Anglo National Bank. Later we even lost our wonderful second Bank of Carmel building when Crocker-Anglo became Crocker-Citizens and erected a new building on the site of the old Purity Grocery. (It is now Crocker National.) The old bank

building, completely remodeled, was turned into another tourist gift store complex.

Though by most accounts Carmel did not suffer as much from the depression years as other areas, an interesting sidelight to its history is the "Carmel Dollars." First issued in 1933, the "dollars" were designed by Catherine Seideneck and Jo Mora, with Mrs. Seideneck doing the stamp and Mora the art work. Devised by the Carmel Business Association (formed in 1931 by Robert Parrott, Thomas Phillip, and Peter Mawdsley) and backed by the majority of merchants, the "Carmel Dollars" script was to be the means of stimulating the local economy, and all those persons working for the City of Carmel were to be paid in "Carmel Dollars." The first week of circulation some seventy-five dollars worth of the script was put into use with similar accounts being introduced over the following weeks until the circulation sum of $1,000 was reached. The success of the plan, under the direction of Howell Byrnes as chairman of the Business Association, depended upon the acceptance of the "Carmel Dollars" by

local residents and their ability to keep the script in fairly constant circulation. They were cautioned not to take it as "souvenirs." There were lists of instructions for the merchants so that they might follow the customary procedure for federal tax and revenue purposes, and the entire village seemed prepared to accept the plan wholeheartedly. However, the "Carmel Dollars" plan collapsed almost as quickly as it had begun, and faded into obscurity.

Just three years before the "Carmel Dollars" came into being, on Saturday, April 26, 1930, the Monterey County Trust and Savings Bank opened its doors for inspection with the following as Carmel's Advisory Board: E. H. Tickle, H. F. Dickman, R. C. De Yoe, Sidney Fish, C. L. Conlon, B. H. Schultz, and J. E. Abernathy as secretary. Its directors were H. E. Abbott, Chapman Foster, L. W. Sanborn, J. H. Gross, H. F. Dickman, George P. Henry, L. A. Wilder, E. E. Hitchcock, and A. C. Hughes, president. Later this building became Wells Fargo Bank and today we know it as the Chinese Museum of Art on Dolores Street.

O ver the years Dolores Street has featured familiar names and businesses apart from those already mentioned, such as the Burnham Building between Seventh and Eighth, and the Studio Theater Restaurant, which opened its doors under the ownership of Royden Martin in 1958. In September of 1926 Paul J. Denny was the only dealer on the Monterey Peninsula for the Oldsmobile and Peerless lines. Denny's sales and show rooms were situated on Dolores next door to the post office site, in the building then known as the Oakes Building.

Oakes Building on Dolores Street, one-time home of the post office.

Later the Monterey County Trust and Savings Bank was built on the site of Denny's showroom. In the building now housing Toots Lagoon were Ernest and Minnie Blood's second grocery and bakery, as well as Romylane Candy Store, later the popular Tom's Cafe, which it remained until 1956.

On the east side of Dolores in 1924 the De Yoe building housed the *Pine Cone* and the Carmelita Hat Shoppe, and next to it the popular "Sally's," also known for a time as the Lark, was erected by

De Yoe Building on Dolores Street housed the Pine Cone offices at one time. Sketch by author.

Once "Sally's," now known as the "Tuck Box."

Hugh Comstock and owned by Bonnie Lee. It is now the Tuck Box. There was El Fumidor and the Cooksleys' Hob Nob (now a gift shop).

Vining's Meat Market shared space with the Carmel Grocery, owned by Ora Minges. Later, across the street was the Dolores Bakery, from which the most delectable aromas would escape. The police department was upstairs above the bakery for a brief period, and what had once been a dirt parking lot and a little studio cottage, in 1965 became the home of Helen and Aage Knudsen's Royal Danish Bakery, which later became a Chinese restaurant. Next to the post office on South Dolores in 1933 was the Dolores Cash Grocery, where spinach was nine cents a tin, raspberries and minced clams sold for nineteen cents a tin, and ten pounds of sugar was thirty-seven cents.

Above the Dolores post office site in 1923, Dr. H. J. Hollison, physician and surgeon, had his practice. In 1922, the site next to the old post office was occupied by Goldstine's women's and children's clothing store, and Arthur Trevor Shand used the

El Paseo Court at Dolores and Seventh, in May 1928. Slevin photograph.

stairway (now long gone) to get to his office upstairs. Shand's friends, Mr. and Mrs. Tad Stinson, opened their quaint little shop known as the Stool Pigeon nearby.

In 1957 an old Dolores landmark disappeared when Robert A. Norton sold the old Tel and Tel Building for "in excess of $100,000" to Barnet Segal for Carmel Savings and Loan Association, now Northern California Savings and Loan Association. The Tel and Tel Building had originally been erected by Percy Parkes for Norton's mother, Mrs. Mary Louise Dummage, at a cost of $8,000, to house the office of the Pacific Telephone and Telegraph Company.

Dolores Street took the spotlight in May 1928, when the *Pine Cone* made this remark: "A cement sidewalk has replaced the dirt walk on Dolores Street. It is with regret that we see these types of 'improvements,' for the turf was much easier on our spines. The unpaved path was fine for our grandmother and her cows to walk on, and it was all right for us."

As Carmel grew so did her inns, rental cottages, and tea rooms. Best remembered were the Sea View Inn, a two-story Maybeck at Camino Real and Twelfth, owned and run by the Misses Stout; the Old Cabin Inn at Camino Real and Ocean; Mayfair House, which took over the site of the old Culbertson home; the old Locksley Hall, which had originally been intended for use as a convalescent home for Christian Science members; and Carmel's first "real" cottage motor court, known as "Carmel Cottages—A Little Bit O' Heaven," at Carpenter Street and Second. It surrounded the old Machado home and was owned by the Van Bibbers.

Other popular spots were Holiday House at Ca-

mino Real and Ninth, run by Mrs. L. A. Dorsey, and the Mission Tea Room on the old Christiano Machado land (now Tevis property next to Carmel Mission), which was run by Clarabel Haydock and was for a time one of the most popular of the tea rooms. However, the one remembered as the best was the Blue Bird. The Blue Bird had two locations in its history, the first on Camino Real in a very old "cobwebbed, ivy-covered" place, and the second, considered the better, on Ocean Avenue where Arne and Dorthe Kippenes later opened their "Scandia." In 1937 the Blue Bird was enlarged to include a banquet room in the adjacent Wilson building on the corner of Ocean and Monte Verde, which had been purchased by Malcomb Macbeth, and where customers were accommodated for fifty cents a dinner. Though it had several owners, best remembered were Medora Schaeffer, Mrs. Herrick, Mrs. Maude Arndt, Imogene Crane, Mrs. Manning, Mrs. Sampson, Mrs. Crawford, and Mrs. Pearl Ridgley. Mrs. Ridgley took over the popular Normandy Inn in 1947. Favorite spots today, in addition to the Pine Inn and La Playa, are the Forest Lodge, bordered by Ocean Avenue, Mountain View and Torres; the Green Lantern, bordered by Casanova and Seventh; and the Stone House. Several places have lost their special charm to time and modernization.

The Old Cabin

Tea Room and Gift Shop

Luncheon
Afternoon Tea
Dinner

↲ ↲ ↲

Oriental Goods

CAMINO REAL
Near Ocean Avenue
Carmel - by - the - Sea

Phone 904-W-3   Closed Sundays

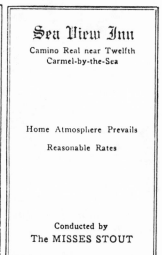

Sea View Inn

Camino Real near Twelfth
Carmel-by-the-Sea

Home Atmosphere Prevails

Reasonable Rates

Conducted by
The MISSES STOUT

One of the few inns left on Ocean Avenue apart from the Pine Inn is the Normandy Inn. The site was first occupied in 1915 by a wooden home-style structure known as Hotel El Monte Verde, run by a Mrs. Hamlin. It was later moved around the corner. The Normandy Inn began as the dream of its owner, Mrs. Ethel P. Young, and was considered in its time to be a "buffer" between the commercial and residential areas in that section of Carmel. When built in 1937, it was, and still is today, a graceful combination of modern convenience and old world charm, with its brick, stucco and timbered effect topped off by heavy tiled shingles. The design of architect Robert Stanton of Carmel, the Normandy is consistent with the quality of design typical of Mr. Stanton in all his undertakings. It was built around a central courtyard, and each section and separate apartment is furnished in keeping with the French Provincial style down to the smallest detail.

The work of Robert Stanton may be seen in several parts of California. A native of Torrance, California, Stanton first came to Carmel on his honeymoon in 1922 and stayed at the Highlands Inn. He returned in late 1925, but did not stay long, after an unfortunate partnership with another man. He acquired a job with Wallace Neff as a traveling superintendent and was associated with Neff in the building of Pickfair and the homes of Kinsley-Gillette, Frederick March and others. Stanton continued to work with Neff for three years, and Neff encouraged him to return to Carmel in 1934 as a licensed architect. ("Sam Morse gave me a room at the Lodge and a telephone.") Within a year Stanton was given the job of designing a new courthouse for Salinas. "I accepted the job on one condition, that I be given the permission to have my good friend and artist Joseph Mora work with me. This was a bold thing for me to do, since it was a federally funded project, but it was agreed that he could. Since I owed a plasterer by the name of Andy Jacobson money, I managed to get him to work on the project also, as payment." The Salinas courthouse was built around a central fountain with Jo Mora's bas relief designs portraying chronologically the people that populated California.

Dr. John Sharp, the administrator of county hospitals, requested Robert Stanton to make a four-month tour from Eureka to San Diego, studying all hospitals and all the aspects that made each of them function, both effectively and non-effectively. After this four-month trip, Stanton designed one of the first tubercular and isolation hospitals in the state. He was called a "leading expert on hospitals," with some sixteen hospitals to his credit. He also designed forty schools throughout Santa Cruz and Monterey counties, including Thomas Larkin and Monte Vista schools, as well as Monterey Peninsula College. Mr. Stanton was also responsible for the introduction of "bilateral lighting" into the field of architecture. He considered the Monterey Penin-

sula College job one of his most challenging. "We did a total of seventy-five site use plans in four days before we ended up with our final plan." Robert Stanton has many other projects to his credit in areas such as Watsonville, Santa Cruz, Petaluma, Greenfield, and King City, where he was responsible for the King City Auditorium, with Joseph Mora again doing the bas relief work. Stanton was also responsible for the first A-frame in Morgan Hill.

Robert Stanton, friend to many, was an especially good friend to Joseph Mora, who was born in Uruguay, came to the United States as a child, and later studied art in New York and Boston. It was in Boston that Mora became a newspaper artist and part time author-illustrator. After service in World War I he came to Carmel, purchasing a full block at San Carlos and First, where his first studio home remains today. Soon after his arrival, Mora was commissioned to do the Serra Sarcophagus for the Carmel mission. Setting up his studio on the mission courtyard, he began work on his now famous commission. The sarcophagus itself depicts the life-size figures of Father Serra lying in state, with his close associates, Fathers Crespi, Lopez, and Lasuén (Serra's successor as president of the missions), grouped around the main body of the sarcophagus. The side panels tell the story of the conquest of Alta California. The medallions of Carlos III, king of Spain, and Pope Pius VI complete the design. There are also seven low, flat bas reliefs in bronze which picture the historical events of Alta California, as well as the Franciscan cord which is interwoven with the Spanish coat of arms. It is a lovely piece of work, as are many of Mora's creations, and at its completion and dedication in 1924, Mora's children, Joseph, Jr. and Patricia, proudly raised the flag from the sarcophagus.

After the completion of the sarcophagus Mora sold his San Carlos and First property and moved to his newly built home and studio, which he had designed, just off Sunridge Road in Pebble Beach, where he lived until his death. He will be remembered for many artistic contributions. In addition to the Serra sarcophagus, he was commissioned to do a monument to Cervantes at the Golden Gate Park, a Bret Harte Memorial at the Bohemian Club, the Memorial Fountain at the county courthouse in Salinas, the bas reliefs on that courthouse, dioramas for the Golden Gate International Exposition and for Sutter's Fort in Sacramento, and a memorial to Will Rogers in Oklahoma. Locally, Mora is also remembered for his model of the Sphinx for the Forest Theater production of *Caesar and Cleopatra* in May of 1922, and his art work and collaboration on Tirey Ford's book, *The Dawn of the Dons*. He made a tremendous hit with the local populace when he was commissioned to paint the murals and design the contented cow for the trademark of the Carmel Dairy, which occupied the corner of Ocean and Mission in the building built by H. C. Stoney in 1932 for Thomas Reardon, now Mediterrean Market.

There have been many tributes to Father Serra locally, including the statue begun by Remo Scardigli and completed by Roy Zoellen in 1938, which was cut from a single log brought up from Palo Colorado and still continues to grace Devendorf Park. Every day many people pass a spot in the Carmel Woods which is marked by a statue of Junípero Serra and never know its significance. Long before Del Monte Company became the owner of this section of land, now known as Carmel Woods, the Franciscan padres often passed through it on their way from Monterey to the Carmel mission. They would pause to rest in the area once known as Serra Circle, and for this reason this particular spot was chosen for the statue. The dedication of the statue, another of Mora's works, not only commemorated Serra, but heralded the official opening of Carmel Woods as a development and captured the entire village for a three-day celebration and a pageant in honor of the event.

The dedication of the Serra statue was preceded by a proclamation issued in the *Pine Cone* on July 20, 1922, with all the "Whereases" and "Therefores" regarding this special event, and signed by then president of the Board of Trustees, Perry Newberry. The Board of Trustees also published the following public notice of the event: "The Serra Memorial will be dedicated on Serra Day, officially proclaimed by the Town Trustees as falling on Saturday, the twenty-second of July. Here again propriety has been constituted with happy results. For Serra Day will fall in the midst of the three days, July 21, 22, and 23 to be signalized by the first production anywhere of Garnet Holme's Carmel Mission Play entitled 'Serra' on the 21st. Truly our first annual celebration of Serra Day will be set in a pageantry of the most appropriate ceremonies."

There were also lengthy articles on the life and times of Serra, and poems by Richard E. White, David Atkins and Robinson Jeffers. Many of those who had participated in *Junípero Serra* (written by Perry Newberry and [then] Father Ramon Mestres) were also anxious to join in the pageant. On Saturday, July 22, 1922, some three hundred people participated in the procession led by Monsignor Mestres, which began near San Carlos on Ocean at a central gathering spot and, moving in solemnity, made its way to the place where the Serra statue was to be unveiled. The crowd of onlookers and participants witnessed the formal dedication and opening of Carmel Woods with the begining prayer by Msgr. Mestres and the opening speech by Mayor Walter Kibbler. A poem written for the occasion by George Sterling was read by Susan Porter, after which the statue was unveiled for all to see. Carved of wood, it was set within a wooden shrine atop a granite rock base and flanked by two benches bearing the following inscriptions:

"In the Immortal Memory of Padre Junípero Serra . . . Servant of Christ, Adventurer, Artist and Engineer" and "Designed and Executed by Jo Mora Sc . . . Dedicated the 22nd day of July 1922 AD"

After the formal dedication of the statue, the day was officially proclaimed Serra Day and was recalled as such in the years to come. On April 3, 1923, the city trustees accepted an offer by the Camp Fire Girls to plant trees and shrubs around the statue, and a memorial fountain was made. However, in the ensuing years the fountain went to ruin and the statue suffered the abuse of vandals and errant motorists. Individuals like Mrs. Walter Burde and Paula Rogers have painstakingly given of their time to its care so that we might all continue to enjoy this spot in the woods, and more recently the City of Carmel has taken over the job of maintaining the statue and the area around it.

The well known engineer and architect Mark Daniels was responsible for the layout of Carmel Woods for Del Monte Properties Company. He already had to his credit Pebble Beach, Forest Hill in San Francisco and Thousand Oaks in Berkeley. The Carmel Woods home sites were separated from Pebble Beach by a small area once called Pescadero Park (after the old Rancho Pescadero, where an old mine shaft and a kiln for the tile used in the old lodge still remain) and from the village of Carmel on the other side. The first lots for the opening sales were standard forty by one hundred foot parcels which sold for $350 each, and the sales of some twenty-two sites were made during the opening of the Carmel Woods. Among the buyers were Agnes D. Signor, William S. Kellogg, Lloyd A. Myers, A. G. Penfield, John T. Black, L. W. De Forest, L. E. Gottfried, Natt S. Head, R. E. Naylor, Professor K. G. Rentdorff, W. F. Gabriel, and Frances McComas. There were many more sales to follow and the "Woods" became the fashionable place to build. Adele Denny and Hazel Watrous built seven Carmel Woods homes with Allen H. Tyler as contractor. M. J. Murphy and McEldowney were others who built there.

Serra Poem
by George Sterling
"The shadows fall from cloud or pine
We, knowing you were great and good
Nearer than we to the divine
Would make you warden of our Wood."

Another memorial monument, which rests near the center of town at Ocean and San Carlos, also has a history. World War I Memorial Arch was designed by Charles Sumner Greene, who also supervised its construction as a gift to Carmel. The memorial was built in 1921 in place of the old Carmel watering trough, plumbed by Thomas Reardon in earlier times. It was built in commemoration of the fifty-six men who left Carmel to fight in the First World War, and was spurred into being by the Carmel American Legion which spearheaded a year long fund raising project. Activities included a dance (Fandango) at the La Playa, and the production of three plays at the Manzanita Theater. On November 11, 1921, the cornerstone was laid, complete with time capsule. Upon completion of the arch, Charles Sumner Greene also donated a "white stone bowl" on which he personally carved a design of breaking waves. Many of us remember that drinking fountain well, and were sorry to see it removed in the 1960s out of fear of vandalism. On August 6, 1977, after fifty-six relatively undisturbed years, the arch was almost totally destroyed when a woman lost control of her car and crashed into the northern portion of the arch. However, it was rebuilt, and in 1977, on the eleventh day of the eleventh month at 11:00 A.M., it was re-dedicated. The 1921 time capsule was resealed and a 1977 version was added.

The architect of the memorial arch, Charles Sumner Greene, at the age of forty-eight, at the height of his distinguished architectural career, retired to a quiet life in Carmel Village, where he continued to live until the time of his death in 1957, at the age of eighty-nine. Beginning his career after graduation from the Massachusetts Institute of Technology in the late 1880s, he later became closely affiliated with his brother, Henry Mather Greene. The Greene brothers brought forth entirely new concepts in their field with treatment of both space and materials in sharp contrast to the Victorian style of that day.

Charles Greene was "a devoted student of all things Japanese, from Zen to architecture." It was never clear why he deserted his successful career.

Perhaps the mechanization which followed World War I and its overshadowing of craftsmanship had something to do with it.

Greene and his English born wife, Alice, were both admired and respected residents of the village, and their Carmel home became the center of "coffee and cake, conversation and music." Of the Greenes' five children, Nathaniel Patrickson, Thomas Gordon, Bettie, Anne, and Alice, two have been linked with Carmel—Anne Greene Roberts, the pianist of early Bach Festivals, and Bettie Greene. In 1916, the Greenes lived in the old Fry house at Carmelo and Twelfth. They later moved to the old Clamphet house where Bettie, a horse enthusiast, was allowed to purchase her first horse. In late 1924, Bettie built her stables on Junipero and Fifth across from the old (now gone) Carmel Laundry, and handy to John Catlin's Forge in the Forest. Bettie housed her own horse (the one I recall was named "Chino") and eight other horses and a frisky pony at her stables, and was visited by at least two generations of friends in the children of the village, who were allowed to watch, learn and help feed and curry her charges. Bettie Greene always had time for children. Her quick smile and a twinkle in her blue eyes always made you welcome, and some of my fondest memories as a child include time spent in her presence and at the Forge nearby. It was over twenty years ago, on February 20, 1958, that Bettie's stables were torn down to make way for a motel, but for some of us it was only yesterday.

Some of Charles Greene's better remembered architectural productions were: the Daniel James home, which Greene spent two years designing and building and for which he imported a stone mason; the Martin Flavin home, "Spindrift," at the Highlands; the Woodside, California home of Mortimer Fleishacker; Greene's own home and studio with its walls in "Flemish bond, eighteenth century and interior carvings of a unique style"; the R. R. Blacker house in Pasadena, built in 1907; the William R. Thorsen house in Berkeley, built in 1908; and the David Gamble house in Arroyo Seco, built in 1909. Greene was also noted for his interiors in which he used special techniques with woods, carving and masonry. In spite of all his accomplishments, Greene's close friends believed that he retained a "bitterness and detached" feeling toward his work, which was in his own time largely forgotten and ignored. In the early 1940s there was a renewed interest in the Greene concept, which ended in professional recognition by the American Institute of Architects. Though years late, it brought a measure of satisfaction to both brothers. In 1952, the

A.I.A. honored Charles Sumner and Henry Mather Greene with a citation which read as follows:

> Your gifts have multiplied and spread to all parts of the nation and are recognized throughout the world. You enrich the lives of the people. You have made the name of California synonymous with simpler, freer and more abundant living. You have helped shape our distinctly national architecture, and in giving tangible form to the ideals of our people, your names will be forever remembered among the great creative Americans.

Several influential architects have established characteristics synonymous with the atmosphere of Carmel. One whose work is widely known and associated with the storybook side of Carmel's architecture is Hugh White Comstock. Comstock was born in 1907 on a ranch in Evanston, Illinois, the youngest of a large family. He later came to live in Santa Rosa, California, and in 1924 came to Carmel to visit his sister and brother-in-law, Catherine and George Seideneck. Through them Hugh met a talented "maker of dolls," Mayotta Brown, and they were soon married. Before the first year of their marriage was over, an event took place which unofficially began Comstock's architectural career. The popular rag dolls which Mayotta created and called "Otsy-Totsies" had gradually become literally stacked throughout their home, and in "desperation" Mayotta exclaimed, "Hugh, can't we build a little cottage to keep the dolls in? We could build it like a fairy house in the woods and the buyers will be able to see the dolls in a house all their own." It was not long after Mayotta's remark that Comstock, who had a natural flair for drawing, created the original Carmel Doll House. He had his own version of architecture for the Doll House, combining usefulness with whimsy. He and Mayotta constructed his fantasy, complete with pine needles in the plaster, which was troweled on over burlap in totally uneven form.

What took place at the completion of the Doll House in 1924 was community reaction which was a total surprise to the Comstocks. Almost immediately many residents requested similar shops and houses for their own use, and this ultimately resulted in a firmly established profession which operated from Comstock's offices at Torres and Sixth. Hugh Comstock was called the "builder of dreams," but was considered by all who knew him to be a delightful, fair, gentle, honest, clean, strong, and generous individual with "irrefrangible integrity." To those with whom he worked closely, the experience was considered "a privilege of incomparable value." Compliments and popularity were both "quietly scorned" by Comstock. His work and the fact that he held various civic posts such as president of the school board and chairman of the sanitary board were matter of fact to him, and scorning publicity, he never sought public office, though his opinions were often sought.

At home the Comstocks generated a warmth and generosity in an environment typically Comstock, felt from your first step into their garden and on to a seat before the hearth.

Some of the structures of Comstock's "storybook" era are listed below, as well as some of those homes built after his 1936 perfection of a then "new form of stabilized adobe" which rapidly won him great recognition as a technical expert in the field of "Post-adobe" architecture.

Hansel (the original Doll House), 1924, Obers', 1925, Gretel, 1925, the Tuck Box, 1926, the Tuck Box Jam Shop, 1929, the Guest House, 1926, "Snow White's Summer Place," 1926, the Wood, 1927, Comstock Studio, 1927, the Torres Cottage, 1928, the Birthday House, 1928, the Dolls House, 1928, Yellow Bird, 1928, Fables, 1928, Curtain Call, 1929, the Twin on Palou, 1929, San Antonio, 1929, the Jordan House, 1929, Great Expectations (outside the city limits), 1929, the Wheeler House (Pebble Beach), 1929, the Chanticleer motor court, the Carmel home built for Jimmy Hatlo, the H. M. Haskins home at Carmelo, 1939, and many other homes and businesses all bear his distinctive mark of both endurance and beauty, contributing so much to the charm of Carmel.

Beauty and charm are words which describe Carmel and its quality of life. Its uniqueness has been created by such things as its architectural heritage; its forest of pines; its beaches and woods, and the sense of freedom they give to both body and spirit; and its cultural originality and vitality.

The city has reached a point in its existence at which maintaining and strengthening the "old" Carmel—so well loved by many—has become increasingly difficult. I have watched as we have become cluttered with a variety of undesirable problems; I have sighed with the commission, growled with the council, and grumbled with the natives, and have in moments in recents years felt the desire to hurl a flower pot at a councilman just as Bertha Newberry once did, knowing full well that there are no expedient means of dealing with choices we now face.

CARMEL VALLEY

Memories are stepping stones to the past.

My early memories are ones I can almost touch and feel... A rushing river, crawdads in a pool, the warm ground under my feet and between my toes, coupled with the smell of oak on a gentle breeze... Golden grass in undulating patterns as I looked across a field to watch a hawk turn lazy circles above a barn... Hot dry days that melted my ice cream faster than I could lick it... Pickles at Rosie's Cracker Barrel that made my mouth pucker... Crickets chirping, curious dragonflies, and the call of an owl in the night.

This is Carmel Valley.

As the seasons and the years have come and gone, the valley has seen much change from those gentle days. I am happy in the knowledge that I first knew and grew to love it as a child.

2

Carmel Valley

The fertile valley of the beautiful El Rio Carmelo once stood in green and golden tones of untouched open space and grandeur. The land beckoned, and to its rolling hills of tawny grass and oak, and its willowed river banks, came those to occupy the land given to them as Spanish land grants. Before them, only a few Indian rancherías—such as Tucutnut and Ichxenta—dotted the countryside.

The Rancho Cañada de la Segunda (second valley) was originally granted to Lázaro Soto in 1839. Consisting of 4,366.8 acres, the grant lay behind what is now Carmel-by-the-Sea Village, including the area known as the Mesa and the hills going toward the Mission San Carlos de Borromeo. In 1851 the United States government confirmed the grant which was then given to an Andrew Randall, who bought the land for $500. After Randall later defaulted in his payments of $35.75, Alexander

Taylor took the land. A year later, in 1857, patent was issued to Fletcher M. Haight, and although Haight filed claim, taking over the payment of judgments against Taylor amounting to $63.11, Andrew Randall regained title when the United States acknowledged the original Spanish grant. Later Randall sold the land to Oscar Shafter for $1,000, while in the meantime Alexander Taylor had sold his 1856 claim back to Randall for a profit, at the price of $125. In 1858, the United States again confirmed the grant which had been given to Randall, and upon Randall's death, patent was reissued to Fletcher M. Haight, in 1859.

In 1861 the land was sold to a syndicate of five men for $1,700 and two months later Haight, who wanted to clear off a foreclosure suit of $1,700, bought out four of the five men for $2,100. By late 1862 Haight was having serious financial difficulties

A panoramic view of the Carmel Valley in 1946, looking up the valley from Rancho Cañada de la Segunda. Photograph by Dale Hale.

and had been given a loan of $10,000 on the land by the old Central Trust Company of California. Later he acquired a second loan of about $4,000 from Lloyd Pacheco Tevis and soon after this, in 1866, Tevis bought the entire ranch holdings for the sum of $11,950 in cash, a bargain considering the loss of his $4,000 loan.

In 1869 Tevis sold the land to Mrs. Dominga Doni de Atherton, mother-in-law of Gertrude Atherton and wife of Faxon Dean Atherton. Faxon Dean Atherton, it is remembered, had already become owner of the old Rancho Milpitas (under protest) and suits had been brought against him by various settlers who had been on the land long before Atherton had come to claim it—suits which became bitter and lengthy. Hard feelings persisted for some twenty-five years after the courts ruled in Atherton's favor. His son George continued to run the old rancho, despite local feelings, after the death of his father in 1877. Eventually the Milpitas was sold to William Randolph Hearst, and today we know it as the United States Army's Fort Hunter Liggett.

The end of the beautiful Rancho Cañada de la Segunda began in 1888, when William Hatton became manager of the rancho for its owner, Mrs. Atherton. In 1890 Mrs. Atherton rented the ranch to Hatton for the sum of one dollar per acre annually. (In 1947 the land rented for $100 an acre to those growing artichokes on it.) In 1892 Hatton purchased the west half of the rancho with $55,000 in cash. He had already gained possession of another 640-acre parcel. In 1925 Hatton heirs sold some 233 acres of high land east of Carmel city limits to Paul Flanders for about $100,000. Flanders was head of a syndicate which included Harry Leon Wilson and Charles Van Riper, as well as several men from the east coast. The land was bounded at its northern point by Second Avenue in Carmel, on the west by the city limits, on the south by the county road that runs in front of the Carmel mission, and on the east by the same road which runs into the roads to Carmel Valley and Carmel Highlands. The purchase was made, in Flanders' words, "for high class homesites." The landscape engineer sent from Mason McDuffie Company of San Francisco was Henry H. Gutterson, well known for having laid out St. Francis Woods.

After William Hatton and his lovely wife, Kate, purchased the land, they built a wonderful eighteen-room Victorian house in the area which is now called Carmel Knolls at the mouth of the Carmel Valley. Today it is difficult for those who remember the charming Hatton Ranch and the beautiful early

The Hatton Ranch in 1918, with Palo Corona (the Fish Ranch) behind it. Slevin photograph.

days of the Carmel Valley to look upon the developments which have taken place there since the early 1950s and not feel both some resentment and nostalgia.

William Hatton was born in Wiclow County in Ireland on June 9, 1849, the fourth of eight children. At the age of thirteen he rebelled against his father's wishes that he should continue working on the family farm. Leaving behind his family and land of birth, Hatton signed on a merchant ship as an apprentice for seven years, at the end of which he settled in Charleston, South Carolina. During his year's stay in Charleston, where he worked as an agent for the United States Revenue Service, he met, courted and married the "charming" Kate Harney, who was herself a native of Charleston, having been born on James Island. In 1870 William and Kate came to California, and William took his first job with the old St. John Dairy Ranch on the outskirts of what is now Salinas. As an apprentice dairyman William gained both valuable experience and sufficient funds to allow him to purchase a 640-acre parcel of the land on which he was working, from the Pacific Improvement Company, along with land just south of the Carmel River mouth on what is now the Odello Ranch.

Part of Hatton's land had once been a part of the Gregg Ranch, owned by Joseph W. Gregg. Son of Aaron Gregg, he was born December 6, 1828, in Virginia, and named after his great-grandfather Joseph Gregg of England, a Quaker. When Joseph was two years old his family moved to Liking County in Ohio, where he grew to young manhood. When he was seventeen he began work as an apprentice at a flour mill near his family's land holdings. In the spring of 1852 he went to Cole County in Illinois, where he superintended the building of two flour mills. Then in March of 1863 Joseph Gregg started for California via the Isthmus of Panama, arriving in Monterey on May 4, 1863. He rented land at first, and then later purchased heavily timbered valley land for $360 from the Snively brothers. Sixteen years later he purchased a squatter's claim of 400 acres, which he later sold for a profit of $7,000. The largest part of the Gregg Ranch consisted of rolling hillsides (later the Fish Ranch) with some 450 acres being valley bottom land which was "in close proximity to the Carmel mission and later occupied by William Hatton." For many years Mr. Gregg owned a fine, large dairy with 180 cows, and was also engaged in general farming and stock raising. His property was valued at $100,000.

Joseph Gregg brought a wife to his valley land in 1869. She was Lola Soberanes of the old and respected Soberanes family of Monterey. Four children were born to the Greggs: Elizabeth Ann, who became the wife of Oliver Thomas of Monterey; Lola M., who married William Garner of Monterey; Mary (Dallie), who became the wife of William D. Steadman (who retained an interest in the ranch with his father-in-law); and a son Joseph, who involved himself in community affairs and at one time was a school trustee, having donated "a primitive sort of building on his ranch" (Bay School) in 1879. In 1889 the board of trustees of the school was made up of John Vierra, C. Machado, and M. Silva.

Returning to the story of Rancho de la Segunda and William Hatton: As manager of the Pacific Improvement Company's holdings, Hatton modernized the dairy operations at the old Boronda adobe at Rancho Los Laureles and improved the stock by the addition of Durham to the Holstein. He built a laboratory to increase the butterfat content of the milk, and at one time it was the best in the United States. By 1890 Hatton had made the Del Monte Dairy the only supplier of dairy products to

the new Del Monte Hotel. With this completed, he built an auxiliary dairy up Carmel Valley, and that building, constructed with a special ventilation tower, still stands today in Carmel Valley Village just before the Robles del Rio Road. It has served as the White Oak Inn, an art gallery, and a real estate office over the last several years.

The Hattons endeared themselves to many, as did their children: Anna M., Harriet, Sarah J., Edward G., William, Jr., Frank D., and Howard. Two other children died in early childhood. Neighbors and friends of the Hattons were the Meadows, Martin, Snively, and Berwick families. Their lovely home was not quite finished when William Hatton died of Bright's disease in 1894, at the age of forty-five. After his death, Kate, with the help of her brother, John Harney, himself a resident of the county since 1881, managed the dairy until the turn of the century, when her sons took over the management with Andrew Stewart. For many years Mrs. Hatton continued to entertain graciously the family's many friends and business associates, and even today there are many who remember with fondness those bygone days at the Hatton Ranch.

The W. E. Martin Ranch in 1917. William Martin was the grandson of William and Agnes Martin and the son of John and Anna Hatton Martin. Slevin photograph.

The land of William Hatton was left in fair division among his heirs. Anna, who was married to William Martin, was given the area known as the Martin Ranch. Harriet, who never married, was given the area known as Rio Vista. Sarah, the wife of Dr. Martin McAuly and a doctor herself, was given the area known as Mission Fields. William, Jr. received the area now east of Rio Vista and bottom land, and Edward became owner of what was later called Hatton Fields and owned by Dudley Swim. (Edward was married to Ida E. McDonald, daughter of Mr. and Mrs. Phillip McDonald, early settlers

Los Laureles Rancho in the Carmel Valley.

in the valley.) Frank owned and lived on what is now Rancho Cañada with Irene, his beloved wife, who for many years was a teacher at Carmelo School. She retired in 1954. Adopted son Flip Hatton was given some sixty-five acres which he later sold to Samuel Smith, and Howard lived for a time on the hill in the old family home with his sister Harriet. After Harriet's death in 1945, Howard continued to see that the house was kept up. He died in a tragic mishap at work at the Fish Soluables Company in Monterey in 1955. In 1963 the house was sold to subdivider and businessman Wright Fisher of Monterey, the original Victorian furnishings were distributed among family members, and its doors were closed forever. Slowly the once lovingly cared for cypresses that had been kept trimmed and in hedge form were no longer groomed, and vandals were responsible for destroying the inside of the house, the windows, and the fences. Also vandalized and destroyed beyond any hope of salvage was the small house which stood nearby, one of the first wooden houses built in the Carmel Valley. It had been built by Henry H. Haight, who was governor of California from 1867 to 1871. Originally Haight had built the little house across the river, but after purchasing it, William Hatton floated it across the river for use as a guest house. The remains of the Hatton home stood in the midst of Carmel Knolls until the bulldozer came along to make way for multiple dwellings and other monuments to man's progress.

Lying between the Rancho Cañada de la Segunda land and the lands of Rancho Los Laureles were some 4,592 acres of land which were given to the daughter and son-in-law of Juan Onésimo, Loretta and Domingo Peralta. Juan Onésimo had a special place in the hearts of the padres of the Mission San Carlos, for as a boy he had helped to build the mission, and they had given him a most precious and treasured violin and had taught him to play, in return for his devotion. Showing their gratitude to Juan once more, the padres also showed favor to Loretta by giving her the gift of land at the time of her marriage. The elder Onésimo lived there with his daughter and son-in-law.

The Peraltas lived peacefully and happily, planting, cultivating and trying to save money enough to purchase cattle. In 1837 James Meadows came to the Peraltas, seeking refuge after deserting his ship in Monterey Harbor, and thus began a strong and lasting friendship.

Born on March 2, 1817, in the small seaport of Clay-next-the-Sea in Norfolk, England, Meadows began a life upon the sea at an early age, serving first

James Meadows of Carmel Valley.

as an apprentice collier. He sailed out of London in March 1835, at the age of eighteen, on the whaler *Indian.* After a two and a half year cruise, under rough treatment, he and a friend, William Anderson, jumped ship in Monterey.

The young Meadows was a "hot tempered" and independent young man who quickly fell into the role of vaquero on the Rancho El Sur, where he worked contentedly for another period of two and a half years. During his time there, he felt compelled to visit the saloon of Isaac Graham, even though it was a known hangout for deserters like himself. On one such visit to Graham's in April 1840, Meadows was rounded up with various other foreigners, arrested and shipped to Tepic, where he spent fourteen months in prison for failure to produce a passport. In July 1840, after much negotiation, he was granted clemency and returned to the Port of Monterey. In 1841 he went to visit the Peraltas, and learned that his friend Domingo was dead. He was told how civil administrator Antonio Romero had made the Peraltas' lives miserable with his constant demands and threats to remove them from their land, and how Loretta had been pressured even more since Domingo's death. It had not been proved how Domingo had met his death, yet all knew that it was not an accident. Meadows felt a great desire to protect Loretta, and found his friendship turning to love, and a year after his return they were married. There was no further question of who owned the land.

106

Isabelle Meadows.

Though James Meadows never lost his testy temperament, he was well known for his generous loans, which more than once helped to see other farmers and ranchers through rough times, along with his words of encouragement and loans of equipment. As his holdings increased to some 4,500 acres, he was responsible for the hiring of many jobless Chinese to work in his dairy. It was Meadows' land, deeded on November 5, 1859, on which the Carmelo school was built. Meadows' sincerity and fellowship endeared him to women and earned him respect among the men of the area.

James Meadows built a charming adobe for his ready-made family, which soon became the center of many gatherings among family, friends, and business associates. One who came often was William B. Post, who later married Loretta's sister Anselmo. James and Loretta had two more sons and a daughter. Madalena Peralta Meadows became the wife of Isaac Hitchcock and continued to live in the valley. Her son, Joseph (Joe) Hitchcock, born January 9, 1881, became a much loved Carmel Valley personality. A remarkably good person, Joe is remembered in later years with his warm, twinkling smile as he sat upon Laurel, his horse, with the ever faithful Pal, his dog, close by. He was an important part of the valley until he died at the age of eighty-seven.

Of James and Loretta's children, their daughter Isabella is probably best known by historians. She was born on July 7, 1846, the date that the flag was raised at the Custom House signalling the American era. It was Isabella who later left us the native tongue of the Costanoan before she died at the age of eighty-nine. The Meadows sons, Frank and Thomas, both lived to be almost eighty, and, like their father, were well liked.

Though not many today know of Satirno Diaz, he was not unlike a son to James and Loretta Meadows. Satirno, or Mike, as he was known, was the son of a Carmel Indian mother and Mexican father. His grandmother had long ago carried stones from the mission quarry. When his parents both died during an epidemic, James and Loretta took Mike in and reared him as their own, and he lived on Meadows land until he died at the age of seventy-three in 1938.

Management of Meadows' ranch holdings passed to his son Edward at the turn of the century, and Edward in turn passed on the land to his son Roy, who was born in 1886. Roy married Rena Beverton, and they raised their children on the family land. The old Meadows family home was torn down in 1924 and replaced with a new eight-room stucco house. At that time it was the property of Mrs. F. V. Northrup.

Born in London, England, on January 25, 1843, Edward Berwick began his business career as a bank clerk in London. In August 1865, at the age of twenty-two, Edward arrived in San Francisco, and almost immediately set out for Monterey County, where he set up stock keeping and a dairy. He nearly failed at his new enterprise, but remained undaunted, and soon sent for his English fiancee, Isabella Richardson. The newlyweds made their home in an isolated area near King City for a time, but the Carmel Valley beckoned, and Isabella expressed her desire to settle someday in such a lovely, more civilized place.

The Berwicks came to Carmel Valley in 1869, and here Edward had unbelievable success. A scholarly person, he taught at the original Carmelo school, which was across the Valley road, opposite the present Carmelo school. At the same time he used the capital he had left from his previous business and land holdings for some experimental farming and planting, having heard from Loretta Onésimo Meadows about the excellent valley soil and the pear orchards which had once been a part of Mission San Carlos. He planted an orchard of his own, using some cuttings from the trees originally started by Padre Lasuén in 1795. The Berwick orchards became universally famous, and his "Winter Nelis" pears were shipped as far as London and

107

Paris, while his vineyards, walnuts, strawberries, and apples were considered some of the best in the country. The original Berwick Carmel Valley home sat off the river bank and was later moved nearer the Valley road. The original little house became the kitchen of a newer one, which included a second story and a windmill to bring up the river water. The Berwicks called their land "Carmel Gardens."

Both Edward and Isabella took active roles in the area's social and political affairs. The tall, blue-eyed Berwick and his small, lively wife were congenial, outgoing people, and Edward, a student of ancient and modern history, with a great love of poetry, was an avid conversationalist. He felt compelled on many occasions to raise his voice in his "battle against ignorance, superstition, and vice," and to express his feelings on "sanitation." A known pacifist, he was given the title of "Honorable Secretary of the International Arbitration Association, which endeavored to show the irrationality and futility of war. He was the author of many articles on his pet subjects which were printed in such newspapers and journals as the *London Times, Examiner, Rural New Yorker, Pacific Rural Press, Argonaut, Overland Monthly*, and the *Century*.

The Berwicks were the parents of one boy and four girls, all born at the valley home: Ada, Ella, Edward, Jr., Mabel, and Isabella. Edward built a lovely home at 1313 Ocean View Boulevard (at Second Street) in Pacific Grove in 1881, and later a second home at 343 Ocean View, both of which have been torn down. He continued to commute from his home to the valley for many years, until he finally turned over the valley property to his daughter, Mabel Berwick Mason, who was part owner with her brother, Edward. They later leased out part of the property for produce farming. Today, Mabel's daughter, Edith Mason, occupies the valley home and continues to lease out the land.

Berwick was witness to the burning of Chinese Village in Pacific Grove, and had this to say on the front page of the *Pacific Grove Review*, as chairman of the board of trustees: "It seems incredible that American citizens could become lost to all sense of moral obligation as to behave as I saw them behaving at the Chinatown fire. Conscience, honor, delicacy, decency seemed thrown to the winds." Outspoken, respected and liked, the Berwicks were very much a part of Carmel Valley's early days. When Edward, Sr. died on January 28, 1934, at the age of ninety-one, another chapter of our local history came to an end.

Chinese settlement at Point Allones, site of the present Hopkins Marine Station. This is like the one Edward Berwick wrote about, before the February 16, 1906 fire.

The Snivelys were three brothers who left their mark not only on the Peninsula, but in the Santa Clara Valley as well. James B. Snively was the oldest of the three, having been born October 21, 1835, in Erie County, New York. In August of 1861, James enlisted in the 38th Illinois infantry. He was mustered out at Atlanta, Georgia, in October of 1864. The life of a soldier left James an invalid, and, seeking a climate conducive to a change of health, he came to California in 1868. He studied law and was a judge in Monterey for a time. Later he engaged in the lumber business with Captain T. G. Lambert near Santa Cruz, at Felton. He later returned to Monterey and was appointed Wells Fargo agent in 1873, and to a position with Western Union Telegraph. He retired in 1896.

Daniel Snively, who was born in 1836, came to California in 1869, and became a successful fruit grower in Santa Clara County.

Richard Collier Snively was born March 24, 1839. He was six years old when he and his brothers were orphaned, after which they lived with their Uncle Richard at St. Catherine, Ontario. After he grew to manhood, not being of sound health and suffering from asthma, Richard was advised to take a sea voyage to California. Arriving in late 1868, he stayed first with his newly settled brother, Daniel, in Santa Clara, where his health improved, and then with James in Monterey.

With his brothers' help, Richard invested in land in the fertile Carmel Valley, in a section which was near Edward Berwick's property. Later, it was Snively land that Joseph W. Gregg first rented for farming, for some sixteen years, before acquiring the property for his own. In March 1896, Richard Snively died unexpectedly at his Carmel Valley ranch.

Daniel Snively came to the Carmel Valley and took charge of his brother's property. He sold a portion of the land, just ahead of the entrance to Robinson Canyon, to Perry McDonald. Later McDonald sold it to a Mr. Payne. Daniel continued to maintain the greater part of his brother's original property for many years. During this time, a man by the name of Sinclair Ollason was in partnership with William Hatton in one of the early valley dairies near Rancho Cañada. Ollason died suddenly, at the age of fifty, of a heart attack, leaving his widow, Mary Bolce Ollason, and two small children. In those days women usually had no knowledge of how to run a dairy, so Mary Ollason sold her husband's land and interest to William Hatton and took her children to live nearer her brother in the Natividad area near Salinas. While there, she met and married William King. Later, after King's death, she and Daniel Snively, who had long been a widower, were introduced through her brother, Harold Bolce, and his wife, Sarah Wright Bolce, whose family lived above the San Francisquito. Daniel and Mary were soon married. Their happiness was short-lived, however, as Daniel died within a few years, leaving the ranch to Mary. She presented the ranch to her son, Stanley Ollason, as a birthday gift. He brought his wife there and they reared two daughters on this lovely spot in the valley.

The Ollason girls had many wonderful memories of their childhood, and Mary Ollason Caporgno of San Juan Bautista recalled her school days with great fondness. "We walked daily to school. The fastest ride we ever had was on a horse-drawn water wagon in summer. We were never late or absent, though we had to run sometimes. We would go to school until the river became too high for anyone to cross, since most of us came from up Robinson Canyon, and then when the river would go down enough we would all go back to school again. Sometimes we would have to stand and whistle or call, and Dad would swim a horse across for us until he could build a new footbridge, which was a yearly chore. We loved our little school house of Carmelo with its wonderful, warm pot-bellied stove in the middle of the room. There was never a dull day in the beautiful valley. What fun! What memories! My heart was broken when our father decided to sell."

Eugene C. Marble became the third deeded owner of the Snively-Ollason property after the Mexican land grant period. Arriving with his family in the spring of 1926 from Winnetka, Illinois, Marble spent a good part of his time during his first year's stay looking for a suitable spot for the family residence and for investment. During this period, Gene Marble and his family also enjoyed "enlarging their circle of friends and taking part in the not-so-serious games of the Abalone League."

Early in 1927, Marble's friend, realtor Trevor Shand, showed him a fifty-acre parcel "rising to a spectacular 640-foot hilltop crown," which lay between Rocky and Bixby creeks some fourteen miles south of Carmel, on what was the old coast highway (now California One). The panoramic vista of hills with the Santa Lucia rising behind them, and the rocky coast line with the ever changing Pacific, constituted "love at first sight." This was what Gene had been looking for. When he bought this land, he resolved to keep it as close to its natural state as possible.

In the fall of 1927, Gene decided on a Carmel Valley ranch property for his family's home. Trevor Shand had shown Marble two attractive sites, one the 288-acre Oliver Ranch, which Sydney Fish of New York subsequently purchased, and the other the 1,843-acre Ollason Ranch, which he selected. The ranch was situated off Robinson Canyon road at the Farm Center "hard by the Carmel River on its Northern boundary and almost to Pinyon Peak [now the location of the Sid Ormsbee fire lookout tower] to the South." The ranch land, some 120 acres of which consisted of fertile farm land, also contained a thirty-acre pear orchard. There were several ranch-style structures which comprised the ranch house and out-buildings, and Mildred Olla-

The home on the Snively-Ollason-Marble Ranch before it was remodeled, circa 1927.

son, the older of the Ollason daughters, remembered her father making Jack cheese in a building near the main house known as the "chalk rock" building.

Under the direction of Carmel designer and contractor Fred Bigland, the main house was remodeled and enlarged considerably over the next six months. A small building near the house became a guest house, and the chalk rock building was converted into a large rumpus room with a boiler and tool room beneath. The lean-to garage was enlarged to a six-car garage with special paneled wood doors designed and made by Bigland. By the spring of 1928, the remodeling work was completed, and the Marble family took up permanent residence. Over the next twenty years the Marble ranch was filled with family life, both typical and noteworthy. Four young Marbles, Mary, Bud, Stuart, and Ted, grew to maturity and moved on to families of their own, but even then the ranch was seldom without visitors or guests. One guest who stayed on a while was Galt Bell, and during his stay he re-created the script of *The Drunkard* which he produced for a record run in Los Angeles. Another visitor to the Marble ranch, before he attained fame, was actor Richard Boone and his wife, Janie, who later became Mrs. Herb Vial. She was the daughter of well-loved author and Carmelite, Jimmy Hopper.

The home on the Snively-Ollason-Marble Ranch after remodeling in 1928.

In 1948 Gene Marble sold his beautiful ranch to Edison Holt of Stockton and turned his attention to his coast property. Eventually, over a period of many months, a plan evolved which would do justice to the spectacular setting the home there was to occupy. Heavy work began, and with the encouragement and help of "old and dear friend, Clay Otto," the house gradually began to take shape. It would be an understatement to say that the house

was Marble's creation. It was indeed a creation from the ground up, as he bought a bulldozer and cleared the homesite and approach road himself. Fieldstone sections for the base of the house were cast and raised into place. "Rough hewn redwood was used for the peaked ceiling, and a six by twelve redwood beam some thirty feet long was hand-roughed for the right effect." The stones for the fireplace and hearth were all individually selected during forays to the nearby coast and brought to the site over a period of time. The front of the fireplace was fashioned of heavy sheet copper. During all of the activity, Gene found time to establish a water supply system for the house by setting a filter tank and pump station by Rocky Creek, which ran freely and abundantly 500 feet below the house. He laboriously laid and camouflaged a pipe between the pump station and the house.

When the house was at last completed, the surrounding spectacular view had been captured. From a picture window which spanned almost the whole living room on the north side, Pebble Beach was visible up the coastline beyond Rocky Point. Each bedroom had its own unlimited view for all those glorious sunsets that Gene and his wife, Marjorie, enjoyed over the years. (A marker left by an 1875 Coast and Geodetic Survey team proclaimed the property to be "Devision Knowl" but it became officially Division Knoll.)

The house can still be seen from Highway One, hugging its hilltop like a part of the terrain, a testimonial to its creator—a kind, gentle, and ingenious man, Eugene C. Marble.

The lovely Rancho Los Laureles, which lay on the other side of the land once belonging to Domingo and Loretta Peralta, and later James and Loretta Meadows, was first granted to Jose Boronda and Vicente Blas Martinez in 1839, and consisted of 6,624 acres. The grant was confirmed by Boronda in 1856. Los Laureles was actually two ranches, the larger joining Rancho Tularcitos on the west, and the smaller 718.23 acres which laid to the west of the Boronda grant. The smaller grant, which was just north of the river, was given to José Agricio in March 1844, and still later was patented to Leander Ransom, in April 1871.

To begin the story of Los Laureles it is necessary to return to Monterey and the primitive conditions of the early days at the Presidio of Monterey, where Corporal Manuel Boronda had retired from his previous position in San Francisco. Taking a risk at that time, Boronda built what was considered to be an adobe of quiet luxury, with its three rooms, dirt floor and thatched roof, on the Mesa, where it remains today as one of the first homes to be built outside the protection of the presidio walls. In 1840, Don Jose Manuel Boronda and his wife, Don Juana Cota de Boronda (who was Gertrude Higuera of Sinaloa, Mexico), their eighteen-year-old son, Juan de Mata, and younger children, Carlotta, Josefa, Isabel, Ascension, Francisco (whose descendants live in the valley as Soberanes), Juan, Tuche, Inazie, Manuel Santos, Juanita, Sybal, Maria, Maria de Los Angeles, and Antonio, all left Monterey, following the trail of the padres, with their belongings on carretas and a pack train. Governor Alvarado had been generous to the Borondas, and on this day Don José would proudly become the first ranchero to set up a permanent residence in the lovely valley of the Rio Carmelo. The adobe to which the Boronda family came rested just below a gentle slope with laurel trees, near the Rio Carmelo. The adobe had been built in 1833 by an Indian family who had taken care of some of the mission cattle in the earlier days. However, Don José and his son had worked, with the help of some of the mission Indians, repairing and making additions to the adobe. When the work was finished, the adobe consisted of three rooms and looked much like the Borondas' adobe on the Mesa in Monterey. The Borondas were industrious and hard working, planting grain and adding gradually to their stock as they prospered. Since milk was plentiful, Dona Juana created a much-loved, round yellow cheese in mounds, which was desired by many households and requested at the many family and fiesta celebrations and get-togethers.

Jack cheese, as it is now called, is a descendant of the Italian semi-soft cheeses that were given to Caesar's armies. The Romans took the cheese to Majorca and from there it was taken to Spain. Franciscan missionaries have been given credit for bringing it from Spain to California in the 1700s. When Monterey had its famine in 1770, milk was credited with keeping the community alive. The cheese was not produced commercially until around 1800. Señora Juana Cota de Boronda was the first to make the cheese in the Monterey area, for the support of her large family of fifteen children, after her husband suffered an injury. At the time she was making the cheese, it was called "Queso del País" (cheese of the region). When David Jacks acquired various dairies, he produced the cheese for American buyers, and it got its name, Jack cheese.

In 1860, the Borondas' son, Juan de Mata, sold his inherited land to Nathan W. Spaulding, thir-

Boronda Adobe, Carmel Valley.

teenth mayor of San Francisco. Spaulding had felt drawn to the spectacular and rich scenery of this yet wild and untamed valley, and he built Los Laureles Lodge in the early 1870s. The lumber was shipped from San Francisco to the Carmel Valley by way of the cove at Point Lobos. Spaulding's brother-in-law, Kinzea Klinkenbeard, was in charge of the construction. With the new house the center of all activity, the old adobe slowly began to fall into a state of disrepair—even being used for a time as a cattle stall. Today some of the fencing built while Spaulding owned the ranch can still be seen along parts of the road, as well as traces of the ditch that was used to bring water to the ranch.

The Pacific Improvement Company became the third owner of the beautiful Los Laureles in 1882, with William Hatton as the manager. He energetically repaired and modernized the dairy, as well as seeing to the installation of vats and presses for the manufacturing of the golden cheese that Señora Boronda had made so long ago. Then in 1896, the Pacific Improvement Company made the addition of several small cottages, and enlarged the newer, main Los Laureles ranch house, turning it into a popular spot for guests of the Del Monte Hotel who desired country air and serenity, along with fishing or hunting, complete with tally-ho's for transportation to and from the Hotel Del Monte.

Finally, between 1903 and 1905, the holdings of the Pacific Improvement Company came under the direction of Samuel F. B. Morse. The accounts of what took place next are all a matter of record, beginning with the decision to subdivide. The first attempt at finding a developer who would consider the entire 10,000 acres at a price of $150,000 failed. In 1923 the land was offered in eleven parcels at sixty dollars an acre, and successfully sold to parties from the east coast. Among those to purchase sections of the beautiful Los Laureles was Samuel Fertig from Pennsylvania, who bought the area that included the Boronda adobe and the nucleus of the future Los Laureles. In 1940 George Sims purchased the acreage with the adobe, lovingly restoring it and living in it—making it once more a family home. By 1926, Frank and Jet Porter of a Salinas syndicate, Porter and Gould, had purchased 600 acres of the southeast corner of the old rancho, calling it Robles del Rio.

Well-known golf champion Marian Hollins purchased the remaining 2,000 acres, which included the upper valley village and the hills behind the Holman Guest Ranch up to the Berta Ranch. Marian, a crack real estate woman herself, is remembered for the time when she took out a prospective buyer, blindfolded, on horseback. After reaching the hills behind the Holman Ranch, Marian removed the blindfold, and the buyer, so overcome with the beauty before him, returned to sign on the line for 400 acres. The buyer was San Francisco broker Gordon Ormsby, who hired the famous and sought-after architect, Clarence A. Tantau, to do his building. Tantau was famous for his Spanish-Colonial style, and shared the credit for the Hotel Del Monte with fellow architect Hobbart. Later he designed the Monterey Peninsula Country Club.

The Holman Ranch was the scene of the only rodeo arena in the Carmel Valley. Old-timers remembered a time when valley herds were combined for cattle drives, "the likes of which have never been seen since, for it took from sun-up to sunset to reach various points to even begin to leave the valley, because the herds were so large." For Clarence Holman it was a dream come true, for in his youth he had been a driver of a tally-ho for the Del Monte Hotel, never dreaming that he would one day be the owner of 400 acres of choice valley land.

Herald newspaper publisher Allen Griffin and Carmel real estate man Ray C. De Yoe bought Los Ranchitos tract from Sam Morse, then president of Del Monte Properties, in April of 1927. Another 1,200 acres, farther up the valley, was sold to a Mrs. Henry Potter Russell, and today is known as the Russell Ranch. D. A. Madeira bought Los Laureles subdivision down to Sam Morse's River Ranch, the scene of some delightful times during my teens.

Later, the Fertig property belonged to Muriel Vanderbilt Phelps Adams, who raised horses there, and the Sanborn Griffins, who became owners of the Hollins acreage, with the exception of a small portion on the north side of the valley which the Frank Porters sold to Byington Ford, brother-in-law to Sam Morse. Ford was responsible for de-

veloping the present Carmel Valley Village. Griffins changed Los Laureles into a popular resort spot, which it remained for many years. It was popular even among the locals, my own family included, who found a warmth and comfortable charm about the place in earlier days.

The acreage belonging to the Porters, Robles del Rio, was a heavily wooded and particularly beautiful 600 acres of hillside. To promote sales on the 75 by 150 foot lots at ninety dollars apiece, a homey, comfortable building, called Robles del Rio Lodge, was constructed atop the tract. Business was slow at first, and then, one by one, cabins for "weekend folks" began to sprout up among the winding roads, and soon homes replaced some of the cabins, lending an air of permanence to the place.

Our family's time came in the early 1940s when, leaving the village of Carmel behind, my parents decided the Carmel Valley was the place to be. My childhood, all of it, was a marvelous thing, and that part spent in the beautiful valley is especially precious. Our neighbors in those days were the Donald Davies, the Virgil Partches, George and Barbara Corrigan, and Cliff and Nadine Garrett. Cliff and Nadine owned the old Bucket of Blood across from the wonderful Arabian horse ranch, Rancho Carmelo. Rancho Carmelo, which belonged to K. D. Mathiot, was on the old stage road that ran between Carmel and Jamesburg, and was California's first dude ranch. Robles del Rio postal boxes were sandwiched in between the shoelaces and pocket knives and were administered to by Rosie. Rosie (William Irwin Henry) had had his nickname since earlier days in Carmel, where he had been a member of the Abalone League. A former Standard Oil employee, Rosie was a part of the "Barrel Gang" which met in the famous back room of the Cracker Barrel for many years. The Cracker Barrel was originally a tract office for real estate, and later, with additions,

"Rosie" at the Barrel in Robles del Rio, 1976.

"It's okay, Rosie. See, he's over twenty-one."

the Robles del Rio Post Office, grocery, and drug store. It became known as such after Beth Frellson, weekly gossip reporter for the *Carmel Cymbal*, used the name in her column.

In those days in the valley, my father would leave my mother and me to go to work in the village (as we have always called Carmel), while my mother and I attended to an endless variety of wonderful projects. In the winter there was the warmth of a fire after a long soaking rain, the inner warmth of sharing hot cups of coffee and tea with friends; there were hobbies and a wealth of mud pies. Summer brought more projects: cooling off in a bathtub of ice cubes; great feasts of boiled crawdads, after an enormous amount of fun catching them; trips down a wonderfully strident river in a raft; snakes; bee stings; and sometimes sitting on an ant hill. I cannot recall an unsmiling face or unfriendly voice. It was a place for families, children and pets, with a camaraderie among those living in the valley that was wonderful. It was a gentle place with rolling hills, oak, willow, aromatic grasses, wild flowers, gentle streams, hoot owls outside the window at night, deer, raccoon, bobcat, and cattle. There was a great sense of belonging. Today, people cannot imagine that from the mouth of the valley to the valley village, we would daily have from ten to twelve wild boar running alongside our car, as there were no walls or fences except where they served a purpose for livestock.

Rancho El Potrero de San Carlos (pastures of St. Charles) began with the original grant of 4,306.98 acres which was given to Fructuoso del Real in December of 1839. It starts on the second ridge to the southwest as you approach it at the entrance to the valley. In 1852 Joaquin Gutierrez and Maria Estefana, daughter of Fructuoso del Real, filed claim, and Maria Estefana was given patent to the grant on June 9, 1862. In 1858 Bradley V. Sargent purchased Rancho El Potrero de San Carlos along with other land adjoining it—the Rancho San José Y Sur Chiquito, and later the San Francisquito. Sargent, a resident of the area for over thirty years, was one of the largest land owners in central California, becoming owner of some 80,000 acres. Originally from Grafton, New Hampshire, Sargent came to Monterey County in July 1849.

Parts of the Rancho San Carlos are hilly, back from the river side, as it stretches along from the mountains to what is now Gregg Hill and the beautiful Stuyvesant Fish Ranch, and opens out upon a place which was once an Indian ranchería consisting of small clusters of adobes, one of which was still partly discernible by a mound and wall until 1940, and considered by historians as a possible second site of Las Vírgenes, considering its nearby spring.

Today the beautiful section of land called Palo Corona (part of the 5,200-acre Fish Ranch) occpies 605.4 acres of the original grant of the Rancho San Carlos, including Gregg Hill. Once belonging to Elizabeth Ann Oliver, wife of Thomas Oliver, the Palo Corona became the property of Sidney Fish on April 28, 1927. Fish, a member of one of New York's oldest families, was a graduate of both Harvard and Columbia universities, with a degree in law. His legal profession was interrupted by World War II, after which he continued his practice until he retired to make his home on the Monterey Peninsula and develop his ranch property. Both Sidney Fish and his wife, Olga, were extremely well thought of and liked on the Peninsula. Their interests in the community were both generous and varied, as were their friends, among whom were Colonel and Mrs. Charles A. Lindbergh, visitors to the ranch when Lindbergh was test-flying gliders there in 1930. Other distinguished guests were George Gershwin, Sinclair Lewis, and Irvin S. Cobb, to name just a few. After the deaths of his parents, Stuyvesant Fish continued their hospitality and is well liked and respected among his many friends on the Peninsula.

The original adobe home of the El Potrero grantees was farther up the Potrero canyon and long ago fell into decay. It consisted of five rooms and a kitchen addition where Indian servants did the cooking.

During Bradley Sargent's ownership of Rancho San Carlos, a couple of retired sea captains, Jonathan Wright and Anson Smith, rented a section of land nine miles up the canyon at San Clemente

113

Jonathan Wright's cabin where Robert Louis Stevenson was taken to recuperate. The white-bearded man is Anson Smith. At the far left are Wright, his wife and youngest child. Smith's wife and daughter are in the middle, and two of Wright's children to the right.

Creek, where they tried their luck at bee keeping, and had a small vineyard, a peach orchard, and a small herd of goats. Of the two men Smith was the hunter, and became well known for his grizzly hunts. The Wright-Smith cabin was the scene of an historical event during Robert Louis Stevenson's visit to the Carmel Valley in 1879. Stevenson had gone into the valley for a couple of days of camping. During one night, the weather took a sudden change for the worse. Stevenson, finding himself unable to move from the cold and the pain he was suffering with it, fell into a "stupor." Off in the distance came the sound of goat bells from Wright's flock, and when Stevenson awakened, Wright was nursing him. Between Wright's and Smith's care, Stevenson was able to recover enough to leave the valley and return to Monterey, but not without crediting Wright with having saved his life, and establishing a lasting friendship.

In 1897, a chapter of the Rancho de San Carlos Potrero story was ended, when Bradley V. Sargent sold a greater part of his holdings to the Oppenheimer family.

Another Oppenheimer holding was the large and beautiful Rancho San Francisquito. Rancho San Francisquito Y San Carlos was first granted to Dona Catalina Manzanelli, wife of Esteban Munras, on November 7, 1835. Joint petition to the land was filed by Don Jose Abrego and Milton Little on behalf of William R. Garner, and patent was given in 1862 for 8,813.5 acres to Jose Abrego.

Southwest of Potrero de San Carlos, the Rancho San Francisquito was believed to be the site of the Carmel Mission Rancheria San Clemente. In 1923

San Francisquito became the property of George Gordon Moore, who bought it from the Bradley V. Sargent heirs. In six short years Moore had invested well over a million dollars in the rancho, building a thirty-five-room Spanish style ranch home, and a race track, polo field, and over ten miles of private road, and introducing boar from his estate in North Carolina. When the stock market crash occurred in 1929 it took with it all of the remaining fortune of George Gordon Moore, and he was forced to sell the lovely Rancho San Francisquito for what was rumored to be a quarter of a million dollars. The new owner was Arthur C. Oppenheimer. He retained the lands as a working cattle ranch, with George King as foreman. King had been a seaman and later a newspaper man. For nineteen years he and his wife managed the Encinal Yacht Club, where he met Oppenheimer. Today the rancho is still one of the most beautiful in Central California.

Rancho Los Tularcitos was granted in 1834 to Rafael Gomez. The largest grant in the valley, it consisted of 26,581.34 acres which were located at the end of the Carmel Valley and east of the present village, extending up Chupines Creek. All who traveled to Tassajara passed through the land of Tularcitos.

Held in great esteem by the local Indians, and later the Spanish and other settlers, the Tassajara springs are situated about forty miles south of Salinas and Monterey. The local Indians were the first to discover the soothing qualities of the spring waters, and it was reported that in 1843 a hunter, while hiking up the valley, met a party of Indians on their way into the Santa Lucia. One Indian, believed to be a Carmel mission Indian, spoke Spanish to the hunter and told of their plan to use the springs to

The Smith-Wright cabin in the Carmel Valley as it looked in 1949. Photograph by Dale Hale.

114

cure a skin disease which had broken out among them. He explained that they would build sweat huts or temescals of mud and branches over the spots where the hot water flowed from the earth. Remaining within the sweat huts until they became so weak they had to be physically removed, they would then scrape their bodies with ribs of deer or other suitable animal bones. Old Gabriel of early mission days followed this practice until old age kept him from the springs, and even then he continued to scrape his body in the old way.

The exact time the Indians stopped using the springs is not known. However, by 1868 a man known as Frank Rust had opened a camp at the site, and in the early 1870s two men, "Rocky" Beasley and "Doc" Chambers, used the caves five miles upstream from which to hunt. The caves they used were those at Church Creek, the same caves that contain several stylized hand prints used as a theme in one of Robinson Jeffers' poems. What tale they tell we may never know, yet the feeling in that cave, for me at least, is that they seem to make a shout of triumph.

The first person to settle the area of Tassajara with business aspirations was a man known as Jack Borden and he changed the name of the springs, then known as Agua Caliente, to Tassajara, meaning a place where meat is hung to dry. In a Government Office Travel Guide of 1875, called "A Handbook To Monterey And Vicinity," Charles A. Canfield described the area and its remarkable curing abilities. Borden had intentions of forming a "joint stock" company for the purposes of developing the area. The first building he erected was a long three-room log "hotel," a shale dining room (today the zendo), and a few scattered cabins along with a shale bathhouse (now storerooms) with wooden tubs.

The journey up the Carmel Valley along a winding trail went past the sparkling waters of the river, meandering through Los Laureles and into the canyon at Robles del Rio and on out through the valley where the silent footsteps of spring still send those wonderful fragrances into the air, stirring reminiscenses of bygone days. Traveling on through the Rancho Tularcitos, the Cachagua, and Jamesburg, the old road eventually passes over a spur of the Santa Lucia, reaching an altitude of 4,500 feet. Finally, traveling southward past forests of pine, madrone, oak, and cedar, it descends into the great canyon where the Tassajara springs are located.

The beautiful canyon setting in which the springs lie is filled with great masses of granite and snowy limestone. It was to this place that the enterprising Charles W. Quilty brought his wife and seven daughters from San Jose in 1884. Improving the area and opening the springs as a commercial venture, Quilty even constructed fifteen miles of road at the cost of some $15,000 (without any assistance from the county), with his partner, John McPhail, as crew boss. The first section, from what was known as the James Ranch, went up to and along Chew's Ridge, and was built by local laborers using plows. Later, as in the building of San Clemente Dam, Chinese laborers were brought in from San Jose, and they all lived at Chinese Camp while they cut the eight-mile downgrade around Black Butte with pick and shovel. With the opening of the road, a wagon could make it down, dragging a large tree behind it, and after 1890, a four-horse, all-day stage made the trip from Salinas three times a week. (Until the 1950s it was necessary to place a telephone call to see if traffic was coming up, in order to make it safely down; then in the 1950s the road became two-way.) Quilty erected, from the natural sandstone of the area, a hotel and fourteen bathhouses, to accommodate those wishing to use some of the eighteen springs which existed then, as well as two large plunges, one each for men and women at the price of three dollars a week, with special family rates. The temperature of the waters, 140° to 150°, was advertised as being "unexcelled natural hot mineral water, wonderful cures of Rheumatism, Kidney, Blood and Skin Diseases. No tuberculars." The waters were reported to be "soft, while containing sulphur, soda, magnesia, lime and iron."

Eventually Tassajara Springs became the property of William and James Jeffery of Salinas, owners of the Jeffery Hotel. In 1904, William, having married one of Quilty's daughters, further improved the place. The months of May through October were those most widely recommended, and they brought patrons from outlying counties as well as locals. There were tennis courts, a bowling alley, and a dance pavilion, and barbecues were held, with moonlight dancing. By 1912 an even better road had been accomplished, cutting the time to Salinas to two and a half hours.

After the Jeffereys' ownership, the springs were under the management of Helen Quilty for twenty-five years. A daughter of Charles Quilty, she married Senator James Holohan of Watsonville in 1931. After World War II, Ralph Meyers was owner of the springs. His tragic death left his widow in charge. She later remarried, becoming the wife of actor Philip Terry, and they continued to run it together. In early September of 1949, tragedy struck again in the form of fire, destroying entirely the old hotel, which was never rebuilt. Later owners were Frank

Sappok and a Mr. Beck, who sold the property to the Zen Center of San Francisco in 1966. Today interest continues in the area, and it is open to visitors during the spring and summer, at certain times.

The old adobe of Rancho Los Tularcitos, now gone except for a worn fragment, was once the way station used by the Search brothers for travelers to the springs. The original grantee of the Tularcitos was a Mexican lawyer named Gómez, and, though he died on his property, the grant was not confirmed until 1855 by his heirs, after his widow, Josefa Antonia Gómez de Wolter, had filed claim in 1853. The property was finally patented, in 1866, to the heirs of Gómez.

The picturesque Tularcitos later came under the ownership of Andrew Ogletree, who lost his holdings in a mortgage foreclosure to Andrew Trescony, the former tinsmith of South County history. In 1924 the largest part of the rancho was sold to John and Robert Marble. It remained in their ownership until recently, when a portion of Robert Marble's holdings was sold.

Perhaps one of the best-known ranchers of the Carmel Valley early days, other than those I have already mentioned, was Eustace E. Swetnam, who came from his native Kentucky in 1866. Born in Bath County, October 19, 1863, Swetnam grew up on the family farm, not leaving it until he was well into adulthood. He eventually drifted west after his older brother, Isaac, had written of the favorable aspects of Oregon and other points on the west coast. At the end of his journey to California, Swetnam arrived in Monterey with the sum of one dollar to his name. He found a job with the Pacific Improvement Company for a four-year period, and also did some grain harvesting in various spots in the Salinas Valley, during which time he met and married Marceline Vásquez. She was the daughter of A. E. Vásquez, an early settler of California and the Salinas Valley, and sister to Mrs. Luis Wolter of Carmel Valley. After their marriage, Eustace rented a ranch in the valley from his brother-in-law. He remained there for five years, until he purchased several lots, valued at $50 to $300, in the New Monterey area, where he later moved his family. He erected a home on one of the newly purchased lots in New Monterey, and worked for a time as a clerk in a grocery store there before opening his own grocery business. Ill health later forced him to sell. In January 1905, he purchased 697 acres of hill and bottom land within the Carmel Valley at a cost of $6,000,

and in later years he sold a portion of the hill land consisting of 610 acres which formed a part of the James Meadows tract. On the remaining eighty-seven acres Swetnam built a roomy house and barn, and planted ten acres of apples, peaches, and apricots. Sadly, at the very time that Swetnam regained his health, his loving wife passed away, on December 16, 1907, at the age of forty-three. Besides her husband she left four children, Elmer Ellsworth, Rebecca Inez, Gladys Mamie, and Clarence Eustace. Mr. Swetnam gained much respect through his public-spirited enterprises, and was personally responsible for helping financially in the construction of several buildings in the Monterey business district, as well as willingly devoting his time and cooperation, gaining him a close circle of friends throughout the remainder of his life in the Carmel Valley.

The story of the Wolter family, whose Hacienda market and farm are an important part of the valley to many, began with a man of the sea. A native of Germany, Captain Charles Luis Wolter was born in the village of Stralund in Throlsenden. He ran away from home at the age of eighteen for a life on the sea. It is known that he came from a family of means, and on his very first voyage the ship was boarded by pirates who took $2,000 in gold from his hidden money belt. With nothing but the clothes on his back, Charles Luis Wolter worked his way up from the bottom ranks until he became owner and master of his own vessel. Eventually he found himself in Peru, where, after a two-year stay, he became a Mexican citizen in December 1833. As a Mexican citizen he was soon sailing from the ports of Mexico as master of the ship *Leonore* from 1833 to 1838; the *Clara* from 1840 to 1843; the *Julia* from 1844 to 1845 and the *El Placer* from 1845 to 1848.

It is known that Wolter became an American citizen in late 1833 or early 1834, at which time he built a large adobe on the site of the old Federal Hotel at what was (before redevelopment) 331 Alvarado Street in Monterey. Retiring and settling at last at El Toro Ranch, a ranch of some 6,000 acres which extended from the present Los Laureles grade to the Salinas River off what is now the Monterey-Salinas Highway, Charles met, courted and married the widow Josefa Antonia Gómez.

Josefa was the daughter of Isabella Argüello, who had married José Mariano Estrada, commandante of the Presidio of Monterey and a relative of Ascension Boronda. Isabella was the daughter of Governor José Dario Arguello and sister to Concepcion, a much-loved nun who took the veil in the old convent in Monterey. José and Isabella's adobe home, which later became a part of the Mission Inn, was full of suitors who came to court their three beautiful daughters. David Spence married Adelaida, Juan Malarin married Josefa, and Charles Luis Wolter took the hand of the widowed Josefa Antonia, and in so doing became father to five children: Felipe, Isabel, John, Rafael, and Mariana. He cared for and educated them as if they were his natural children. Five more children were born to the Wolters: Joseph, who was marshal of Monterey at one time; Manuel, who later started another branch of the Wolter family tree when he married Lucretia (Lucy) Catherine Little (descended from Milton A. Little, a member of the first wagon train to enter California and one time owner of all of New Monterey); Luis, of Carmel Valley; Charlotte, who became Mrs. Fitton of New Monterey; and Laura, who became Mrs. Brown of San Francisco.

It was Luis who continued the story of the Carmel Valley Wolters. He was born in the family home in Old Monterey on August 8, 1849, and was only seven years old when his father died suddenly at the age of fifty-six, on September 26, 1856. Fortunately for the family, Josefa had also inherited the El Toro Rancho from the Estrada family, and it was there that Luis was sent at age eleven, to herd sheep that his mother had also inherited. He remained there for almost nine years. Returning to Monterey, Luis later met and married Juana Ma Luciguela Vásquez, who was born June 12, 1859. She was the daughter of another native Californian, Antonia Marie Vásquez, and the sister of Tiburcio Vásquez. The young Wolters settled on land which was later called the Jacks ranch. Two years later they moved to the 320 acres of the Vásquez estate in the Carmel Valley which they had earlier purchased. Here they established their home and later added more stock and some 113 acres to their holdings which they devoted to fruit orchards and hay.

In 1897 Josefa Wolter died at the age of seventy-seven, and Luis, who had been a great source of pride to his mother, continued the traditions of the family. By 1902 he had established an apple orchard of some nine and a half acres as well as a large dairy business. Fourteen children were born to Luis and Juana. The twelve who lived to adulthood, and the years of their birth, were: Arthur L., 1880; Lucretia A., 1881; Adelaina E., 1881; Florence L., 1883; Agnes P., 1886; Gustave, 1888; Jose E., 1890; Julia, 1892; Luis Federico, 1894; David P., 1896; Robert, 1898; and Irene E., 1903. All except Arthur were born at the Carmel Valley homestead, and all of them displayed talents in the arts and music. Today's Wolter family has reason to feel great pride in

their heritage. The Wolters' wonderful generosity has extended down through the years and seems reflected in their yearly bounty of pumpkins and cornstalks, in fields complete with scarecrows which continue to delight children each fall.

John Freitas, whose name is linked with the early days of Carmel Valley, was brought as a baby by his parents from the Azores, where he was born on May 13, 1871. The family sailed into the port of Boston on their journey west to California. Coming directly to Monterey, John Freitas's father, who had great ability as an agriculturist, received many offers of employment. He was engaged in stock raising and farming for many years. John Freitas's earliest recollection of his youth in the Carmel Valley were of days spent assisting his father, when not attending the Carmelo school. He learned well from his father, and set out on his own in 1898 for the 140 acres of land which he had rented in Spreckels, where he contributed substantially to the sugar beet industry. John also raised some of the finest draft horses of the area, beginning his stock with a stallion Percheron, valued at $3,600, imported from France. During his many trips to the Carmel Valley to see his parents, he met, courted and married the dainty Lottie Machado of Carmel Valley, daughter of Christiano Machado. To the marriage of John and Lottie were born four children: Louise, Grace, Roy and Inez, who attended the public school at Spreckels and later became residents of the Salinas Valley.

The Machado family from which Lottie Machado Freitas came was a family linked in many ways to the story of the Peninsula. Christiano Machado, Jr. was born on July 14, 1838, on the Azores Islands, where his ancestors had lived and flourished for many generations. While still a young man he im-

Old pear orchard adobe on the Machado-Tevis property, 1979.

Machado-Tevis property as it looks today under the ownership of Richard Tevis.

migrated to the United States and Monterey County. First becoming a whaler with the Carmel Whaling Company at Point Lobos, he made the acquaintance of the priests at the Carmel mission and arranged with them to live in the old pear orchard adobe and operate a farm on that property. He lived there for over thirty-seven years. He was married to Mary Dutra, and they had fourteen children: Antonio, of Carmel; Mary, later Mrs. Suckow of the Blanco area in Salinas; Jessie, who became Mrs. De Carlie of Monterey; Kate, who became Mrs. Martin; Lottie, who married John Frietas; Manuel, of Chualar; Mary Ann, who became Mrs. Charles Goold; John, who became a Carmelite; and Emily and Christiano III—these ten lived to adulthood. They attended Bay School, often crossing the Carmel River when it was full, along with the De Amarals, the Hattons, the Felicianos, the Martins, and others.

By the age of nineteen Christiano Machado III showed great aptitude for ranch life. He and his brother-in-law, John Frietas, formed a partnership and raised sugar beets for the Spreckels Sugar Company. This partnership continued successfully until 1905. After its dissolution, Christiano once more engaged himself on the John Olsen ranch, which consisted of 110 acres. During his first successful year there, he added another seventy acres of land. He married Olsen's daughter Christina, and the land became the property of Christiano and Christina. They had three children, Mildred, Melvin, and Christiano IV.

Another part of the Carmel Valley is that land which was first called, and is still referred to, as Martin's Valley. William and Agnes Martin and their six children emigrated from Strahaven, Scotland in 1840, and first settled in Canada. News of the

gold strike in California brought them west and they reached the port of Monterey in 1856. Their long and roundabout journey took them down the Mississippi to New Orleans, across the Gulf of Mexico to Nicaragua and via the Pacific Ocean to San Francisco and Monterey. Undaunted by the trip, the Martins promptly took a picnic of cheese and crackers to a spot on a "gently-curving hillside where they looked down upon the tiled roofs of Monterey." They were immediately captivated by the beauty and the climate of the area, and as the schooner sailed away, William and Agnes gathered their children—William, John, James, Robert, Thomas, and Mary—and their belongings and set out for their property three miles up the Carmel Valley at Martin's Canyon. Their roots became deeply embedded in the land which William had purchased at the mouth of the Salinas and Pajaro rivers, as well as in their homestead. The family prospered as a result of their diligence and hard work.

When not working with his father, John Martin took odd jobs, including one at the old sawmill located at Sawmill Gulch between what is now Pacific Grove and the Country Club. By 1859 the industrious John and his brother Robert had developed a dairy and were raising stock, and had taken over their father's interests in the land at the Salinas and Pajaro rivers. They purchased what is now Mission Ranch land from L. F. Loveland. This land had originally been held by loose deeds belonging to Juan Romero. In 1852 it was acquired by William Curtis. In 1856 it was transferred from Curtis to L. F. and Annie Loveland, and from them to John Martin in 1859.

One of the two small adobe buildings adjoining the mission became John Martin's homestead. It consisted of an adobe kitchen with a cookstove and a lean-to living room of large proportions for those times. Through his generosity and kindness to those around him, including the Indians of the area who survived the diphtheria epidemic that swept through the Carmel Valley, John Martin learned the history of the land.

Stripped of its precious relics by vandals, the mission which John Martin knew was vastly different from the one we know today. Its land long since confiscated by Mexico and divided into grants, its priests stripped of their power, and its neophytes scattered into rancherias, the mission lay in ruins. John Martin learned that the land on which he lived had been used to make the original tiles for the mission, and that the building he now lived in occupied the space used for the tannery and making of tallow. Skilled as a cabinetmaker, John was called upon to build the coffins and to help bury the dead in the old mission quadrangle during the terrible diphtheria epidemic.

On the open range outside the walls of the mission quadrangle were some very large boulders which obviously contained silver. Samples sent to San Francisco for tests proved to be high in silver content, furthering the legend of a lost silver mine belonging to the padres. While clearing some of his land Martin found an old abandoned shaft, adding to the tales that a hidden mine exists somewhere near the mission, and it is generally known that an aged Indian woman, when asked of the mine, simply smiled and replied, "All who come and go near the mission pass over it." In still later years a bulldozer leveling land for the Walker Tract uncovered still another shaft and abandoned mine.

On a visit to Canada John met and married the petite, blue-eyed blonde, Elizabeth Hislop Stewart, daughter of Andrew and Isabel Hislop. Elizabeth, a widow with three sons, John, Joseph and Andrew, provided John with the sons he had wished for, and it was a happy family which left Canada for the return to California. They arrived in Gilroy, where the railroad terminated, and a spring wagon brought them to the end of a rough journey which coincided with the arrival of the rainy season. Even part of John's land was inundated. It was remembered that the youngest of the boys, little Andrew Stewart, took one look at the flooded land and said, "Look, Mother, we can't go any further. We've come to the end of the world."

It certainly was not the end of the world, and the boys soon took to their new surroundings with the typical energy and enthusiasm of boys.

John and Elizabeth brought seven more children into the world. James, William, Thomas (who died as an infant), and Robert were all given family names, but when their fifth son was born, they named him Carmel for the Rio Carmelo which was near the doorstep of the place they had grown to love. The sixth child was Roy, and the last and smallest bundle was the only daughter, Isabel.

The Martin children had many carefree and interesting moments mixed with the more serious ones. They went hunting and fishing, and searching for relics, shells and choice bits of driftwood after a storm, just as we do today. As they grew to adulthood there was time for dancing and theatricals, held within the family home which had been enlarged as the family had grown, and in the homes of neighbors.

The Valley Social Club, now the Farm Center, was built by the Martins, Berwicks, Snivelys, Stewarts and Hitchcocks, among others, under the direction and design of Delos Goldsmith, at the entrance to Robinson Canyon in 1890. It was the scene of many get-togethers and happy memories for the entire Carmel Valley population of those days. The women of the valley would work long in advance of the socials, making preserves, cakes, and other homemade specialties. The entertainment and the music for dancing came from a fiddle and accordion. Besides the good food and the dancing, there was poker for the men and boys, with the day's catch of fish used as chips, general chit-chat and good-natured exchanges. By 1926, the center was considered the best agricultural club in the county. There were also Sunday baseball games, when the "Sandfleas" would get together with the "Rattlesnakes" from the Jamesburg and Cachagua areas and the "Woodtics" from the Farm Center, all congregating at the Martin place.

The Martin family worked hard and prospered. All of their food was raised on their own land, and butter and eggs were used as barter in Monterey for those things which they could not supply for themselves. The Martin children all attended school. The two eldest went by horseback daily six miles up the valley where Edward Berwick was their teacher. The younger children attended Bay School which was built in 1879 at San Jose Creek just about the time they became school age. Fred Feliz was their first teacher there and later Thomas Work's wife was their teacher. In youth, John and Joseph were the more serious-minded, while Andrew was remembered for riding his horse in races up and down Alvarado Street in Monterey with young Spanish boys, and working at the old coal mine in Malpaso Canyon south of the Carmel Highlands.

When Andrew Stewart grew to manhood he married Catherine Roseboom, the daughter of the A. H. Rosebooms, whose little home still stands at the corner of Lincoln and Santa Lucia, complete with additions and modernization over the years. Andrew and Catherine settled in their wonderful Carmel stone house in the valley, later becoming the proud parents of a daughter, Mary. Andrew often had a hand in civic activities, and was vice-president and a director of the Bank of Carmel from January 1929 until his retirement in June of 1940.

Andrew recalled that among the many friends who called at the Martin family ranch was Jack Swan, builder of the First Theater in Monterey. Jack had hard times, and when he was old he would make his way from one friend's home to another, staying long enough to wear out his welcome. As he became even older and more eccentric he also became more deeply in debt. In order to terminate his debts to John Martin, he gave title to the theater to the Martins, who remained its owners for several years. Later John Martin's descendants passed the property to William Randolph Hearst, who in turn deeded it to the State of California.

In June 1918, Mr. and Mrs. Willis J. Walker of Pebble Beach purchased the 216-acre Martin Ranch adjoining Carmel on the south and southwest at a price said to be $150,000. Mission San Carlos was situated near the center of the ranch, which was bounded on the north side by Santa Lucia Avenue. On the east it was bounded by Hatton Fields, on the south by the Carmel River, and on the west by subdivision number seven of Carmel. At the time of the sale, most of the land was being used as pasture for dairy herds.

James Martin, the oldest of the second set of children, was a successful farmer who acquired ranch lands in both the Salinas and San Joaquin valleys. He had one son, James H., who was killed in an automobile accident in the late 1930s. William Martin married Anna Hatton, as I mentioned in the Hatton story, and had a beautiful ranch in the valley in the midst of oaks, with their mixed orchards. They had two children who lived to adulthood: Emily, who later became Mrs. Leonard Williams and owner of her father's property, and Hatton Martin, who resided in Gilroy. Robert, the third son of John and Elizabeth Martin, became a rancher, too, and the father of two children, Kenneth Martin and Vivian Martin La Pierre, both of whom continued to live on their father's land.

Carmel Martin was the only one of John and Elizabeth's children to choose a professional career, seeking an education at San Jose Normal after which he taught first in Salinas and then Oregon. Later he studied law at Ann Arbor, Michigan. Carmel Martin was an excellent sportsman, especially in baseball, and a decision between a baseball career in Virginia and homesickness overtook him in a train station at one point in his life. The desire to see his family and the decision to stay with the profession he had studied brought him home to Carmel. He strayed briefly into real estate subdividing, and eventually he joined Fred Treat and George Hudson, law partners, creating the firm Treat, Hudson and Martin, which later became Hudson, Martin, Ferrante and Street. Carmel Martin's career was long and lucrative, and he was the first mayor to be elected by the people of Monterey. Later he met and married Lydia Wahl, and their marriage brought five children into the world:

Douglas, John, Stewart, Carmel, Jr., and Ann.

Roy Martin, Sr. became an experienced and prominent Carmel Valley rancher. He married the charming Metta Schulte, daughter of another valley landholder, H. B. Schulte, and they were blessed with three children, Royden, Jr., John (Jack), and Ann Elizabeth. Royden, Jr. became a well-known pastel and oil painter, who credited George Seideneck with his success, while Jack took over his father's land and Ann Elizabeth Martin Hackbarth, widowed with one child, later became Mrs. Stephen Grant.

The last of the children of John and Elizabeth Martin, tiny Isabel, became the wife of Robert Leidig, and they had three children. Two of their sons were war casualties. Their daughter Jean and her husband had Draper's on Ocean Avenue until they sold to Gordon Robertson, who now has Robertson's in the same location.

When Frank Powers and J. F. Devendorf established the village of Carmel, it was said jokingly that Devendorf, who knew the Martins well, borrowed Carmel Martin's name for the village. Powers and Devendorf bought all of the land between Twelfth Avenue and Santa Lucia, including land on the east side of the present highway as well as the entire Carmel Point, from John Martin. Then in the early 1940s Willis Walker purchased all the land between the mission and Santa Lucia and east of the highway adjoining the Hatton property, subdividing it into what is known as the Walker Tract. James Doud also purchased property at this time, securing some of the land adjacent to the mission.

Time has changed much of what the Martins held dear. What began as an adobe kitchen with a lean-to became in the end a night spot which had its grand opening with Allen Knight and his orchestra, in January of 1937. It was known as the "Valley Ranch Club" and later the "Mission Ranch," first owned by the Willis J. Walkers who bought it from Muriel Vanderbilt Phelps. After the Walkers it was owned by Margaret and Bert Dienelt. Following Mr. Dienelt's tragic death, Margaret continued to run the Ranch until recently. For years it was a place of enjoyable memories for many, with a homey restaurant and piano bar, with nights of dancing in the barn—the place Carmelites and Valleyites meant when they said, "See you at the Ranch."

Other family names of the Carmel Valley in the early days were Moore, Berta, James, Blomquist, Steffani, Robinson, McDonald, Bruce, Wilder, Selfridge, Tice, McClurg, Scarlett, Fry, Tomassini, Condon, Cooper, McKenzie, Branson, Soberanes, Piazzoni-Forani, Johnson, and Schulte.

Simon Moore came to the Carmel Valley in the late 1800s and married into the well-known Feliz family. Coming from England, with the salt of the sea still in his veins, Simon purchased a parcel of excellent ranch land adjoining the Potrero on the northern fringe of the San Francisquito. Five other ranches lay on the southern side of the Carmel River and the Potrero, and it was said that Simon's was on the best and most fertile land. The others belonged to his son, and to Ernest Michaels, one-time Justice of the Peace in Monterey, Luis Tarango, and Austin Holmes.

Andrew B. Blomquist, who was born in Monterey County in 1885, took over the 7,162-acre Rancho Los Conejos from his father, Andrew, Sr., who was a nineteenth century Swiss immigrant.

Henry Schulte, who came with his son Bernard to Carmel in 1910, established pear orchards which were maintained until 1946. Bernard followed in his father's footsteps and was a founder and served for twenty years as manager of the Carmel Valley Fruit Growers Association, which shipped both fall and winter pears through the Blue Anchor Organization. He and his wife, Viola Lee, provided leadership to 4-H clubs on and around the Peninsula, among other varied civic contributions. Bernard passed away in August 1971 at the age of eighty-one, leaving his wife, a daughter, Virginia McClurg of Salinas, and a son, Bernard, of Berkeley, along with five grandchildren and three great-grandchildren. The name Schulte marks the road where pear orchards once filled the air with perfume.

There are those who remember fondly Perry McDonald and his wife, Mary. Born December 4, 1869, in Ontario, Canada, Perry was a valley resident at the Farm Center and Robinson Canyon for seventy years. He came to California in 1887 after reading glowing reports from his uncle in Monterey, and was a steam engineer in charge of the heating system of the old Hotel Del Monte. He became a United States citizen in Salinas in 1901. For a time Perry was in San Francisco, and during this period he met Mary Lillian, his "Irish Rose." After a long courtship, including survival of the 1906 San Francisco earthquake, they were married. Between 1919 and 1932, Perry and Mary owned the Carmel Valley Dairy Depot, and it was Perry who originated the milk shrines and later tokens for Carmelites. Although the original milk shrines slowly disappeared, newer, more modern ones took their place, designed by the householder, and large companies like Foremost, Challenge, and Meadow Gold drove their delivery trucks through our Carmel neighborhoods. Home milk delivery stopped in early 1959.

Perry McDonald on his one hundred and first birthday, riding his tractor.

Perry and Mary farmed some forty acres of their land as orchards from 1932 until 1966, when Perry decided to retire his Case tractor and the familiar figure of Perry McDonald, complete with hat, driving his tractor through his orchards, was never seen again. Perry died in the valley he loved so much just two weeks short of his one hundred and fifth birthday, leaving three children and nine grandchildren.

Some of the last of the native inhabitants of the valley were the sons of Rumsen Indians Manuel "Panocha" and Manuela Onésimo—Berthold Carlos, Juan (Little Johnny) and Alejandro (Alex)—who together owned a small piece of land on the old Meadows holdings. They had worked on the Meadows Ranch until the Meadows family gave up ranching. Their sisters, Mary, Maggie and Joan, married and moved away. The brothers were well liked and familiar figures. They liked parties and wine, sometimes too much, and they became occasional guests at the Monterey police station. However, they will long be remembered, especially for their continual offers of help to Harry Downie in the restoration of the Carmel mission, continuing to link the name of Onésimo with the heritage of the past. Alejandro is the last surviving Onésimo as of this writing.

In addition to stock raising and fruit growing, farming was an important part of Carmel Valley business. One of the early tillers of the land was Kumahiko (Papa) Miyamoto, who came to the Monterey Peninsula in 1900. He was born in Kumamoto, Ken, Japan on August 7, 1879. Employed first as a woodcutter in Pacific Grove, Kumahiko was later hired by Frank Devendorf and the Carmel Development Company, and he helped to clear the forests for the beginning of the Carmel Village. Kumahiko was not without friends in a new land, for with him were several of his countrymen, eleven to be exact. He remembered well the reception they received when the train pulled into Salinas from San Francisco. Never having seen Japanese before, children threw rocks at them and adults stared. Undaunted, Kumahiko became a pioneer of another kind as he quietly worked hard. Little by little, he and his countrymen were accepted by the community, and Kumahiko became a friend to many people.

When Kumahiko first came to Carmel, there was only one store, the Carmel Development Company store. As he cleared out trees for streets and worked on what was to be Ocean Avenue, he became friends with a small boy who grew up to be police chief of Carmel from 1935 to 1940, Robert Norton. Kumahiko helped to build additions to Chris Jorgensen's studio, turning it into the La Playa Hotel, when Agnes Signor bought it in 1907. In 1909, he began his lifelong occupation of vegetable growing on Hatton land, where the new shopping center at the mouth of the Carmel Valley stands today.

In 1913 Kumahiko sent word to Japan that he wished to marry, and in the custom of his home land, two families agreed on a suitable bride, a picture was sent for his approval, and soon Hatsu arrived as Mrs. Miyamoto. Hatsu spent long, hard hours in backbreaking work beside her new husband, as well as bringing five strong sons into the world: Takahisa (Ky), Hoshito (Oyster), Maya, Gordon, and Archie. The Miyamoto family gained love and respect from all who came to know them well. Their hard work brought the first artichokes to be grown in the valley, and their business grew as their produce gained popularity. For a full year there was a setback for the Miyamoto family when they were told without warning that an alien could not pay rent in cash. The family sadly left the Hatton Ranch. A friend came to their aid, and his name was Carmel Martin. Martin settled the family on his property where the Carmel Little League Park now stands, and the Martins figured out a method by which Papa Miyamoto could continue his farming. He gave money to Andrew Stewart, who in turn gave it to William, his half-brother, for rent of the land.

All of the sons of Kumahiko and Hatsu contributed to the community through their personal and community-minded efforts, and when the war came, Archie and Gordon joined the service. Not long after the war began, evacuation orders came, and the Miyamoto family received only twenty-four hours' notice. They packed what they could with the help of friends, and said heart rending goodbyes. They were first sent to an internment camp in Central California and then to Arizona, where Gordon completed high school. (His diploma is authorized by an official of the Indian Affairs Department of Interior.)

When at last the Miyamoto family was allowed to take up the threads of their lives once more, feelings were still high in some places, but not so much so on the Peninsula. Their many friends encouraged them to return, which they did. Though a part of their lives was gone forever, they preferred not to dwell on those times, but instead were thankful for the good, dear and numerous friends who made their return a welcome one. Papa Miyamoto continued to gain awards for his produce, and his sons continued to bring him honor. Hatsu died in 1958. Papa Miyamoto died in 1975 at the age of ninety-five, leaving four sons: Takahisa and Hoshito of Monterey, and Maya and Gordon of the Carmel Valley, as well as a total of fifteen grandchildren and five great-grandchildren. His son Archie had died in 1972.

I remember a clean, unbroken view of artichoke fields which stopped just short of the Carmel mission where the Carmel Little League Field is today, and swept through what became Mission Fields in the late 1950s, across to the opposite side of the river, where they stopped short of the rise which has

Carmel River beach in 1949. Adjacent land at this spot is a portion of the Palo Corona Ranch and Odello land. Dale Hale photograph.

122

been developed more recently as Carmel Meadows. It was a sea of green from the old mission pear orchard slope to the Fish Ranch and beyond. This unbroken line of green and river marsh greeted pioneer artichoke grower Battista Odello when he came to Carmel in June of 1924. He leased 302 acres of bottom land from Mrs. Elizabeth Ann Oliver, then owner of the Palo Corona Ranch.

Born October 20, 1885 in Micetto, near Turin, Italy, Battista Odello came to the United States in 1909. Working for a period of four years in the mines near Redding, California, Battista returned to his native Italy in 1913 to marry Josephine Carnazzone, who was to be his wife a few years short of fifty years. They returned to the United

Battista Odello.

States and lived in Redding until 1919, when the family moved to San Francisco where Battista was employed in the steel works for a five-year period. The land which Battista Odello leased from Mrs. Oliver was mostly swamp land and totally useless for cattle grazing, but, living by his motto, "If you are honest and work hard, the good Lord will fulfill your dreams," Battista worked until he cleared the land and planted his artichokes. His fields grew and he developed the largest independent business of raising and shipping the ever-popular artichoke to different parts of the world, a position which Castroville was to take several years later. Battista and

Josephine Odello reared two sons, Bruno and Emilio, both of whom took pride in the land which their father had worked.

In 1945, Battista passed the general management of the ranch on to his sons, though he remained their advisor until his death at the age of seventy-seven on May 13, 1963. Battista had purchased the land outright from Mrs. Oliver in 1952-53. In the ten years after his death, plant disease coupled with soaring property taxes brought changes for the Odello family. The land could not be sprayed by crop dusters due to the population growth and housing, which intensified the loss of crops due to the plume moth. The Odello family announced in 1970 that they would gradually "phase out" their artichoke growing. Various plans as to how the land would be used were discussed by the family. One plan, for a $60 million resort-hotel and residential development, created great controversy. In August 1974, the State of California took formal title of some 155 acres for use by the Department of Parks and Recreation, but the battle of what to do with the remaining 137 acres continued. On October 22, 1974, Emilio Alfred Odello died, leaving his wife, Bruna Rita, at the family's ranch home, two daughters, his brother Bruno, and his mother, Josephine Odello, who died in November 1979. Today Bruno Odello continues to await the decision concerning the 137 acres. In any event, an era of farming at the mouth of the Rio Carmelo has ended.

Today much of the valley has given way to housing developments and commercialism, but I carry with me many memories collected over the years—moonlight swims; climbs to the tops of hillsides and mountain tops where the view was breathtaking and words were not eloquent enough; a bumpy ride on an early morning bus to the village of Carmel, and the return ride in the evening; picnics and barbecues at White Rock, Prince's Camp and the Cachagua; horseback rides; trips to see the river in winter flood; steelhead fishing on cold frosty mornings at the river mouth, when the frozen sand cracked beneath your feet. There is joy in having known a beautiful place when the pace of life was slower and more mellow, and the road, still a country road complete with bumps, undulated and curved past rolling hills as it crossed the river into quiet canyons and open space.

◆

BIG SUR

I have scaled her cliffs, and rested on her mountain tops, in meadows of fragrant grasses that rustled with the breeze, and looked upon the sea, its sound carried up to me.

I have watched the fog as it comes to hug the land in damp caress and filter out the color of the sky.

I have wandered in her evergreen forests, and seen the sun's silvery sheen upon the leaves, and known the variety of odors that hang there. I have felt the spongy mass of carpet of soft leaves at my feet.

I have sat on a rock misted with spray, while the river crashes through the gorge to trace its way to gentle pools and slower streams—a tonic in its wild vast features, it stands witness to man's limits.

My restless eye can flit to only one point of contact at a time, as nature's phenomena register their many moods upon my mind. The landscape laid out before me in fertile, eloquent silence—clean, pure, alive—is an argument for immortality.

Yesterday, today—it is always the same, yet always a new adventure, and the thought excites me.

3

Big Sur

El pais grande del sur—the big country to the south. This land, marked and stamped upon a map with the seal of the Spanish crown in 1769, was so-called after Don Gaspar Portolá returned to Spain. One year later Father Junípero Serra blessed the region and raised the cross at Mission San Carlos Borromeo del Rio Carmelo.

The history of the local ranchos began at the time of the secularization of the missions. Land was plentiful, the population small.

El Sur Rancho, an 8,949-acre grant to Juan Bautista Alvarado in 1834, was deeded in 1840 in a 6,000-acre grant to Juan Bautista Cooper (Captain Roger Cooper), grandfather of Andrew Molera. A second grant of 8,876 acres was given to Teodoro Gonzales in 1835. The Gonzales grant, which Teodoro called Rancho San José Y Sur Chiquito, stretched from the Rio Carmelo to Palo Colorado Canyon. When this grant passed from Teodoro to his uncle Juan Bautista Cooper, it became an established cattle ranch.

Captain Roger Cooper had come to Monterey in 1823 on a trading vessel. A native of England, he was half-brother to Thomas Oliver Larkin. Baptized Juan Bautista Cooper before his marriage to Encarnation Vallejo (younger sister of Mariano Vallejo), Cooper acquired large land holdings in addition to the El Sur Rancho, such as the Moro Cojo Rancho between Salinas and Castroville, as well as grants in Sonoma County. Headquarters for the rancho were in an old house in Little Sur Canyon made from timbers brought around the Horn. Juan Bautista Cooper's daughter married into the Molera family, and her children were a son Andrew and a daughter Francis. Cooper's son and namesake, John Baptiste Henry Cooper, married Martha Brawley from Illinois and Castroville, and they had four children: John, Arbolado, Fred, and Mabel. The Cooper house was built in 1832 at the mouth of the Big Sur river land near the present stand of eucalyptus trees.

In 1967 Francis Molera requested through her estate that some 2,200 acres be sold to the State of California for what is now Molera Park. It was opened to the public in 1972. At that time the Nature Conservancy Association bought and held the Molera land west of Highway One from Miss Molera's estate until the State of California could obtain funds through appropriations to repay the group for the land. Miss Molera also donated a beautiful site for the Big Sur School which, at her request, was named Captain Cooper School.

The ever popular Jack cheese was produced by Andrew Molera on land held by the Cooper family. He hired Swiss dairymen to make the cheese. A part of the original creamery is standing today along with Captain Cooper's original log cabin, despite efforts by campers to obtain wood from these sites for campfires.

After J. B. H. Cooper died of a heart attack on January 31, 1928, Harry Hunt of Pebble Beach purchased the Cooper holdings, taking possession of the coast ranch from Mrs. Martha Cooper Hughes at a purchase price understood to be upwards of $500,000. Hunt retained Alvin Dani as manager. The remaining 4,000 acres of the old Rancho El Sur was a working cattle ranch until 1955, when Harry Hunt sold Rancho El Sur to Cortland T. Hill, grandson of James J. Hill, a Canadian Pacific and Great Northern Railroad tycoon.

Come with me on a journey into the Big Sur. To begin it is necessary to realize fully the rugged and often impassable reaches of this land, where it was necessary for the early settlers to take heart in one hand and courage in the other. The whims of nature ranged from rock slides to washouts. At best it took eleven to fourteen hours of travel to reach the Big Sur by wagon from Carmel. There were no bridges at any of the many crossings of the Big Sur River until the 1920s when a bridge was built near the Big Sur post office. Only the hardy came before the days of the coastal steamer.

A group of school superintendents hike the Coast Ridge Trail during a 1921 trip to the south coast. Slevin photograph. (Courtesy Monterey County Library)

The topography of the Big Sur begins with a slow rise of the Santa Lucia at Mount Carmel, until it reaches Junípero Serra Peak at 5,862 feet, near the middle of the range, and then begins to slope gently toward the south on the coast toward San Luis Obispo—one hundred miles of varied geographical features and native species of flora and fauna that surpass limited description and cannot be found anywhere else in such concentration and variety.

The climate of the Big Sur seems to be the result of a perfect recipe. Its weather combinations are high humidity, cooling winds, early rains, summer fog and summer droughts. Winter bursts upon Big Sur with hard driving rains and the Pacific offshore winds in late November and December. The summits may have occasional snow. With the same suddenness, spring follows, bringing its lush new promise, replenished streams, and fragrant flowered meadows of peonies, poppies, violets and ceanothus. Summer is a brief, hot, dry season, sprinkled with cooling fog. In autumn nature's paintbrush creates vibrant yellows, oranges and reds among the green.

Leaving the beauty of Point Lobos behind, we pass those long-ago holdings of Bassett, Emery and Doble, and come to Gibson Beach, named for a man who hauled redwood there long ago. As we pass the lovely Highlands where the families of Victorine and Heath once lived, we come to Yankee Point, cross Malpaso Creek, pass Soberanes Point, and go through Granite Canyon to Garrapata, coming to Palo Colorado. There the log house built by Isaac Newton Swetnam still stands, its hand-hewn logs, dark with age, in contrast to its white plaster seams.

Next is Notley's Landing where the redwood groves begin, then on to Bixby Creek, Hurricane Point, and across the Little Sur, and as we round the curve, the Point Sur Lighthouse upon its granite throne comes into view. The road slowly leaves the shore past the lighthouse and turns inland, passing Andrew Molera Park and Cooper Point. Following the river, we arrive inland from Pfeiffer Point and come to Big Sur Village and Pfeiffer State Park, where the road moves slowly toward the sea once more, passing Sycamore Canyon and coming out at Posts. From Posts the journey takes us past Grimes Point on to Julia Pfeiffer Burns State Park, where, passing over Andersen Creek, we travel on to Slates Hot Springs and John Little Park. The sea to our right now gives us a view of Dolan Rock, as we look ahead to Big Creek and Mining Ridge. After passing Gamboa Point, we come to Lucia, Harlan Rock and Harlan Landing. Once past Limekiln Creek, we continue until we come upon the Nacimiento Road which leads to the Jolon Valley. Our journey through the Big Sur more than half over, we come to Plaskett Rock, Plaskett Ridge Road, Jade Beach, Cape Martin, and the road to the old Los Burros mining region. Next come Gorda, Alder Creek, Villa Creek, and the Salmon Creek Station.

Big Sur above Bixby Creek. William C. Brooks photograph.

128

At the headlands of the Big Sur, a place to feed the soul, we can look down upon the crags to the shimmering sea and beaches below. We can watch the endless parade of gulls, terns, cormorants, sandpipers, grebes, oyster catchers, phalaropes, murres, sanderlings, plovers and willets, as well as many species of ducks, swiftly diving brown pelicans, whales in migration, harbor seals and the wonderful sea otters. There is a rhythm to all this activity, like the constant rhythm of the sea.

The sea comes to meet the land in a swirling, pulsing froth, restless, ageless, ever changing. The beaches and landings are as varied as the moods of the ocean. Some are sparse and sandy, others full of rocks. They are another world of hundreds of species of animal and plant life, from kelp and seaweeds to the barnacles, limpits, snails and hermit crabs, mussels, abalone and oysters. Here and there occasional lovely fluorescent sea snails and sea cucumbers among the sponges lie trapped in some tidal pool, and you may chance upon a shell cast like a prize upon the sand, a miniature world of its own.

Beside the creeks where the land is interrrupted by trickles, fast-running streams, or the Big and Little Sur rivers, you will find a different pleasure in the poppies, daisies, succulents, nightshades, lavender, monkey flower, grasses and black sage, as they hug the land near the sea.

Leaving the sea and lower chapparal-covered slopes and tawny grasses behind in places like Andersen Creek and Partington, with the climb to the giant redwoods, the scenery changes to one of the buttercups, furry curled fiddlehead ferns, shamrocks and mariposa lilies. The ground becomes a thick carpet, as mosses, lichens and fungus spring near our feet to cling to dew-moistened rock and fallen logs, while maidenhead ferns bow their heads to the forest richness there. Garrapata, Palo Colorado, Kirk Creek, and Plaskett Creek all offer scenery unique and varied, an endless choice.

In Andrew Molera Park there is much to enjoy including glimpses of history. After a journey to Pfeiffer State Park and a hike to the gorge, the road at Kirk Creek will beckon, and climbing almost a mile to the summit of the rugged Santa Lucia we will enter a different world, leaving the sea behind. The narrow and winding Nacimiento Route will take us past California laurel, madrones, maple, yellow pines, and yucca, as well as rich and abundant undergrowth. If we are lucky, as I have been over the years, we may happen upon fox, bobcat, boar, deer, quail, and an abundance of lizards pausing to sun themselves before slithering away. On increasingly rarer occasions, it is possible to come eye to eye with

House built by Isaac Swetnam at Palo Colorado, Big Sur.

a tawny cougar or to see a condor, its shadow looming large upon the ground. As the road descends slowly past ridges and outcroppings of granite and scrub oak, the San Antonio River leads into the San Antonio Valley and we will have left the coast and sea to enter on yet another adventure, while circling buzzards, hawks, and occasional majestic eagles mark our passage.

You must see the land in all its seasons and come to know it well to love it best, and yet one visit will linger long in your mind. To see the sun's slow sparkling rise that lights the sea while it bathes the land in yellow morning tones, and at day's end to see the scene as the sun sets, the grasses all aflame, to linger in its mellow afterglow, and to see the stars nearer, brighter and quietly magnificent, is to have been caught full circle in the beauty of the land.

El pais grande del sur has called to many, those who came briefly and passed on to other places, and those who came to build their dreams and live out their lives there, and these are the people who bring to life the history of the Big Sur.

By the middle of the nineteenth century people were coming and going from the Port of Monterey in a steady stream, and some of them ventured south to the rugged coastal areas on the fringes of the wilderness.

The California legislature, always on the lookout for new frontiers, sent a party to survey the mineral deposits of the coastal area. The leader of the party was Professor William H. Brewer. They left Los Angeles on mules and followed the inland route until they reached the area just south of Point Lobos where in his notes from an earlier trip Brewer had discussed the great abundance and variety of flora and fauna. The year was 1862.

Because of the ruggedness and inaccessibility of the coast land, it was not settled quickly. One of the few who came was a hardy soul by the name of George Davis. Davis came alone and built his rough cabin alongside the beautiful Rio Grande del Sur, where he pitted his survival against the land by hunting and trapping for almost eight years. It was said that he arrived with a beehive on his back and stayed the eight years because of an argument with his wife. When he decided to return to her and to his properties in Monterey in 1869, he sold his claim under "settlers rights" to Emanuel Innocenti, a Santa Barbara Indian vaquero, and his wife Francisca for fifty dollars.

The Innocentis lived long in the Big Sur. The 3,000-foot Mt. Manuel is named after Innocenti. Both Manuel and Francisca had been educated by the mission padres in Santa Barbara. Over the years Francisca was to tell of life with the tribe and with the padres. She said that on some occasions she and Manuel were allowed to leave the mission and go with their tribe for a period of time, but she remained faithful to her religious education, and as a devout Catholic could recite the mass just as the padres did.

Manuel Innocenti was a good vaquero and often traveled between Santa Barbara and Santa Cruz on cattle drives. It was on one of these cattle drives that he first came to know of the Davis holdings. Manuel eventually settled for a time at Castroville Landing (now Moss Landing), where his first two sons, Juan and Manuelito, were born. Learning that Davis wished to sell his land, Manuel returned to Big Sur where he became a vaquero for Cooper and purchased the land and crude cabin from Davis. The Innocentis planted additional fruit trees and vegetables, along with grapes from the mission at Santa Barbara and a rose garden.

The Innocentis' first neighbors and friends were the Pfeiffers, who had come to settle in the area. Seeking help for one of their sick children, Manuel came to the Pfeiffer cabin "where he was given a measured dose from a bottle of precious castor oil in a special horn cup that Michael had made." The

Innocentis lived where Pfeiffer State Park now is, near where Mt. Manuel Trail begins. To this couple were born seven children: Juan, Manuelito, José, Rosa, Julio, Cornelio, and a child who died in infancy. As the sons grew they worked for their father and Captain Cooper, breaking horses, cutting fence posts, and clearing land.

When William and Anselmo Post came to homestead, Anselmo and Francisca, both Indian by birth, formed a mutual comradeship that cemented a lasting friendship between the families. Francisca received comfort from Anselmo at the loss of her children, five of whom succumbed tragically to what was believed to be tuberculosis. Beginning with Manuelito, they developed "wracking coughs" that could not be "soothed or cured with native herbs or remedies." Manuelito died at the age of eighteen, Rosa at fifteen, then Juan, José and Cornelio. Only Julio was left. Manuel and Francisca both lived long lives. At the age of almost eighty, Manuel was found by Post wandering around, unable to distinguish fact from fantasy. He was taken to Napa, where he died shortly afterwards.

After Manuel's death his son Julio tried to finalize the claim but died before doing so. Francisca was given final claim rights by the United States Land Office.

When Francisca was alone after the deaths of her children and husband, she often visited the graves and placed fresh flowers there. She spent long hours alone. Many times the Posts asked her to come and live near them, which she finally did, moving into a little cabin that Post had built for her. Francisca sold a small piece of her land to William Post and the rest to Garcia Martinez. At an advanced age, she knew, in the way of her people, that her life was nearing its end, and she called Mary Post de la Torre to help her go over her possessions. After giving away her dish towels and some personal possessions, she sat by the fire in her little cabin and, following the custom of her people, burned all of her family keepsakes. A week later, on May 17, 1907, she passed away. In keeping with her wishes, she was buried in the dress she was wearing. John Pfeiffer made arrangements for her burial near her family, saying "the land is mine and all her children are buried here."

Today the graves of the last Indian family to live in the Big Sur are marked by simple river stones on a flat in an oak grove near the Mt. Manuel Trail. It takes a steady climb of 3,100 feet in four and a half miles to reach the site, where there is a view of the coastline and the Ventana Wilderness—a fitting resting place.

130

Barbara and Michael Pfeiffer.

The name Pfeiffer is woven forever into the history of the Big Sur, the land for Pfeiffer State Park having been made available by John Pfeiffer.

Michael Pfeiffer was born in Illinois on September 18, 1832. His wife was Barbara Laquet of Alsace-Lorraine, France, born April 20, 1843. Michael and Barbara joined an emigrant wagon train in Illinois in 1858. Arriving in Vacaville, California, with "several well selected brood mares," they rented a small ranch and began farming. Their family began with two sons, Charles and John. Through their diligence they prospered; however, their landlord, seeing the fruits of their labors, decided to raise their rent, which was to send them one step closer to Big Sur. Passing through Tomales Bay, where they found that Spanish land holdings made it impossible to obtain clear title to the land, the Pfeiffers heard of the land to the south of Monterey along the coast.

Arriving "lock, stock and barrel" on the freighter *Sierra Nevada* in Monterey Bay in 1869, the Pfeiffers began the final leg of their 700-mile journey. When they reached the Soberanes Rancho, they rested briefly and then headed toward the mountains ahead. With Point Sur rock on the horizon, they descended into the Little Sur Valley, Rio Chiquito, where they rested for the night at the Cooper Rancho. Traveling a short distance farther to Sycamore Canyon, they rested in the flats near the spring in Deer Ridge Canyon. Unsure of the terrain ahead and with winter coming, they decided to remain at the site near the mouth of Sycamore Canyon. Michael constructed a cabin from rough hand-hewn redwood. The area around them contained open spaces or flats, which Michael cleared and plowed. The cattle were doing well on the available grasses, wild oats and water, and by spring were in excellent condition. The Pfeiffer children, Charles Alexander, nine, John Martin, seven, Mary Ellen, three, and Julia, less than a year, were thriving, and Michael and Barbara decided to make this their final home.

It took grueling work and tremendous endurance to clear the land for further settlement and to make the cabin livable on a long-term basis. Barbara, small and strong, cured the meat, made all the clothing, saw to the milking and churning, and planted the garden, along with the normal daily tasks that were necessary to their survival. When Michael was away hunting or fishing, his other tasks fell to Barbara, too. In addition to all the other labors, there was the problem of keeping the stock alive under repeated threat of attack from grizzlies, who on two occasions took the lives of new colts. And from time to time mountain lions preyed on the sheep.

Despite the hardships encountered and the grief sometimes caused by setbacks, there were many compensations. Four more children were born to Michael and Barbara: William Nichols in 1873,

Michael and Barbara Pfeiffer on the steps of their Big Sur home, showing a quilt handmade by Mrs. Pfeiffer.

131

Frank Anthony in 1876, and twins Flora Katherine and Adelaide (Lyda) Barbara in 1879.

In addition to the livestock of pigs, sheep, cattle and chickens, and the meat provided for the table by hunting and fishing, there were also trout from the streams and mussels and red abalone from the sea. What nature, hard work and busy hands could not provide was collected and packed on horses across the terrain back to Sycamore Canyon from Monterey in three to four days of travel time, of crossing both dry and flooded streams, crossing and re-crossing trails and canyons. On some of these trips extra butter and eggs were packed into small oak barrels to be exchanged for much-needed items such as cloth, tools and harness goods. Coffee was a luxury and tea was brewed from the yerba buena plants. It was necessary to plan well ahead and collect what was necessary for winter, when the trip was impossible. When extra money was needed Michael Pfeiffer would make the trip to Monterey for odd work, or to the Salinas Valley, where he would find work during the harvest season. He made many friends and was respected and admired.

Barbara was known for her clever and resourceful ways and her generosity to all who might pass by or need her. Being a skillful mother with a large family of her own, she was often called upon to act as midwife for the settlers' wives. Francisca Innocenti made special visits to Barbara, bringing flowers, seeds, or some useful gift, after traveling the ridge trail barefoot, her shoes in her hand until she came within sight of the Pfeiffer cabin, when she would pause to put them on. Francisca chose the ridge trail because it was the safest in avoiding meetings with grizzlies or mountain lions. She would come early in the morning, stay for lunch, and make her goodbyes to her "white sister" in time to be at home before nightfall.

When Charles and John were old enough they began to accompany their father on his supply trips to Monterey, and John made his first trip alone at the age of ten over the trail back to Monterey. This same trail took the boys to Monterey for their first real schooling.

After the Partingtons came in 1875, the Castros in 1876, and the Posts in 1877, there were enough school age children in the area to warrant the beginning of a real school. The first school site was at Sycamore Canyon at the Pfeiffers' home. They generously housed the children of the different families at their home for the school term. The second schoolhouse was built on land near the Posts' house. It was this little school at the Posts' that Esther Pfeiffer first attended school. The teach-er was a Mrs. Houston from King City, who taught all the grades. The school was later moved to the Community Hall in Sycamore Canyon and was called Pfeiffers, as at one period in time all the trustees, teachers and pupils were Pfeiffers.

When Charles and John were old enough each secured a 160-acre parcel through the "preemption" clause with the option of making "final proof." If final proof were made, then another 160-acre parcel was usually obtained as a homestead where a five-year residence was necessary before title was given.

John was the first to set claim, and the preemption was on a mountainside between Sycamore Canyon and the Big Sur River, while his homestead sat on the river where the state park is now located. During the time he set about to prove his claim, the Wurld brothers, who had adjoining acreage, decided they wished to return to the East, and so John borrowed money to purchase their 160 acres. Eventually John was also to purchase the Snow, Pheneger, and Bradford properties.

In 1918 John Pfeiffer went to Alaska with an eye on greener pastures, traveling with hand sleigh and pack over the Chilcote Pass from Dyes to Lake Bennet. (Years later, in 1934, he took his first plane ride for pleasure over the same route from Skagway.) Things did not work out for him in Alaska, and he returned to his holdings and met his future wife, Zulema Florence Swetnam Brown. She was the daughter of Isaac Swetnam, who lived at the north fork of the Little Sur River, where the Boy Scout camp was later located. He was a brother of Eustace Swetnam of Carmel Valley. Florence was the young widow of Guy Brown, and lived at Palo Colorado with her two small children, Ellen and Kyle.

Florence and John Pfeiffer were married in 1902, and a daughter, Esther Julia, who later became Mrs. Hans Ewoldsen, was born in April 1904. A son, John Ivan, was born in 1906. John and Florence had a good life together, their only real arguments stemming from John's open hospitality to fellow ranchers, hunters, and fishermen who happened upon the Pfeiffer ranch. None ever offered payment of any kind, which put a heavy drain on the household budget and on Mrs. Pfeiffer's patience and stamina. However, the story goes that on a particular occasion a guest stirred Mrs. Pfeiffer's ire with his behavior, and without pausing she walked directly up to him and announced that in the future he and his friends would have to pay for their room and board. All of this of course led to the future resort.

The attraction of good food and clean, comfortable surroundings in a ranch-style setting made the

Wurld brothers' cabin, which became John Pfeiffer's. He brought his young bride, Florence, to live here in 1902. Slevin photograph.

Pfeiffers' resort a continually popular place over the years, with its beautiful climbing rose arbor which once covered the porch.

Across the river from Pfeiffers', in 1908, Dr. Charles Wayland from San Jose established a private campground of approximately forty camp sites across from the old Big Sur Lodge on land leased from Pfeiffer. In 1912, in the area now called Wayland Campgrounds, Dr. Wayland built redwood cabins. Families usually stayed for one or two months each summer season. During this same period the families of the Castro and Post ranches also opened their homes to paying guests.

Over the years John was given many blue ribbons for the quality of honey produced by his bees. He fished and hunted and rode over the ranges he loved, but he loved best the Big Sur Valley. On many occasions John would visit the wharf in Monterey, where friends had boats.

A familiar scene in John's youth was one which his mother described in her journal as follows: "A lion is rather timid, but very bold when driven by hunger; grizzlies were bold, hungry or no, and they were powerful . . . the bear's method was to slap an animal (beef cattle) on the side and knock it down, the blow being so heavy the ribs were usually crushed inward; then the bear tore open the abdominal cavity and the fat off the stomach first, next

the brisket was eaten, always the fattest portion consumed first. If dirt was scratched over the kill, the bear expected to return for another meal. To get rid of grizzlies, the method was to take the fat from the stomach and intestines of a freshly killed animal, make it into a ball as big as two fists, in the center of which was placed a certain amount of strychnine, the ball of fat to be hung from a branch . . . oak was preferred because of the outstretching branches and it was high enough so it was beyond the reach of dogs. The oak trunk was smeared generously with fresh fat, and the bear was soon attracted by the odor of the new kill and soon licked off the fat. Still smelling the fat and being hungry it did not take long to find the hanging ball of fat, and since, while standing upon their hind legs they have a long reach, they got the ball of fat and it was hastily consumed."

John was also descriptive in telling how his wife took care of the problem of unwanted skunks: "She grabbed the skunk by the tail, called for the ax and held the skunk against the tree while one of the boys quickly cut its head off. Held in that position it could not throw its scent and so the chickens were saved and no disagreeable odor." John had many varied and interesting memories about a trip from Big Sur to Monterey. "Driving hogs from Rancho El Sur to Monterey is about the hungriest work a man can do, and this was over such rough country and mostly on foot. It was dark when the men arrived, a fire was soon made outside, the coffee set to boil, some steaks cut from the hanging meat and broiled over the open fire. The men found the meat tough and a little strong, but they ate heartily, then bedded down. In the light of the next day they found they had eaten off the carcass of a mountain lion, the venison hanging next to it was untouched."

In later years Florence Pfeiffer recalled, "when the road was first made up the Big Sur Canyon it crossed the river thirteen times, but the people thought they had really accomplished a great deal to be able to come in a wagon as far as Posts' Rancho. Even in 1920, it took a man with two good horses and a light spring wagon eleven hours to make the trip from Big Sur Post Office to Monterey, and thirteen hours with four horses and a lumber wagon."

Esther Ewoldsen remembers that her parents "had a very good vegetable garden, and a beautiful flower garden with many unusual flowers and plants. There were blackberries, logan berries and pie cherries which all did well at their place. On the land they owned in the Big Sur River Valley (now called Ripplewood), they had a large orchard with many fine varieties of fruit—apples, pears, peaches, grapes, plums, walnuts and chestnuts, persimmons and loquats. They of course raised cattle, milking many in the spring while making butter which was stored for use when they didn't milk or churn. There were a few hogs and chickens also. I can remember in the years 1908 to 1914 that their home was often a lively place on Sundays when neighbors or relatives came visiting, and there was perhaps a short walk to the beach, maybe ocean fishing or gathering abalone or mussels . . . a bountiful meal served at midday . . . young folks gathering in the parlor around the organ to sing together."

When fires swept through the land, people like John Pfeiffer were called upon for their knowledge of the land and means of fighting the fires successfully. More than once John offered his help in what seemed hopeless situations.

In the early and middle 1920s a great deal of interest was shown toward John Pfeiffer's holdings, one man offering $240,000 until the stock market crash sent him into bankruptcy. Another man offered $210,000 so that he could subdivide the entire area. John flatly refused that offer. The State Park Commission wanted the land and promised it would always bear his name if he would sell. After several years of negotiations, in 1934 just a little over seven hundred acres of Pfeiffer's 1,200 acres were sold to the State. John Pfeiffer paid dearly, for he donated half the purchase price of $171,260. He kept his timber claim and 120 acres near the State Park, as well as fifteen acres two miles down the river, where he and Florence built a home in 1936. They lived there quietly until John passed away in 1941. The remaining land was given to the Pfeiffer children, Esther and John, Jr., and a small portion to each of his stepchildren, Ellen and Kyle.

In February of 1937 Florence Pfeiffer left on a trip around the world with the Andrew Stewarts of Carmel Valley. John could not be coaxed to go. While Mrs. Pfeiffer was in China in March, she received word that her husband had suffered a stroke. She was given assurance that he was doing fine, and that she should continue her journey. Then on April 8, word reached her that a blood clot causing gangrene had occurred, making an amputation necessary. Florence sent word that she was returning as quickly as possible, and she arrived back in the United States on April 16, coming by a Dutch freighter and then an airplane.

There were many anxious days; however, in time John did grow better, and all appeared normal (except for some memory lapses) for about two years before he gradually began to worsen. His long illness continued for another two years. Florence, ever loving and continually by his side, was with him

when he passed away in his sleep at the age of seventy-nine on May 11, 1941.

Florence Pfeiffer died in 1956 at the age of eighty-four. Their son John Ivan died in 1973 at the age of sixty-seven. Kyle Christopher Brown, Mrs. Pfeiffer's son, had died in 1936. It is interesting to note that, since the time of John Pfeiffer's death, out of the original large properties in Big Sur, the only remaining ones are the Rancho El Sur, the Post Ranch, the relatively new 1,200-acre Boronda Tract and the 8,000-acre John Nesbitt Ranch to the south of Partington Ridge. Half the Nesbitt holdings were sold in 1954 to two King City cattlemen.

Ellen and Isaac Swetnam.

The story of the Swetnam family began when Isaac Swetnam, born March 8, 1846, married Ellen Jane Lawson, born October 6, 1848. They were both from Kentucky. They farmed in Kansas for a time and then came to California, arriving in Felton, where Isaac was involved in timber production. They stayed there until 1885. They moved to the north fork of the Little Sur River in 1887, hoping to get others to settle so that they could form a school there. This didn't work out, so they then moved to Garrapata, some distance up the canyon, so that the children could all attend school at Granite Creek. Their children were Florence Zulema, Vivia Alice, John William, Lou Ellen, Julia Trinvilla, Leonora Josephine, Mary Belle, Manoah Newton, and Elfrieda Inez. Some were born in Kentucky, some in Kansas, and some in California, and there were twenty years between the oldest and the youngest.

Finally in 1896 the Swetnams moved to Palo Colorado where the wonderful log house still stands, and the children all went to school at Bixby Creek, then called Mill Creek. Esther Ewoldsen recalled that the Swetnam children, "all being redheads," suffered the following taunt from other children: "Red-headed matches, ten cents a pack." It certainly seems mild in comparison to today's exchanges between children.

When the Swetnams moved to Palo Colorado, to quote Esther Ewoldsen, "they had a fine garden, including strawberries, a small dairy for milk and butter as well as an apiary. Sometimes fresh meat from butchered animals on the ranch was taken to Monterey for sale. Trips were made to Monterey several times a week by team and wagon. Overnight guests (travelers) were also welcomed at the log house after it was built, some staying for a week or longer. It was a good life and they prospered, but Grandmother's health was not good so eventually they moved to Monterey so she could be nearer a doctor's care. Yet, in spite of poor health, Ellen Jane Lawson Swetnam lived to be seventy-eight years old. When Swetnams moved to Monterey they bought the adobe on Hartnell Street and had a two-story house built on the same lot but set back somewhat with flowers in front and a small vegetable plot at the back." Before moving to Monterey, Isaac Swetnam had built a nice house for his family at the north fork of the Little Sur and they had a good vegetable garden and more than one milk cow. At Garrapata Isaac built another house and they had a good garden as well as a small orchard before moving to Palo Colorado. "It was all hard work but everyone expected to work in those days if they wanted a good life."

The Post story began when William Brainard Post, age eighteen, and a friend enroute to San Francisco left the ship they were on to row ashore at Baja California while the ship took on supplies. The two young men returned to find the ship had sailed without them. The year was 1848. There was nothing to do but go to the nearest ranch and wait for another ship, whose captain agreed to take them as far as Monterey. Post found his first job with the Whaling Station near Point Lobos where he worked for two and a half years, two months spent at sea. Later Post lived and worked at Castroville, and eventually found his way up the Carmel Valley. He went to work for James Meadows and met and married Anselmo Onésimo, the sister of Mrs. James Meadows.

Both of William and Anselmo's sons were born at the old Soberanes Ranch, which was later known as the Doud Ranch, below Carmel Highlands. Charles Francis (Frank) was born on March 1, 1859, and Joseph William was born on July 28, 1862.

William Post earned the reputation of being an excellent bear and deer hunter, saving the hides for

William Brainard Post.

trading and sharing the meat on many occasions with the Indians of the area. He served as an agent for the Goodhall, Nelson and Perkins Steamship Company and established the first butcher shop in Castroville, across from what is now the old Franco Hotel. The Posts' daughters, Mary and Ellen, were born in Castroville.

Returning in 1877 to Big Sur and the 640-acre homestead he had acquired while working as foreman at Rancho San José Y Sur Chiquito, Post built the original family home with the help of his son Frank. Ten years later his son Joseph helped with an addition. Five generations of Posts have lived in this home.

William Brainard Post died in Monterey in 1908 at the age of seventy-eight. His wife Anselmo had died in 1902. Both rest in El Carmelo in Pacific Grove.

The children of William and Anselmo were solid and self sufficient people and loved the land they grew up on. They worked with their father, and at the age of twenty-one each homesteaded 160 acres.

In 1894 Frank Post married Miss Annie Pate whose family had been among the early home-

135

steaders in the area, on Serra Hill, having come from Lodi, California. Frank and Annie lived all their lives in the Big Sur, with the exception of the time they lived in Monterey so that their children could attend school there. Frank was known as a big man in heart and stature, and was well liked. He remained vigorous and active until he died at the age of ninety-four in March of 1953, having lost his beloved Annie three years earlier.

At the time of his death, Frank Post left a son, Edmond B. Post, daughters Frances Muller and Alice Jargar, three grandchildren and one great-grandchild.

The second son of William Brainard and Anselmo Post, Joseph William, worked on the Molera Ranch as foreman while he helped his father and proved his land. He married Mary Elizabeth Gilkey of Monterey. They occupied the little house in Post Canyon that Joseph built. Their son, William (Bill) Post, was born on December 8, 1896 in Monterey, and he attended the little school house which replaced the original at Sycamore Canyon.

The daughters of William and Anselmo Post married men who homesteaded just south of Castro land. Ellen married an Englishman, Edward Robert (Bob) Grimes, a nephew of James Meadows, and gentle Mary became Senora de la Torre as the wife of José de la Torre.

Joseph Post had many memories of the Big Sur: "Neighbors from all up and down the coast gathered at our place, to pick, peel and slice the apples, to dance at night and sing the old songs, to exchange whatever news there was and to talk about the need for a good all-year road from Monterey." Other recollections included grizzly hunts, all night rides to Castroville for a doctor, the first hand-carved road to Point Sur, which took a government contract and eighteen months to complete, and the early post office on his ranch, first called simply "Posts," then "Arbolada" before finally becoming officially Big Sur. For several years Joseph carried the mail without compensation from the government.

When William Post could no longer manage his holdings, his son Joseph took over the running of the Post Ranch, which at one time was between 1,200 and 1,600 acres of land, including the area of the Coast Land Development beyond Post Summit, sold in later years. Joseph Post died on June 5, 1951, at the age of eighty-eight.

William Post II learned much from his father Joseph. When he was only fourteen he began taking pack trips into the wilderness, and later worked for the Forest Service, building trails into the Big Sur area. While he was in the employ of the Forest Service, word came that he had been chosen driver for the mail stage between Monterey and Big Sur. Bill remembered how his mother, a hearty outdoors person, took on the job of packing for his trips, while he would "ride all night" to reach Monterey so that he could begin the route at seven o'clock in the morning. In 1918, Bill joined the army and almost immediately came down with a case of typhoid pneumonia from which Dr. Martin McAuly of Monterey was not sure he would recover. He did, and in 1919, at a Cooper Ranch Rodeo, he met Irene Elizabeth Frederick, who was working for the Pfeiffers at their resort and cafe at the time. They were married in Monterey on May 8, 1919, and in 1969 celebrated their fiftieth wedding anniversary. When Bill and Irene were newly married they lived in the original Post homestead with Bill's parents. In later years Bill used the lumber from the original house to build the home that stands today behind the cafe and service station at Post Summit, later Rancho Sierra Mar. Bill was remembered as having killed the last recorded bear of the region, a 200-pounder in June of 1938.

Bill and Irene brought two children into the world: Mary Fleenor, who operated the Post Cafe and Campgrounds, and William (Bill) Post III, who became an electronics engineer in Santa Barbara. Irene Post passed away on October 5, 1975, and the property was then sold to the Ventana Company. Bill died at the age of eighty-one on May 23, 1978.

The Post Cafe was opened for business in 1945, and became a popular stop on the coast route. The campgrounds were opened in 1955, and Bill Post III designed the home for his parents on the west side of the highway. In 1968, 160 acres of Post land was retained when the cafe and campgrounds were sold.

There is another interesting addition to the Post story which deals with the Point Sur Lighthouse and its history.

The Point Sur Lighthouse was established in 1889 on the summit of Punto del Sur. Sitting atop its rocky site, its beam mounted fifty feet above the ground and 322 feet above sea level, its light can be seen from twenty-five miles away. The 1,000-watt power electric light globe magnification comes from eight bullseye ground glass lenses in the tower. The beautiful lenses, prisms and polished brass mechanisms and fittings were all Parisian-crafted and transported to America in 1887. The blinking light was powered by a weight suspended by a cable through a hole under the center of the light. An eight-horsepower electric motor now replaces this. Blinds surrounded the lenses to keep concentrated sun rays from causing lens burns.

Post Ranch home at Post Summit, Big Sur.

The distance to the base of the lighthouse is six-tenths of a mile from the coast road. Joseph William Post was given the contract to build the road to the lighthouse point. The contract stated that "a wagon with a four-horse team should be driven to the top, turned around and come down with witnesses present." Post followed the contract to the letter, and the Government not only accepted the road but gave him the contract to haul all the rock needed to construct the original building, which still stands today.

There have been many keepers of the lighthouse through the years since it was erected. The first was John F. Ingelsal, whose assistants were Charles Howland and Peter Hansen. There were three families living beneath its beam from 1935 until the Coast Guard took over its maintenance in 1938. Members of these families remembered when the new coast road was built, and how the sand covered areas the men had cleared, before they went to bed at night, one of the frustrations encountered in the building of the coast route. A lighthouse keeper who was to call public attention to the lighthouse was A. T. Henderson, who was a witness at the formal hearing and Naval inquiry into the crash of the dirigible *Macon*, having been witness to the tragedy.

On February 12, 1935, the *Macon*, leading an impressive flotilla of ships full steam ahead up the coast from the south, hit squally weather at 5:18 p.m., just as she approached Point Sur. Within minutes, the upper fin on the dirigible had become twisted and crumpled, pulling its struts and girders loose, which in turn punctured the two aft gas bags which kept such airships afloat. At 5:21 p.m. the radio operator's message was, "We have a casualty," then, almost immediately, "S.O.S. . . . Falling." The last message, received at 5:31 p.m., was, "We will abandon ship as soon as it lands in the water. We are twenty miles off Point Sur." At 5:40 p.m. the airship gently collapsed, stern first, in the Pacific. Calcium flares lighted the sea as the eighty-three member crew struggled into rubber lifeboats, with the exception of the radioman, who had leaped out at 125 feet above the sea and sank on contact, as did the *Macon*, in 250 fathoms. The cook, who had been unable to get out, came down with the wreckage and was rescued.

The *Macon* was 787 feet long, flew at an altitude of 3,000 feet, and was built at the cost of $2,450,000. The captain of the airship was Lieutenant Commander Wylie, an experienced officer of dirigible flight, having survived the crash of the *U.S.S. Shenandoah* over Ohio in 1925, in which fourteen lives were lost, and the loss of the *U.S.S. Akron* off New Jersey in 1933, which took seventy-three lives. With the loss of the *Macon*, an end came to the dirigible or fixed airship with a rigid frame, and a new airship, the type B (limp), was produced in five sizes and in considerable quantities, and became distinguished during World War II as anti-submarine patrol ships on the shores of North America, South America and the Mediterranean countries. This was the type of airship, without a frame, which my own father flew and trained men to fly at Lakehurst, New Jersey, and later at Moffett Field, California.

There were other wrecks. Official records show that since 1896 a total of twenty ships have been wrecked in the coastal area from Point Joe on the Monterey Peninsula to the San Luis Obispo County line, even after the lighthouse was built, when the sea played tricks and men made errors in judgment. Wrecked vessels were the bark *Robert Sudden*, the steamship *Ventura* and the steamer *Los Angeles*, the *Majestic*, *St. Paul*, *Celia Roderick Dhu*, *Triton*, *Sybil Marston*, *Pt. Arena*, *Casco*, *Scotia*, *Thomas L. Ward*, *Roanoake*, *Babina*, *Orowaite*, *Crescent City*, *Anne Hanify*, *San Juan*, *Rine Maru*, *Nipon Maru*, and *J. B. Stetson*. In the case of the *Majestic*, the Community Hall in Sycamore Canyon where Pfeiffer School was held for a number of years bore the ship's name board over its doorway for many years.

In all things there is change, and the early 1950s saw the end of casual visits to the lighthouse when the Navy took charge of its operations and the surrounding property. However, I remember trips across the partially sand-covered road to the foot of the lighthouse rock, and the cautious climb up the narrow road that wound up to its top. Sometimes in conversations among friends and family members,

137

we remember when the lighthouse rock was completely cut off by the sea in winter, while the road stretched off from the highway and disappeared into the sea before it reached the rock. It is amusing to us that so many statements have been made to the contrary, when so many of us, including those who manned the lighthouse, remember these times well. It has been some years now since we last saw this happen, and every now and then we wonder when the time will come again.

Lucia, as it is named, sits twenty-four miles south of Big Sur at the foot of the Lucia Range. It was to this place, following a brief stay with his sister Hester Todd in Santa Cruz, that Wilbur Judson Harlan came in 1882. He was born December 14, 1860, in Rushville, Indiana, the son of Aaron Harlan.

Wilbur Harlan in front of the cabin he built in 1884. In 1902 he replaced it with a two-story home, which was razed by fire in 1926.

Harlan arrived in Soledad with a German friend and companion, Philip Schmidt, wearing the handmade leather shoes and pack he had started out with. Hiking from Soledad to San Lucas and on to Jolon, Harlan continued to follow the Nacimiento River until he reached the inland side of the Santa Lucias. Crossing the Lucias over a bear-track trail, which was as narrow as eighteen inches in some places and as high as 1,800 feet, Harlan walked onto the Big Sur land on which he was to live out his life, just a mile and a half north of Limekiln Creek, at the age of twenty-two. It was 1882, the same year the families of Lopez, Olivas, Boronda, and Artellan arrived.

By nature Wilbur Harlan was a naturalist and this was to give him an advantage against the land he settled. With no machinery, only bare hands and a mattock, Harlan began to clear the land, using the rocks as a foundation for his home, and the redwood for timbers, floors, frames and shakes. He constructed a cleverly-devised redwood flume to carry water to his homesite from a natural spring. Slowly, but steadily, the 167 acres began to show good pasture land, orchards and the first citrus fruits of the area, as well as a sizable garden. Harlan even produced his own salt and tobacco. He never smoked, but he delighted in giving the tobacco to friends and passersby.

The claim proved, Wilbur Harlan took as his wife Ada Amanda Dani, age sixteen, in Santa Cruz on July 7, 1889. To these two hearty, self-sufficient, generous and respected people were born three daughters and seven sons. Most were born at their grandmother Dani's. The girls were Lulu Mae, Hester, and Ada. The boys were Aaron Wilbur, George, James Arthur, Albert Victor, Frederick, Paul Drummond, and Marion. Each of the children was raised as an individual in the Harlan tradition of self-sufficiency, and each learned to care for and love the land by clearing, plowing, milking, growing vegetables, barley, and fruit trees, and raising pigs and chickens.

What could not be produced by the families of the region was supplied once a year when Wilbur Harlan went to San Francisco to purchase supplies such as sugar, salt, flour, rice, macaroni, thread, woolens, bedding, seeds, tools, and sometimes the luxury of coffee or tea. All of these items would arrive on the two-masted *Bonita* at Lucia Cove. A cable operated by mule or horse was used to haul the supplies up the cliff where they were unloaded, sorted and given to the rightful owners. George remembered two Indians who lived in the area when he was small and delighted in coming to see the *Bonita*'s arrival. They were David Moro and Pablo, both of whom lived to over one hundred years of age.

Over the years, as some of his neighbors moved out of the Big Sur, Wilbur bought them out. One was Philip Schmidt (or Smith, as they called him), his German friend, who moved to King City in hopes of curing his arthritis. Schmidt's claim consisted of 160 acres. In time Harlan became the owner of some eight hundred acres. For a while, Wilbur Harlan had a timber claim for which he hauled heavy machinery parts over a thirty-mile trail from King City, and it was during this time that he built the larger two-story house the growing Harlan family was to occupy. In the new home there was ample room for ten children, with four bedrooms in the upper story, and kitchen, living room and dining room downstairs. There was always room for one

Harlan clan, April 1921. At the top are Lulu, left, and Alice Stewart, the teacher. At the bottom, left to right, are Hester, Wilbur, Marion, Fred, and Ada Dani, who became Mrs. Wilbur Harlan. Slevin photograph.

more, and the one more was usually a school teacher who lived with the Harlans. The teachers provided by the school district usually came from the San Jose area, and two of these young women later became members of the Harlan clan.

It was often said that a teacher seldom left the Big Sur since she was usually courted and wed by one of the young men of the many coastal families. Alice Stewart later became Mrs. Paul Harlan, and Mary Esther Smith was to become Mrs. George Harlan. George married Mary Esther in 1916 after first meeting her three years earlier when she came to teach in the little one-room school house. Mary Esther continued to teach until 1943, taking time out when each of her three sons was born—Eugene, Donald and Stanley.

With a growing family George took on the added responsibility of a mail route which often took two to three days to complete. The mail came to King City where it was switched to pack horses and

brought into Jolon, then along the Nacimiento River and over the Lucias and home. George remembered being caught in some pretty wild storms on some occasions, as well as suffering the dry dust and heat, not to mention the fact that he had to keep track of as many as seven animals when the load averaged about 1,400 pounds a week. There were times when it was necessary to make the trip twice a week, depending on the number of pickups and deliveries. George, it was said, was most like his father in his deep love for the land and for the work he put into it. In 1920 he bought 246 acres next to his father's land, and he would go to work for fifty cents a day for a ten-hour day at the lime kilns when he needed a little extra money.

In 1968 George lost his Mary Esther. He lived alone in the home he had built for her with his own hands and, with a little help from his sons, he continued to manage his land until 1970, when he was seventy-seven. Of his father's land Don was quoted as saying, "I know every bush and rock on this place and love it. So does Dad. The reason that there is an island of open space here is that my father had the guts to hang on to it against horrible odds. Making a living here has always been a terrible fight."

The rest of Wilbur Harlan's children have a story, too, except for Albert Victor, who died of pneumonia just before his sixteenth birthday. He lies in a small family plot in a field near Lulu's and next to his grave are those of his mother, Ada Dani Harlan, who passed away July 4, 1942, and his father, Wilbur Judson Harlan, who died on February 3, 1947.

At the time of this writing, Lulu Mae Harlan occupied the split redwood place that the Harlans

A 1922 visit by the school superintendent to the Harlans. Left to right in front are the superintendent, Lulu, Mama Harlan, Hester, Ellen Fink, and an unknown man. Behind Lulu is Miss Hadden. The other person in back is unknown. Slevin photograph.

had to build to replace their lovely two-story home, which burned to the ground in December of 1926. Hester had her own little place not far from Lulu, and found much to occupy her time, one of her interests being photography. Ada Alice, after many years of homesteading during her marriage to Ernest Delvey, moved to Pacific Grove while their children were growing up. Marion lived in a house near his sisters. Aaron, James, Paul, and Frederick are all gone now from the land they worked and loved.

Of the third generation of Harlans (George's sons), Eugene became an astronomer of merit at Lick Observatory; Don became a construction foreman for the State Highway Department and made his home not far from his father's; and Stanley became a teacher and lives with his family in Monterey.

John J. Partington was born of English parents in Buffalo, New York in 1831. As a young man Partington was an engineer in charge of an exploration company drilling for oil in the Santa Cruz mountains. No oil was found so Partington returned with his crew to the company base in San Francisco. He was introduced to Laura Harmon Longfellow, who had been born in Machias, Maine, on February 28, 1841. In Maine she met and married Franklin Longfellow in 1860, and they had a child who died soon after Franklin enlisted in the Union Army in 1862. While in the service, he died of injuries, leaving Laura alone in the world except for a brother living in San Francisco.

Leaving Maine behind, Laura traveled to San Francisco in 1864, coming by sea and through the Isthmus of Panama. She and John J. Partington were married the following year and they became the parents of two sons and three daughters. In 1873 Partington heard the news of the successful tanbark operations to the south at Big Sur, and he and his family decided to collect their belongings and start on a new adventure in hopes of greener pastures and a better life for them all.

In 1874 the Partingtons arrived in Monterey, where they acquired fifteen mules for the purpose of packing themselves, their children, supplies and household goods on the journey south. Beyond Monterey they picked up the wagon trail south along the coast, and after traveling ten miles they reached the area where the wagon road became narrow, and the rough and hazardous trail began. Not far along on this trail, in the early morning hours, one of the mules lost its footing and fell over a

150-foot enbankment, taking with it supplies and the precious sewing machine which was to help furnish all the clothing for the Partington family. To compound the tragedy, Thomas Slate, who, along with James Andersen and Phillip Dolan, had come to help the Partingtons over the rough trails, was pulled over the edge by the panic of the animals and lay badly bruised and unconscious at the bottom of the bank. Andersen and Dolan rescued Slate and what belongings they could save, and buried one mule. Slate had to be carried to Palo Colorado ranch, where it took several weeks for him to mend.

Three days after they reached the ridge with the little valley behind it that would be their new home, the sad word reached the Partingtons that the schooner carrying their remaining household goods and belongings had foundered and sunk off Point Sur. The earlier trials and tribulations coupled with this latest news would have totally discouraged people of lesser fortitude, but not the Partingtons. Once again putting heartbreak and disappointment behind them, they gathered their family together from the oldest child to the baby in arms, and began to tackle, with the help of neighbors like Slate, Dolan and Andersen, the hewing and sawing of lumber for the seven-room house they were to build, along with the dairy, barns, cellar and school house. The ranges were stocked with hogs and cattle, gardens were prepared and orchards set out, along with vineyards and berries. The Partingtons came to be well known for their abundant gardens and their generosity. They prospered and their children grew strong and healthy in the little valley. The children—Millicent, Ollie, Fred, May, and John—had their own private school and the best of available teachers.

John Partington, an enterprising man who was not content to do things halfway, established a partnership with Sam Trotter just as soon as the government survey was completed. Partington and Trotter began construction of rails and a landing at the foot of the cliffs down from the Partingtons' so that heavy equipment and supplies could easily be shipped and received by means of a cable and supporting framework at the top of the bluff above the cave landing.

The tanbark industry grew, and with it the population came and went down the coast, making the blacksmith shop and general store at Notleys a busy place. Tanbark was cut down when the sap was ascending, so that the bark could be removed easily. Loosened and slit lengthwise, the bark was removed in cigar-shaped pods and dried in the sun. Each pack mule carried 500 pounds to the trail and then onto the landings from there. Partington himself described the operation as follows: "Bark was corded and made ready for shipment. A cable was taken out over the waiting schooners to three bouys, was pulled tight on shore and attached to a large tree. A donkey engine was anchored to another tree and endless small cables were attached to a platform which was loaded with one tier of bark. About six men worked on shore to load the sleds or platforms which were lowered on the cables with pulleys until they were over the deck of the schooners. A cord was fastened so that it could be tripped and the bark would drop safely on deck. The cable was about six hundred feet long and the donkey engine was operated by John Waters most of the time."

John Partington died in 1888, leaving his sons to carry on the business, which at its peak in 1902 included a crew of forty men and produced over ten thousand cords of tanbark. After many years, the Partington sons sold the business and moved to Monterey. Their mother lived to be ninety-two.

Millicent, the oldest of the Partington children, married Percy H. Dolley, a ranch superintendent for David Jacks, and they made their home, where their daughter Mildred and their son Forrest were born, next door to the Stevenson House.

Since I have mentioned the name Trotter, it is time to tell of the man himself. In 1872 Samuel Trotter came from Carolton, in Jefferson County, Missouri, to the Big Sur. He became a partner to John Partington in 1874, having sold his earlier interests and holdings at Godfrey Notley's Landing to Corbett Grimes. Sam Trotter sledded many loads of tanbark down Partington Canyon, and saw to the making of tunnels at Partington Landing. He was a big man whose booming voice and laughter rang across the hills. Trotter married Adelaide (Lyda) Pfeiffer (his second wife), and they lived at Palo Colorado for many years in the log house that Isaac Swetnam had built. Their children were Roy, Henry, Lillian, Frank, and Walter.

Trotter built his second home out of an old barn on the site of the present day Nepenthe. Later he built the log house, originally part of Nepenthe, for co-owners Elsa Blackman, E. Russell Field, and Mrs. Valentine Porter, who in turn sold it to Orson Welles in May of 1943 as a honeymoon retreat for Welles and his bride, Rita Hayworth, for the sum of $10,000. There have been rumors that Rita did not ever stay there, but let me set the record straight— she did indeed reside there for a short period with Welles.

The cabin Trotter built for the three-way partnership was known for many years as the Trails Club Cabin, until Welles sold it to William (Bill) Fassett and his wife Lolly. They turned it into Nepenthe Restaurant after having Frank Lloyd Wright design it for them. Nepenthe is remembered for evenings of musical variety and dancing, laughter and casual meetings of friends and neighbors.

"Old Sam Trotter," as he referred to himself, had four big sons and a daughter, and was quoted as saying that "every Sunday I whip my boys just to keep them in shape."

The large chest in the original log house at Nepenthe, which remained for many years after Sam had moved to Partington Ridge, was put there originally by the Trotter boys—Henry, Roy, Frank, and Walter—who, like their father, were all strong men, and it must be noted that it was said "ten men" could not budge it when it came time to move it.

Sam Trotter died at the Field Ranch three miles south of Big Sur at the age of sixty-seven.

David Castro came to the Big Sur and extended the wagon trail yet another steep mile south. David and his brother Spirit Castro were the sons of José Castro, who came from Spain during the Gold Rush, crossing the desert instead of taking the usual route around the Horn. Arriving in 1852, too late for the Gold Rush, José Castro took up ranching at Big Sur in 1876, where he later died.

David Castro stayed on the land his father left behind, and took a bride, Amanda Vásquez, whom he met in Monterey. They had six children, four boys and two girls—Rojelio (Rochie), Alex, Tony, Danny (who was accidentally shot and killed while deer hunting at the age of eleven), Carrie, and Rebecca. They all attended the Pfeiffers' school in the 1890s with Billie Post, Frances Post, Angie de la Torre, Ellen Grimes, Lupe de la Torre, and Bill de la Torre.

Alex Castro married Maria Gamboa of the Big Sur family, after meeting her at a large barbecue celebration at her family holdings when she was sixteen. "It was love at first sight, though no words were spoken." Alex returned to Santa Cruz where he had been working on the timber lines for a year. "Having saved all his money, he purchased a ring and returned to the Gamboa Ranch where he met Maria in the garden saying, 'I have brought the wedding ring.'" Soon after their marriage they returned with several swarms of bees to the holdings that Alex had acquired. Young Alex built his wooden house, his hinges fashioned from rawhide, and his door handles and levers made of natural wood shapes, while his chimney was made from stone and river rock. Years later Alex and Marie lived in Pacific Grove.

Carrie married Frank Rico of another coast family, from whom she was later separated. Rebecca married Charles Collins, divorced him, and married Manuel Bullene of Pacific Grove. After his death she stayed in Pacific Grove to raise their family. Tony Castro married Margaret Artellan and they had two children, Bernice (Bessie) and David Antonio.

A part of the old Castro property was sold to Ralph Newell in 1932, and on it was the old Bee House which so many years before Alex had built for his young bride and which had fallen into ruins. Newell hired Harrydick Ross, who had come to Big Sur to live not long before, to put the old place back together again, and in 1937 Helmuth Deetjen, a native of Norway, also settled on a part of the old Castro property.

When the American occupation of California took place there were those of Spanish heritage who did not care for the "gringo." One such man was Vicente Avila. Vicente worked on the Soberanes Rancho, later the Doud Ranch at Big Sur, until he moved to Monterey and married and raised his family, still retaining a small holding near what is now called Vicente Creek.

The story which is claimed to be true by descendants was that during the American occupation beginning in Monterey, Vicente lost both his Monterey ranch and home in a wild gamble in a game of cards. Thoroughly disgusted with the turn of events in his life and the abundance of "gringos," Vicente salvaged what was left—his stock of cattle and horses, family and belongings—and headed for the old coast trail vowing that he never again wished to see another "gringo" in all his life. Passing by the Boronda, Rico and Diaz family holdings, and continuing down the coast about sixty miles, Vicente then crossed over to the Santa Lucia range via the old Indian Trail where he spotted a small valley below him. The little valley was surrounded on all four sides by the steep slopes of the mountains, and had a small stream flowing into it. Vicente decided right then that this was the place to live in peace, and it was to be called Sal si Puedas, a term used often throughout California by the Spanish meaning "get out if you can." The adobe that Vicente built served for several generations as the family home, passing from Vicente to Cypriano, and from Cypriano to his

son Sam, who, when he moved to King City, passed it on to his son, Sam, Jr. and his wife, who lived there until the 1950s when they moved to King City and the Pine Canyon area.

An interesting little story about the elder Vicente Avila and his dislike for anything "gringo" was relayed through the years. The story says that one day Vicente sent his son, Bautista, to Monterey for the purchase of a new wagon. Not knowing that the new wagon required axle grease, the young Bautista drove it home, burning out all four axles. When the elder Avila heard the news, he simply hauled the wagon off the side of the road, leaving it there in total disgust as another "gringo" invention, while he returned to the use of the carretas or ox carts.

Thomas Benton Slate and Phillip Dolan both came to the Big Sur as bachelors in 1876, and the two became good friends and neighbors.

Thomas Slate originally came to the Big Sur at the age of sixteen when he developed the "rumatiz" (arthritis) as a wood cutter working in the Santa Cruz mountains above Felton, in connection with the "Jerkline teams" in 1870. He had heard of the hot springs through the Indians of the area.

Five years later Thomas made arrangements for the purchase of a thousand acres from B. S. Andrews, who had acquired large holdings through "squatter's rights." Thomas brought with him some cattle and horses to stock his land. His friends, Phillip Dolan and William (Bill) Waters, offered their assistance when possible.

Thomas Slate was persistent and a hard worker, and developed his land and built a much admired home for the lovely Bersabe Remiga Soberanes, whom he had long courted, having met her on the Soberanes Ranch, where he had worked at roundup time.

Years later, in 1893, Thomas Slate sold his land to John Little. Later a relative of John, Milton Little, retained a portion of the original property for several years. Some thirteen acres had been purchased by an Elizabeth Livermore. However, before her death her portion of land had also been donated to the State while she retained a life tenancy to insure the total twenty-one acre John Little Park. John Little had also sold a portion of the land which he had purchased from Slate to Dr. H. C. Murphy, a retired Salinas physician with great plans for a future sanitorium on the land.

In 1939 Dr. Murphy built his new resort which he referred to as "Tok-i-Tok." It was designed by Palme, constructed by Maynard McIntyre of Carmel, and plumbed by Edward Burnam of Carmel. Belvail Electric of Carmel did the wiring on several small redwood cabins and open air baths, with old porcelain bathtubs set on platforms in the areas over the cliffs. Since the water turned green if it was left to stand for very long, it was considered a courtesy to clean and at least partially refill the tubs so that the water would not be too hot and thus suitable for the next person. A system to alert bathers that tubs were in use (before they reached the tubs) was devised—it consisted of a raised flag along the path to the tubs.

After selling their holdings in the Big Sur to John Little, the Slates moved to Monterey, where they built their home on Pacific Street next door to "The House with the Blue Gate," the lovely Casa Soberanes. The Slates continued to return to the Big Sur for gala family events often held at the Soberanes Rancho, and also to visit the Waters family who had been their good friends and neighbors.

The first family of American-born stock to come to the Big Sur were the Danis. Gabriel Dani had been a scout for early wagon trains across the United States, and it was on one of these trains that he met his future wife, Elizabeth.

Born in England, and having arrived in St. Louis in 1860, Elizabeth joined a wagon train for Salt Lake City. The Danis were married in Missouri, on the way to Salt Lake City, where they lived for a period of time. It was there in Utah, as they were leaving in 1867, that Ada Amanda Dani was born in a covered wagon. After her birth, the Danis made their way to California. They settled in San Juan Bautista until Ada was nine, then in 1876 set out for Soledad. Uncomfortably cramped in a stagecoach with their family, which now numbered five children, they had three days of dangerous travel before they reached the Hotel Dutton at Jolon, where they rested. The hardest part of the journey still ahead, they set out from Jolon on the dusty, dangerous ascent into the Santa Lucia. The children, who were strapped onto horses, clung to the horses' manes as they all climbed steadily higher. Years later, Ada Dani recalled vividly how on that climb her feet were "often at the level of the horse's ears." After their tortuous journey, the Dani family finally arrived at the site of their future homestead, which today is the site of the Camaldoli Hermitage. A total of almost ten years was to pass before another American came to settle near the Danis.

Gabriel and Elizabeth's first Big Sur home and their furniture were crudely constructed of young redwood trees. It was difficult, dirty, backbreaking

The Dutton Hotel in Jolon, 1896.

work for the Danis, but both were strong willed and physically able individuals who were willing to learn all the skills necessary to live in this new way of life they had chosen. The Borondas, their neighbors, were all affable, generous and extremely helpful whenever possible, showing Gabriel the best ways to plant, plow, and harvest in the Big Sur climate. Elizabeth, besides raising eight children—Ada, Jane, Alvin, Riel, Mary, Amelia, Anthony, and Lucia—learned to milk cows, feed hogs and attend to the regular duties of sewing, washing, mending, cooking and chopping wood. She also found time to help others in their times of need or illness, often acting as a midwife.

The Danis' success inspired the Nes Swending family, cousins of Elizabeth, to come to the area. They settled just above the Waters' holdings.

The Dani children all married into families of other early day coastal settlers. A granddaughter of Gabriel and Elizabeth, Electa Dani Grimes, was said to be the best woman with a horse that any of the south coast families ever had. The Dani children married into the families of Lopez, Twitchell, Pfeiffer, Harlan, Gamboa, and Boronda, and when the Pfeiffer family of Big Sur had a reunion in June of 1968, there were present-day Danis from King City, Big Sur, and various other parts of California, Indianapolis, Idaho, Alaska, and Oklahoma. Other names at the reunion, besides Pfeiffer and Dani, were Brazil, Trotter, Ewoldsen, de la Torre, Grimes, Fortman, Kelch, and Veach.

On May 24, 1852, Edward Alvin Grimes was born in England. Arriving in San Francisco in the early 1870s, he went to work for his uncle, James Meadows. In 1879, while working for his uncle, he met and married Ellen Post, and they homesteaded in 1880 at what is now called Grimes Point. Grimes

143

Canyon, named after Edward, is four miles south of the old Post Ranch.

Of the marriage between Edward and Ellen, there were three children, Isabel, Edward Robert, and Ellen. The children had a wonderful childhood, and in later years recalled many fond memories. As they grew they attended the school on the Post Ranch, originally known as the Pfeiffer school, with the Pfeiffer, de la Torre, and Castro children. The students attending the little school in 1890 were William (Billie) Post, Jr., Francis Post, Angie de la Torre, Ellen Grimes, Lupe de la Torre, Rebecca Castro, and Rojelio Castro. The teacher was Nimpha Narves, who later became Mrs. Jack McWay.

Ellen Grimes Peace kept a journal of family events, and she recalled in particular the family trip to Monterey each Fourth of July by horse and wagon. Each year the family would stay at the old Underwood Hotel on Alvarado Street, which at that time was owned by José de la Torre, who was married to Ellen Post Grimes' sister Mary.

Edward Grimes suffered ill health in 1905 and was forced to sell his holdings, which he did, to Alejandrino Boronda and Castro. They later sold to a Mr. Hathaway. Edward and Ellen settled in their new home on Belden Street just before the twelfth birthday of their daughter Ellen. Ellen, who was named after her mother "at Father's insistence," and her brother and sister all attended school in Monterey. In later years Ellen recalled when she began work with the telephone system in Pacific Grove, and how, after ten years with them, she was transferred to Monterey where the new "light system" had just been installed on Alvarado Street. Later she met Robert F. Peace, who was with the Eighth Infantry at the Presidio of Monterey. During World War I, on August 28, 1917, they were married. In 1967 they celebrated fifty years of married life. They had one child, a son, Franklin Peace, who was living in the Carmel Valley in 1978.

Edward Grimes died April 8, 1921. Edward Grimes' nephew was Corbett Grimes, who came from England and later sent for his sister Ethel. Corbett Grimes married Electa Dani, daughter of Katherine Pfeiffer and Alvin Dani.

In 1883, Peter G. Andersen set up homestead on 240 acres on what is now called "Anderson" Canyon. Peter Andersen's nearest neighbor apart from his brother Jim, who owned some five hundred acres nearby, was the McWay family. Peter Andersen was involved in the tanbark industry for almost

seven years before he left the Big Sur, selling his land in 1889 to a man whose name he could not remember years later.

At the time of a return visit to the Big Sur, almost fifty years later, Andersen expressed his amazement over the spelling of his last name, which somehow ended up on the maps with an "o" instead of an "e," and the most noticeable of all changes, the present coast road, which had been the narrow wagon road those many years before. He and John Pfeiffer, after nearly fifty years, enjoyed a visit and noted all the changes that had occurred. Peter Andersen recalled putting in all the cables and booms necessary to load and unload the goods and supplies when the steamers from San Francisco anchored off shore, because it had cost him eight dollars a ton to get all his machinery, plows and other cargo up and down from the landing. The spot that marked Andersen's home looked entirely different, as the hundreds of tanbark trees in the canyon had all been cut down and shipped away long ago, and there were no traces to recall the labor camps' having been there or the men who worked on the road.

Like Peter Andersen and others, the McWay family did not stay in the Big Sur once the tanbark period passed, leaving only their names behind to become a part of the history of the Big Sur. The McWay children were Jack, Katie, Nettie and Rachel. Nettie married John Little and lived for a long time at Slates before moving to Monterey with their two sons, John, Jr. and Deal. Rachel became John Waters' wife.

The Waters ranch was called Saddle Rock Ranch because of the shape of the rock at the mouth of McWay Canyon, named after the McWay family. Saddle Rock Ranch was later managed for twelve years by Hans and Esther Ewoldsen, and today is known as Julia Pfeiffer Burns State Park.

The Waters story began in 1868 when William and his wife Mary Ann sailed on the S.S. *Golden Gate* with their five children, Joseph, Martha, John, William, Jr., and Edmond, out of New Bedford, Massachusetts. Arriving in San Francisco, they were greeted by a relative already living on the coast, Anne Cerina Heath, who journeyed with them to what is now Carmel Highlands. The property they homesteaded, sold to Thomas Work in 1890, is where the present Highlands Inn stands.

Of the Waters children, John and Joseph took "settlers claims" at Saddle Rock Landing eighteen miles south of Pfeiffers'. John Waters took a bride,

Rachel McWay. Joseph never married, and William, Jr. became a doctor. Edmond Smith Waters later went to King City, as one of the Dani sons had done, and there rented 3,000 acres of land on the Rancho San Bernabe, where he raised hops, cattle, barley and alfalfa, and also operated a dairy.

On September 17, 1890, Edmond married Rosa Laura Soberanes, whom he had long courted. Edmond and Rosa had one child, a son whom they named Edward, born in 1892. Edward's uncle, Ezequiel Soberanes, Rosa's brother, and his wife were his godparents. Edward had many recollections of his youth, one of which was the time he helped his uncle John Waters fill five-gallon cans of honey and load them onto horses and burros for the trip to Posts, where William Post had established the original post office, known simply as "Post," then "Arbolado," and finally Big Sur. The honey came from the 125 swarms on the property of Joe and John Waters at Saddle Rock. Edward remembered that this particular job had to be done every other week when the mail was collected for the return trip to Monterey. The honey was sold in exchange for needed supplies and groceries. Edward also recalled that the exchange was not always fairly balanced, yet "no one stood short." On one occasion "we got fifty pounds of butter in exchange. That butter was cut into slabs and put into brine crocks and placed in the streams where it stayed ice cold until needed." It was difficult to raise some fruits at Saddle Rock, and the honey was also a means of exchange for canned fruits.

Edward's youth was not different from that of the other early day settlers' children, including both hard work and fun, but he remembered with particular fondness the twice a year meetings when all the coast ranchers collected at Malpaso Canyon to break horses and socialize. The Waters family would

Coal shed, Malpaso, February 13, 1919. Slevin photograph.

first meet up with their neighbors the Victorines and then set out for Malpaso. Edward's father could easily be coaxed to bring his accordion to play at such affairs.

Edward Waters married Juanita Agnes Soberanes of the Soledad Soberanes family, and they lived in King City. Years later Edward still had the accordion his father had played so many years ago at those happy get-togethers. At the time of this writing, Violet Waters King told me her father Edward died in January 1973 and is buried in the King City family plot, and her mother (eighty-six in 1977) was still in good health, though not strong.

On April 22, 1837, in Livingstone County, New York, Charles H. Bixby, the son of William Bixby and Sarah Adams (cousin of John Quincy Adams), was born. William Bixby, an enterprising man, built for himself a manufacturing business in textiles. His woolens in particular earned him an enviable reputation among his colleagues.

On the advice of Sarah Bixby's doctor, William sold his woolen mill and they began their journey west with a very ill Sarah riding in the wagon. Her health improved gradually and she was walking several miles a day by the time they reached Salt Lake City, where they remained for a short time. They finally arrived in Placerville, California, where Bixby tried his hand at mining, which led to the ownership of a grocery store and hotel.

In the meantime, young Charles Bixby had traveled on the long overland journey with a wagon train to California, where he stayed for five years before returning to his native New York.

In 1863 Charles came west again and joined the Seventh Arizona Volunteers. After he was mustered out he set up stock raising in Healdsburg, California. Five years later, in 1868, he made his way to Monterey County.

Charles followed in his father's footsteps in his business ability, and he soon established a prolific lumber industry, logging with oxen during the tanbark period in Big Sur. He acquired several acres of land where he built his home on a gentle slope above what is known as Bixby Canyon, just above Bixby Landing, where he also established a school and mail stop. During this time, Charles Bixby took on two partners, one in business, a man called McClellan, and a wife, Miss Barbara Sammons of Alisal, the daughter of Ira Sammons, who himself crossed the plains from New York in 1864.

Bixby and McClellan built a new sawmill, with a landing and loading chute, from which great quantities of redwood, oak, shingles and shakes, along with tanbark and railroad ties, were shipped. The area was to be known later as Mill Creek.

In 1870 Charles and Barbara sent word to the older Bixbys in Placerville (old Hangtown), asking them to join them in the Big Sur, which they did. Charles and his father built the road from the Carmel mission to Bixby Landing some eighteen miles down the coast with a total of twenty-three bridges crossing the creeks.

William died at the age of eighty-seven, and his wife at seventy-five. Both were buried in the Big Sur.

Charles Bixby was roadmaster for the building of the road to the Big Sur lighthouse in 1888. He hired men at a dollar and twenty-five cents a day, plus food and a place to sleep.

Over the years Charles accumulated 1,100 acres of Big Sur land and large investments in livestock. When the lumber supply slowly depleted, and the small community at Bixby Landing began to dissipate, he sold out his holdings and moved to Monterey, where he lived out the remainder of his life.

The area around Bixby Landing was quiet for some while after the tanbark era; then between 1904 and 1910 the forest again filled with the sound of wood being timbered and shipped, when the Monterey Lime Company operated at Bixby Point. From Long Ridge, by a chute consisting of elaborate pulleys and cables, lime was transported in kegs down from the kilns to the warehouses built at Bixby Point. Loading three barrels of burnt lime at a time on trams to the company boats below kept a crew of Chinese laborers busy. The manager of the company was Frank D. Shields. The kilns produced an estimated 75,000 tons of limestone during their period of operation. Eventually the lack of readily available wood for firing the kilns brought to an end the Monterey Lime Company, but the mail stage still stopped at Hogues near Bixby Creek, where the early post office was, in the little, sharply-roofed building.

Charles and Barbara Bixby had two children, George and Alta. George married Reba Knox-Andrews, who was the sister of Bart Knox of King City and the daughter of Charles W. Knox, an early settler of Hilby Avenue in Seaside, California. Alta Bixby became Mrs. Charles Gregg, wife of a county road builder in Monterey County.

Just before the turn of the century Dr. John L. D. Roberts dreamed a dream for the coast which came true when the construction of 143 miles of roadway was completed in 1937. Dr. Roberts had come to Monterey in 1887 at the age of twenty-six, and he was to say, "All I had in my pockets was one dollar and a medical certificate." He not only had a love for his chosen profession, but a deep and lasting love of nature which took him on hundreds of horseback and wagon trips into the Big Sur territory. Dr. Roberts dreamed of a road which would allow others to enjoy the beauty of the south coast range. He made a trip on foot from Monterey to San Luis Obispo in 1897, mapping the land as he walked. The roadway, which Dr. Roberts thought could be built for $50,000, actually cost $10 million. He had years of frustration in attempting to convince others of the merits of his plan, and at one point took Frank Powers on a trip on which Powers took the earliest known color slides of the area. Equipped with the slides, Dr. Roberts finally found someone who would listen to his idea—Senator James Rigdon of San Luis Obispo County. Senator Rigdon arranged for Dr. Roberts to appear before a legislative session in Sacramento. On that day in 1915 the legislature voted to include $1.5 million in a bond issue for the purpose of beginning construction. In 1917 the State Legislature's Committee on Defense decided that all roads of military significance should be given priority. With this decision, the term "scenic" was deleted, and the Carmel-San Simeon project was then specified "necessary for defense." The people of California passed the bond issue in 1919 and the $1.5 million was appropriated for the construction of what was to become the coast highway.

Actual construction began in 1922. State Highway Department engineer Lester J. Gibson recalled the planning and survey phase as being "the most interesting part of the project." He and his crew were responsible for making surveys for the road atop mules and horses. Gibson had the highest regard for the natural conservation of scenery and told the *Monterey Herald* "we attempted to preserve the scenic factions of the coast line by means of balancing yardage." This meant, he explained, "that when rock material was blasted out for a cut, this material was then transported to another area where it could be used for fill. It would have been cheaper to merely let the cut material spill down the cliff after blasting, but such a process would have left permanent scars."

The original funds ran out before three years had passed, resulting in the cancellation of the contract between the State of California and the builder, who sued the State and won. To finish the project, prison labor was used (some of the cabin quarters still remain), and more money was acquired through

During the construction of Bixby Bridge in 1932. Lewis Josselyn photograph.

bond issues. The road had been built as far as Andersen Creek in one direction and up from Salmon Creek in the other direction in 1931, leaving thirty miles yet incomplete.

The most publicized bridge of all was the "Rainbow" bridge or Bixby Creek Bridge, as it is known today. When the bridge was being built in the 1930s, nineteen miles south of Monterey, it was considered an engineering triumph. Stretching the length of 714 feet and rising 285 feet above the sea, the structure contained 6,600 cubic yards of concrete and 600,000 pounds of steel reinforcement.

The entire project was felt not only in Sacramento, but hit the coastal residents when it encroached on their land, changing boundaries and making huge dents in the landscape that they had for so many years considered their domain. Many felt that the best way to view anyone from the highway department was from "the business end of a double-barreled shotgun."

The new highway's first contractor, George Pollack, and resident engineer Irwin T. Johnson, who made base headquarters at Slates Hot Springs, remembered many interesting things in regard to the project. Johnson in particular remembered the time there were arguments over the esthetics of the bridge planned to span Wildcat Creek (now on Highway One). Photographer Edward Weston (who was our neighbor in the Highlands at Wildcat Canyon) casually drew a sketch of what he thought was a suitable bridge on the back of an envelope, which finally ended up on an official's desk in Sacramento and became the basis for the design of the bridge.

Irwin Johnson, who settled in the Carmel Valley after retirement, recalled the kindnesses of the Pfeiffers. Each time they made a trip to Monterey they would take requests for supplies from the crew members. Gibson retired in 1949 and lived in San Luis Obispo, and, as did Johnson, had a sense of pride in his involvement with the highway project.

The Big Creek bridge was completed in April 1937, and the last of the highway was completed by June 27, 1937, at the total cost of $10 million. The official dedication of the coastal route began at San Simeon, and ended at Big Sur, where Governor Merriam cut the ribbon and there were appropriate festivities.

Dr. Roberts' career included other activities apart from his devotion to medicine and nature. He served for forty-two years as Seaside postmaster, and was on the Monterey School Board for thirty-six years, beginning in 1892. He was chairman of the Monterey County Board of Supervisors from 1908 to 1928.

Dr. Roberts made the thirty-mile trip from Monterey in three and one-half hours (the fastest anyone had ever made it) to aid those from the shipwreck of the steamer *Los Angeles* off Point Sur. When he arrived, he found "150 people thrashing around in the surf, some trying to climb rocks, some already dying." He spent three days and nights without rest or sleep, administering to the injured and embalming the dead. He later submitted a bill for $150 to the steamship company, who refused to pay. Dr. Roberts raised his bill to $300 and the company contin-

Bixby Bridge in 1947, from the original Coast Road. Rosa Lee Hale photograph.

ued to refuse payment. He then threatened to impound one of the company's ships which was docked in Monterey, and this brought prompt payment and much delight to the good doctor.

Soon after the Spanish-American War, the government wished to establish a Veterans' Hospital somewhere in the interior of Monterey County, and Dr. Roberts convinced officials that the climate of our area would be better suited to the welfare and recovery of the patients than that of a proposed interior location. The government already owned the Presidio property, and in 1902, the Veterans' Hospital was established in Monterey, bringing with it a new and modernized presidio. Dr. Roberts died in Monterey at the age of eighty-eight, on November 21, 1949. He had truly left his mark upon the Monterey Peninsula, and had a place in the hearts of many coastal residents.

The driest year that any of the earliest settlers of the Big Sur could remember was 1869, and the most dramatic story about that year was told by Robert (Bob) Cruess. Bob was born in the Indian Valley in 1860, and at the age of nine, during that dry year, he accompanied his father on a journey to move a herd of sheep from the Indian Valley to Monterey. The sheep were in a weakened condition, and the drive took three months. At the end of it, there were less than five hundred of the original ten thousand sheep, and Bob and his father were parched, with bleeding and cracked skin. The elder Cruess rented the entire Monterey Peninsula, Carmel Highlands, and Pacific Grove for $125 for one year, from landowner David Jacks, for pasture for his sheep. Bob remembered that on the three-month journey, every watering hole and stream was dry and empty, as was the Carmel River when they reached it. the Carmel Valley was called a "glut of stinking thirst-dead cattle" that year.

While in the Monterey area, Bob's father met Michael Pfeiffer, who had come up from the Big Sur to do his trading for the winter, and Pfeiffer told him of the clear water and free grazing available near him. Bob and his father drove what remained of their flock up the Carmel Hill and made their own trail over the hazardous terrain of the Big Sur until they reached the Little Sur River. There he remembered meeting someone called "Old Leather Britches," who was unloading winter supplies from her horse, and who gave them a wonderful hot home-cooked meal and directed them to the ridge trail.

After three days of travel south, they finally spotted the landmarks that Pfeiffer had mentioned, and they came to rest in the high pastures above Torres Canyon. They built a crude but livable cabin,

and ate grizzly bear and deer until the end of the winter came, along with the end of their stay in the Big Sur.

We know only a little about other early settlers of Big Sur, except that they had to be hardy and courageous.

Donny Smith first came to the Big Sur at the age of seventeen in 1887, to his first paying job with Demos Soberanes on the Big Sur Rancho. He was one of the last of the old buffalo hunters and a sailor as well, having sailed on the British bark, the *Falls of Hallandale*. Smith's parents settled between Palo Colorado and Rocky Creek, calling their place Westmere—this name was retained by the Hogues when they lived there. Smith's brother Dick bought land from a man named Dexter, where he lived until 1891 with their sister Josephine.

Donny Smith remembered Charlie Gregg, who packed tanbark, and the Gibson family, who had three pretty daughters and a son and lived between Point Lobos and the Highlands. Mr. Gibson also packed tanbark. Smith himself lived at what was then called Souza Creek, between Soberanes and Palo Colorado, and his neighbors were the Vaudall family. The two Vaudall sons, John and Ned, helped

John and Ned Vaudell with their father at the Vaudell Apiary in Big Sur, 1893. Slevin photograph.

their father with the family's large apiary. Donny Smith eventually moved to New Monterey, and his daughter Hazel married P. O. James. They lived in Pinnacles, California, and in Big Sur in the 1920s, with their son Sammy.

A man named Sterrit lived near Garrapata and had a mill there which he used to grind his and his neighbors' corn by using water from the creek.

The tale was told of an old hermit who appeared

regularly from above Post Summit to meet the stage, until the early 1930s when he seemed to vanish without a trace. He was believed to be the fugitive Bauman of the Los Burros area.

There was a man called Uncle Al, another loner, with a long white beard and two long white braids. There was Pong Hong (Jim Fatt), who lived briefly between Point Sur and the Brazil Ranch, living a serene and lonely life among his jars of preserved rattlesnakes and other assorted things, befriended by his neighbors, the Bershires.

Then there was Johnny Pate, blinded by buckshot, and married to the sister of the bandit Vásquez of Monterey. In spite of his handicap, Johnny could play the banjo, and did so, to the delight of all, whenever the opportunity presented itself. His parents, Mr. and Mrs. Edmond Pate, crossed the plains from Indiana in 1852 and settled in Lodi, California before coming to Big Sur. (Their daughter Annie was the wife of Frank Post.)

When Johnny Pate played his banjo for gettogethers, Albert Clark, who lived alone, played his banjo, too. Manuel Vasquez played his guitar and Edward Burns would delight everyone with his accordion. Saturday night get-togethers and once-a-year celebrations would find them all performing together, to everyone's pleasure.

At the north fork of the Little Sur were the Harry Moreton and Isaac Swetnam homes. The Dolan family lived at the mouth of the Little Sur, and where their house stood, today cypress trees grow. Jim Williams and Joseph Schmidt were on the north side of Pico Blanco, and a man called Pierce was on the south side along with Albert Clark and Johnny Pate and family. There was also "old lady Heath," the "Old Leather Britches" of the Bob Cruess story. Her place later became the Artellan place, where twenty-two Artellan children were raised.

A man named Martínez married a Gibson girl and bought part of the original Innocenti land, and a family by the name of Walker lived at Bixby Creek (now the Brazil Ranch). An old one-armed bachelor named Vogler lived up Palo Colorado, and a family called Picks lived on the east side of the Coast Ridge above Partington Canyon. Farther down from the Cooper Rancho near Moro Rock (named after David Moro), lived a loner of a man named Nidever, who made his living killing seals and otters.

On past the lighthouse lived a man called Snow and his companion, a man named Pheneger, who was remembered for his two large and beautiful bloodhounds. Pheneger lost his life when his team overturned his wagon on him alongside the coast trail. A little farther down were the Wurld and Bradford brothers, who attempted a sawmill together and failed, and the Cunninghams, who lived on Serra Hill near the top where cypress trees still stand.

Another hardy soul was an old man named Gschweind, who settled at Little Sur in the 1870s and called his place Little Switzerland. Three men, Hopkins and Soliday, who were supposed to have come from South Africa, and a Mr. Keeyler, lived at the north fork of the Little Sur. Keeyler took up land on a preemption near the hot springs. He had a sawmill and sold lumber, and it was remembered that he was related to Donny and Dick Smith. Keeyler sold the lumber to Gschweind for his home.

A Mrs. Leewaldt had a feed store in Monterey, where she also sold groceries and merchandise and loaned money. She lived for a time near Gschweind, and once collected on a debt by buying out Soliday, who at the time had some one hundred and sixty acres, most of which he sold to a man called Hopkins. Hopkins later sold the land to a man named William Baker and his partner.

In 1887 there was a population of almost one hundred in the Big Sur.

Since the opening of the highway in 1937 many others have come to the Big Sur—new settlers of a different era, naturalists, writers, poets, artists, entrepreneurs of the unusual, and the ever-present real estate investor. Some have cared deeply and fought beside the old guard to preserve, in farsighted plans, what has become rare and precious in this hurry-up world. A master plan was drawn and adopted in 1963 requiring strict zoning regulations along the coast, and the coast highway, Highway One, was removed from the list as a future freeway.

Each time I leave the Big Sur there is a need to glance back, to capture a mental picture to take away with me, for the changes have been many. An example is the lonely grave near Bixby Landing which was recognizable for many years, until Gallatin Powers built his Crocodile's Tail Restaurant on the site—now both are gone.

Gone are the Indians and grizzlies and many of the once-familiar names. Forlorn rusted bits of cable and pulley wheels have come to light, vegetation has crept upon the kilns, covering them in green silence, and lilies mark the place where once a cabin stood.

DANI FAMILY

Gabriel and Elizabeth.

Their children:

Jane, who married William Twitchell.

Ada, who married Wilbur Harlan.

Alvin, who married Mary Ellen Pfeiffer and after her death married her sister Katherine (Kate).

Reil, who married Fredricka Welker, who was a school teacher, and after her death married Josie Boronda.

Mary, who married Nes Swending.

Amelia, who married William Pfeiffer.

Anthony, who married Eliza Hidalgo, and later Cipriana Lopez.

Lucia, who moved with her parents to San Lucas in 1905. She also ran the post office on the coast which had been named after her.

Gabriel died in June of 1908 at the age of seventy-six and was buried in San Lucas.

Elizabeth and Lucia went to England in 1909 to visit Elizabeth's sister, and in 1912 they moved to Monterey. Elizabeth died there in 1931 at the age of ninety-five.

Alice Amelia Dani Pfeiffer, William Pfeiffer, and Mary Ellen Pfeiffer Dani are all buried in the Big Sur family plots. Present Dani family members are living in the King City-San Lucas area.

PFEIFFER FAMILY

Michael Pfeiffer. Born September 18, 1832 at Centerville, Illinois, fifteen miles from St. Louis. Died October 10, 1917 at Big Sur. Married Barbara Laquet. Born April 20, 1843 at Hautcloche, Alsace-Lorraine, France. Died March 4, 1926 at Big Sur.

Their children:

Charles Alexander. Born March 6, 1860 in Solano County, California. Died February 26, 1936 in Challis, Idaho. Married Ellen Olson of Challis area. Their children: Frank, Charles, Lyda, and Gladys.

John Martin. Born March 13, 1862 in Vacaville, California. Died May 11, 1941 in Big Sur. Married Florence Swetnam Brown. Born July 7, 1871 in Kentucky. Died February 5, 1956 in Big Sur. Their children: Esther Julia and John Ivan.

Mary Ellen. Born July 14, 1866 when family was enroute to Tomales Bay. Died September 24, 1900. Married Alvin Dani. Their children: Electa and Alvina.

Julia Cecelia. Born November 20, 1868 in Tomales Bay. Died January 25, 1928. Married John Burns. No children.

William Nicholas. Born September 28, 1873. Died March 8, 1920 in Big Sur. Married Alice Amelia Dani. Their children: Charles Michael, Oscar Sebastian, Wilhelmina, Richard Dewey, and Joseph Alexander.

Frank Anthony. Born August 7, 1876 in Big Sur. Died September 15, 1935. Never married.

Flora Katherine (twin to Frank Anthony). Born August 7, 1876 in Big Sur. Died ? Married Alvin Dani. Their children: Katherine, Albert, Stanley, Donald, Margaret, and Helen.

Adelaide (Lyda) Barbara. Born August 19, 1879 in Big Sur. Died 1922. Married Samuel Marshall Trotter. Born 1871. Died 1938 in Big Sur. Their children: Roy Martin, Henry Marshall, Lillian Ruth, Frank Alexander, and Walter Samuel.

SWETNAM FAMILY

Isaac Newton Swetnam. Born March 8, 1846. Died October 12, 1917 in Monterey. Married Ellen Jane Lawton. Born October 6, 1848. Died December 15, 1926 in Monterey.

Their children:

Florence Zulema. Born July 7, 1871 in Kentucky. Died February 5, 1956 in Big Sur. Married Guy Brown. Their children: Ellen Olive and Kyle Christopher. Florence and Guy were divorced. She married John Martin Pfeiffer. Their children: Esther Julia and John Ivan.

Vivia Alice. Born November 30, 1872 in Kentucky. Died January 28, 1955. Married Adam Mowat. No children. Vivia and Adam were divorced. She married Thomas Carlyle. No children.

John William. Born April 10, 1874 in Kentucky. Died July 1898 on San Juan Hill in Cuba. Never married.

Lou Ellen. Born January 1, 1878 in Kansas. Died November 6, 1954 in Nevada City. Married Horatio Parmelee. Their children: Spencer Newton, Leslie, Mary Ellen, and George Vivian. Lou Ellen and Horatio were divorced. She married Samuel Scarlett. Their children: Severn, Irene, Sarah (Sally), Truman, Ariel (Bill), and Eunice.

Julia Trinvilla. Born January 21, 1879 in Kansas. Died ? Married William E. Loftus. Their children: Lou Ellen and Owen. Julia and William were divorced. She married Edward K. Ernst. Their child: Edward K. Ernst, Jr.

Leonora Josephine. Born August 5, 1880 in Kansas. Died ? Married Robert Emmons. Their children: Leona Josephine, Edna Ethel, Dorothy Pearl, Robert Lee.

Mary Belle. Born February 26, 1882 in Kansas. Died December 1939. Married Howard Severance. Their children: Howard, Harriet, Esther Louise, and Ellen.

Manoah Newton. Born July 10, 1888 in Garapatos. Died February 22, 1961 in Washington, D.C. Married Elsie Hunting. Their child: James Manoah.

Elfrieda Inez. Born March 29, 1891 in Garapatos. Died ? Married Robert Daniel Drinkwater. Their child: Ruth Edna.

POINT LOBOS

In the summer, the morning air hangs warm and pungent with the smell of moss and fog-damp wood within the forest parts.

In the fall, the cool crisp air greets you and invigorates your zest for life, and each tidepool from Sandhill to China Cove becomes your own special place for rediscovery of nature's extravagant bounty.

In the winter, the crashing, swirling waves along the Blue Fish Cove make a pleasant pounding in your ears. The early morning and afternoon fog steals quietly into Cypress Grove and often touches some long forgotten chord within your soul.

In the spring, there is a quiet peace in the meadows, where you can watch the honeybee at work in the honeysuckle and the squirrels in the trees, while the deer pluck tender morsels nearby. At China Cove there is the quiet blue-green lapping of the waves, sometimes punctuated with the call of sea birds from Bird Island.

4

Point Lobos

How Punta de los Lobos Marinos, the hauntingly beautiful Point Lobos, came to be a reserve is a lesson for future generations if we are to save what is left that is natural and beautiful for all the tomorrows.

On its way to becoming a reserve, Point Lobos survived the following: a granite quarry, its granite being used in the Old Monterey Jail and San Francisco Mint; a whaling outpost and Chinese fishing village, from 1861 to 1884; and a loading and shipment outpost for the Carmelo Land and Coal Company from 1888 to 1896. The latter was linked with tragedy from its beginning, first when a steamer loading coal from Coal Chute Point exploded and all hands were lost, and shortly after that when seventy Chinese laborers were buried alive in a cave-in, bringing to a close, for all practical purposes, its history as a mine. In 1863 an interest in mining was shown by a group of citizens calling themselves the San Carlos Mining Company.

Point Lobos was once the proposed townsite of "Carmelito"; it was the scene of cattle rustling; and it suffered a range fire. It was first occupied by the local Indian settlements at San José Creek and Gibson Creek, mainly the Ichxenta and Pitchi tribes, with the Excelemac, Ekkheya and tribes from farther south as visitors to the area. These gentle people are gone forever, having left behind them bedrock mortars and abundant shell mounds to mark their existence.

During the mission period the padres, including Serra, who was a "great walker," probably visited the area often, and through early records of the Mission San Carlos Borromeo, we know that mission herdsmen often grazed their herds in the area.

After secularization, mission "pueblo" lands became available to private ownership, and at this time a part of Point Lobos fell within the boundary set up in the grant of July 30, 1834, awarded to Juan B. Alvarado and called Rancho el Sur. One year later, in 1835, Teodoro Gonzales applied for a grant, Rancho José Sur Y Chiquito, which did include

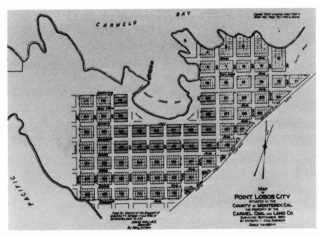

Map of Point Lobos City, surveyed in September 1890.

Point Lobos as we know it. The patent was given on April 16, 1839 to Don Marcelino Escobar, a Monterey official, and confirmed in 1840. This land grant was bound on the north by the Rio Carmelo and on the east by the mountains; the south boundary was at Palo Colorado Canyon, while the west boundary was the Pacific Ocean. Don Marcelino's two sons, Juan and Augustin, obtained the rancho soon after the grant passed to their father, and they in turn deeded it to Dona Josefa de Abrego on August 26, 1841 for $250, half the amount being paid in merchandise. For a brief period in the rancho's existence, its story is a little puzzling. It is known that it was granted to a group of about ten soldiers of the Presidio, and the land was held in their names until June 7, 1844.

In June 1844, General José Castro was given the claim deeds by the soldiers holding title and filed a petition for claim to Rancho Y Sur Chiquito which was rejected. Castro's claim was later appealed in the United States District Court, over a period of years. From then on there were many conflicting claims, several of them squatters' claims. In 1880 a suit was filed on behalf of several claimants, and a final agreement recorded on June 5, 1882 gave the land as follows: Ashley heirs, one-ninth; William T.

Baggett, one-ninth; Joseph S. Emery, two-ninths; William T. Bassett, two-ninths; Sidney L. Johnson, two-ninths; W. Van Dyke, one-ninth. Joseph Emery was the man after whom Emeryville was named, and whose daughter married Fred Farr, uncle to one-time State Senator Fred S. Farr, father of present county supervisor Sam Farr.

The Gregg claim to the land north of San José Creek was finally recognized along with the claims of twenty-seven others. At one time there was a small village which included the Roadhouse, rebuilt by Alexander Allan as his residence, a blacksmith shop, and a general store. It was located at the future site of the Thomas Frances Riley dairy. After some thirty-five years, title was confirmed to Castro's successors, W. T. Bassett and Nathan W. Spaulding, on December 24, 1885, and on May 4, 1888, patent was signed by President Grover Cleveland.

On September 6, 1888, the owners of Point Lobos sold their claim interests to Carmelo Land and Coal Company for one dollar with retained interests in shares.

Between 1861 and 1884, Point Lobos and its Carmelito Cove, now called Whalers Cove, were the focal point of whaling operations by thirty-five to forty Portuguese under the direction of a Captain Verisimo. Whalers Knoll was the area from which whales were sighted, and the whales were brought to Whalers Cove where they were "flenced." All that remains of that period are the cauldrons for boiling whale oil, the derrick rings embedded into the rock inside the cove, and a lone weathered whaler's cottage, once one of several, standing beside the lovely old cypress tree planted in 1875 and serving today as a ranger's cabin. The ninety-foot Fishback whale skeleton put up by the Japanese fishermen in 1917 stood in the quarry at Whalers Cove until it was dismantled in the 1950s, thousands of names

Columbia Park Boys in 1917 at Point Lobos in front of a whale skeleton.

penned, painted and carved upon its surface, our own family names among them.

A history of Point Lobos and environs would not be complete without the story of the Victorine family, which began in the village of Fayal in the Azores. A whaler by trade and tradition, Antonio Victorine sailed from the Azores around the Horn on his way to the whaling station at Monterey in late 1863, where he became attached to the whaling company at Point Lobos under the direction of fellow countryman Captain Verisimo. Soon after his arrival, Antonio was operating a dairy ranch at the mouth of San José Creek, as well as whaling. Antonio Victorine established himself firmly and then sent for his wife, Mary Nunes, and sons Tony and Joseph. They arrived in Monterey in 1870.

When he grew up Joseph married Louisa Correia, who had come from the Azores to be the cook for Joseph's uncle and his wife in their saloon. Joseph acquired a 2,000-acre ranch south of the Highlands, known as San Remo. He was active on his ranch until 1923, when he retired and established a home in Seaside, California. The children of Joseph and Louisa were Joseph, Jr., Lillian, Avelino, Mary, Bradley, Angelas, and Ernest. The family had many friends, among them the Frank Mathies and Serpa families.

The old homestead still stands in the eucalyptus grove near the beach and the historic Bay School

This picture of whalers from Point Lobos and Moss Landing was taken in 1918. The flencer was William Lehman.

154

site across from the Carmelite Monastery. In 1928, Joe, Jr., with the help of his brother Ernest, built the rock house in the Highlands with stone from Malpaso Creek a mile away. Later Joe's daughter Alice and her husband, Ed Brewer, were its owners. There was a beautiful daily fare of nature's bounty in those days, the hills and meadows a sea of poppies, lupines, johnny-jump-ups, and rich fern. Joseph once said, "When a man was all alone he could not help but marvel at what a gardener God is." This beauty brought visitors who became family friends, one of them Dr. D. T. MacDougall, who discovered the method of measuring the age and growth rate or trees by tree rings, and was also founder of the Carnegie Institute in Carmel Village.

The Victorines were a close family with aunts, uncles and cousins living nearby. Some later married into other local families such as the Hitchcocks of the coast ranch (later Brazil Ranch), and the de Amaral and Artellan families. Frank Victorine, a nephew of Joseph, Jr., married Lillian (Lena) de Amaral on October 18, 1902. Lillian was born on November 15, 1883 on the old family ranch at Point Lobos, above the present Riley Ranch. Her parents were Jacinto and Anne de Amaral, who pioneered in the Santa Clara area for a time and returned to the Point Lobos area in the late 1920s to live out their lives. In January 1940, Joseph Victorine, Sr. died, leaving his three sons to carry on the name of Victorine, and his daughters, Lillian (Mrs. Ferriera) of San Martin, California, and Mary, who became Mrs. Angelus Harlan of Aromas, California. Today two Victorines remain on the Peninsula, Ernest and Joseph, Jr.'s son, Walter.

The story of the abalone industry at Point Lobos began with one of the first Japanese to come to the Peninsula. His name was Otosaburo Noda, and he came after farming for a while in the Castroville area. He began his fishing career with the search for salmon, and before long he was employing many of his fellow countrymen, who came to live and work at his camp in New Monterey. Highly successful at his new profession, Otosaburo wrote home to Japan to his government with impressive reports of his success and the abundance of abalone. Convinced by his statements, the Japanese government contacted a seasoned abalone diver by the name of Gennosuke Kodani. Kodani was already well respected in the fishing industry of Japan, having helped to develop a highly specialized diving suit for abalone fishing which replaced the standard white bathing suit, cap, net bag and goggles. Kodani

Abalone drying on racks at Whalers Cove, Point Lobos, in the area between Coal Chute Point and Granite Point, 1905.

arrived in Monterey in late 1897 and began a search up and down the west coast for a suitable place to begin his abalone business. He looked over the Abel Cannery below the present Highlands Inn, and decided on Point Lobos. He soon brought many divers from Japan to work for him.

Kodani began a partnership with Julian Barnett and Alexander M. Allan, who built the cannery at Whalers Cove and was grandfather to the late Thomson Hudson. They opened the Point Lobos Canning Company, which existed for twenty-five years, shipping many tons of canned abalone back

Gennosuke Kodani in the diving suit he perfected.

to Japan and supplying abalone to hundreds of California restaurants. When the State took over the 1,250 acres of Point Lobos in 1933, all of the cannery buildings were removed except for the whaler's cottage.

Kodani and his wife had a good life at Point Lobos. Their son Seizo and his wife, Fumiye, have continued to live at Point Lobos. Their daughters are Eugenie, Lucinda, and Marilyn, who teaches school locally.

Seizo Kodani and the sons of Kumahiko Miyamoto of my Carmel Valley story were boyhood friends and, being cut off from the Japanese settlement in Monterey, they had mostly Caucasian friends. Seizo attended Bay School and fished in the Carmel River with his friends. After World War II was over, the Kodani family returned to the area from a relocation camp, as the Miyamotos had. However, Seizo found that to continue in the abalone industry was not economically possible. Having worked as a volunteer for the Carmel Highlands Fire Department since its inception in 1932, Seizo returned to work there again, first part-time and later full-time. His last position with the department was as fire chief.

The site of the abalone cannery, where the whaling station had been, was a part of the 1890 plan for Point Lobos City, or Carmelito, as it was later known. It was the dream of the Carmel Land and Coal Company to set up a resort community made up of twenty-five-foot wide lots, many of which were actually sold. Some, it is said, were purchased by Mrs. Robert Louis Stevenson and her sister. The streets of Carmelito were planned and named: Bassett Avenue, Emery, Doble, and Baggett, after the early property holders and company owners of Carmelo Land and Coal Company. Fortunately, however, the dream failed, and the beautiful Point Lobos has retained its original character.

Alexander MacMillan Allan and his wife, Sarah Bradley Morgan, were introduced to this area by their friend Joseph Emery. Allan was born in Pittson, Pennsylvania, and was graduated in 1888 from the University of Illinois. He became involved in race tracks and was associated with building the early Santa Anita and Lucky Baldwin. He was also involved in the Ingleside Track as well as the construction of the tracks at Ascot Park in Los Angeles, Tanforan, and Emeryville. He was later a partner of Kodani in the fish canning company, and was a banker.

On January 14, 1898, Allan purchased 640 acres

Alexander Allan of Point Lobos.

of the Carmelo Mining Company's land. Despite battles and suits to force Allan from the land, he held on to his ranch (the original Allan homestead and dairy remain today) and in 1897 he began repurchasing the lots once sold for the Carmelito subdivision, a total of 1,000 acres, which brought his acreage to 3,000. Sarah Allan loved the beauty of Point Lobos deeply and in order to protect it from unwelcome picnickers who trampled its beauty and left behind their garbage, she convinced her husband to charge a toll. A toll gate was set up, with the following charges: one-horse buggy, twenty-five cents; two-horse buggy, fifty cents; and four-horse tally-ho, one dollar. It was never mentioned whether the toll helped or not.

During the time that Allan was repurchasing land, a forester, G. Frederick Schwartz, made a formal study of the cypress groves at Point Lobos and wrote to Allan, "You might perhaps see your way clear to add your beautiful cypress holdings at Point Lobos to those at Pescadero Point, if the latter were established as a State Park." Despite his varied interests, Allan continued to live at his ranch from 1897 until he died in 1930, at the age of seventy.

With the increase of visitors there grew a desire to save and protect the beauty that abounded at Point Lobos, and at a Save-the-Redwoods meeting on January 5, 1925, Point Lobos was mentioned as a possible park area within the State Park System. A year later an investigation was launched by Dunbar McDuffie and Frederick Law Olmstead in regard to areas worthy of preservation. In 1929 Olmstead's report stated the following: "[Point Lobos is] the most outstanding example on the coast of California of picturesque rock and surf scenery in combination with unique vegetation, including typical Monterey Cypress."

October 19, 1932 marks the date when State Park bonds were issued by the State Park Finance Board for the purchase of 400 acres at Point Lobos for $631,000. Transfer took place on February 8, 1933. In agreement with the Allan heirs, the Cypress Headland was a gift in memorial to Allan and his wife. On April 15, 1960, 750 acres of underwater reserve were established, creating the first reserve of its kind in our country, and in 1975 the State Parks Department bought forty-eight adjoining acres from the Hudson-Riley heirs.

The author and her father in 1947 at Point Lobos. Rosa Lee Hale photograph.

The flora and fauna of Point Lobos are astonishing and unique, not because of the number of separate species found within the reserve, but for the unusual varieties and groups of plant and animal life found in close association with one another.

So that you may become acquainted with some of the marvels of nature within the reserve I have listed some of the species you will encounter, as well as those you may not chance to see due to the seasons.

There are 147 varieties of sea and shore birds, and almost all of them are dependent upon the sea or its surrounding area. A few of them are the Pelagic cormorant, Brandt's cormorant, western gull, oystercatcher, sanderling, pigeon guillemot, brown pelican, chickadee, pygmy nuthatch, Allan's hummingbird, sparrow, finch, bush-tit, owl, eagle, hawk, Steller's jay, bush jay, Oregon junco, thrasher, killdeer, and meadow lark.

Following are lists of fauna and flora of Point Lobos.

AMPHIBIANS AND REPTILES
Arboreal salamander—*Aneides lugubris*
Oregon salamander—*Ensatina eschscholtzii*
Slender salamander—*Batrachoseps attenuatus*
California toad—*Bufo boreas*
Pacific tree toad—*Hyla regilla*
Alligator lizard—*Gerrhonotus multicarinatus*
Fence lizard—*Sceloporus occidentalis*
Garter snake—*Thamnophis ordinoides*
Gopher snake—*Pituophis catenifer*
Yellow-bellied racer—*Coluber constrictor*

SEA MAMMALS
Sea otter—*Enhydra lutris*
California sea lion—*Zalophus californianus*
Elephant seal—*Mirounga angustirostris*
Harbor seal—*Phoca vitulina*
Steller sea lion—*Eumetopias jubata*
Gray whale—*Eschrichtius gibbosus*
Killer whale—*Oricnus orca*

LAND MAMMALS
Brush rabbit—*Sylvilagus bachmani*
Jack rabbit—*Lepus californicus* (now rare)
Black-tailed deer—*Odocoileus columbianus*
Brown bat—*Eptesicus fuscus*
California bat—*Myotis californicus*
Gray squirrel—*Sciurus griseus*
Ground squirrel—*Citellus beecheyi*
Gray fox—*Uroeyon cinercorgenteus*
Harvest mouse—*Reithrodontomys megalotis*
House mouse—*Mus musculus*
Meadow mouse—*Microtus californicus*
Pocket mouse—*Perognathus californicus*
White-footed mouse (deer mouse)—*Peromyscus maniculatus*
Long-tailed weasel—*Mustela frenata*
Mole—*Scapanus latimanus*
Oppossum—*Didelphis marsupialis*
Pocket gopher—*Thomomys bottae*
Raccoon—*Procyon lotor*
Striped skunk—*Mephitis mephitis*
Wildcat—*Lynx rufus*
Wood rat—*Neotoma fuscipes*

TREES
Monterey pine—*Pinus radiata*
Monterey cypress—*Cupressus macrocarpa*

WOODY BASED SHRUBS
WHITE
Gray locoweed—*Astragalus Nuttallii*
Douglas' nightshade—*Solanum Douglasii*
YELLOW
Mock heather—*Haplopappus ericoides*

Bush lupine—*Lupinus arboreus*
Northern sticky monkey flower (bush monkey flower)—*Mimulus aurantiacus*
Lizard tail—*Eriophyllum staechadifolium*
RED OR PINK
Dune erigonum (wild buckwheat)—*Eriogonum parvifolium*
California wild rose—*Rosa californica*
BLUE
California lilac—*Ceanothus thyrsiflorus*

HERBS
WHITE, REDDISH WHITE
Star lily—*Zygadenus fremontii*
White Chinese houses (lanterns)—*Collinsia bartsiaefolia*
White globe lily (white fairy lantern)—*Calochortus albus*
Soaproot—*Chlorogalum pomeridianum*
Milkmaid—*Dentaria integrifolia* var. *californica*
Coast morning glory—*Convolvulus cyclostegius*
Common manroot (wild cucumber)—*Marah fabaceus*
YELLOW OR ORANGE
Golden brodiaea—*Brodiaea lutea*
Golden mimulus (common large monkey flower)—*Mimulus guttatus*
Coastal gumplant—*Grindelia latifolia* ssp. *platyphylla*
Cream cup—*Platystemon californicus*
California poppy—*Eschscholzia californica*
Bluff lettuce—*Dudleya farinosa*
Johnny jump-up—*Viola pedunculata*
Sun-cup—*Oenothera ovata*
Footsteps of spring—*Sanicula arctopoides*
Tidy tips—*Layia platyglossa*
Sand-hill dandelion—*Agoseris apargoides*
Coast tarweed—*Hemizonia corymbosa*
California buttercup—*Ranunculus californicus*
RED OR PINK
California bee plant—*Scrophularia californica*
Checker bloom—*Sidalcea malvaeflora*
California hedge nettle or wood mint—*Stachys bullata*
Hill Clarkia (Farewell to spring)—*Clarkia bottae*
Sea pink—*Armeria maritima* var. *californica*
Seaside painted cup—*Castilleja latifolia*
Escobita (Owl's clove)—*Orthocarpus purpurescens*
BLUE
Dwarf brodiaea—*Brodiaea coronaria* var. *macropoda*
Blue dicks—*Brodiaea pulchella*
Blue-eyed grass—*Sisyrinchium bellum*

Douglas' iris—*Iris Douglasiana*
Large-flowered star lily (Mariposa lily)—*Calochortus uniflorus*
Seaside daisy—*Erigeron glaucus*
Common California aster—*Aster chilensis*
GREEN
Checker lily (Mission bells)—*Fritillaria lanceolata*

OTHER FLOWERING PLANTS
Yellow sand verbena—*Abronia latifolia*
Beach sand verbena—*Abronia umbellata*
Yarrow or Milfoil—*Achillea borealis* ssp. *californica*
Yarrow—*Achillea millefolium*
Chamise—*Adenostoma fasciculatum*
Leafy bent-grass—*Agrostis diegoensis*
Western bent-grass—*Agrostis exarata*
Hall's bent-grass—*Agrostis Hallii*
Hairgrass—*Aira caryophyllea*
Lady's mantle—*Alchemilla occidentalis*
Tumbleweed—*Amaranthus graecizans*
Fiddleneck—*Amsinckia intermedea*
Seaside Amsinckia—*Amsinckia spectabilis*
Pimpernel—*Anagallis arvensis*
Blue pimpernel—*Anagallis arvensis* forma *caerulea*
Chaffweed—*Anagallis minima*
Pearly everlasting—*Anaphalis margaritacea*
Mayweed—*Anthemis cotula*
Sticky snapdragon—*Antirrhinum multiflorum*
Wild celery—*Apiastrum angustifolium*
Celery—*Apium graveolens*
Crimson columbine—*Aquilegia formosa* var. *truncata*
Tower mustard—*Arabis glabra*
Pine mistletoe—*Arceuthobium campylopodum*
Monterey manzanita—*Arctostaphylos Hookeri*
Shaggy-barked manzanita—*Arctostaphylos tomentosa*
California sagebrush—*Artemisia californica*
California mugwort—*Artemisia Douglasiana*
Dragon sagewort—*Artemisia Dracunculus*
Beach sagewort—*Artemisia pycnocephala*
Broad-leaf aster—*Aster radulinus*
Lady fern—*Athyrium felix femina* var. *cyclosorum*
Seaside saltbush—*Atriplex californica*
White-leaf saltbush—*Atriplex leucophylla*
Fat hen—*Atriplex patula* ssp. *hastata*
Wild oat—*Avena fatua*
False everlasting—*Baccharis Douglasii*
Dwarf chaparral broom—*Baccharis pilularis*

Coyote Brush—*Baccharis pilularis* ssp. *consanguinea*
Bowlesia—*Bowlesia incana*
Field mustard—*Brassica campestris*
Summer mustard—*Brassica geniculata*
Charlock—*Brassica Kaber* var. *pinnatifida*
Cabbage—*Brassica oleracea*
Rattlesnake grass—*Briza maxima*
Little quaking grass—*Briza minor*
White brodiaea—*Brodiaea hyacinthina*
California brome—*Bromus carinatus*
Ripgut grass—*Bromus diandrus*
Soft chess—*Bromus mollis*
Sterile brome grass—*Bromus sterilis*
Cheat grass or Downy cheat—*Bromus tectorum*
Cheat grass—*Bromus tectorum* var. *glabratus*
Red maids—*Calandrinia ciliata* var. *Menziesii*
Pacific redgrass—*Calamagrostis nutkaensis*
Water starwort—*Callitriche marginata*
Large-flowered star lily—*Calochortus uniflorus*
Shepherd's purse—*Capsella Bursa-pastoris*
Bitter cress—*Cardamine oligosperma*
Sand mat—*Cardionema ramosissimum*
Round-fruited sedge—*Carex globosa*
Monterey sedge—*Carex montereyensis*
Clustered field sedge—*Carex praegracilis*
Foot-hill sedge—*Carex tumulicola*
Indian paint brush—*Castilleja affinis*
Carmel ceanothus—*Ceanothus griseus*
Warty-leaved ceanothus—*Ceanothus papillosus*
Monterey ceanothus—*Ceanothus rigidus*
Tocalote—*Centaurea melitensis*
Canchalagua—*Centaurium Davyi*
Field chickweed—*Cerastium arvense*
Mouse-ear chickweed—*Cerastium viscosum*
White goosefoot—*Chenopodium album*
Mexican tea—*Chenopodium ambrosioides*
Soap plant—*Chenopodium californicum*
Nettle-leaved goosefoot—*Chenopodium murale*
Red goosefoot—*Chenopodium rubrum*
Diffuse Chroizanthe—*Chorizanthe diffusa*
Douglas' spine flower—*Chorizanthe Douglasii*
Water hemlock—*Cicuta Douglasii*
Indian thistle—*Cirsium brevistylum*
Bull thistle—*Cirsium vulgare*
Canyon Clarkia—*Clarkia unguiculata*
Chinese houses—*Collinsia heterophylla*
Poison hemlock—*Conium maculatum*
Field bindweed—*Convolvulus arvensis*
Horseweed—*Conyza canadensis*
California corethrogyne—*Corethrogyne californica*
Common corethrogyne—*Corethrogyne filaginifolia*

Branching beach-aster—*Corethrogyne leucophylla*
Creek dogwood—*Cornus occidentalis*
Pampas grass—*Cortaderia Selloana*
Brass buttons—*Cotula coronopifolia*
Coast cryptantha—*Cryptantha leiocarpa*
Tejon cryptantha—*Cryptantha microstachys*
Gowen cypress—*Cupressus Goveniana*
Western dodder—*Cuscuta occidentalis*
Umbrella sedge—*Cyperus Eragrostis*
French broom—*Cytisus monspessulanus*
California wild oatgrass—*Danthonia californica*
American wild oatgrass—*Danthonia californica* var. *americana*
Rattlesnake weed—*Daucus pusillus*
Dichondra—*Dichondra repens*
Salt grass—*Distichlis spicata* var. *stolonifera*
California wood fern—*Dryopteris arguta*
Sea lettuce—*Dudleya caespitosa*
Goldman's dudleya—*Dudleya cymosa* ssp. *minor*
Creeping spike-rush—*Eleocharis macrostachya*
Giant ryegrass—*Elymus condensatus*
Western ryegrass—*Elymus glaucus*
Alkali ryegrass—*Elymus triticoides*
Northern willow-herb—*Epilobium adenocaulon* var. *Parishii*
Coast cottonweed—*Epilobium watsonii* var. *franciscanum*
Giant horsetail—*Equisetum Telmateia* var. *Braunii*
New Zealand fireweed—*Erechtites arguta*
Coast eriogonum—*Eriogonum latifolium* ssp. *auriculatum*
Golden Yarrow—*Eriophyllum confertiflorum*
Red-stemmed filaree—*Erodium cicutarium*
White-stemmed filaree—*Erodium moschatum*
Coast eryngo—*Eryngium armatum*
Beach poppy—*Eschscholzia california* var. *maritima*
Chinese caps—*Euphorbia crenulata*
Six-weeks' fescue—*Festuca dertonensis*
Rat-tail fescue—*Festuca myuros*
California filago—*Filago californica*
Sweet fennel—*Foeniculum vulgare*
Wood strawberry—*Fragaria californica*
Beach bur—*Franseria chamissonis* ssp. *bipinnatisecta*
Goose grass—*Galium aparine*
California bedstraw—*Galium californicum*
Climbing bedstraw—*Galium Nuttallii*
Coast silk-tassel—*Garrya elliptica*
Salal—*Gaultheria Shallon*
Cut-leaved geranium—*Geranium dissectum*
New Zealand geranium—*Geranium retrorsum*

Many-stemmed gilia—*Gilia achilleaefolia* ssp. *multicaulis*
Bioletti's cudweed—*Gnaphalium bicolor*
California everlasting—*Gnaphalium californicum*
Cotton-batting plant—*Gnaphalium chilense*
Weedy cudweed—*Gnaphalium luteo-album*
Purple cudweed—*Gnaphalium purpureum*
Pink everlasting—*Gnaphalium ramosissimum*
Coast piperia—*Habenaria elegans* var. *maritima*
Sawtooth goldenbush—*Haplopappus squarrosus*
Sneezeweed—*Helenium puberulum*
Rush-rose—*Helianthemum scoparium*
Chinese pusley—*Heliotropium curvassavicum*
Toyon (Christmas berry)—*Heteromeles arbutifolia*
Alum-root—*Heuchera micrantha* var. *pacifica*
Seaside heuchera—*Heuchera pilosissima*
White-flowered hawkweed—*Heiracium albiflorum*
Velvet grass—*Holcus lanatus*
Meadow barley—*Hordeum brachyantherum*
Mediterranean barley—*Hordeum geniculatum*
Foxtail barley—*Hordeum jubatum*
Wall barley—*Hordeum leporinum*
California horkelia—*Horkelia californica*
Wedge-leafed horkelia—*Horkelia cuneata*
Leafy horkelia—*Horkelia frondosa*
Tinker's penny—*Hypericum anagalloides*
Smooth cat's-ear—*Hypochoeris glabra*
Hairy cat's-ear—*Hypochoeris radicata*
Toad rush—*Juncus bufonius*
Bog rush—*Juncus effusus* var. *brunneus*
Spreading rush—*Juncus patens*
Brown-headed rush—*Juncus phaeocephalus*
Western rush—*Juncus tenuis* var. *congestus*
Iris-leaved rush—*Juncus xiphioides*
Junegrass—*Koeleria cristata*
Coast goldfields—*Lasthenia chrysostoma* ssp. *hirsutula*
Woolly goldfields—*Lasthenia minor*
Common Pacific pea—*Lathyrus vestitus*
Pitcher sage—*Lepechina calycina*
Common peppergrass—*Lepidium nitidum*
Wayside peppergrass—*Lepidium strictum*
Australian tea—*Leptospermum laevigatum*
Flowering quillwort—*Lilaea scilloides*
Common linanthus—*Linanthus androsaceus*
Toad-flax—*Linaria canadensis* var. *texana*
Narrow-leaved flax—*Linum bienne*
Hill star—*Lithophragma heterophyllum*
Sweet alyssum—*Lobularia maritima*
Italian ryegrass—*Lolium multiflorum*
Small-leaved lomatium—*Lomatium parvifolium*

Hairy honeysuckle—*Lonicera hispidula* var. *vacillans*
Twinberry—*Lonicera involucrata* var. *Ledebourri*
Bentham's lotus—*Lotus benthamii*
Slender or Coast lotus—*Lotus formosissimus*
Woolly lotus—*Lotus Heermannii* var. *eriophorus*
Rush lotus—*Lotus junceus*
Bird's foot trefoil (Hill lotus)—*Lotus micranthus*
Spanish clover—*Lotus purshianus*
Deer weed—*Lotus scoparius*
Bishop lotus—*Lotus strigosus*
Chile Lotus—*Lotus subpinnatus*
Douglas silver lupine—*Lupinus albifrons* ssp. *Douglasii*
Douglas annual lupine—*Lupinus nanus*
Lindley varied lupine—*Lupinus varicolor*
Common wood rush—*Luzula subsessilis*
California loose-strife—*Lythrum californicum*
Grass poly—*Lythrum Hyssopifolia*
Little tarweed—*Madia exigua*
Slender tarweed—*Madia gracilis*
Bull mallow—*Malva nicaeensis*
Cheeseweed—*Malva parviflora*
Horehound—*Marrubium vulgare*
Bur clover—*Medicago hispida*
Smooth-burred medic—*Medicago hispida* var. *confinis*
Western melica—*Melica bulbosa*
Small-flowered melica—*Melica imperfecta*
Indian melilot—*Melilotus indicus*
Sea fig—*Mesembryanthemum chilense*
Common ice plant—*Mesembryanthemum crystallinum*
Hottentot fig—*Mesembryanthemum edule*
Yellow gentian—*Microcala quadrangularis*
Coast microseris—*Microseris Bigelovii*
Thintail—*Monerma cylindrica*
Miner's lettuce—*Montia perfoliata*
Wax-myrtle—*Myrica californica*
Water-cress—*Nasturtium officinale*
Skunkweed—*Navarretia squarrosa*
Variable-leaved nemophila—*Nemophila heterophylla*
Baby blue-eyes—*Nemophila Menziesii*
Pacific oenanthe—*Oenanthe sarmentosa*
Beach primrose—*Oenothera cheiranthifolia*
Evening primrose—*Oenothera Hookeri*
Small primrose—*Oenothera micrantha* var. *Jonesii*
Broomrape—*Orobanche californica*
Paint-brush orthocarpus—*Orthocarpus castillejoides*

160

Dwarf orthocarpus—*Orthocarpus pusillus*
Oso berry—*Osmaronia cerasiformis*
Wood cicely—*Osmorhiza chilensis*
Hairy wood-sorrel—*Oxalis pilosa*
Sickle grass—*Parapholis incurva*
Florida pellitory—*Parietaria floridana*
Bird's-foot fern—*Pellaea mucronata*
Squaw root—*Perideridia Gairdneri*
Wild heliotrope—*Phacelia distans*
Stinging phacelia—*Phacelia malvaefolia*
California canary grass—*Phalaris californica*
Fiesta flower—*Pholistoma auritum*
Scouler's surf-grass—*Phyllospadix Scouleri*
Torrey's surf-grass—*Phyllospadix Torreyi*
Goldenback fern—*Pityrogramma triangularis*
Artist's allocarya—*Plagiobothrys Chorisianus* var. *Hickmanii*
Annual coast plantain—*Plantago Bigelovii*
Mexican plantain—*Plantago hirtella* var. *Galeottiana*
California plantain—*Plantago Hookeriana* var. *californica*
Common plantain—*Plantago major*
Goose-tongue—*Plantago maritima* var. *californica*
White plectritus—*Plectritus macrocera*
Annual bluegrass—*Poa annua*
Douglas bluegrass—*Poa Douglasii*
California polycarp—*Polycarpon depressum*
California milkwort—*Polygala californica*
Common knotweed—*Polygonum arenastrum*
California polypody—*Polypodium californicum*
Rabbitfoot grass—*Polypogon monspeliensis*
Sword fern—*Polystichum munitum*
Black cottonwood—*Populus trichocarpa*
Silverweed—*Potentilla Egedii* var. *grandis*
Sticky cinquefoil—*Potentilla glandulosa*
Catalina cherry—*Prunus Lyonii*
Slender woolly-heads—*Psilocarphus tenellus*
California tea—*Psoralea physodes*
Brake (Western bracken)—*Pteridium aquilinum* var. *pubescens*
Pterostegia—*Pterostegia drymarioides*
Coast live oak—*Quercus agrifolia*
Wild radish—*Raphanus sativus*
California coffeeberry—*Rhamnus californica*
Poison oak—*Rhus diversiloba*
Canyon gooseberry—*Ribes Menziesii*
Pale red flowering currant—*Ribes sanguineum* var. *deductum*
Red flowering currant—*Ribes sanguineum* var. *glutinosum*
Thimbleberry—*Rubus parviflorus* var. *velutinus*

California blackberry—*Rubus vitifolius*
Sheep sorrel—*Rumex Acetosella*
Green or clustered dock—*Rumex conglomeratus*
Coastal dock—*Rumex crassus*
Curly dock—*Rumex crispus*
Fiddle dock—*Rumex pulcher*
Willow dock—*Rumex salicifolius*
Western pearlwort—*Sagina occidentalis*
Pickleweed—*Salicornia virginica*
Arroyo willow—*Salix lasiolepis*
Scouler's willow—*Salix Scouleriana*
Chia—*Salvia Columbariae*
Black sage—*Salvia mellifera*
Blue elderberry—*Sambucus mexicana*
Gambleweed—*Sanicula crassicaulis*
Coast sanicle—*Sanicula laciniata*
Yerba buena—*Satureja Douglasii*
California Saxifrage—*Saxifraga californica*
Pincushions—*Scabiosa atropurpurea*
Three-square—*Scirpus americanus*
Low club rush—*Scirpus cernuus* var. *californicus*
Keeled club—*Scirpus koilolepis*
Panicled bulrush—*Scirpus microcarpus*
Marsh scorzonella—*Scorzonella paludosa*
Bigelow moss-fern—*Selaginella Bigelovii*
Redwood—*Sequoia sempervirens*
Common catchfly—*Silene gallica*
Many-nerved catchfly—*Silene multinervia*
Milk thistle—*Silybum marianum*
Tumble mustard—*Sisymbrium altissimum*
Hedge mustard—*Sisymbrium officinale*
Fat Solomon—*Smilacina racemosa* var. *amplexicaulis*
Slim Solomon—*Smilacina stellata* var. *sessilifolia*
Douglas' nightshade—*Solanum Douglasii*
Black nightshade—*Solanum nigrum*
Common goldenrod—*Solidago californica*
Dune goldenrod—*Solidago spathulata*
Prickly sow-thistle—*Sonchus asper*
Sow-thistle—*Sonchus oleraceus*
Corn spurrey—*Spergula arvensis*
Large-flowered sand spurrey—*Spergularia macrotheca*
Purple sand spurrey—*Spergularia rubra*
Hooded ladies' tresses—*Spiranthes Romanzoffiana*
Common chickweed—*Stellaria media*
Tall stephanomeria—*Stephanomeria virgata*
Nodding stipa—*Stipa pulchra*
Dwarf snowberry—*Symphoricarpos mollis*
New Zealand spinach—*Tetragonia tetragonioides*

Many-fruited meadow rue—*Thalictrum poly-carpon*

Cut-leaved thelypodium—*Thelypodium lasio-phyllum*

Sand pygmy—*Tillaea erecta*

Star flower—*Trientalis latifolia*

Bladder clover—*Trifolium amplectans*

Colony clover—*Trifolium barbigerum*

Pin-point clover—*Trifolium gracilentum*

Double-headed clover—*Trifolium Macraei*

Maiden clover—*Trifolium microcephalum*

Tomcat clover—*Trifolium tridentatum*

Cow clover—*Trifolium Wormskioldi*

Hoary nettle—*Urtica holosericea*

California huckleberry—*Vaccinium ovatum*

California vervain—*Verbena lasiostachys*

American brooklime—*Veronica americana*

American vetch—*Vicia americana*

Slender vetch—*Vicia exigua*

Chain fern—*Woodwardia fimbriata*

Spiny clot-bur—*Xanthium spinosum*

Eel-grass—*Zostera marina*

A formidable number of intertidal creatures and organisms live in an almost totally ideal natural aquarium, including many varieties that are common forms and many that are becoming increasingly rare.

Rocky shores, protected coves, sheer cliffs, and sandy beaches—all in abundance at Point Lobos—soon make you aware that certain plant and animal forms are found in areas which nature has seen fit to restrict by tidal zones. It is necessary to know each tidal zone so that you can enjoy as well as protect what is there in order to conserve the ecology of the beach. There are three distinct areas of intertidal life, which can be divided as follows:

High-Tide Zone is the name given to the area that is submerged only during high tides, and is exposed for considerable periods of time. Such creatures as barnacles, mussels and small anemone are found in this area, as well as the common seaweeds called nailbrush and yellow rockweed.

Mid-Tide Zone is the area exposed at least once a day for a long period of time, and contains within its territory a great variety of animals and algae. Most of the seaweeds in this zone appear green in color.

Low-Tide Zone is the name of the area which is exposed for very short periods of time, and the living creatures within this zone are the most abundant and varied of all. Red colors—seaweeds, sea urchins and abalones—are a sign of this zone.

The three distinct tidal zones are caused by natural interaction of the sea, the force of the waves, the beaches, sand, and mud, the lengths of exposure, and the relationship of other organisms which may or may not be present.

Though I wish you "good hunting," I entreat you to leave the specimens where you find them. Being able to observe what is beautiful and natural is far more meaningful for all of us than collecting. Please pick up animal life that moves, carefully, if you must, and admire the rest, being certain to put things back as you found them, for as my daughter said at a very early age, "You wouldn't want someone to lift the roof right off your house and then not put it back!" It is important to remember that we are the intruders on nature, and are intruding on a delicate, well-ordered environment. We are all responsible for seeing that nothing upsets the balance.

Leaving Point Lobos, we will pass very quickly into the Carmel Highlands, which was included in the Spanish grant called San José Y Sur Chiquito, belonging to Marcelino Escobar. The historical setting of Carmel Highlands includes Indians, legends of pirates, hidden caves, Scottish sailors, whalers, Chinese coolies, a coal mine at the site of the present Highlands Inn, and pioneer ranchers.

The Highlands can boast of artists, scientists, writers, architects, photographers, poets, actors, and actresses, and has an unmistakable flavor of Scottish traditions. It was first developed by Franklin Devendorf and Frank Powers of the Carmel Development Company. One place there that is special within my own heart is our old home, which is now the home of well-known attorney Francis Heisler.

CARMELITE MONASTERY

A sublimely beauteous spot built in glory to His name...
Behind the walls in cloistered life, yet sheltered not from the outside...
In calm communion above a world of strife,
*   voices raised to God are still at night.*
These gentle souls His love does guard,
*   till quiet morning's golden light brings forth the first stirrings of those*
*   who go about their chosen tasks in prayer Divine...*
*   for love,*
*   for peace,*
*   for hope,*
*   and life.*

5

The Carmelite Monastery

Many a traveler driving along the beautiful coast highway near Carmel-by-the-Sea has been intrigued by the sight of a large, impressive white building nestled serenely in the folds of the rolling hills. The tall, cross-tipped tower, the huge round amber-glass window, the form and height of the building seem to exercise a magnetic force upon people, and when they drive into the grounds, they discover that it is a Carmelite monastery in which a group of cloistered nuns live a strict life of contemplative prayer and work.

The monastery was built in 1931, the first home for the women who started this community of praying sisters. In 1925, five Carmelite nuns came from the Carmelite monastery in Santa Clara, California, to begin what is called a "foundation." A new monastery usually begins on a small scale; then as more young women are called to the contemplative way of life, a larger building becomes necessary and arrangements are made over a period of time to construct one.

Each Carmelite "foundation" has a different reason for being made. In this instance, the moving force was a new bishop beginning a new diocese. Bishop John Bernard MacGinley had been called from the Philippine Islands to become the spiritual leader of a newly formed diocese to be known as Monterey-Fresno Diocese. He traveled to Rome to be present at the canonization ceremony declaring a young French Carmelite as a saint—Saint Therese of the Infant Jesus and of the Holy Face. The bishop was very devoted to this holy Carmelite, so he asked Pope Pius XI if he might have this new saint as patroness of his new diocese. At the time, he requested permission to establish a foundation of Carmelite nuns who would follow the same way of life as St. Therese and pray for the priests and people in his fledgling diocese.

At the time of his requests, which were both approved by the Pope, it was early spring—May 1925. As soon as he returned to California, he contacted Mother Augustine of the Mother of God, O.C.D., prioress of the Santa Clara Carmel. (Each monastery is called a "Carmel.") He told her of his plan and asked her if she could send some of her sisters to begin a new foundation.

"Mother Augustine was a woman of great vision, deep spirituality and poetic insight. What's more, she had a keen appreciation of history, and she immediately grasped the significance of this request." She was being asked to send Carmelite nuns to a place that had been named by priests of the Carmelite Order more than three hundred years earlier.

When the Spanish explorer Sebastian Vizcaíno sailed north up the coast of California in 1602, he had three Carmelite priests aboard, to say mass and act as chaplains for the men who sailed with him in the ships he was commanding. The patroness of this voyage was the Blessed Virgin Mary under her title of Our Lady of Mount Carmel. Her picture had been enshrined in the bow of the main vessel. When the ships dropped anchor in what is now Monterey Harbor, two of the Carmelite priest-friars went ashore to explore this new land. After celebrating mass under an old oak tree near the sandy beach, they hiked south and found an area that resembled the place in Palestine where their religious order had its first foundation. Point Lobos reminded them of Mount Carmel, where the great prophet Elijah lived a prayerful life in a cave, going forth from time to time to preach the message of the one true God. In 1153, a group of laymen and priests from Europe journeyed to Palestine for the purpose of living a life similar to that of Elijah's hermit existence. Like the great prophet, these men living around Mount Carmel often went forth on apostolic preaching missions. Eventually they formed to migrate to Europe, and the Carmelite friars of Vizcaíno's expedition were two of their successors in the Order of the Blessed Virgin Mary of Mount Carmel, as their religious group was officially titled.

The first Carmelite monastery at Carmel Point.

Returning to the ship after their explorations, the two priests, Father Andrew and Father Anthony, suggested that the areas south of Monterey might be named "Carmel" in order to honor the patroness of their safe voyage and to acknowledge the close resemblance to Mount Carmel. Vizcaíno acquiesced, and the name was duly entered upon the maps by the expedition's cartographer. Centuries later, Mother Augustine decided to honor Our Lady, also, and gave her new foundation the title "Carmel of Our Lady and Saint Therese."

In order to proceed with her plans, Mother Augustine got permission to leave her Santa Clara cloister and journey by car to Carmel-by-the-Sea. "Mother and her companion, Mother Agnes of Jesus, looked in vain for a suitable building for a monastery, so they decided to build a very simple wooden structure on a fair-sized lot far from the village where the nuns would have the privacy and silence they needed for their prayerful way of life." They purchased a lot on the west side of Isabella Avenue near Scenic Drive, near Carmel Point. (After that first house was torn down, the property remained a vacant lot for over fifty years; now new homes are being constructed on it.)

On October 23, 1925, the five Carmelite nuns who had been chosen to make the new foundation traveled from the Santa Clara Carmel to their new home. The five who set out on this adventure in faith were: Mother Alberta of St. Theresa, Sister Elizabeth of the Trinity, Sister Marie Aimee of Jesus, Sister Therese of the Infant Jesus and of the Holy Face, and Sister Rose of Nazareth.

The first mass was celebrated on October 24 by Bishop MacGinley, who had welcomed them to

their new monastery. For three days, the public could visit the building and talk to the sisters who had come into their midst. Hundreds of local residents and visitors inspected the simple dwelling and were impressed by the joy of the sisters who had voluntarily chosen to live such an austere and secluded way of life. The next five years passed quickly as the nuns followed their regular routine of prayer and work, fast and feast days. They began to receive applications from young women who wished to join their order. The small foundation house did not have much room for new members.

In 1930, Francis Joseph Sullivan, the father of Mother Agnes, died in San Francisco. He had made possible the first foundation of Carmelite nuns on the west coast, bringing a group of sisters from Boston to San Francisco. Then he had been instrumental in moving them to a better location in Santa Clara. Mother Agnes knew that his desire had been to "build new homes for Our Eucharistic Lord" so she asked that her share of his estate might be used to build a larger monastery and chapel in Carmel. Eventually, her inheritance was more than sufficient to establish Carmelite monasteries in San Diego, Berkeley, and Taiwan, Isle of Formosa.

The site for the new monastery in Carmel was carefully chosen, and construction of the building was scheduled for March 19, 1931, "because that was the feast-day of Saint Joseph, the spouse of Mary and the foster-father of Jesus Christ."

The plans for the building were drawn by a firm of Boston architects, Maginnis and Walsh. This firm had also made the plans for the Carmel of Santa Clara. Mother Agnes asked that a place be made in the chapel for a final resting place for her father, so a side altar dedicated to St. Joseph was included in the plans. Mr. Sullivan's body was transferred to a crypt beneath this altar in 1931, when the five foundresses moved to the new monastery on November 1, the Feast of All Saints.

"Another request was honored. Bishop MacGinley told the nuns that all he wanted in return for arranging for this foundation was a final resting place for himself when God called him home. He died at the age of ninety-nine and was buried in a beautiful sunlit tomb in the south rear corner of the chapel. There is a statue there of his favorite saint, St. Therese."

The entire monastery—chapel and living quarters—is made of concrete, steel and wood. Cut stone and terra cotta are used extensively in the chapel and sturdy marble columns brought from Italy enhance the beauty and authenticity of the Romanesque interior. The high clerestory windows are also features of this particular style. Mother Augustine chose appropriate texts from Scripture to be carved in stone above the doors of the chapel.

In contrast to the elegant beauty of the chapel, the living and working quarters of the nuns were constructed and furnished very plainly, according to Carmelite custom. "The monastery contains some seventy rooms, including a 'choir,' a large room directly in back of the reredos of the altar in the chapel, where the nuns recite the Liturgy of the Hours, the public prayer of the Church. In this room, unfurnished except for built-in benches along the walls, the nuns also make their daily hours of mental prayer, kneeling directly on the floor facing toward the Blessed Sacrament reserved in a monstrance above the altar." Other rooms are the refectory, or dining room, the kitchen, the laundry, the recreational room, and the chapter room, where the nuns meet to conduct the business of the monastery and discuss ways and mean to improve their observance of their Carmelite life, and small offices of various kinds.

On the second and third floors are located the cells—rooms in which the sisters sleep, work and pray. Each sister has a room furnished with a table, chair or bench, and a simple wooden bed—two boards laid across two low wooden trestles. A thin but adequate mattress, usually filled with straw, is placed on the boards. The nuns lead a monastic life, which means they spend a great deal of time in solitude, like the hermits of old. The term "cell" refers to the idea of living alone, yet in community, as in a honeycomb where all the small "cells" join to make one larger unit. Generally, each monastery is limited to twenty-one nuns, although a few more may be permitted to enter if some of the sisters are unable to keep the full schedule due to illness or age. If a foundation is many years in the planning, the monastery may take up to thirty nuns so that the departing group of sisters will not deplete the home community. This was the case when the nuns were preparing a new foundation in San Rafael, California. Nine sisters were sent to the new foundation, so the nuns were allowed to have a community of twenty-nine during the preparatory years.

The comparatively small number of nuns in each monastery stems from the desire of the foundress of the Discalced Carmelites, St. Teresa of Avila, to maintain a family spirit among her nuns. She lived for many years as a member of the Calced Carmelites in a convent outside the walls of Avila called the Incarnation. There were well over one hundred nuns in this convent, and as a result, there was very little silence or solitude available to foster the life of prayer. St. Teresa wished to give herself more completely to a life of praise, worship and petition, so she received permission to begin a small foundation with just four young women whom she trained in the ways of prayer, gradually leading them into the paths of contemplative prayer and even writing books for their guidance and encouragement. Her works have become classics enjoyed throughout the world: "Way of Perfection," "Interior Castle," and her autobiography are outstanding examples of her writing, although she did not write them specifically for wide publication.

It might be interesting to mention at this time how it happened that women became part of the Carmelite Order. In the year 1452, Father John Soreth was the General of the Order. He came to know a group of truly religious women living in community in Belgium. They asked if they might be affiliated with the Carmelite Order as they wished to pursue a life of prayer and contemplation. Their request was granted and soon communities of Carmelite sisters were making foundations in other countries, including Italy and Spain. They followed what was called a mitigated Rule—the original Primitive Rule had been modified during the time of the plagues, when the health of the men and women religious was greatly threatened, and the fasts of the order were lessened, even to the permitting of meat in their diet. An increasing number of women desired to enter these monasteries, but not all of them had genuine religious vocations. St. Teresa wanted to have only those women who were serious in their desire to pursue a life of prayer, and she petitioned to use the earlier form of the Carmelite Rule—the Primitive Rule in all its pristine vigor. There had to be some adaptations, of course—the nuns were not living in caves—but in general the main themes of prayer, solitude and silence were stressed. The date of her reform was 1562, after she had spent over twenty years living in the larger, less austere Convento of the Incarnation.

Through the years, the requirements of becoming a Carmelite nun have changed very little. The life of prayer, of "praising God and praying for all," as one of the Carmelites once wrote, is simple yet profound. Because the life has its communal aspects as well as its erimitical spirit, the women who are best suited to "lead the life are those who enjoy solitude but also like the companionship of others at recreation time. The age span is from twenty-one to thirty-five, for entrance. Good health and a strong desire to help others through praying for the graces they need are two very important requirements for prospective Carmelites."

If the tests, which include psychological screening, are successfully passed, the young woman enters and becomes a postulant for one year, wearing a dress similar to the religious habit, and observing the life by participating in the various religious exercises. At the end of that time, she may become a novice for two years. She is clothed in the Carmelite habit during this period and wears a white veil. If all goes well she is accepted by vote and she makes a temporary Profession of Simple Vows, for three years. The next step will be her petition for Solemn Vows, which are the most binding vows in the Catholic Church for cloistered nuns. By that time, she will have lived the daily life for six years and both she and the Community should know if she has the necessary qualities to persevere in the Carmelite vocation of prayer and penance. If she is accepted, she makes her Solemn Profession and receives a black veil as a sign of her total consecration to God. This is a ceremony open to the public.

Visitors often inquire about the daily schedule of the nuns. The usual rising time is 5:40, giving the sisters twenty minutes to prepare for the first prayer action of the day, at 6:00 a.m. After the recitation of the Angelus, Morning Prayer, or Lauds, is recited in the choir. At 6:20, having finished the first of the Liturgical Hours, the nuns have an hour of silent prayer. After this, they return to their cells to tidy them up before daily Mass begins at 8:00 a.m. The entire Community assembles in the preparatory room in the rear of the choir, to don the white mantles and veils which they wear for the celebration of the Holy Mass. They assist in an oratory at the side of the sanctuary, where they can see the altar and the priest very clearly, the shutters being opened

for this important daily ceremony. The nuns sing hymns and the proper parts of the Mass on feast days. After Mass, all return to the choir for ten minutes of silent thanksgiving for the privilege of having assisted at Mass and receiving Christ's Body in Holy Communion. "The Real Presence of Christ in the tabernacle is something that many visitors to the chapel sense but do not always know what it is." After ten minutes, the nuns recite Mid-morning Prayer, the second of the seven Liturgical Hours that are prayed at intervals throughout the whole day. After this recitation, the nuns take their first repast of the day—they break their fast from the evening supper of the night before, with toast or cereal, and a choice of tea or coffee.

"By this time, it is usually close to 9:30, when the daily manual work begins according to assignment. Some Sisters will help in the kitchen, preparing the noon-time meal, others will work in the sewing offices, the letter room or perhaps the garden. Vestment making is one means by which they earn their living. Some of the Sisters make beautiful leaf cards which are very popular with visitors. At noon, it is time for Mid-day Prayer, or Sext as it used to be called. The Sisters leave their work and go to the choir to recite this Hour, after the Angelus is said once again. At the conclusion of the vocal prayer, a hymn is sung in honor of Our Lady, the Blessed Virgin Mary . . . Then daily prayers honoring the Carmelite Saints and asking their help to live the Carmelite life worthily.

"Seven minutes is then taken to look over the morning's work, mentally, to see how each one accomplished her assigned work. This is known as the Examen, and each Sister does this privately, for the purpose of making new resolutions to improve herself in various ways, not only in the area of work but also in her attention to prayer and her attitudes toward her Sisters. When the bell for dinner is rung, the nuns go in procession to the refectory, reciting a psalm for the souls of those who have died.

"In the refectory, after grace has been said, a reader mounts to a small pulpit and announces the reading for the day. Perhaps the Rule of Carmel, the Declaration for updating the Constitutions, and a spiritual book will be read while the nuns eat their mid-day meal, which is ample and well-cooked. Although no meat is eaten, there is a well balanced diet provided to keep up the strength of the nuns—fish, eggs, fresh vegetables given by kind friends and benefactors, and a variety of fruit in season, also the gifts of good friends. After dinner, the nuns do the dishes, then assemble for an hour of recreation: sewing during conversation, or playing a game such as croquet or perhaps volleyball. Indoor games such as Scrabble are enjoyed on occasion, although friendly family conversation is the favorite activity for this hour."

After recreation, the nuns disperse to their assigned tasks for the afternoon's work. During these hours, "they will spend time doing their spiritual reading which St. Teresa considered was 'no less necessary for the soul than food is for the body.' She wanted her daughters to be well-instructed in their faith and in the obligations of their vocation. During this time, the nuns also recite privately the mid-afternoon Hour which used to be called 'None' (ninth hour)."

At 3:00 p.m. a bell rings, and the nuns stop their work to kneel down and pray for all those who are dying that day, "a beautiful custom going back to the early days in the Order. At 5:00 p.m. the nuns assemble once again in the choir to begin the evening hour of mental prayer. At 6:00 p.m. Evening Prayer, or Vespers as it is sometimes still called, is recited, after which the supper bell is rung. The simpler meal of supper, which often consists of soup, salad and fruit, takes but a shorter time. After chores, the sisters again come to the recreation room for an hour. St. Teresa wanted her daughters to develop an amiable spirit which is very helpful to growth in the spiritual life and makes living in community much more pleasant. After evening recreation, the sisters return to the choir for the night prayer of the Church, Compline, now simply called Night Prayer. The bell is rung after this for Great Silence which means no one except the prioress is permitted to speak and all strive to be as quiet as possible in order to maintain the deep silence so conducive to prayer and rest. At 9:30, the bell rings again, calling the nuns back to the choir for the Office of Readings which used to be called Matins. St. Teresa always wanted her nuns to begin the night office 'when people began sinning most' rather than at midnight as she said the 'women do not pray well in the middle of the night.' After the Office is finished the nuns retire to their cells for rest around 10:30 p.m." It is a full day and the sisters are glad for the opportunity to sleep a few hours before beginning a new day of prayer and work.

"People often ask about the penitential aspect of the life, having seen movies that depict cloistered nuns doing all kinds of strange penances. The penances of self-denial in matters of food, talking, helping one's sisters generously in unobtrusive ways—these are the penances that are most meaningful to the young women of today. Older forms of corporal penance seem unrelated to today's need for

more compassion for oneself and others. To practice promptness, fidelity to Rule, attention to the many details of community living—all these entail considerable penance when lived day after day in the same surroundings, with the same people. When lived for many years—fifty or sixty years—such as several of our Sisters have lived it, the life is very demanding and requires much correspondence to God's grace.

"Another question people often ask is: what have the nuns done by way of updating their life? One answer is the introduction of a hermit day once a week. It gives the nuns more time for solitude and prayer, and allows them a space of consecutive time to work on a painting or some other hobby that requires an hour or two of steady application. The nuns make their lunch in the morning, take it to their place of work, and do not return to the choir until Vespers. It is during days like these that the Sisters make the lovely leaf cards and other religious objects such as rosaries and relics that are offered to the public in one of the local shops. The cards are also kept for sale in the external area of the monastery but there is not a gift shop as such.

"Each nun, in addition to the hermit day, has a Day of Recollection on which she has more time for prayer and reading, and has a visit with the prioress for spiritual refreshment and direction. This is a monthly experience . . . the day being spent away from the community, an opportunity for distancing and evaluating the different aspects of Carmelite living and how one relates to them."

It is difficult for the non-religious and even for those who are religious as ordinary people to understand the life the sisters have chosen for themselves, yet their lives are full of great happiness. A sister speaking for all of them once said: "Our life leads to an intimacy with God which produces as great a happiness as can be found. We feel no need for anything else. As St. Teresa said, 'God alone suffices.'" The happiness and serenity of the sisters are obvious in their presence and in the sound of their voices, and their faces mirror the depth of their faith.

The joy of the sisters is most readily seen on the occasions of special celebration, the Jubilee Days of the sisters. The Silver Jubilee is celebrated on the twenty-fifth anniversary of receiving the Carmelite habit, and the Golden Jubilee on the fiftieth anniversary of that memorable day in the life of a sister. In February 1950, the nuns celebrated the Golden Jubilee of the foundation's first prioress, Mother Alberta of St. Teresa. "Mother was eighty-one years old at that time, and it was said by those who saw her that her face appeared to be 'one of a woman less than fifty, alternating in expression between sparkling gaiety and serenity seldom seen in the faces of our troubled times.' Mother Alberta's memory remains fresh and green in the community, an inspiration to all who knew her."

Visitors are often curious to know how the community gets its superiors if they live a cloistered life and do not transfer from one Carmel to another. "The Chapter Nuns, those with final vows, each have a vote, and every three years, they elect a prioress and four council members. These may be re-elected for one more three-year term; in fact, except for the prioress, all may be re-elected again as council members the next time. Only the prioress has to wait another three years, after two terms of consecutive office, before being elected again. Each Carmel is autonomous, having no central motherhouse, but the nuns look to the Father General of the Carmelite Fathers for guidance. St. Teresa founded the men's branch of the Discalced Carmelites to be spiritual advisors and directors for the nuns. A true family spirit!"

The chapel and grounds of the monastery are open to the public daily from 7:30 a.m. to 5:00 p.m. Daily Mass is at 8:00 a.m. and on Sundays it is at 9:00 a.m. Benediction is given each Sunday at 4:30 p.m. and on the first Friday of every month at the same time—4:30.

Another question frequently asked is if the nuns ever see their families or friends. "The parents, brothers and sisters, may come once a month for an hour's visit, if they live close enough to travel here. After final profession, a friend or two may visit, but ever since St. Teresa began her reform to give the nuns more time for prayer, the visits of too many friends has been discouraged. Silence and solitude are important aspects of the prayer life of Carmelites and too much talking dissipates their spirit. The two Sisters who are assigned to help in the outquarters return to the cloister whenever they are free from answering the bells." Besides these two sisters, visitors may also speak to the Turn Sister who is in charge of the interesting-looking wooden half-pillar or revolving cylinder which is in the wall in the

The present Carmelite monastery as seen from Point Lobos. Dale Hale photograph.

extern hall. Friends who bring offerings or want to leave notes requesting prayers place their gifts or letters on the Turn, which then literally turns around so that the sister on the other side may take the things placed there to the proper station in the monastery—Reverend Mother's office or the kitchen. Each petition is placed on a bulletin board where the nuns may see it on their way to prayer.

When I was younger, I found the beauty of the monastery and its surrounding setting enhanced by occasional glimpses of the sisters walking quietly to the monastery beach and upon the hills nearby, something they are no longer allowed to do.

Two of the sisters who made the original foundation are still leading prayerful lives within the cloister—Mother Marie Aimee and Sister Rose, both of whom celebrated the sixtieth anniversary of their Profession in 1979. "Their joyful spirits are a constant source of edification to the younger members especially—sisters in their twenties who look with admiration upon these pioneers who are still so faithful to their promises!"

Should you visit the monastery you will find it both beautiful and compelling, and, as many do, you may feel a "personal presence"—an impression which will remain with you long after your visit to this peaceful place beside the sea.

LOS BURROS

*To the mountains they came—brave, strong in body and spirit, clinging
to hopes and dreams of what was yet to be . . .*

*They fought the elements—and sometimes each other—the call of the
gold and silver, and their promise of wealth, urging them on.*

*Now, amid lofty peaks, shaded canyons, and meadows of bleached grass,
there is stillness.*

*Now, aged, forgotten timbers from countless seasons past are all but
dust, and licking flames have left dark open tunnels, while ancient
hulking machines bring forth in mute appeal
the ghosts of bygone days.*

6

Los Burros

Los Burros—the name conjures up a variety of visions today, much as it did in those long-gone days when many tantalizing tales were told of gold, silver, and lost mines in the region.

The lore of the Los Burros began with the tales told by the neophytes of the coastal region, coupled with the story which was spread in about 1833 by a Scotsman named David Douglass in which he claimed to have found gold "flakes" for the taking.

Among the many tales is the legend of the Dutra Creek Pear Orchard. (In late 1968 only one pear tree remained to identify the area which was once referred to as a location point for the "Priest Mine.") The story states that the coastal Indians found silver at Dutra Creek, and later the padres of the Mission San Antonio de Padua set aside quarters for the Indian workers at the northwestern fork of the San Carpojo Creek, and the silver was transported to Mission San Antonio. It was also from this point that the creek flowed to the sea. Though the Indians did describe the location of the mine on many occasions, and strong though scant evidence has been found to indicate various places of excavation, no silver has ever been discovered. Naturally, due to the inaccessibility of the area and rough existing trails, more up-to-date investigation is sporadic and has not been common in the region, as many think.

The most elusive of all the tales of the Santa Lucia is the legend of the Los Padres Mine and a secret cave which is said to be the entrance to this well-hidden mine, reported to have been "filled with nuggets." The descriptive landmark which was repeatedly used as a guide to the now lost mine is the Ventana Double Cone, 4,853 feet high. Ventana in Spanish means window, and it was the geographical location of the Ventana Double Cone, twenty-one air miles south of the Mission San Carlos de Borromeo, that make it possible to see the bell tower of the mission from the summit of the peak, as the legend states, as the "window" or opening of the way to the mine.

The only cave to be discovered and recorded as having any signs of Indians native to the area is the one called "Massacre Cave," found in 1962 near Cape Martin. The cave was stumbled upon quite accidentally by some prospectors from San Francisco, who were able, with much effort, to remove enough rock to open the passage into the cave, allowing them to explore. During exploration the cave was found to have various depths and levels. However, in exploring the first of these levels, the prospectors found the remains of at least ten people. Local news reporters and specialists were called to observe the discovery site and examine the findings of bones, and it was brought to light at the time that the cave had not been lived in by any Indians previous to the massacre. Nine Indian skulls and one believed to be of a Spaniard showed signs of having been cracked "as if by a blunt object." One large bone which did not belong to the humans was found in the cave; it could have been the weapon used to kill them. Death was reported to have occurred approximately one hundred years prior to discovery. There were many theories then and have been since about how and why the massacre came to be. The strongest theory was that the Indians did indeed find gold but were exploited and later attacked by eager prospectors seeking to obtain the claim. The bodies' having been secreted in the cave for over one hundred years, and the abundance of prospectors approximately one hundred and twenty years ago make the theory a plausible one. Someday perhaps the mystery will be solved.

The Los Burros Mining District, as we know it today, at the southern end of the Los Padres National Forest, began in 1875. Though there was earlier activity, mining records do not show us accounts of any organized activity until the 1850s. Records and reports vary in their accounts of early mining in the region, but hard-rock mining did occur in the summer of 1853. Early newspaper accounts state that in 1869 some $100,000 in gold was taken from the Santa Lucias. However, when William Brewer came through in 1861 he did not mention any mining activities to substantiate any claims, and at the time of the encampment at Jolon there were only a sheep ranch and post office. Whatever the amount of activity, the accounts are forever lost, yet it is known that the Los Burros Mining District was officially formed in 1875 at a local miners' meeting. The "official" organizational meeting took place at the New Year Company's claim on February 5, 1875, with H. C. Dodge as chairman, A. C. Frazier as secretary, and W. T. Cruikshank as recorder. The following was the official statement of boundaries:

"Commencing at the Mouth of the San Kapoko following the Pacific ocean Northerly to Premits Trail. Thence following said trail to McKerns. Thence following the Nassimienta to the mouth of the Los Burros Creek. Thence to the place of beginning."

The newly elected recorder, W. T. Cruikshank, had a "busy time of it" in 1875, recording a total of sixty-seven claims, and working his own claim. His son William D. (Willie) discovered the Last Chance on April 7, 1887, at the head of Alder Creek. The Last Chance was later reported as having been the largest for sheer yield of all the mines.

Ten claims were recorded in 1876, six in 1877, and fifteen in 1878. By 1880, there were some five hundred claims within an eight-mile area; this number eventually rose to an estimated two thousand.

In 1887 Cruikshank crushed some twenty pounds of ore in a hand mortar and in just four short months completed a horse arrastre and a crude dragstone mill for crushing ore. By the end of those four months he had also earned enough to build a three stamp mill with a two-horsepower engine. Four tons of ore came through the mill in just twenty-four

hours. Fifteen men were employed around the mill and in the mine. The ore itself was assayed at $200 a ton, though some reports stated that it assayed at from $100 to $8,000 a ton. There were some five hundred feet of tunnels and shafts in which five well-defined leads were found. From November of 1887 until June of 1888, when it was flooded, the mine was continually worked. The Last Chance was reported to have yielded some $62,000 in precious gold ore, though various accounts place that sum as well below the actual amount taken from the mine before it was abandoned.

Some of the marvelous names for mines of the area were the Mars, None Such, King, Queen, Beacon Light, Charity, Lions' Den Ledge, Good Boy Placer, Mud Soring Mine, Old Bill Quartz Mine, Nip and Tuck, Scorpion, Comfort, Turtle Dove, Black Mare Claim, Rough and Ready, Buckeye, Worlds Pride Vein, Home Stake Claim, Gold and Silver Lead Lode, Eureka, Pacific Quicksilver, Grand Pacific, Jack Rabbit Quartz Claim, Golden Eagle Quartz Claim, Lucky Cuss, Grizzly Mine, Yellow Jacket Claim, Sea Side, Melville, Logwood, Old Man of the Mountains, Ajax, Ophir, and Plumed Knight.

Hotel Ganoung in Jolon, circa 1897.

It was also noted from early accounts that George Dutton and Captain John Tidball, owners of the Dutton Hotel and Hotel Ganoung, took some twenty-five hundred dollars between 1877 and 1878 from Chinese customers of the area who were working in the placer mines. The Jolon area was later closed to mining when it became known that the land belonged to the Rancho Milpitas Grant.

Simply to begin mining in the area, not to mention transporting the ore out or much-needed supplies in, was a monumental undertaking. The road from Jolon went through the Milpitas and Pyojo ranges and across the San Antonio Creek to the

This photograph of the New York Mine cabin of Willie Cruikshank was taken in about 1900. From left to right are Jim Tickle, Walter Basham, John Lazier, John Harbolt, David Harbolt, and Willie Cruikshank, founder of the "Last Chance."

174

Nacimento River, and there the wagon road came to an abrupt halt. From there it was through non-existent trails and impossibly thick types of vegetation, and today anyone hiking in the various areas of the Santa Lucia can imagine what these earlier mining pioneers were up against. Mules were the order of the day, as the trail ascended the mountains, winding ever higher. The mules were prodded, sweet-talked, cursed and coaxed to perform their duty to man. On the return trip they made their way back out of the Pyojo Range into the Los Robles Valley, and beyond to Jolon and King City, where the final leg of the journey of the gold ore was by rail to San Francisco.

Gold taken from the Los Burros region was estimated to be in excess of three million dollars. James Krenkel was responsible for finding one of the largest gold nuggets in the Los Burros region, valued at $1,100, from the Gorda Mine. A nugget from the Ralston Mine was reported to have been cashed at a value of $1,400. There were other reports of finds that were of high value, but no substantiating records.

Imagine, if you can, the sounds of hammers, men shouting, the grinding noises of machinery, the braying of mules, dogs barking, and women talking as they worked at chores and discussed the gossip of the day, while the shouts and laughter of children punctuated the air, and you will have set the scene of the small town of Manchester, where a field of tawny grass and wild oats now exists.

It is hard to comprehend the hopes and dreams, successes and failures that took place in this proud little community of 350 persons. From the few pictures we have, we know a little about how the town looked, with its hotel, two general stores, post office, blacksmith shop, barbershop, restaurant, a one-room school, a dance hall, and various saloons,

The Gem Saloon in the town of Manchester in 1885. It was owned and operated by Edward Caldwell.

not to mention the usual conglomeration of mess halls and bunk houses in addition to the family homes and cabins which dotted the countryside.

It was said that Manchester was named in much the same way as most mining towns, yet there is one popular tale which gives this version: "During the early days a huge blacksmith, bearing the name of Manchester, who was comparable in strength to a grizzly, got into a fight with one of the miners. As the fight advanced, Manchester's thumb was clawed clean off in the middle. When Manchester realized he was minus his thumb, he got all the madder and, with one mighty blow, laid the miner out on the hard cold ground." In what was apparent awe of the blacksmith, Manchester was the name chosen for the town. Other stories credit a miner by the name of Manchester as having been the person the town was named for. In any event, the tales of fact and fiction are numerous.

Today the Los Burros region is almost as inaccessible as in those days of long ago. Los Burros region is bounded by the wonderful Los Padres National Forest on one side, and the U.S. Army's Fort Hunter Liggett on the other, and can only be reached by a steep, narrow, hazardous seventeen-mile dirt road which is totally impassable in the winter for anything other than a four-wheel drive vehicle. The turn-off for the Los Burros is a few miles past Cape San Martin on the coastal side, or through Fort Hunter Liggett from the Jolon side.

One of the many settlers who came to this area was William T. Cruikshank, mentioned earlier. He came to California in 1849 from Troy, New York, and lived until early 1872 in Calaveras County. Seeking a different way of life and climate, Cruikshank found his way south and settled at Villa Creek. He built a small cabin, planted an orchard of plums and apples, and lived rather simply and quietly until he was elected claims recorder, at which time he also took up mining. From that time on, the name Cruikshank was to be forever linked with the Los Burros mining region, and both William T. and his son Willie are considered by historians to be true mining pioneers of the area. The younger Cruikshank not only discovered the Last Chance Mine but also the New York Mine, which he worked with miners John Harbolt, Jim Tickle, David Harbolt (son of John), Walter Basham, and John Lazier. Willie Cruikshank's cabin at the New York Mine was often the scene of informal get-togethers among the miners.

The deaths of William T. and Willie Cruikshank, who were much alike in life, were strikingly similar. In 1907 the senior Cruikshank left the Los Burros region on a trip to San Francisco. He appeared to all who knew him to be in both good health and spirits, yet he was never seen again, nor was there ever a trace or clue to explain what might have happened to him. Thirty years later, Willie, at the age of eighty-one, was seen leaving the area, just as his father had, well and in good spirits. He stopped to rest with the road gang in the area, and the foreman gave him a new pair of boots, which he was wearing as he rode out of sight, on his way to the ranch home of Adrian Harbolt for a holiday party. In earlier times, Adrian, the son of John Harbolt, had been a partner to the younger Cruikshank and had once given Willie a silver watch with the inscription of his, Adrian's, name. Some years after Willie's disappearance, soldiers of the Hunter Liggett Military Reservation found human remains, which were found to be those of Willie Cruikshank. With them were the silver watch and new boots.

One other member of the Cruikshank family who came to the Los Burros was John Cruikshank, the nephew of William, Sr. He mined for his uncle and James Krenkel in the early days of the Last Chance.

James Krenkel came to the Los Burros from that familiar and marvelous old mining town of Sonora, California in 1887, after hearing of the Last Chance. He went to work with the young Willie Cruikshank at the Last Chance for a while. When the mine was sold to the Buclimo Mining Company, Krenkel was in charge of digging a 2,100-foot drain tunnel, until lack of funds discontinued the project. After leaving the Buclimo, Krenkel had considerable success in working at the Oregon Mine for a long period of time. During that time he also worked another claim, where he found one of the largest nuggets ever to be taken from the Los Burros. Other large

The Krenkel children, Miss Hadden, and the school superintendent, 1921. Slevin photograph.

Mrs. Krenkel and five children, to the left, pose with Miss Ellen Fink, a guide, and the school superintendent during the superintendent's visit in 1921. Slevin photograph.

nuggets were reported, but the old-timers of the region were sure that Krenkel's nugget was the largest they remembered.

James Krenkel married a woman named Margaret, whom he had met in 1901 on a visit to the south county town of Pleyto. Before their marriage, he brought Margaret "over the mountains" to see the area she would later call home, and to inspect the cabin of logs that James had built for their home. James and Margaret Krenkel had five children: Marjorie, Bill, Jim, Jr., Charlie, and Doreen. They all attended the little school the mining community had provided. The entire family endeared themselves to the mining community, and Margaret was referred to with much affection as the "Matriarch of the Mountains," as she willingly served as nurse and friend to the "people of the peak" for over fifty years.

Tragedy clouded the life of this family when young Jim was killed. As in all mining communities, arguments and disagreements took place over boundaries, trespassers, and a variety of other issues, and it was a dispute involving trespassing that led to Jim's death. A man by the name of Ernest Bauman, who was originally from Russia, arrived in the Los Burros district in 1913 and staked his claim. From the beginning Bauman was disliked by many members of the community and was given the name of "the mad Russian." A burly, solidly built man of dark complexion, weighing 190 pounds, with long arms, big hands, and huge shoulders, he reminded the locals of a bear ambling over the countryside. Having great strength, Bauman was known to lift two hundred pounds of equipment or supplies on his back and climb effortlessly up and over the hills.

In 1937 Bauman had some serious quarrels with

neighbors who, he claimed, had trespassed on his mining claims. He became enraged by motorists who, though having every right to use the community road, repeatedly refused to close his gates, which in turn allowed cattle from the Hearst ranch to ruin his gardens. To strike back he scattered "bent horseshoes and old nails" in the road.

On one occasion an unsuspecting motorist found himself with several flat tires and walked to the home of Jim Krenkel. He had to awaken Jim to explain his plight, and Jim in turn summoned the help of a neighbor by the name of Clarence Webb. The three men returned to the stranded car and found that "various sharp metal objects had caused the flattened tires." It seems, though details were sketchy, that Bauman was called to "come out and talk," but his reply came from a gun which lodged a bullet in the right breast of Jim Krenkel, who died by the next morning.

Ernest Bauman was captured, after having fled the area, on the tenth of November, as he was walking along a riverbed near the south county town of King City, and a trial was held in the early part of 1938. Though Bauman was reported in the King City newspaper as having made the statement, "I planted the nails, and shot him with a .35. I aimed high for the breast just like you would kill a deer," he was acquitted after a plea of "self-defense"! The ending of the story came in late 1954 when the bullet-ridden body of Ernest Bauman was found in northern Butte County. Though Bauman's death was reported to have happened at the hands of an "escaped mental patient," proof of which was never found, there were those who felt that a type of justice had been served.

There have been stories of other miners and settlers, many of whom did not record their stories for future discovery. Among them was Edward Caldwell, a popular owner of the Gem Saloon and a hotel keeper in the old town of Manchester. Caldwell

Sam Pugh's Los Burros cabin in 1900. It was lost to the 1970 fire.

claimed to have started to dig a well, only to find "gold in every bucketful he examined." Another early miner, Paul Acquistapace, worked the old Brewery Mine which was discovered in 1888. A miner for over thirty years, Acquistapace had some two thousand feet of digging and four tunnels to his credit, yet he never struck it rich and continued to eke out only a small living while remaining philosophical about the whole thing, believing mining to be exactly like gambling.

Owner of the stamp mill used at the New York Mine and also a miner was a man called Samuel Pugh. Another miner was Frank McCormack, who hung on to his claim for too long, selling it for a mere

The old Melville home in Los Burros as it looked before the 1970 fire.

$300 instead of the original $20,000 he was offered. The Plaskett brothers, Lauren and Dudley, have been credited with the rediscovery of gold in the Los Burros. One chilly February evening in 1911 they stopped to rest beside what is now called Plaskett Creek on their way home and found small flakes of what appeared to be gold. The brothers quickly set about recording a total of twenty-three claims. The sample of ore sent to San Francisco proved to be of high grade and the rumors began to spread regarding the Plasketts' strike. The Plasketts did do well mining, as family members will tell, as the Ocean View Mine gave up some $18,000 in free gold. However, when the gold gave out it was the family's large land holdings and farming that put the bread and butter on the table. Today there are no Plasketts along the coast nor in the Los Burros region, but there are seven Plaskett families in the King City area.

In more recent years new prospectors have come in hopes of finding the elusive Los Padres Mine, or striking it rich on their own, and though many claims are still held, only a small handful of old-timers still cling to the land. Before the 1970 fire some were even living in the old homes and cabins of the Melvilles, Pughs, Krenkels, and Cruikshanks. Mining became very sporadic until around 1902 when there was attention given to a larger operation on Spruce Creek.

In 1914 there was a placer mine on the old Milpitas in what was called "Old Man's Canyon," three miles northwest of Jolon. During World War I, mining ceased, and in 1925 it was resumed once more. The depression somehow stimulated mining, and during that period William Cruikshank became a partner in the New York Mine, and the test shipment of ten tons sent to San Francisco at a cost of four dollars a ton sold for some eighty dollars a ton when it reached its final destination.

In April of 1939 at Bear Creek, R. F. and Marvin Lane filed a claim at what they believed to be the "Priest Mine," and in May 1948, King City prospectors Elmo Sellemoir and Wiley (Lucky) Likens made a strike near the old town of Manchester. Ore from their diggings assayed at $221.50 a ton. Today their claim is still being mined, although it has changed hands twice since that first lucky strike. In 1959 Jim Pauley and partner Gerald Doyle made a strike at the old Brewery Mine, the ore selling for $2,690 a ton, but the mine quickly ran out. Another miner, Virginia L. Swanson, has over twenty claims though none are on a paying basis. Of all the gold found in the Los Burros there is a consistent characteristic—it is rough, coarse and angular, with fragments of quartz adhering to it, and requires hard mining efforts by those who seek to find it.

Among those in search of the treasure of Los Burros since the late 1940s, holding out against time and the elements, was a peninsula old-timer and ex-policeman, Hickey Stalter, who mined in the Gorda area. He was a friend of a Seaside, California, barber, Thomas Grover, who became a miner of the district in September of 1946 and spent his weekends there. He found an old tunnel on his stake which lacked good timbering, but had been carved by very crude methods many years before, all of which led to speculation that perhaps these later miners were indeed discoverers of the Los Padres Mine.

One man, Howard Hilton, has mined for many years in the Los Burros, and knows it better, probably, than anyone else alive. Hilton named his mine the Lucky Mo Mine, and lived in a cabin on a hill leading up to the area called Manchester Flat. It was from this spot that he could see the comings and goings of all who passed on the community road across his land. A thin, white-haired man of many years, but erect and strong, with a firm shake and a twinkle of mischief in his eyes, Howard was known for his ready smile. It was he who discovered a secret passageway to the Last Chance Mine on the opposite side of the hill. He was a good friend to Paul Acquistapace and to present generation members of the families of other early miners, one of whom rescued him from the terrible fire in 1970. Charles Krenkel and another neighbor, Jim Collard, not only saved the historical Krenkel cabin but Howard Hilton's life. That dreadful fire destroyed much of historical interest and beauty, leaving little in its path but blackened metal and the ghostly remnants of a once proud mining community.

The lost mines of the Los Burros will continue to haunt us, and the aura of mystery that surrounds the area will linger on.

7

Pebble Beach

The original Pebble Beach Lodge in 1919. Julian P. Graham photograph, courtesy William Curtis Brooks.

The year was 1915. The grandnephew of the inventor of the telegraph, ex-Yale football captain Samuel F. B. Morse, had been called in by the Pacific Improvement Company (the "Big Four"—Leland Stanford, Mark Hopkins, Charles Crocker, and Collis P. Huntington) to see what could be done with the land. Riding across it on horseback, Morse fell in love with the land before him. He soon took two very important steps for the Pacific Improvement Company: he hired an excellent manager for the foundering but fashionable Hotel Del Monte, and then began work on the forest holdings of the company, re-routing the Seventeen-Mile Drive and picking up the deeds on choice waterfront locations, including an old Chinese fishing village. In its place he had the original Del Monte Lodge and the golf course constructed. The golf course was designed by architect Douglas Grant, the father-in-law of Howare Bobbs, the prominent artist. The physical lay-

Samuel F. B. "Sam" Morse. Courtesy William C. Brooks.

The second Pebble Beach Lodge, circa 1929.

out, with modifications, was done by Russian-American Ilya Rudneff.

By 1919 the company's holdings were so lucra-tive that a syndicate from the East had offered $1,200,000 for the acreage, but Morse declined the offer, deciding he would make the land his own. With the backing of Herbert Fleishhacker and other friends from San Francisco, he purchased the holdings for $1,300,000. With Morse as its president and chairman of the board, the company was renamed Del Monte Properties. Two more golf courses, Cypress and Monterey Peninsula Country Club, were developed, and in 1929 Pebble Beach became the home of the National Amateur Open Championship Golf Tournament and eventually the Bing Crosby Pro-Am, the Pebble Beach Road Races, Steeplechase, and the Concours D'Elegance. Morse also brought the addition of shops to the second Del Monte Lodge in the 1950s, always striving for quality and maintenance of the forest. He was a special breed of man.

Facts and Quotes

1859
An 1859 list of students of Carmelo School included the following names: Wilder, McKenzie, Williams, McClurg, Tomasini, Coleman, Selfridge, Meadows, Wolter, Branson, Martin, and Tice.

1864
Outlaw Gregorio Oresco was hanged from the porch of "El Cuartel" in Monterey for the ambushing and shooting of John Martin of the Martin Ranch. Martin, who survived the incident, remained a partial invalid because of the bullet injury to his spine. The tragedy caused great public outrage, as Martin, a mild-mannered man, was at the time going about his business and did not provoke the attack.

1887
James Krenkel arrived in the Los Burros region, where he was a miner and remained a resident until his death in 1944.

1888
The Brewery Mine of Los Burros was discovered.

1911
A small Presbyterian chapel was built on the southeast corner of Dolores and Eighth under the supervision of the Reverend Hicks. It was used by the local Chinese.

1914
Carmelo School students were Hatton Martin, Joe Onesimo, Leo and Ora Vasquez, Mary Ollason, Alice Meadows, and Irene Wolter. The teacher was Mrs. William Rhyner.

1915
T. B. Reardon advertised Edison Mazda lamps.

The John Martin Ranch was sold, with the exception of the area bounded by Santa Lucia and the Carmel mission, Carmelo Street and the main highway.

Leidig Brothers advertised "Hot Point" range service.

The Wermuth family lived in the old Hansen house on San Carlos.

On September 29, F. M. McAuliffe took over the management of the Pine Inn from George Shields. The mortgage on the property was still held by the Carmel Development Company.

The old Carmel Hall at Ocean and Mission underwent extensive alterations in October. M. J. Murphy did the work and the Manzanita Theater used the upstairs for movies.

1916
The Carmel-Monterey highway was macadamized.

S. J. Wyatt advertised he was "½ block east of the Post Office," and carried "glass, cement, hardware, oils, paints and brushes" in "The Little Hardware Store."

In March, the lot between J. W. Hand's building and that of Delos Curtis's Carmel Candy Store was turned into a children's playground, with Mr. Curtis doing the work.

On March 21, the Carmel Bathhouse was the scene of a special birthday party for the niece of Dr. and Mrs. J. E. Beck, Julia McEldowney. Guests for the occasion were Helen Hicks, Irene Goold, Vera Basham, Fay Murphy, Dorothy Smith, Evelyn and Myrtle Arne, Roslyn and Kathleen Murphy, Waldo Hicks, Franklin Murphy, George, Martin and Teddy Leidig, and Chauncey Owens.

1917
Miss Alice Beardsley gave instruction in English in her apartment at El Monte Verde Hotel.

Between 1917 and 1920, special duty officers who assisted Marshal Englund were Harry Aucourt, E. A. Arne, C. S. Beck, David Machado, and Robert H. Durice.

On July 5, Carmel's Board of Health was established, its members J. E. "Doc" Beck, George Beardsley, Catherine Morgan, and H. P. Larouette.

On December 20, the following was a news item: "The Carmel Fire Department, a Volunteer organization, which for the past two years has been operating under the state and county authority, is now a municipal organization."

1918

Pebble Beach Golf Course held its grand opening on Washington's Birthday.

New city officers were installed on April 15, as follows: Grace P. Wickham, clerk; Fraser (re-elected), president; Johnson, fire and police commissioner; Taylor, streets, sidewalks and parks; Kibbler, health and safety; Fraser, finance.

On August 6, C. W. Bowen applied for a permit to operate automobiles, auto trucks, or auto stages within the City of Carmel-by-the-Sea. On the same day, Harry Aucourt was hired for special police services while Ed Romandia took charge of burying a dead horse.

On November 6, Mrs. Philip Wilson gave permission to the fire department to use the roof of her garage for erection of a frame for drying the fire hose.

1919

Zink and Huseman advertised the "New Carmel Bakery."

Frank Hellan had a little tobacco store on the southwest corner of Dolores and Sixth.

1920

Philip Wilson, Jr. advertised "The Carmel Saddle Livery," with horses for rent.

On April 19, newly installed city officers were: trustees, T. B. Reardon, F. R. Bechdolt, Mrs. G. M. Cooke, and J. E. Nichols. City clerks were Saidee Van Bower and R. H. Durice, and the city treasurer was L. S. Slevin.

On August 3, the undersigned merchants petitioned for enactment of an ordinance to require a license of all peddlers operating in Carmel: John L. Williams, Robert G. Leidig, Robert A. Norton, Brewer and T. L. Elder, Mrs. Delos Curtis, F. A. Wermuth, G. L. Carroll, E. S. Schweniger, W. C. Overstreet, Stella Guichard, and J. W. Hand. A motion was made and carried.

On October 5, Henry Fisher of San Jose accepted the office of city engineer and Harry W. Groff took over trimming of trees, with R. W. Hicks taking over the care of all electrical labor and materials for the city.

1921

B. W. Adams advertised "Mission and Craft Furniture" at Dolores and Eleventh.

On March 1, City Trustee C. Dorwart nominated Robert A. Smith for "garbage man" for the City of Carmel at twenty dollars a month. Passed.

On April 5, the following signed a protest notice against paving: Bertha Newberry, Andrew Stewart, Margaret Taylor, A. P. Fraser, D. W. W. Johnson, Wm. P. Silva, Laura Maxwell, Emiline Harrington, Mr. and Mrs. William Watts. Speaking in protest were Grace McGowan Cooke, Mrs. A. P. Fraser, A. H. Roseboom, and H. P. Larouette.

In July, the city clerk was ordered to inform the following that they must file with the city a "Master Electricians License Board" to cover operations in the city: Holman's Department Store, Noggle Electric Works, S. J. Tice, W. H. McConnell, E. E. Sirlee, Thomas B. Reardon, and H. Larouette.

On October 11, a communication from the Community Club to the Board of Trustees was read at a board meeting, requesting permission to lay the cornerstone of a proposed memorial to the veterans of the World War. A sketch was presented.

On November 7, voting was unanimous in favor of the purchase of the Sand Dunes by the city.

In November, W. T. Dummage was named secretary of the Sanitary Board. Albert Otey was placed in charge of general hauling, Ernest Jimenez of street labor, and Walter Basham of team and street labor.

1922

Cabbages and Kings, Ltd., advertised a weekly special of typewriter paper at $1.25 per ream.

The Walter Bashams announced "our brand new place is open at the Bathhouse now."

In June, Thomas Bickle and his wife Eva came to Carmel so that he could take over the management of the newly opened Palace Drugstore.

Miss Stella Shaw became the owner of the Highlands in July.

On July 6, the *Pine Cone* observed, "There have been nine additions to Carmel-by-the-Sea in the space of a few years, the last being the most interesting and most significant of all, Carmel Woods."

Thomas Vincent Cator had two studios, one at the Arts and Crafts Hall in Carmel and another on Dutra Street in Monterey.

Charles C. Smith had a taxi service in front of the Pine Cone. He made special daily trips to scenic points Big Sur, Big Trees, and the Seventeen-Mile Drive.

The following were the charter members of Carmel's Businessmen's Association: T. L. Edler, R. C. De Yoe, R. G. Leidig, C. O. Goold, J. L. Williams, C. C. Hogle, L. S. Slevin, J. B. Jordan, W. L. Overstreet, and H. P. Glassell.

It was announced that Thomas H. Reardon and Fred Leidig would build an equipment station of mission type architecture on the northeast corner of San Carlos and Sixth. The building was leased as Grimshaw's Flying A.

Donald L. Hale, son of Mrs. F. R. Bechdolt, went into the contracting business with his brother-in-law, L. E. Gottfried, in May.

In May, Miss Marie Mai Guichard was married to James B. McGrury of Hollister. Miss Guichard, one of seven sisters, "has been a teacher at Sunset School and is sister to our own Stella Guichard."

The "Mission Tea Room" in the El Monte Verde Apartments opened formally, with the Misses Esther and Louise Hayes as proprietors.

Stella's Dry Goods, owned by Stella Guichard, opened in the new Leidig Building on May 1. The building had the first tiled roof on Ocean Avenue.

S. Ruthven of Monterey was awarded the contract for paving Ocean Avenue for $27,984.00, on May 23.

In June, Albert Otey and Ray Ramsey, owners of Carmel Transfer, advertised that they were "able to move anything, anywhere."

In June, Calvin Hogle, who was in real estate and handled land in the Highlands, boasted a "new convenience station with all the modern conveniences excepting a mirror and a vanity box, as well as a map of Carmel and directory of Carmel with stage information."

In July, Delos Curtis allowed Mrs. Jennie Coleman to set up her real estate business in the front of his own business. C. J. Arne shared with Elizabeth White for a short period at about the same time. Daisy Bostick once remarked that she had long since lost track of the various locations at which she was allowed to light for periods of time.

On July 22, the statue of Junípero Serra by Jo Mora was unveiled by Father R. Mestres. Dr. D. T. Mac-Dougal was chairman of the play committee, with C. A. McCollom, M.D., and Edward G. Kuster.

On December 27, C. O. Goold offered to use his team and go over the streets "rounding up the gravel," if a grader could be rented from the county.

In August, B. G. Newell took over the grocery of J. Davis.

1923

"Doc" Beck's residence was on San Carlos between Eighth and Ninth, near the Wermuths' residence, and the J. W. Hands also lived nearby.

Carmel's first Sir-cuss Day was held during this year.

J. W. Hand's real estate and insurance office was also the agent for Star Cleaners of Monterey and Del Monte Laundry.

Carmel's popular beauty shop was "Ye Carmel Beautie Shoppe" at the Pine Inn.

On February 6, C. O. Goold offered to be superintendent of streets without compensation.

On March 10, the Carmel Shoe Repairing Shop, conducted by J. Burch, moved to a new location on San Carlos which had formerly housed John Williams' grocery. It remained at this location until 1977, with several changes in ownership. The last owners were the Anthony Gomez family.

Ground was broken in May for the new post office on Dolores near Seventh.

On June 5, the distribution of the estate of Mrs. E. Reid Harrison was read. She left a library of two or three thousand books, a collection of Japanese art, and a collection of furniture and etchings. F. A. Wermuth, a volunteer of the fire department, was responsible for storing the books until the library was built in 1925.

In July, Marshal Gus Englund turned in expenses of twenty-five cents for postage, fifteen cents for office expense, sixty cents for postage, and one dollar for postage, amounting to two dollars altogether.

Louie Lewis erected the seven-room Praeger home on Carmel Point in August.

Mrs. Ada Howe Kent became the owner of White Cedars in September.

In September the city paid Luis F. Wolter $100.80 for hay and Arthur Wolter $30.00 for street labor.

In October the Bloods moved their grocery into the Parkes Building, and the Minges took over the Ocean Avenue location.

On November 6, Delos Curtis asked the city to bear part of the cost of his telephone because it was being used for fire alarm calls. He was paid $12.60.

1924

Carmel's Masonic organization was founded by the following Masons: Walter L. Basham, William Titmus, M. L. Wild, A. F. Meckenstock, the Rev. F. W. Sheldon, C. L. Burke, Ross E. Bonham, and William T. Kibbler. They met at the annex of the Carmel Community Church with the Rev. Sheldon as their temporary chairman and Mr. Titmus as secretary. Later they purchased the cottage on Lincoln.

Robert Leidig advertised "Fry Fyster Service" extinguishers for sale.

Franklin Devendorf's mother, Mrs. Grace Aram, died in Pacific Grove.

The popular footbridge across the gulch on North Lincoln was torn down to avoid its use by automobiles.

Eva Bickle, wife of Thomas Bickle, and Mary Hayden had a dressmaking business at Junipero and Eighth.

Miss Dorothy Bassett, daughter of Willard K. Bassett and Dorothea Castlehulman Bassett, opened Carmel's first boarding kennels at Alta and Junipero.

Harris D. Comings and Allen Jeckham bought the Carmel Garage. Later it belonged to William Frolli.

Mrs. Sidney Yard closed out her "Ye Olde Shoppe" on Dolores in July.

1925

Clay Otto had his office and studio upstairs in the Wilson Building.

Vinings Meat Market and Minges Grocery were together on Dolores. The Dolores Grocery and Romylane Candies were both sold during the year.

Albert and Emma Otey became owners of the Carmel Thermolite Company in partnership with Ella Maugh.

Reis and Down opened the Bootery on Ocean Avenue in January.

In June, 233 acres of Hatton land were sold to a group headed by Paul L. Flanders. Other partners were Charles Van Riper, author and baseball enthusiast, and Harry Leon Wilson, author. "The land was bounded at its northern boundary by Second and in Carmel on the west by west city limits; on the south by the county road that runs in front of the Carmel Mission and on the east by the same road into which converges the road to Carmel Highlands and the Carmel Valley."

1926

Hugh Comstock built the five-room irregular residence at Dolores and Twelfth for Milton H. Douzensky.

In March, Gottfried and Hale erected an English style home on Carmel Point for Mrs. Rhoda Long and a Norman-French style chalk rock residence for the Joseph Schoeninger family.

George Seideneck was elected second president of the Carmel Art Association.

Kindergarten units were added to Sunset School at Tenth and San Carlos.

The Merrill Building was constructed at Dolores and Seventh. It housed the Hob Nob Restaurant and El Paseo.

Los Ranchitos Valley Estate Homesites project was officially opened.

Mr. and Mrs. B. C. Jessena moved to Carmel Point. They were the proprietors of the Holiday House, considered a "charming family hotel with an excellent table." It later became Hollyhock Court and then the Holiday Inn.

On January 24, Carmel began its first reforestation program with the planting of pine seedlings along the city streets, under the direction of Alfred Fraser, superintendent of streets.

The second Serra Pilgrimage took place on September 9, with and 8:00 p.m. staging of the historical pageant, *Fray Junipero Serra*, written by Perry Newberry and Monsignor Ramon M. Mestres.

1928

The "Barnacle" on the west side of Lincoln was the home of Mrs. Sidney Yard.

Crazy Plunge, held on Washington's Birthday, was begun this year. Dr. Ray E. Brownell, who was eighty-eight years old in 1979, was one of those who participated and has continued to take part every year. Other well-known plunge participants are Ted Durein and Gordon Campbell.

On July 26, Dorothy Green Chapman opened a business in a new shop located in the Sun Dial Court on Monte Verde between Ocean and Seventh. She advertised a line of pianos, radios, and sheet music, and called her business the Carmel Music Shop.

In December, telephone cables were removed from overhead poles and placed underground at the cost of $30,000. The poles became the property of the electric company.

1929

The formal ground breaking ceremony for the Grace Deere Velie Metabolic Clinic was held at one o'clock on January 9. Mrs. Velie lifted the first shovel of dirt.

Walter Basham died in Grass Valley, California, in March.

Early pioneer builder and painter Enoch Lewis, father of Louie Lewis, died in May.

On September 27, Margaret and Kay Lial opened a music shop for Carmel villagers in the newly opened Leidig Building.

1930

The Boy Scouts occupied a log cabin on property purchased from George Seideneck on the east side of Junipero between Seventh and Eighth.

The Sundial Apartments opened in May. The builder was M. J. Murphy; the designer was Albert Farr.

184

In September the Carmel Fire Department rented the William McPhillips Building at Fifth and San Carlos for forty dollars a month to use as a firehouse.

William T. Dummage died following an operation in December.

1931
Mary De Neale Morgan donated a painting depicting a scene from *Evangeline* (a Point Lobos production) to Sunset School. Other paintings were given by Ferdinand Burgdorff, Elizabeth Strong, and William P. Silva.

Mrs. Harriet Dorr Doulton sold the El Paseo building and Holiday House in May.

1932
Jose Bernabel died at the age of 104. He had lived the last ten years of his life in an old tent at Tortilla Flats.

The *Pine Cone* stated that Carmel had officially grown to ten times its original size.

The Market Del Mar opened its doors in March. It was run by Walter Nielsen and Byron G. Newell. Percy Whitworth, formerly of Vinings Market, was in charge of the meat market.

On March 4, between 1:00 and 2:00 a.m., about five hundred dollars worth of goods were stolen from Imelman's Sport Shop.

A report from the local health official stated that there was one case of scarlet fever and one case of influenza in November.

1933
Lynn Hodges opened the San Carlos Riding Academy at Junipero and Ocean.

Charles Delos Curtis advertised "Christmas-New Year Turkey Dinner—11:30-7:30, 65¢ with Mince Pie, Pumpkin Pie, Plum Pudding and Icecream."

Carmel Realty advertised themselves as being "Carmel's oldest licensed Real Estate & Insurance Co. Rental Office."

1934
The Carmel Grocery Cupboard, where Orange Julius is today, was considered Carmel's first "co-operative grocery." It was organized by J. Howard Brooks, president of Carmel Grocery Cupboards, Inc. The secretary-treasurer of the organization was E. Fae Miller, and Herbert Heron was vice president. Capitalization was $15,000 in shares at a par value of $100,000, with the Bank of Carmel as trustee.

1936
This was the last year that candy was passed out at the annual tree-lighting ceremony at the corner of Junipero and Ocean. The old pine tree in the center of Ocean was strung with lights and everyone sang carols, a practice started in 1926. The Curtises gave each child a gift of candy for the first ten years.

Mr. and Mrs. W. G. Bulinger bought "The Green Lantern."

1937
Fortier's boasted the following "cut-rate" drug specials: 50¢ Woodburys liquid shampoo for 29¢; 10¢ cocoa almond soap, four for 25¢; 75¢ imported bay rum for 39¢; and 35¢ Woodbury shaving cream for 23¢.

Mrs. Carr Thatcher lived in the old Call residence on Scenic.

On January 24, three to four hundred guests attended the opening ball of the Valley Ranch Club. The completely renovated complex of buildings was on the edge of the river valley west of the mission.

On January 26, "one of the biggest real estate deals at the sum of $30,000 took place . . . when broker Barnet J. Segal sold 75 feet of frontage on Ocean Avenue between San Carlos and Mission belonging to George W. Wagner of San Jose to a Carmel resident."

Bee and Ora Minges sold the Carmel Grocery to Fred McIndoe and E. D. Shepard, in February.

1938
The Storie Building was dismantled in May and the wood taken by Charles G. Stoops to Carmel Valley, where it was used in the building of apartments. Work on the second Bank of Carmel was begun on the site where the Storie Building had stood.

In September, the last major bridge on the Carmel-San Simeon Coast Highway was completed. It crossed the canyon ninety feet above the stream bed and was over five hundred feet long. It was known as Big Creek Bridge.

1939
The first Artists Ball was held on Saturday, January 20, with Byington Ford in charge.

Frank B. Porter of Salinas sold the Robles Del Rio resort to David Prince, a San Francisco and San Diego hotel man, and William Woods of San Francisco, in February.

1940
The old J. Culbertson house at the corner of Seventh and Lincoln was torn down and the Mayfair House was built on the site. It was designed by Jon Konigshofer.

Margaret Lial opened the Carmel Branch Music Store on Dolores Street in June, in the former location of the Spencer House of Cards. She had had a business at the same location ten years before.

In July, Barnet Segal moved his Carmel Investment Company into the old Carmel Bank building. It later became the second location of Wells Book Store.

1942
Rose De Yoe, who had come to Carmel in 1909, died on March 24 at the age of eighty-eight.

1944
Grace McGowan Cooke died in January at Carmel. Her sister Alice lived with their niece Kathryn (Mrs. John Ryan) in Los Gatos until her death.

1946
The Fee Building, once the location of Kramer's Specialty Shop, was remodeled. It had been built in 1926 by M. J. Murphy, and also housed a business known as Rittmaster.

1947
Willard K. Bassett, outspoken publisher of the *Pine Cone Cymbal*, died from injuries received when he was struck by a car in Hawaii. He was sixty-six years old.

The last undeveloped tract of land in Carmel was sold in January. The Carmel Land Company sold 400 acres where Carmel High School is located, to the Carmel Company, headed by C. A. Fuller. Included in the deal were all the unsold portions of Hatton Fields Tract, consisting of forty to fifty lots. The purchase price was between $150,000 and $200,000, and the 400 acres extended from the Carmel Valley Road along the east side of Highway 1, to a line opposite the now old Carmel hospital.

On January 18, Cynthia Dragoo and Virginia Lemon opened the Fairy Story Candy Shop at Ocean and Mission, next door to the present Tiki Hut, where Dock Lor's Chinese restaurant now is.

On January 25, "the sturdy old pine tree that has stood in the middle of Lincoln Street just south of Ocean ever since the village was founded, blocking the thoroughfare to motorists since the invention of the automobile, has been removed amid wails of anguish."

On October 20, tax bills were mailed to Carmel property owners at the low rate of 92¢, for which City Clerk Peter Mawdsley was given credit.

1948
Mrs. Robinson Jeffers, Dr. Remsen Bird, Matthew Jenkins, and Mrs. Ernest Morehouse were the executive committee of Carmel's chapter of the American Red Cross.

Benito Soberanes, who was born in a little adobe hut in the Carmel Valley on March 21, 1853, died on November 11. He was a descendant of Jose Marie Soberanes.

1949
Los Padres Dam and Reservoir was built at the cost of $1.5 million.

1954
Clifford and Wilma Cooke were the owners of the Pine Cone on Dolores between Ocean and Seventh.

1955
There was a Blum's where the Wine Cellar is today.

The lovely old stone home on the ocean side-bend leading to Carmel Point was torn down. Built by Colonel Dutton, it had massive iron doors and was referred to as "the Castle" and "the Warehouse." A new house for Mrs. Gladys Hosking was built in its place.

School enrollment in Carmel in October was 1,081.

1956
The property owned by the Leslie Fentons and the San Carlos Canning Company became the Carmel Plaza, replacing M. J. Murphy's lumber yard and the Carmel Theater and adjacent shops.

In January, the California Water and Telephone Company opened in a new location in the Los Cortes Building on Dolores near Fifth.

In May, the Carmel Laundry at Fifth and Junipero was sold to Mareses Ina of San Jose by Leonard and Frances Carey, who had owned it since 1946. It is now gone.

1957
On May 7, county supervisors approved the Hatton Canyon Freeway agreement over the objections of residents of Hatton Canyon. The new freeway was to cover the area from Veijo Road south of Monterey to the Carmel River, with three interchanges and a crossing at Rio Road south of Carmel Valley Road.

1962
The Studio Theater began operating as a dinner theater. It was founded in July 1958 by Betty Hackett Martin and Royden Martin and has changed hands four times since then.

1966
Carmel's first Sand Castle Contest was held in October.

1968
On October 3, Frances M. Molera, the great niece of General Mariano Guadalupe Vallejo, died at the age of eighty-eight in San Francisco.

1969
On April 25, the Cachagua Valley earth station of the Communications Satellite Corporation was dedicated with a ribbon-cutting ceremony.

1978

Del Monte Properties sold the 1,600-acre San Clemente Ranch to a private group for $315,000.

1979

The Big Sur Land Trust announced the purchase of 3,040 acres of the Potter Ranch (also known as Circle M or Gamboa Point Ranch). Many benefactors contributed to the transaction, the purpose being for the preservation of the property. The purchase price was approximately $1.8 million.

The subject of annexation of the unincorporated areas of Carmel came before the voters of Carmel for the third time and was defeated again, 555 to 453.

The population of Carmel was 300 in 1908; 1,000 in 1922; 2,837 (within the city limits) in 1940; 4,000 in 1943; 4,600 in 1956; and 4,756 in 1977.

Big Sur Postal History

1889 - October 30	"Posts" post office established by William Brainard Post as postmaster.
1905 - November 18	Zulema Florence Pfeiffer took office and it was later entered in the official records on January 31, 1905.
1919 - April	The name of the post office was changed to "Arbolado."
1912 - January 24	Money orders were started.
1915 - March 6	The name of the post office was changed to "Big Sur."
1915 - May 5	Zulema Florence Pfeiffer was commissioned.
1915 - October	Corbett Grimes replaced Charles Howland as mail carrier between Monterey and Big Sur.
1934 - April 30	J. C. Smith took office.
1935 - March 29	J. C. Smith was commissioned.
1943 - August 17	J. C. Smith made last entry.
1943 - September 20	Tillie Pollack took office, to September 23.
1943 - September 28	Esther Ewoldsen was commissioned.
1947 - July 1	Post office was promoted to third class commission.
1947 - July 21	Esther Ewoldsen was given third class commission.
1959 - June	Esther Ewoldsen gave resignation.
1959 - June	Florence McQueen took office.
1972 - April 27	Florence McQueen retired because of ill health.
1972 - April 28	Bette Sommerville became acting postmistress.
1972 - August 1	The sheriff advised Bette Sommerville to evacuate because of fire. Bette and Loretta Dengate took mail, stamps, and cash home for safekeeping.
1972 - October 15	There was minor water damage to post office interior because of flooding after fire.
1972 - November 15	Post office was flooded with mud and water.
1972 - November 16	Post office was moved to navy base at Point Sur after loss of building.
1972 - December 5	Post office was moved to a trailer.
1973 - April 1	Nunnie Whitfield was appointed postmistress.
1975 - December 5	Nunnie Whitfield was transferred, and Bette Sommerville was appointed officer in charge until July 26, 1976.
1976 - July 29	John Giza was appointed postmaster.

Ranchos of Carmel, Carmel Valley and Big Sur

CANADA DE LA SEGUNDA
(Second canyon)
4,367 acres

Granted to Lazaro Soto 1838 and patented to Fletcher Haight 1859. Held by Haight until patent was given to William Hatton in 1875.

EL POTRERO DE SAN CARLOS
(The pastures of St. Charles)
4,306.98 acres

Granted to Fructuoso del Real December 12, 1839. In 1852 claim to this grant was filed by Joaquin Gutierrez and Maria Estefana, daughter of del Real, and patent was given to them on June 9, 1852. This property was purchased by Bradley V. Sargent in 1858, and remained his until 1897.

LOS LAURELES
(The Laurels)
6,625 acres

Granted to Jose Manuel Boronda and Vicente Blas Martinez by Manuel Jimeno on September 19, 1839. Patent was given to Don Jose Manuel Boronda and his son Juan de Mata Boronda on August 9, 1866.

LOS LAURELITOS
(Ricon de los Laureles)
(Little Laureles)
718.23 acres

Granted to Jose Agricio March 4, 1844. Patent was given to Leander Ransom on April 18, 1871.

JAMES MEADOWS TRACT
(Lomas del Carmelo)
4,592 acres

Granted to Antonio Romero 1840. Patent was given to James Meadows in 1851.

SAN FRANCISQUITO
(Little St. Francis)
8,814 acres

Granted to Catalina Manzanelli de Munras November 7, 1835. A joint petition for patent was filed by Jose Abrego (for himself et al.) and by Milton Little, for the minor heirs of William R. Garner. Patent was given to these claimants in 1862 for 8,813.50 acres.

LOS TULARCITOS
(Little Tules)
26,581.34 acres

Granted to Rafael Gomez on December 1, 1834. In April 1852 his widow, Josefa Antonia Gomez de Wolter, and his children filed claim for the property and were given patent in 1866.

CANADA HONDA
(Deep canyon)
270 by 750 varas
(A vara is 36 inches or one yard; therefore this rancho was approximately 42 acres.)

Granted to Angel Ramirez 1835. Held by "loose deeds," no claim filed, absorbed into Pescadero.

EL PESCADERO
(The fisherman)
4,426 acres

Granted to Fabian Barreto on February 29, 1836. John C. Gore filed claim on February 9, 1853, and was rejected. Patent was given to David Jacks in 1868. An 1864 survey shows that John C. Gore had a home on the property.

EL SUR
(The South)
8,949.06 acres

Granted to J. B. Alvarado 1834. Patented to Juan B. R. Cooper 1866.

SAN JOSE Y SUR CHIQUITA
(Saint Joseph and Little South)
8,876 acres

Granted to Marcelino Escobar on April 16, 1839. Claim filed by Jose Castro on February 2, 1853. After lengthy arguments the tract was patented on May 4, 1888 to Joseph S. Emery and Nathan W. Spaulding, administrators for the will of Abner Bassett and his widow, successors in interest to the deceased Jose Castro.

EL TORO
(The Bull)
5,668 acres

Granted to Jose Ramon Estrada on October 17, 1835. In 1852 Charles Wolter filed claim to the grant and received patent in 1862.

Index

195

201